# The Bible Untangled

# The Bible Untangled

Read the Texts that Were Edited Together
to Form the Early Books of the Bible

edited with commentary by
Charles Siegel

Omo Press

adolescentium alunt
senectutem oblectant

Published by:
Omo Press
Berkeley, California
omo@omopress.com
www.omopress.com

Cover: Rembrandt, Moses Breaking the Tablets of the Law, 1659

Publisher's Cataloging-in-Publication Data
Names: Siegel, Charles Neil, 1947- , editor.
Title: The Bible untangled : read the texts that were edited together to form the early books of the Bible/ edited with commentary by Charles Siegel.
Description: Berkeley, CA : Omo Press, 2019. | Summary: Presents parallel texts of early source documents for the first four books of the Bible, along with extensive commentary and historical context.
Identifiers: LCCN2019903812 | ISBN 9781941667200 (pbk.)
Subjects: LCSH: Bible. -- Pentateuch -- Criticism, Interpretation, etc. | Documentary hypothesis (Pentateuchal criticism). | E document (Biblical criticism). | J document (Biblical criticism). | P document (Biblical criticism). | BISAC: RELIGION / Biblical Studies / History & Culture. | RELIGION / Biblical Studies / Old Testament / Pentateuch.
Classification: LCC BS1181.S54 2019 | DDC 220.4 S54--dc23
LC record available at https://lccn.loc.gov/2019903812

# Contents

# Part I:
# The Authors and Their Times

# Chapter 1:
# The Texts Behind the Bible

The first five books of the Bible—called the five books of Moses, the Pentateuch or the Torah—are hard to read because some of their stories are long-winded, and they contain long lists of ritualistic commandments. These books are even harder to understand because many stories are self-contradictory, and different passages seem to have very different views of God and of our religious duties.

But most of these difficulties disappear when we separate the Torah into its source texts.

The idea that the Torah was edited together from source texts is called the "documentary hypothesis" because it claims that the Torah is made up of several independent documents. The documentary hypothesis has been important to Biblical scholarship for over a century, but this edition is the first to arrange the three parallel texts of the Torah in parallel columns. You can read across the columns to compare the different versions of the same story in the different documents. You can read down the columns to read the documents from beginning to end.

This book is an experiment to test the documentary hypothesis. When you read down the columns, you can see whether each text is a cohesive whole with a consistent view of God and our religious duties. When you read across the columns, you can see the contradictions among the texts.

There are still disputes among scholars about which source text many passages of the Bible should be assigned to. As part of its test of the documentary hypothesis, this edition assigns disputed passages in the way that makes the source texts as continuous and cohesive as possible. Some critics of the documentary hypothesis say that we cannot divide the Torah into cohesive source texts, and in this edition, you can read down each column to judge for yourself whether each text could be taken from a single, cohesive document.

## The Source Documents

The traditional view is that the entire Torah was revealed to Moses on Mt. Sinai or Mt. Horeb.

Many people questioned this view over the centuries, including the philosophers Thomas Hobbes and Baruch Spinoza.[1] The modern approach to Bible criticism began in the eighteenth century, when scholars identified what they called "doublets," places in the Bible where the same story is told twice with differences between the two versions. Scholars also noticed that, within these doublets, one version referred to God using the word *Elohim* (Hebrew for God) while the other referred to God using the four-letter name YHWH, which is translated as "the Lord" in most English versions of the Bible.

For example, the Bible begins in Genesis 1 with the well-known story of the creation in six days, but then it repeats the story of the creation briefly in Genesis 2 before going on with the story of Adam and Eve. The order of creation is different in these two versions. In Genesis 1, which uses the word "God," God creates the birds (Gen. 1:20), then creates the animals (Gen. 1:24), and then creates both man and woman (Gen. 1:27). In Genesis 2, which uses the name "Lord God," God creates man (Gen. 2:7), then creates the trees (Gen. 2:9), then creates the animals and birds (Gen. 2:19), and then creates woman (Gen. 2:22). These two versions of the creation story are easy to identify because they are presented one after another.

A bit later, in the story of Noah and the flood, the two versions are intertwined, with fragments of one version alternating with fragments of the other. If you separate the two different versions, you see that they both give complete accounts of Noah and the flood but that they contradict each other in many ways. The version that uses the word "God" says that Noah took one pair of each kind of animal (Gen. 6:19), that the flood lasted about ten and a half months (Gen. 7:11, 8:13) and that Noah sent a raven to see if the flood had ended (Gen. 8:7). The version that uses the word "Lord" says that Noah took seven pairs of clean animals and one pair of unclean animals (Gen. 7:2), that the flood lasted during 40 days of rain (Gen. 8:6) plus another seven days before the water receded (Gen. 8:10), and that Noah sent doves to see if the flood had ended (Gen. 7:6).

In 1711, Henning Bernhard Witter was the first to discuss doublets, but his work had little influence. In 1753, Jean Astruc, a French physician, anonymously published a book defending Moses' authorship against the criticisms of Hobbes and Spinoza by saying that Moses wrote the books of Genesis and Exodus in four columns, which used these different names for God and which scribes later combined,[2] but he also had little influence. In 1780, Johann Gottfried Eichhorn said that the Bible was compiled after the death of Moses from two sources; he called one source E because it used the word *Elohim* (God), and he called the other J because it used the four-letter name of God, which is written as JHWH in German.[3] Eichhorn could not be ignored because he was a well known scholar and a professor in the Faculty of Theology at Jena University, and his work was the beginning of the modern documentary hypothesis.

Shortly afterward, scholars realized that there were also doublets within the texts that used the word Elohim and that these doublets had different concerns and used different language. They concluded that there is a third source, and because this source was often concerned with the rituals that priests performed, they called it P, the priestly source.

To make things even more complicated, scholars later found that E and P use the word *Elohim* in the early parts of the Torah, but both of these texts say that God revealed His four-letter name to Moses, and after this revelation, both texts use His name, translated as "the Lord," as well as using the word "God."

The E, J, and P texts were combined by editors to make up the first four books of the Bible, and scholars also found that almost all of the fifth book of the Bible, Deuteronomy, differed from these three sources in language and sometimes contradicted them, so they attributed it to a separate source, which they called D.

Thus, we have four sources, called E (from *Elohim*), J (from JHWH), P (from Priestly) and D (from Deuteronomy).

Redactors (editors) combined all these source texts into the single text that has survived to our time. Scholars found that J and E were combined into the JE text by a redactor whom we call RJE, who often discarded material that was duplicated in both of these texts, leaving gaps in what has survived of the J and E texts. Later, the JE and P text were combined by a redactor whom we call R, who kept almost all the material in his two sources.

This theory explains many of the contradictions in the Bible. To give just one example, the Torah says that Moses received the law both on Mt. Sinai and on Mt. Horeb. Why does the Torah contradict itself? Because the J and P texts say it happened on Mt. Sinai, while the E text implies and the D text says it happened on Mt. Horeb in the wilderness of Sinai.

Julius Wellhausen was the great scholar who synthesized the earlier work and created a definitive version of the documentary hypothesis. However, Wellhausen was influenced by the ideas of the philosopher Georg Wilhelm Friedrich Hegel, who believed that history was the story of the inevitable progress of ideas, so he characterized these sources by saying that J and E represented the earliest phase of the Israelite religion, which was family-based and polytheistic, D represented an intermediate phase, when religion began to be centralized under the kings and priests, and only P (the latest text, which he placed after the Babylonian exile) had a monotheistic religion under the control of the priesthood.[4]

As we will see, it was an error to lump together J and E as two examples of the early primitive phase in the inevitable progress of religion. Today's scholars are not Hegelians, but they have not freed themselves entirely from the error that both J and E represent primitive versions of the Israelite religion. In reality, E is remarkably advanced for his time, while J's religion is much more primitive—and when we read the E text, we have to wonder how a people as primitive as the early Israelites developed such an advanced religion.

To understand the four source documents, we have to look briefly at the historical events that shaped Israel when the four authors lived.

# The World of E and J

The E and J texts were written when the Israelites lived in two kingdoms, the northern kingdom of Israel and the southern kingdom of Judah, between about 930 BCE and 722 BCE. To understand this era, we have to step back and look at how all of Israel became a unified kingdom and at how that kingdom broke in two.

Archeologists have shown that a group of nomadic herders arrived in Canaan and began farming in the unoccupied hill country around 1200 BCE, about the time of the exodus from Egypt, with an initial population of about 45,000 people at about 250 sites.[5] These nomads were different from all the surrounding peoples because the bones remaining at their settlements show that they did not raise pigs, implying that they were the Israelites. They peacefully settled unoccupied highlands rather than conquering Canaanite cities as the book of Joshua claims, but they occasionally clashed with Canaanites who lived in parts of the valleys of these highlands.

The book of Judges tells us that the Israelites did not have any centralized government for the first couple of centuries after they arrived in Canaan. Each tribe was independent. When it was necessary to fight other nations, a tribe or alliance of tribes would muster up an army.[6] The tribes also would fight among themselves occasionally.[7]

A unified kingdom replaced this collection of tribes because disunited tribes could not face the growing threat of the Philistines, who probably settled the coast of Canaan at about the same time that the Israelites settled the highlands. In the book of Judges, the tribes are sometimes conquered by surrounding nations, but they often wage war successfully and avoid being conquered, or they free themselves after being conquered. But the final war in the book of Judges is against the Philistines, and the leader of the Israelites was the judge Samson, who died after being captured by the Philistines.[8] Behind the mythology of Samson having supernatural strength that he lost because of the treachery of his Philistine wife Delilah, we can see the historical fact that the Israelite tribes had fought and ultimately defeated other enemies but could not defeat the Philistines.

At this point, Israel needed to have a king with a standing army rather than forming impromptu armies when the need arose. Saul was the first king to form a standing army, but he failed to beat back the Philistines. David, a member of the tribe of Judah who had been part of Saul's army, assembled his own army, called the "mighty men," and he unified the twelve tribes into one kingdom through a series of military victories that conquered territory for Israel.

David also conquered Jerusalem, and he made it the religious center of the unified kingdom. The most important religious object at the time was the Ark of the Covenant, which the Israelites believed their ancestors had carried through the desert to the Promised Land. At first, the Ark was kept at the main religious center of Israel at Shiloh, in the territory of the tribe of Ephraim.[9] But when the Israelites carried it into battle against the Philistines thinking it would protect them, the Philistines captured it.[10] David brought the Ark to Jerusalem, and the Bible presents a very vivid image of David forgetting his dignity and dancing before the Ark as it was carried to his new capital.[11]

David worked hard to promote unity among the twelve tribes. During the period of the Judges, the tribes had not conquered Jerusalem, which was called Jebus and occupied by the Jebusites. David made this city his capital after his army conquered it, avoiding jealousy among the tribes by locating his national capital in a city that had never been part of the territory of any tribe.

David also promoted unity in the religion by having two sets of Levites (priests) control the religious center in Jerusalem. One high priest was Zadok, the leader of the Levites of Jerusalem, who are called the Aaronid priests because they traced their ancestry to Aaron. The other was Ahimelech, the leader of the priests of Shiloh, who are called the Mushite priests because they traced their ancestry to Moses.[12] Though David moved the ark from Shiloh to Jerusalem, he maintained unity by bringing Mushite priests from Shiloh to join the Aaronid priests in Jerusalem.

Solomon was more firmly entrenched in power than David, so he made less of an effort to unite the people. His divisiveness began at the beginning of his reign. Because Zadok, leader of the Aaronid priests, supported Solomon's bid to become king after David died,[13] while Abiathar, leader of the Mushite priests supported David's son Adonijah's,[14] Solomon gave Zadok and the Aaronid priests exclusive control over Jerusalem's religious rituals, and he banished Abiathar to Anathoth,[15] one of the cities of refuge where people who killed others by accident could go to avoid revenge. This division between the Aaronid priests and the Mushite priests, the two most influential groups of priests in ancient Israel, is crucial to understanding the Bible, much of which was written by these two groups of priests.

In another divisive move, Solomon hired King Hiram of Tyre to build the temple in Jerusalem and to build a royal palace that was much larger than the temple. He forced large number of Israelites to work on these building projects[16]—and when both projects were finished, Solomon gave Hiram twenty cities in the Galilee,[17] on the northern edge of Israel's territory. David had been careful to locate his capital in the newly conquered city of Jerusalem, so as not to put it in one tribe's territory and offend the other tribes. Solomon came from the southern tribe of Judah, like his father David, but did not care whether he offended northern tribes by giving their land away in order to build a temple and a palace for himself.

When Solomon died, his son Rehoboam became king. The Bible says that, when people from the northern tribes asked him whether he would continue Solomon's oppressive policies, Rehoboam answered, "My father made your yoke heavy, but I will add to your yoke; my father chastised you with whips, but I will chastise you with scorpions."[18] Rehoboam planned to be even crueler than his father, Solomon.

(In fairness to Solomon, we should mention that this history of his reign comes from I Kings, part of the Deuteronomistic history that was compiled by a descendent of the Mushite priests, who disliked him because he took away their authority over the Temple. The book of *Chronicles*, written later by an Aaronid priest, does not say that Solomon gave northern cities to Hiram; instead, it says that Solomon paid Hiram with grain, wine, and oil.[19] But *Chronicles* does give away the fact that Solomon was cruel and oppressive when it tells the story of the people complaining to Rehoboam and has him reply with the same line: "And now whereas my father did lade you with a heavy yoke, I will add to your yoke; my father chastised you with whips, but I will chastise you with scorpions."[20])

Though Rehoboam wanted to be crueler than Solomon, he was not as entrenched in power as Solomon had been. Jeroboam, who had led an unsuccessful rebellion against Solomon and had fled to Egypt, returned and led a successful rebellion against Rehoboam.[21] As a result, the unified kingdom of David and Solomon split into two kingdoms. Rehoboam continued to rule in the kingdom of Judah, the southernmost part of David's kingdom, which was made up of the tribe of Judah and the small tribe of Simeon that had been absorbed by Judah. Jeroboam became ruler of the new kingdom of Israel, which included the rest of the tribes and their territories. In addition, the tribe of Levi had no territory of its own: the Levites were spread through the territories of the rest of the tribes and served as priests for the other tribes. Though the Bible speaks of Israel and Judah as two similar monarchies, archeologists have found that Judah had a very backward and undeveloped economy at the time of the split,[22] so it is not surprising that the Judean Rehoboam could not dominate all the other tribes.

In the southern kingdom of Judah, Jerusalem remained the capital and religion centered on Solomon's temple in Jerusalem, which was run by the Aaronid priests. In the northern kingdom of Israel, Jeroboam created two new religious centers: one in Dan at the northern edge of this kingdom, and the other in Bethel at its southern edge. He built a statue of a golden calf at each of these religious centers, and he claimed that God was enthroned on top of these two statues, just as the Aaronid priests claimed that God was enthroned on top of two statues of cherubim in the temple in Jerusalem.

(Note that "calf" is a bit of a misleading translation that gives the impression that these were statues of weak young calves; actually, they were calves who had almost grown to be mature bulls and were symbols of potency. Likewise, "cherubim" is a bit misleading to modern readers because we think of cherubs as infants with wings; these cherubim were more like winged sphinxes and were much more intimidating than the cute cherubs of Rafael.)

In both kingdoms, there was an ongoing struggle between the worship of God and the worship of the Canaanite god Baal. A series of prophets denounced Baal worship and called for a return to exclusive worship of God, but they were ignored by most of the rulers of both kingdoms. This struggle against pagan worship may have begun during the united monarchy: the book of Kings, compiled by Mushite priests, tells us that Solomon introduced the worship of pagan gods in Jerusalem late in his reign.[23]

In the centuries that followed, there was a series of ruling dynasties in the northern kingdom of Israel, as rebellious pretenders toppled kings and took their places. But there was only one ruling dynasty in Judah: descendents of David remained on the throne throughout Judah's history, leading the people of Judah to believe that God had loved David so much that he promised him that his descendents would always remain on the throne in Jerusalem, though God punished them for worshiping other gods by taking away most of David's territory and leaving them with only the territory of Judah.

# Who Wrote the E and J Texts?

Now we have enough background in the history of the time to understand the people who wrote the E text and J text.

## The E Text

Most scholars who accept the documentary hypothesis believe that the E text was written by a Mushite priest, one of the priests who believed they were descended from Moses, who had controlled the early Israelite religious center in Shiloh, and who were exiled to Anathoth by Solomon. E's stories of the exodus emphasize the exclusive importance of their supposed ancestor, Moses, and downplay the importance of Aaron, the supposed ancestor of their rivals the Aaronid priests. E's stories focus on the northern kingdom and particularly on the territory of Ephraim, where Shiloh was located.

Solomon expelled the Mushite priests from Jerusalem. With the division of the kingdom, these priests might have expected Jeroboam to restore their religious center in Shiloh, which was in the northern kingdom, but instead Jeroboam created the new centers in Dan and Bethel. Solomon had taken away the Mushite priests' religious authority when he removed them from the temple in Jerusalem, and they were still dispossessed under Jeroboam. Though some scholars have suggested that Jeroboam installed Aaronid priests at Bethel and Mushite priests at Dan,[24] this is uncertain. It does seem clear that an important group of Mushite priests remained in

Anathoth, where Solomon had banished them, since the Bible tells us that Jeremiah, writing hundreds of years after Solomon, was identified as one of "the priests that were in Anathoth."[25]

The Mushite priests were resentful about their loss of authority, and the best sign of this resentment is the story of the golden calf in the E text of the Bible. This is a familiar story: when Moses went up to Mt. Sinai or Mt. Horeb to receive the law, the people complained to Aaron that they wanted a new god to worship, and Aaron built a golden calf and officiated at the sacrifices to it. When Moses came down from the mountain, he was so angry to see this pagan worship that he threw down and smashed the two tablets of the Ten Commandments and killed about three thousand Israelites as punishment.[26] This story was meant to criticize two groups we would expect the displaced Mushite priests to resent. It criticized the Aaronid priests who controlled Judah's religious center in Jerusalem by showing that their ancestor Aaron promoted pagan worship. It criticized Israel's religious centers in Dan and Bethel by showing that the golden calves, which were so prominent at these centers, were pagan symbols that Moses himself had condemned.

The story of the Israelites worshiping the golden calf in the desert is well known today, but it obviously was not well known at the time. If the golden calf had been a well-known symbol of heresy, Jeroboam would have used some other symbol at his new religious centers. Perhaps there was a little-known tradition about the golden calf in the desert, which the Mushite priests made much more prominent after Jeroboam built his golden calves, but there certainly was not a well-known tradition.

As we will see later, it is possible that the story of the golden calf was written later than most of the E text, but it is the most striking example of the attitude of the Mushite priests who wrote the E text toward the Aaronid priests in Jerusalem and toward the religious centers of the northern kingdom of Israel.

## The J Text

Most scholars who accept the documentary hypothesis believe that the J text was written by a member of the royal court of Judah. This text focuses largely on events in the south, in the territory of Judah, and even gives origin myths for subtribes of Judah. It has Jacob give a blessing that raises Judah above his older brothers.[27] It makes Judah sympathetic and even heroic in the story of Joseph and his brothers.[28] It does not focus on the sort of legal matters that priests were interested in: the E and P texts both include extensive legal codes, but the J text has no legal code at all apart from its version of the Ten Commandments.

The authors of the other texts were priests, which means they must have been men, but as a member of the Judean court, J could have been a man or a woman. The stories in the J text include many strong women who control the action. Lot's daughters get him drunk so they can have children by him.[29] Rebekah deceives Jacob and manipulates Isaac to make Jacob steal Esau's blessing.[30] Rachel tricks her father Laban after stealing his *teraphim* (household gods) by telling him, "I cannot rise up before thee; for the manner of women is upon me."[31] Tamar manipulates Judah by posing as a harlot and tricking Judah into giving her his signet, cord and staff, which let her prove Judah was the father of her illegitimate child.[32] Yet J also degrades women: J assumes that it is fine for Lot to have absolute power to dispose of his daughters and sees nothing wrong with Lot offering his daughters to the men of Sodom who threaten his guests.[33] J has God say to Eve, "…thy desire shall be to thy husband, and he shall rule over thee."[34] And, of course, God is masculine in J as in the other texts. Based on these examples, it seems that J might have been a woman who took for granted the male domination that was typical of her society but who also knew that clever women could manipulate and control men.

It is hard for us to imagine how women might have thought in a society so different from ours, but it does seem possible that J was a woman. This book follows Harold Bloom's lead by referring to J as "she" and "her."[35] It is possible but by no means certain that J was a woman, and this book uses "she" and "her" because it is awkward to constantly say "he or she" and "him or her."

It is difficult to determine the dates of the E and J texts precisely. Most scholars have traditionally believed that J is the earlier of the two. But there is actually little enough evidence that the best we can say is that they were both written during the period when there were two kingdoms, between about 930 BCE and 722 BCE.

The exact date of the two texts is not very important to our purposes in this book. It is important that we understand the world in which they were written. There were two kingdoms: Judah's religion and government centered in Jerusalem, and Israel's religion centered in Dan and Bethel. Aaronid priests controlled the temple in Jerusalem. There was a group of displaced Mushite priests who still had strong opinions, though they had lost their formal religious authority when Solomon banished them to Anathoth and gave control of the temple in Jerusalem to Aaronid priests. E was written by a Mushite priest, and J was written by a member of the royal court in Jerusalem.

# The World of D and P

This world changed dramatically when the Assyrian empire, which was centered in the northern part of Mesopotamia, northeast of Israel, became powerful enough to threaten and conquer nearby nations.

In 740 BCE or a bit later, Assyria began conquering some Israelite cities and exiling their people.[36] In 722 BCE, Assyria conquered the northern kingdom of Israel entirely and exiled many of its people.[37] Some residents of the northern kingdom must have fled from the advancing army and become refugees in Judah. Most residents of the northern kingdom went into exile, as we can see from later prophecies that predicted they would return.[38] But they never returned and became known as the ten lost tribes of Israel—"lost" because they assimilated into the nations where they were exiled and lost their identity as Israelites.

After conquering Israel, Assyria wanted to expand further south by conquering Judah. Hezekiah, king of Judah from about 715 to 686 BCE,[39] prepared to survive an Assyrian siege by building a tunnel to carry water into Jerusalem from the spring of Gihon. More important to the history of the Bible's texts, Hezekiah also prepared to resist the Assyrians by leading a religious revival based on the idea that Israel had been conquered as a punishment for worshipping other gods. To protect Judah from a similar fate, he suppressed all pagan religion and allowed only the worship of God.[40]

Hezekiah was probably also the one who first banned the creation of images. What is called "the covenant code," an early version of the law quoted by E, says you should not create images of gods to worship, not that you should not create any images: "[EX 20:20b]gods of silver, or gods of gold, ye shall not make unto you." The early Israelites created many images: in the Temple, the ark of the covenant rested on the wings of statues of two cherubim,[41] there was a molten sea (a large basin of water) that rested on the backs of twelve oxen,[42] with a base ornamented with figures of lions, oxen, and cherubim.[43] And when the Israelites were attacked by serpents in the desert, God told Moses to make a serpent of brass and put it on a pole, and any Israelite who was bitten by a serpent would be healed when he looked at this brazen serpent.[44] A relic in the Temple was supposedly this brazen serpent made by Moses, and as part of his reform, Hezekiah broke this serpent in pieces when he found the Israelites were worshipping it.[45] Hezekiah destroyed this image, even though it was attributed to Moses, because he found that making it led the Israelites to worship it, so it is plausible that he originated the general ban on making images. This ban seems to be in the Ten Commandments, which say "[EX 20:4]Thou shalt not make unto thee a graven image, nor any manner of likeness, of any thing that is in heaven above, or that is in the earth beneath, or that is in the water under the earth; [5]thou shalt not bow down unto them, nor serve them," which seems to condemn making images as well as worshipping them. The commandment against making images clearly was not in effect when the Temple was first built, since none of the prophets condemned its images.

The Judeans apparently believed that Hezekiah's religious revival worked. The Bible tells us that the Assyrians invaded Judah, conquered fortified cities, and received tribute from Hezekiah.[46] But when Assyria besieged Jerusalem, an angel came and slaughtered 185,000 Assyrians while they slept, making the Assyrians abandon the siege.[47] This angel may have been a plague that killed Assyrian soldiers, since another text of the Bible identifies a plague with an angel.[48]

The next Judean king, Manasseh, abandoned Hezekiah's religious reforms, as did his son Amon. The Bible tells us that they, like many earlier kings, did "evil in the sight of the Lord"[49] by worshipping other gods. Amon's son, Josiah, was king from about 649 to 600 BCE, during the time when the Babylonian empire replaced the Assyrian empire as the main power in Mesopotamia and the main threat to Judah.

To protect Judah, Josiah, instituted a religious reform even stricter than Hezekiah's. Josiah not only banned worship of all other gods, but also banned sacrifice anywhere except in the temple in Jerusalem.[50] Josiah's reform was inspired by the discovery of a new book of the Torah while the Temple was being repaired,[51] a book that supposedly had existed since the time of Moses but had not been known before Josiah's time. Scholars generally agree that this new scroll makes up most of what we now call the book of Deuteronomy, the fifth book of the Torah where Moses delivers a farewell address to the Israelites that summarizes all their obligations under the law.

Many hoped that Josiah and his reforms would save Israel, but in 609 BCE, Josiah was killed by Egyptian archers during a battle resisting the army of Pharaoh Necho II,[52] and his successors abandoned his reforms. After Josiah's death, a series of kings with short reigns sometimes resisted and sometimes submitted to the Babylonians. In 586 BCE, the Babylonians conquered Jerusalem, destroyed the Temple, and carried away the prominent Judeans to Babylon as captives, leaving only manual laborers. They killed the sons of the last Judean king, Zedekiah, while he watched and then blinded him and imprisoned him in Babylon.[53] They installed a pro-Babylonian Judean named Gedaliah as their governor, but he was killed by anti-Babylonian Judeans, leading many of the remaining Judeans to flee to Egypt to escape Babylon's revenge.[54]

This exile in Babylon did not last long. In 538 BCE, Cyrus the Great, King of Persia, conquered Babylon and allowed the people who had been exiled there to return to their homelands. Judea became a province of the Persian Empire, but the exiles returned slowly because many had become comfortable in Babylon and stayed there. In 457 BCE, the Persian king Artaxerses let Ezra, a scribe and Aaronid priest, lead a large group of exiles back to Jerusalem, where Ezra was shocked to discover that Jewish men had been marrying non-Jewish women and dissolved these marriages. In about 445 BCE, Artaxerses appointed a Jewish member of his court, Nehemiah, to be governor of Judea and gave him permission to rebuild the walls of Jerusalem. After the walls were rebuilt, Ezra read what was probably the entire Torah that we have today to the assembled Jews of Jerusalem.[55]

# Who Wrote the D and P Texts?

Now, we have enough background to understand who wrote the D text and P text.

## The D Text

As we have seen, the D text is the book of Deuteronomy, which most scholars who accept the documenary hypothesis believe is the scroll found in the temple during Josiah's reign that inspired Josiah's religious reform. Deuteronomy is supposed to be Moses' farewell speech, delivered before he died, so when the editor R compiled the entire Torah, he put it after the combined E, J and P texts, with only brief passages from these three texts about the death of Moses after the D text.

The D text was written by Mushite priests, like the E text, but E was written before the fall of Israel, while D was written after the fall of Israel and inspired King Josiah's religious reform. It talks about exile, which had already happened to Israel and which threatened Judah, when Moses says to the Israelites:

> DEUT 4:25 When thou shalt beget children, and children's children, and ye shall have been long in the land, and shall deal corruptly, and make a graven image, even the form of any thing, and shall do that which is evil in the sight of the Lord thy God, to provoke Him; 26I call heaven and earth to witness against you this day, that ye shall soon utterly perish from off the land whereunto ye go over the Jordan to possess it; ye shall not prolong your days upon it, but shall utterly be destroyed. 27And the Lord shall scatter you among the peoples, and ye shall be left few in number among the nations, whither the Lord shall lead you away.

Scholars generally believe that the history books that follow Deuteronomy in the Bible (Joshua, Judges, I and II Samuel, I and II Kings) are a continuation of Deuteronomy, and they call these books "the Deuteronomistic history."[56] This history seems to be made up partly of a compilation of earlier texts and partly of new text. Much of this history, beginning with I Kings 10, after Solomon has dedicated the Temple, and continuing through the end of II Kings, seems like a morality tale illustrating the main point of Deuteronomy: one king after another leads the Israelites to "do evil in the sight of the Lord" by worshipping other gods, and as a result, God punishes either him or his descendents and the kingdom where they ruled. Hezekiah and Josiah abolish the worship of other gods, and God rewards them and the kingdom of Judah.

It seems that most of this history was written when Josiah was still alive. The author expected the morality tale to culminate when Josiah established a secure kingdom as a reward for his reform, but the author's hopes were crushed when the Egyptian army killed Josiah in battle. The original hopeful version of the Deuteronomistic history was revised later to include the stories of the faithless kings who succeeded Josiah and of the destruction of Judah, and some revisions were made to the earlier text of Deuteronomy. The two authors are called Dtr1, who wrote before Josiah's death, and Dtr 2, who revised the work later.

This edition includes the E, J, and P texts, which tell parallel stories and were intertwined with each other by redactors. It does not include the D text, which was not intertwined with the other texts but was kept separate in the book of Deuteronomy. The division of Deuteronomy into its law code, Dtr1, and Dtr2 is available elsewhere.[57]

Incidentally, Deuteronomy includes some admirable laws, such as the familiar "Thou shalt not steal," "Thou shalt not kill," and "Thou shalt not bear false witness against thy neighbor"[58] But it is also known for its bloodthirsty passages saying that, when they enter the promised land, the Israelites should slaughter all the people living there:

> DEUT 7:1 When the Lord thy God shall bring thee into the land whither thou goest to possess it, and shall cast out many nations before thee, the Hittite, and the Girgashite, and the Amorite, and the Canaanite, and the Perizzite, and the Hivite, and the Jebusite, seven nations greater and mightier than thou; [2]and when the Lord thy God shall deliver them up before thee, and thou shalt smite them; then thou shalt utterly destroy them; thou shalt make no covenant with them, nor show mercy unto them; [3]neither shalt thou make marriages with them: thy daughter thou shalt not give unto his son, nor his daughter shalt thou take unto thy son. [4]For he will turn away thy son from following Me, that they may serve other gods; so will the anger of the Lord be kindled against you, and He will destroy thee quickly.

This call for ethnic cleansing was a panicked reaction to the threat of destruction and exile at a time when many believed that Israel and Judah had worshipped other gods because they married foreign women and so believed that Judeans had to avoid foreigners to survive.

Before this time, there are prominent examples of intermarriage. Joseph married an Egyptian who bore his children Ephraim and Manasseh,[59] and Moses married a Midianite.[60] Thus, two of the most admired men of Israelite history married foreigners, the two largest tribes of early Israel (Ephraim and Manasseh) were descended from Joseph and his Egyptian wife, and the Mushite priests who presided over the early religion of Israel were descended from Moses and his Midianite wife. Ethnic exclusiveness was a later attempt to maintain religious purity, a reaction to the threat of national destruction.

As we have seen, ethnic exclusiveness was also enforced after the exile, when Ezra dissolved marriages between Jewish men and non-Jewish women, but there was also controversy about it at the time. The book of *Ruth*, written around this time, tells the story of a Moabite woman who married an Israelite, followed his religion, and—the book reveals at the very end—was the ancestor of King David. Thus, King David himself, the greatest of the Israelite kings, was not the product of the sort of ethnic exclusiveness that Ezra was promoting at the time of the return from Babylon.

## The P Text

The P text was written by Aaronid priests. Much of it, including the entire book of Leviticus, describes the design and rituals of the Temple in Jerusalem, which the Aaronid priest presided over, saying they were based on the design and rituals of the Tabernacle, the tent that the Israelites carried through the desert and used for worship and sacrifice.

The P text gives a very prominent place to Aaron. The E text, written by Mushite priests, says that God spoke only to Moses; the P text often says that He spoke to Moses and Aaron. When Moses says he is not good at speaking, the E text has God tell him not to worry because He will speak through him;[61] in the P text, by contrast, God tells Moses that Aaron will speak for him[62]—implying that the Aaronid priests inherited this authority. The notes to the three texts in this edition mention many other examples where P gives Aaron a more prominent place.

Sometimes P goes further by denigrating Moses. For example, there are two stories of Moses striking a rock with his staff at Meribah to get water from it. In the E version, God tells Moses to strike the rock with his staff, water flows from the rock, and Moses is praised for this miracle.[63] In the P version, God tells Moses to speak to the rock, but Moses is angry and strikes the rock with his staff instead; because he acted in anger and disobeyed, God punishes Moses by saying that he will not be allowed to enter the promised land and incidentally punishes the innocent Aaron in the same way.[64]

P often attacks the Midianites, denigrating the Mushite priests who believed they were descended from Moses and therefore also from his Midianite wife. P says that the Midianites led the Israelites to worship a pagan god called the Baal of Peor[65] and that the Israelites should attack the Midianites to punish them.[66] By contrast, J says the Moabites led Israel to worship Baal of Peor.[67]

P does not mention Moses' Midianite wife and father-in-law. By contrast, both E and J look favorably on Moses' Midianite father-in-law, whom E says was named Jethro[68] and J says was named Reuel.[69] E in particular says that Jethro gave Moses good advice by telling him to establish judges,[70] and in this story, Jethro seems to be a more important priest than Aaron: "[EX 18:12]And Jethro, Moses' father-in-law, took a burnt-offering and sacrifices for God; and Aaron came, and all the elders of Israel, to eat bread with Moses' father-in-law before God."

It is easy to understand P's attitude as an Aaronid priest, but it is hard to pin down exactly when he wrote this text. Most scholars have said that he wrote during the Babylonian exile or shortly after the exile, and that he described the temple's design and rituals in such detail so they could be restored when the second temple was built. But a significant minority have argued convincingly that P was written before the exile, around the time of Hezekiah,[71] which implies that it described the rituals in such detail to help carry out Hezekiah's religious reform. The first of these theories would make P later than D, and the second would make P earlier than D.

This unsettled point is not very important to this book. We can understand the character and bias of P as an Aaronid priest without knowing at which of these times he lived. This book does not include the D text because it is not intertwined with the E, J and P texts, which are the texts that this book untangles.

# The Two Redactors

The E, J and P texts were woven together by two redactors (editors).

The first redactor combined the J and E texts, so he is generally called RJE and the combined text he created is called the JE text. We can see that these were combined earlier, because parts of P seem to have been written as a response to JE. In some cases, it corrects JE by retelling a story with a less anthropomorphic God. In some cases, it corrects JE by retelling a story in a way that gives more prominence to Aaron. Overall, P's responses to JE make it seem that its writer was familiar with the combined JE text.

Most important to any attempt to untangle the texts, RJE did not consider it necessary to keep his complete source texts. If a passage in J and a passage in E described the same event, RJE might avoid repetition by including only one of them or by including parts of one and parts of the other. Thus, there are many gaps in what has survived of the J and E texts. Most of these gaps are in E, because J was a more compelling and dramatic writer. In some cases, however, RJE does keep both texts: for example, E says that, when Jacob and Laban made a covenant, they set up a pillar,[72] while J says that they set up a heap of stones,[73] and RJE intertwined these two stories.

The second redactor combined the JE, P and D texts and some shorter independent texts to form the first five books of today's Bible. He combined JE with P and inserted some earlier texts to form the first four books of the Bible, and he formed the fifth book of the Bible from D with a bit from the other texts about the death of Moses added at the end. He is generally called R, because he was the main redactor who combined everything.

R tried to keep as much as possible of his source texts. With only a few exceptions (discussed in Appendix 3), he kept both the version from JE and the version from P, even if they contradict each other.

In some cases, R put intact passages from JE and P next to each other:

we have seen that the creation story from P in Genesis 1 is followed by the creation story from JE in Genesis 2, with each story preserved as a whole. R could have gotten rid of the inconsistency between these two stories by editing out just a few verses in J that repeat the creation in a different order than the story in P, but he apparently considered it more important to preserve the entire source texts than to avoid inconsistency.

In some cases, R intertwined passages from the two texts in intricate ways: we have seen that the story of Noah alternates passages from JE with passages from P. Again, R could have gotten rid of the inconsistencies by editing out contradictory details from the P text so the final text said that it rained forty days and then Noah sent out doves, but he apparently considered it important to keep the complete source texts, including the details in the P text that say the flood lasted about ten and a half months and then Noah sent out a raven.

In some cases, R put the two source texts a distance from each other: the E text of the story about Moses striking the rock to produce water is in Exodus 15 while the P text is at Numbers 20, with the entire book of Leviticus and large chunks of Exodus and Numbers between the two, making it difficult for readers to notice the inconsistency. This edition tries to make it easy to compare doublets by moving those that have been separated so they are next to each other whenever possible.

In all these cases and many others, R included information from both the JE and the P texts despite the contradictions. Apparently, he had such respect for the source texts that he felt compelled to include virtually everything they said, even when it weakened his final product. The story of Noah and many other stories show that he was willing to intertwine the source texts in a way that sometimes made it hard to discern their original meaning, so he apparently thought that respecting the text meant preserving the letter even at the cost of preserving the spirit. Yet there are some cases where R removed parts of his source texts (discussed in Appendix 3), presumably because the contradictions were too blatant to include.

RJE and R sometimes added brief passages of their own to tie together or supplement the source texts. Passages written by the redactors are in parentheses in this edition, and readers should ignore them if they want to get the sense of the original source texts.

# Chapter 2: Comparing the Texts

Each of the three texts, E, J and P, has its own distinct view of religion. The texts contradict each other but each is consistent within itself. There are some problems with the continuity of these texts, but these problems can be explained as results of how each text was changed in the course of being written or revised. Reading the three texts separately supports the documentary hypothesis by revealing that each one is unified and each one has its own distinct character that distinguishes it from the others.

Here, we will give a few examples of the character of each of these three; there are many more examples in the Notes column that is next to the texts in this edition. We will also look at whether the texts are continuous.

Up to this point, we have been summarizing the opinions of scholars who accept the documentary hypothesis. Now, we will begin talking about some new things we can learn by arranging the texts so it is easy to read through them from beginning to end and by separating the Bible's text in a way that makes the source texts as coherent as possible.

## E's Religion

Because E is the earliest priestly text, written by Mushite priests who claimed to be descended from Moses, it is closer than the other texts to the original religion of the Israelite priests. Of course, it was written hundreds of years after the Israelites arrived in Canaan, so there were undoubtedly vast changes. Nevertheless, it is striking how different the religion of the E text is from pagan religions—and from the J text, which is much closer to pagan religions.

The E text begins with Abraham, and the stories that it tells about the patriarchs and the journey through the wilderness are specific to the Israelites. E says that Abraham worshipped a new God, different from pagan gods, and that this God later revealed His name to Moses. Thus, this text distinguishes the Israelite religion sharply from other religions.

E's religion is both moral and ritualistic. His version of the law quotes an older document called the Covenant Code (Ex. 20:19-23:33), which is made up partly of moral commandments, partly of ritualistic commandments, and partly of the sort of rough laws that are needed to regulate a relatively primitive society.

E's God is not anthropomorphic. God does not change His mind or regret

His decisions.[74] He does not walk on the earth. He speaks to most people in dreams or through angels. Moses is the only person He speaks to directly, and even Moses can see only His back and not His face.[75]

One striking feature of the E text is that it does not include any of the earlier myths that are at the beginning of the Bible: creation, Adam and Eve, Cain and Abel, Noah's flood, the tower of Babel. The E text starts with Abraham, and it is concerned with the patriarchs and Moses, particularly with their experience of God and also with stories of the patriarchs that justify the relations of the Israelite tribes. The earlier myths are from the J text, which was strongly influenced by the religions of surrounding peoples, and some were included in the P text as a response to J. E might have known some or all of these myths, but he left them out of his text of the Bible, showing that he did not consider them important to the Israelite religion.

Some have speculated that E might have written versions of these earlier myths that RJE did not include, but this idea is not plausible. Since E's view of God is much less anthropomorphic than J's, there would undoubtedly have been many differences in their versions of these early myths, so RJE would probably have included some of the material from E. Much material from E is included in the stories of the patriarchs and of the exodus, so it is hard to believe that E wrote a version of the earlier myths and that nothing at all was included from it. It is far more plausible that E did not include these myths because he was focused on the Israelite religion, which was rooted in the patriarchs and Moses.

This fact is important because the creation myth has discredited the Bible. We now know that the different species of living organisms were not created in the beginning; they were formed by evolution and have changed over time. Fundamentalists who believe the entire Bible is literally true look foolish when they contradict the scientific consensus about evolution, but in fact, creation is not part of the E text, the text of the Bible that represents the religion of the earliest Israelite priests.

This fact also makes the E text unique. Every other early religion includes some sort of creation myth. We cannot help wondering why E is so different from other early religions, with no creation myth or other early myths, with a religion that is ethical as well as ritualistic, and with a God that is not anthropomorphic and cannot be represented by images.

## Is the E Text Continuous?

There are many gaps in the E text because RJE often preferred J's version of stories over E's, but what we have shows that the E text told a continuous and coherent story of the early history of Israel, extending from the time of Abraham and the other patriarchs through the exodus and wandering in the desert, to the death of Moses.

There are places where E interrupts the narrative to give information about rituals or laws. For example, as the Israelites are about to leave Egypt, E gives a lengthy description of their Passover ritual;[76] and when Moses gives the law to the Israelites, the E text quotes the entire covenant code, an earlier document of the Mushite priests that states the law.[77] But these interruptions are exactly what we would expect from a priestly source who is telling this story to strengthen his people's religion. They do not mean that the E text lacks the integrity that we would expect from a document by a single author.

Yet there are a couple of possible exceptions to the continuity of the E text.

We have seen that E told the story of Moses breaking the tablets of the Ten Commandments when he saw the Israelites worshipping the golden calf, implicitly criticizing the golden calves that Jeroboam set up at the two religious centers he created in the northern kingdom of Israel. But, apart from this story, there is no other mention of the Ten Commandments in the E text. E describes Moses smashing the tablets but says nothing about his receiving the tablets or about his replacing the smashed tablets with new ones, and E does not include a text of the Ten Commandments.

This story also seems out of place in the E text, since it comes after the Israelites accept the covenant.[78] It seems more plausible that Moses would give the Israelites all the commandments, including the Covenant Code and the Ten Commandments, and then would ask them to accept the covenant.

It is possible that the original E text included the rest of the story of the Ten Commandments and the reason why they were given after Israel accepted the covenant but that RJE removed these stories because he preferred J's version of events. It is also possible that the story of the golden calf is a later addition.

Another passage in E is even more problematic:

> NUM 12:1And Miriam and Aaron spoke against Moses because of the Cushite woman whom he had married; for he had married a Cushite woman. 2And they said: 'Hath the Lord indeed spoken only with Moses? hath He not spoken also with us?'

In response to their complaint,

> NUM 12:5... the Lord came down in a pillar of cloud, and stood at the door of the Tent .... 6And He said: 'Hear now My words: if there be a prophet among you, I the Lord do make Myself known unto him in a vision, I do speak with him in a dream. 7My servant Moses is not so; he is trusted in all My house; 8with him do I speak mouth to mouth, even manifestly....

As a punishment, Miriam becomes leprous and she is cured only after Moses prays for her and she is isolated for seven days.

This claim that God speaks only to Moses is typical of E, but, apart from this passage, the pillar of cloud appears only J. In J, the Israelites are led out of Egypt by God in the form of a pillar of cloud in the day and a pillar of fire at night, but in E they are led by an angel (Ex. 23:20, Num. 20:16). In J, God comes down to the door of the tent of assembly repeatedly as a pillar of cloud, but in E He does not. God appearing to all the Israelites as a pillar of cloud is typical of J and contradicts E's belief that God appears directly only to Moses. This passage itself is self-contradictory: God speaks directly to Aaron and Miriam in order to tell them that He speaks directly only to Moses. This is the only place in E where God speaks directly to someone other than Moses, rather than appearing in a dream or a vision.

How can this strange passage have been written? The most plausible explanation is that it was written later by someone who was a Mushite priest like E but who knew the combined JE text rather than the E text itself. The JE text has so many references to God coming down to the tent of assembly as a pillar of cloud that this later Mushite priest might have taken it for granted and assumed that it does not violate the principle that God speaks directly only to Moses.

The theory that this passage was written by a later author also explains why it says Moses had a Cushite wife, while all the other mentions of Moses' wife in the Torah say she was a Midianite. Many commentaries on the Bible, both scholarly and popular, say that this must have been Moses second wife: in addition to the wife he took in Midian, Moses must have married an African, since Cush was south of Ethiopia. But rather than meaning someone from Cush, Cushite could mean someone from Cushan, which is another name for Midian. We see that Cushan is the same as Midian in a poem in the book of Habakkuk: "[HAB 3:7]I see the tents of Cushan in affliction; The curtains of the land of Midian do tremble." Ancient Hebrew poetry commonly repeats the same statement using different words, and in this case, the second half of the verse clearly repeats the first half by using "the curtains of Midian" to mean the same thing as "the tents of Cushan." Since the rest of E uses the word "Midian" and was written before 722 BCE, and the other early use of Cushan to mean Midian is in the book of Habbakuk, written in the mid-to-late 600s BCE, it seems likely that Cushan was not used in early times to mean Midian and that this passage about Moses' Cushite wife was written later than most of E.

This theory that there was a second and later author of E would also explain E's story of Moses breaking the Ten Commandments. If this story was written by a later Mushite priest who knew the combined JE text, then it would fit right into JE's narrative of the Ten Commandments, which comes from J, explaining why the Ten Commandments are mentioned in this story but not mentioned anywhere else in E.

It would also explain why this story has an anthropomorphic view of God that is typical of J but not of E. In this story, God wants to destroy Israel and make a new nation just from Moses, but Moses convinces Him not to do this by saying that it would make people think badly of Him, appealing to His vanity.[79] Nowhere else in the E text does God change his mind in this way, so it seems reasonable that this passage was written by a later Mushite priest who was influenced by J's stories about God changing his mind, which he had read as an integral part of the JE text.

Thus, it seems possible that a later Mushite priest modified the JE text and added a few passages—including these two passages, which are more hostile to Aaron and Miriam than anything else in the E text.

This possibility needs more discussion. For now, we can say that, apart from a few problematic passages that might have been added later, the E text seems to be a continuous narrative written by one person.

# J's Religion

J was a member of the court of Judah rather than being a priest. Because the kings of Judah made alliances with surrounding countries by taking wives from those countries, this court was multi-cultural, so J was influenced by the religions of other countries. J also tells us that Judah had three sons with a Canaanite woman,[80] which indicates that there was a considerable mixture of Canaanite ancestry in the tribe of Judah, so we would expect pagan influences in Judah's culture and religion even before they had a multi-cultural court.

As a result of these influences, J conflated the Israelite religion and other religions. Both E and P say that the God of Israel first revealed Himself to Abraham and the patriarchs as El and first revealed His real name, YHWH, to Moses. By contrast, J says that the worship of this God goes much further back in history: before the time of Noah, in the days of Adam's grandson Enosh, people began "[GEN 4:26]to call upon the name of the Lord [=YHWH]." J also speaks of the "[GEN 31:53]The God of Abraham, and the God of Nahor, the God of their father," showing that she thinks Abraham continued his father's and family's religion, rather than making a decisive break with earlier religion, as he does in the E and P texts.

J begins her narrative with pre-Israelite myths, unlike E who begins with Abraham. Adam and Eve, Cain and Abel, the flood, and the tower of Babel are influenced by myths that are earlier than the patriarchs and that come from non-Israelite sources. Appendix 5 discusses possible sources of these myths.

J's religion does not have a moral element. J presents a version of the Ten Commandments that is purely ritualistic, with commandments such as "The feast of unleavened bread shalt thou keep" and "Thou shalt not seethe a kid in its mother's milk."[81] She does not include the familiar moral commandments such as "Thou shalt not steal" and "Thou shalt not kill." Apart from these ritualistic Ten Commandments, there are no Israelite religious texts incorporated in J, as there are in E and P.

In line with her amoral religion, J admires tricksters. When we considered whether J was a woman, we saw that she described Lot's daughters,[82] Rebekah,[83] Rachel[84] and Tamar[85] as tricksters who are more or less dishonest. J also makes Jacob himself a trickster: Jacob and Rebekah use fraud to steal Isaac's blessing from Esau,[86] and Jacob responds to Laban's attempts to swindle him by out-swindling Laban, feeding the herd in a way that makes them give birth to the speckled, spotted, and dark goats and sheep that Jacob can keep.[87] In E, by contrast, there are no admirable tricksters: in E's story of Jacob and Laban, God makes the herd give birth to animals that Jacob can keep, apparently because God cares about justice, as Jacob says:

> GEN 31:7 And your father hath mocked me, and changed my wages ten times; but God suffered him not to hurt me. [8]If he said thus: The speckled shall be thy wages; then all the flock bore speckled; and if he said thus: The streaked shall be thy wages; then bore all the flock streaked. [9]Thus God hath taken away the cattle of your father, and given them to me.

J has a primitive religion with an anthropomorphic God. God changes his mind, regrets his decisions, and even seems to fear competition from humans. He seems to worry that if Adam and Eve eat the tree of life, they might compete with Him and the angels.[88] He has to go and visit locations to see what is happening there: He goes down to see the tower of Babel,[89] and He tells Abraham that He has to go to Sodom to see whether the accounts he has heard about are true and it should be destroyed.[90] So much for omniscience!

In J, God speaks and appears directly to many people, and He meets people while He walks on the earth. He walks in the Garden of Eden to talk to Adam and Eve,[91] and He even walks right up to Abraham's tent with two angels, looking like three men, and stays to have a meal.[92] He talks directly to a long series of people, beginning with Adam, Cain, and Noah. After God gives the Ten Commandments, seventy of the elders of Israel go up to Mount Sinai to see Him.[93]

J loved telling dramatic stories. She seems to tell stories just for the joy of story telling, and she added details to traditional stories that make them more dramatic by describing the characters' emotions; for example, she includes an intense description of Joseph's emotions when he sees his brother Benjamin.[94] She often used repetition to heighten drama: for example, she had Abraham ask God to spare Sodom if it has fifty righteous men, and then has Abraham gradually lower the number until, after six repetitions, Abraham finally convinces God to agree to spare Sodom if it has ten righteous men.[95]

She is a bit like Sophocles or Shakespeare, who use their imaginations to dramatize traditional material from myth or history. It seems likely that she knew of a tradition that Abraham bargained with God about saving Sodom, and she dramatized it by imagining the bargaining and inventing the details that it began with fifty, then went down to forty-five, and so on until it went down to ten in six steps.

It is strange that, after her pagan myths and her imaginative dramatizations were combined with E and later with P, they were taken as revealed truth and became part of the basis of the Israelite religion. Like the J text, Shakespeare's *Romeo and Juliet* was based on history, on the actual feud between the Montecchi and the Cappelletti families of Verona; later writers invented the story of two tragic lovers from these two families; and Shakespeare himself added drama to this story by inventing touches such as the balcony scene. It would be very strange if people came to believe that Shakespeare's story was completely true, so that all the standard histories of Verona said that the balcony scene actually occurred and the family names were actually Montague and Capulet. What happened to J's dramatizations of traditional material is even stranger: for over two millennia, people have believed that her imaginative embellishments and her anthropomorphic God are revealed truth.

J was a great writer, which presumably is why RJE was more inclined to preserve J's version of stories than E's. Harold Bloom has said "J's cognitive power is unmatched among Western writers until Shakespeare."[96] But because she is influenced by pagan cultures, her writing is not the best source for understanding the earliest Israelite religion, any more than Shakespeare is the best source for understanding the history of Verona.

The contrast between E and J disproves Wellhausen's theory about the inevitable stages of the evolution of religion. E is closer to the religion of the early Israelite priests than J is, but J's religion is clearly much more primitive than E's. Much theorizing about the early Israelite religion simply assumes that the earlier religion must have been more primitive. But when we untangle the early texts and read E and J separately, we can see that this is not true. When J and E were combined to form the JE text, including J's primitive myths and anthropomorphic God, there was clearly a decline from E's earlier version of the Israelite religion.

# Is the J Text Continuous?

The J text is a continuous and very readable story that begins with creation and continues to the death of Moses. It has a distinct view of religion that contrasts with the religions of E and P by being closer to paganism. The text is episodic, with one event after another, which is what we would expect from someone like J who cannot resist telling a good story, but if you read it from beginning to end, it reads like a continuous text by a single author.

The Biblical scholar Richard Elliott Friedman has argued convincingly that this text extends beyond the book of J and was also incorporated in the books of Joshua, Judges, Samuel and Kings, providing a continuous story from the creation to the time when Solomon became king. He points out that it is unified because later episodes echo and refer back to earlier episodes.[97]

There is one major interruption to the continuity of the J text. Its story of Joseph is interrupted by its long story of Tamar lying with Judah.[98] The story of Tamar seems to be by J, because it reflects her usual concern with the tribe of Judah and her usual admiration for tricksters, but it does not seem plausible that skilled narrator like J would interrupt the very dramatic story of Joseph and his brothers with a different story. It is possible that a redactor changed the order of J's stories or that a later source from Judah wrote the story of Tamar and a redactor inserted it. The story begins with a clumsy transition, "GEN 38:1And it came to pass at that time, that ...," which sounds like some redactor is trying to make it look like it belongs in a place where it obviously does not really belong.

Yet this one interruption to the continuity of the J text does not destroy the overall impression that it was originally a single text by a single writer, as the documentary hypothesis claims.

# P's Religion

P was one of the Aaronid priests who presided over rituals at the Temple in Jerusalem, and his religion is ritualistic. The P text includes lengthy descriptions of how to build the ark of the covenant, the tabernacle, and other items used by priests, of different sacrifices performed on different occasions, and of laws about what food can be eaten, laws about sacrifices needed after one becomes impure, and other laws that regulate priests' behavior

In P, religion is a matter of performing the right ritual at the right time. If you perform the wrong ritual, you can be killed, as in:

> LEV 10:1And Nadab and Abihu, the sons of Aaron, took each of them his censer, and put fire therein, and laid incense thereon, and offered strange fire before the Lord, which He had not commanded them.
> 2And there came forth fire from before the Lord, and devoured them, and they died before the Lord.

Apart from the detailed information about ritual matters, another characteristic of the P text is its precise and even pedantic attention to detail. For example, it often gives people's age when events occur, and its version of the flood story tells the exact measurements of the Ark, the exact month and day when important events occurred, and Noah's age when these events occurred.

P believed that the Aaronid priests were the only ones who could legitimately perform sacrifices, so he does not include stories of sacrifices that are in the other texts but were not performed in the tabernacle by priests. In J, for example, Noah took two of each type of unclean animal and seven of each type of clean animal on the ark so he could sacrifice clean animals after the flood,[99] but in P, Noah took only two of each type of animal[100] and did not need the extra clean animals because he did not make a sacrifice after the flood. Likewise, the patriarchs make sacrifices in the other texts but do not make sacrifices in P.

When we talk about P's religion, we have to add the qualification that the laws that P himself wrote are ritualistic, but he also incorporated an earlier priestly document called the Holiness Code into his version of the law,[101] and this earlier document that he quotes is moral as well as ritualistic. For example, it includes:

> LEV 19:13Thou shalt not oppress thy neighbour, nor rob him; the wages of a hired servant shall not abide with thee all night until the morning. 14Thou shalt not curse the deaf, nor put a stumbling block before the blind, but thou shalt fear thy God: I am the Lord. 15Ye shall do no unrighteousness in judgment; thou shalt not respect the person of the poor, nor favour the person of the mighty; but in righteousness shalt thou judge thy neighbour. 16Thou shalt not go up and down as a talebearer among thy people; neither shalt thou stand idly by the blood of thy neighbour: I am the Lord. 17Thou shalt not hate thy brother in thy heart; thou shalt surely rebuke thy neighbour, and not bear sin because of him. 18Thou shalt not take vengeance, nor bear any grudge against the children of thy people, but thou shalt love thy neighbour as thyself: I am the Lord.

Likewise, P incorporates a priestly version of the Ten Commandments:[102] unlike J's ritualistic Ten Commandments, it includes the familiar moral commandments, such as "Thou shalt not kill" and "Thou shalt not steal." (Though some scholars disagree, this edition attributes this version of the Ten Commandments to P because it differs from the version in Deuteronomy by saying that we should observe the Sabbath because God created the world in six days and rested on the seventh day, referring back to P's story of the creation.[103])

We can speculate about why the text that P himself wrote focuses narrowly on ritual while the earlier documents that P quotes, the Holiness Code and the Ten Commandments, also have a moral element. Perhaps the Aaronid priests changed over time, putting less focus on morality and more on ritual. Or perhaps the P focused on describing temple rituals during the exile so they could be performed properly in a rebuilt Temple, while the earlier documents were written before the destruction of the Temple.

The difference between the ritualistic religion of the text that P himself wrote and the more moral religion of the older texts that he quoted makes P's religious views seem a bit inconsistent, but this inconsistency can easily be explained as the result of P incorporating earlier documents. It is not an argument against the P text being written and compiled by a single author.

# Is the P Text Continuous?

The continuity of the P text is a bigger problem. At first sight, its does not seem like a coherent whole. The only lengthy narratives it has in Genesis, for example, are the story of the creation,[104] the story of Noah,[105] the story of the covenant of Abraham,[106] the story Abraham buying the tomb of the patriarchs at Machpelah to bury Sarah there,[107] the story of Isaac and Rebekah sending Jacob to get a wife from their relative Laban,[108] and the story of Jacob legitimizing Joseph's sons Ephraim and Manasseh, making the tribes that descended from them equal to the tribes descended from Jacob's own sons.[109] These stories are linked by genealogies or very brief summary histories; for example, P just provides a list of Jacob's children and says nothing about their birth. It does not seem clear at first why P would tell these particular stories at greater length and just give a few verses summarizing other events that seem equally important.

Yet it is possible to find a coherent structure underlying the P text. The author focused on the four events that he considered the most important in history: the creation, the covenant of Noah, the covenant of Abraham, and the covenant of Moses and Aaron. He wrote lengthy narratives about these four events, and he tied them together with genealogies or with very brief summary narratives of intervening events. The genealogies and summary narratives provide a continuous timeline that extends from the creation of the world to the Israelites' arrival at the Jordan River just before entering the Promised Land, and the four key events are all dated on this timeline. For more details about this timeline, see Appendix 1.

These four key events are critical to history. The creation tells the story of the earliest ancestors of all the animals and all the people who have ever lived. Noah and the animals he saved are the ancestors of all the animals and all the people who have lived since the flood. Abraham is the ancestor of every Israelite. Moses and Aaron are the ancestors of the Mushite and Aaronid priests.

P emphasized that these stories are critical to our ancestry by having God use the word "fruitful" during each one.

In the creation story, after creating fish and birds, "GEN 1:22God blessed them, saying: 'Be fruitful, and multiply, and fill the waters in the seas, and let fowl multiply in the earth.'" After creating man and woman "GEN 1:28God blessed them; and God said unto them: 'Be fruitful, and multiply, and replenish the earth, and subdue it....'"

In the story of the flood, after the waters receded, "GEN 8:15God spoke unto Noah, saying: 16'Go forth from the ark, thou, and thy wife, and thy sons, and thy sons' wives with thee. 17Bring forth with thee every living thing that is with thee of all flesh, both fowl, and cattle, and every creeping thing that creepeth upon the earth; that they may swarm in the earth, and be fruitful, and multiply upon the earth'" and in addition, "GEN 9:1God blessed Noah and his sons, and said unto them: 'Be fruitful and multiply, and replenish the earth."

In the story of Abraham, God told Abraham "GEN 17:6I will make thee exceeding fruitful, and I will make nations of thee, and kings shall come out of thee." And God reaffirmed this blessing when He appeared to Jacob as he returned from Paddan-aram: "GEN 35:11And God said unto him: 'I am God Almighty. Be fruitful and multiply; a nation and a company of nations shall be of thee, and kings shall come out of thy loins; 12and the land which I gave unto Abraham and Isaac, to thee I will give it, and to thy seed after thee will I give the land.'"

In the story of Moses and Aaron, there is a long list of blessings that the Israelites will receive if they obey and a long list of curses they will receive if they disobey. One of the blessings is: "LEV 26:3If ye walk in My statutes, and keep My commandments, and do them... 9And I will have respect unto you, and make you fruitful, and multiply you; and will establish My covenant with you."

All of these quotations are from the P text, and as the P text progresses, it becomes progressively harder to get this blessing of being fruitful.

The story of the creation does not mention any requirement. God just tells man and woman to be fruitful and multiply. (The requirement of not eating the apple is from the J text.)

The story of Noah mentions two requirements, not to eat the blood of animals and not to shed human blood, which P seems to think of as one requirement:

> GEN 9:3Every moving thing that liveth shall be for food for you; as the green herb have I given you all. 4Only flesh with the life thereof, which is the blood thereof, shall ye not eat. 5And surely your blood of your lives will I require; at the hand of every beast will I require it; and at the hand of man, even at the hand of every man's brother, will I require the life of man. 6Whoso sheddeth man's blood, by man shall his blood be shed...."

Eating animals' blood is conflated with shedding human blood because P has a very strict requirement in Leviticus that animals must be brought to the Temple to be butchered and the blood must be sprinkled on the altar to atone for the killing; anyone who slaughters an animal himself or who eats blood incurs blood guilt similar to the guilt of a murderer and is cut off from the people.[110]

God made a covenant with Noah that He would not destroy all flesh again, which is symbolized by the rainbow,[111] and a covenant implies that there are obligations on both sides.

God also made a covenant with Abraham that had an additional obligation, circumcision, and an additional promise, that they would be the fathers of a great nation that would possess the land of Canaan.[112] Presumably, Abraham was also bound by the covenant of Noah, since he was Noah's descendent.

Finally, God made a covenant with the children of Israel at the time of Moses and Aaron that imposed many more obligations on them if they were to keep the land—obligations that fill up the book of Leviticus—and He threatened them with curses if they break the covenant as well as promising them prosperity if they keep the covenant. This final covenant also incorporates the covenants of Noah and Abraham: today's orthodox Jews are still forbidden to eat blood and must be circumcised.

All of these covenants are from the P text, and there is a clear progression from no obligations at the time of the creation, through increasing obligations for Noah and the patriarchs, to an exhausting set of obligations for the Israelites—obligations that made them dependent on the priests.

These four narratives form a coherent whole. P did not choose these events at random. He chose them because they are key events in the history of all living animals, of humanity and of Israel, and because they are key points in the history of God's covenant with Israel.

P was probably familiar with the JE text, and he created a new synthesis of pagan myth with Israelite religion by modifying two of J's myths to make them key events in religious history. We can see how he modified the earlier myth in the creation story. God seems anthropomorphic in J's creation myth, creating Adam by molding the soil and breathing life into him.[113] P responds to JE by rewriting this myth to make God more powerful and more remote: God created the world purely by speaking.[114]

P's synthesis represents a change in the Israelite priests' view of God. The E text sees Him as the source of revelations to the patriarchs and to Moses. The P text also sees Him as the Creator, and the idea that God is Creator has been central to the religion ever since, though it was not important to the Mushite priests' earlier version of the religion, so it was left out of the E text.

Thus, there does seem to be a unified core to the P text, centering on these four key events, which are connected with genealogies and brief summary histories, but there are also other lengthy narratives that interrupt this core narrative. It is easy to imagine reasons why people would want to add these other narratives.

The first extraneous story is P's long account of Abraham's purchase of a burial site for Sarah at Machpelah, which became the tomb of all the patriarchs, emphasizing that Abraham paid full price with all the Hittites gathered around as witnesses;[115] and it is easy to imagine why people would want to include this to establish the Israelites' legal right to this religious site.

The second extraneous story says that Isaac and Rebekah were saddened when Esau married Hittite women, so they sent Jacob to Laban to find a wife among their relatives,[116] and it is easy to imagine why they would want to include this at a time when the priests were trying to end marriages with non-Israelites.

The third extraneous story, the final one in Genesis, shows Jacob legitimizing Joseph's sons Ephraim and Manasseh, making the tribes that descended from them equal to the tribes descended from Jacob's own sons, and then shows Jacob being carried back to Canaan to be buried in the cave of Machpelah,[117] and it is easy to imagine why people would want to include this story to legitimize all of the twelve tribes and to show that all the patriarchs are buried at Machpelah, even Jacob who died in Egypt.

These extraneous stories in Genesis are easy to identify. It is harder to identify which passages in P are extraneous in the books that follow, because these books are all about the covenant of Moses and Aaron, but presumably some of its stories were not part of the original core of the P text.

There are clues that the final extraneous story in Genesis, the story of Jacob legitimizing Ephraim and Manasseh, was a later addition to the P text. A bit earlier, the P text implies that Jacob died, using the typical summary style that we expect P to use in everything except the four key events: "[GEN 47:28]And Jacob lived in the land of Egypt seventeen years; so the days of Jacob, the years of his life, were a hundred forty and seven years." But immediately afterwards in P, beginning with Genesis 48:3, Jacob is still alive to bless Ephraim and Manasseh. This story is out of place coming after the summary of how many years Jacob lived, making us suspect that it was added later. There is another piece of evidence that this final P passage about Jacob was added later: before this passage, in Genesis 46, P lists the sons of Israel who came to Egypt and gives many details about them; then after this passage, in Exodus 1:1, P repeats the list of the sons of Israel without the added details. This sort of repetition is often used before and after an inserted passage, to reestablish the continuity of the original text.

Thus, there are two telltale signs that this passage was added later, raising the possibility that other extraneous passages were also added later.

One possible explanation of these extraneous passages is that the P text might have been a book written by a bureaucracy. The priest who was the lead writer had a clear idea of the unified structure of the book he wanted to write, with four key events tied together by genealogies and brief summary histories, but other priests insisted that it was very important to add the story of Abraham's purchase of Sarah's tomb before many witnesses in order to solidify Israel's claim to the cave of Machpelah, and others insisted that it was very important to add the story of Isaac and Rebekah sending Jacob to marry a relative in order to reinforce their campaign against intermarriage with Canaanites, and others insisted that it was very important that he add the story legitimizing Ephraim and Manasseh.

Another possible explanation is that the P text might have been revised by a later writer or writers who were Aaronid priests and so shared the point of view of the original author. The initial writer might have written a book that was the unified core of the P text. Then other priests might have added other stories to the P text that they considered too important to leave out.

Thus, the P text is not as unified as the E or J text, but it does seem plausible that it began as a single document by one writer with a unified plan, and it became less unified as others added passages to it or demanded additions.

# Chapter 3: Why It Is Important

A reevaluation of the Bible is not just an academic exercise in restoring an ancient text. The Bible remains important today.

## Two Implausible Extremes

On one hand, many people still believe that the Bible is the revealed word of God. This belief leads some to deny the science of evolution, and it leads some to say that Israel has a right to take over the West Bank.

But this view becomes totally implausible when we compare the source documents and see the contradictions among them. As we have seen, Genesis 1 says that God created the animals and then created Adam and Eve, while Genesis 2 says God created Adam, then created the animals, and then created Eve. It is impossible for both of these to be true, and there are similar contradictions throughout the text.

The documentary hypothesis shows that the Bible was written by people who were biased, and that it reflects the motives, resentments, and interests of its authors.

On the other hand, many scholars believe that the Bible was produced by people with a primitive religion and that it is filled with vicious ideas, such as Deuteronomy's commandment to slaughter all the Canaanites. Some scholars, accepting the common idea of inevitable progress, believe that the early religion of the Israelites was polytheistic and it did not evolve into monotheism until the time of the prophet Amos or Isaiah.

This view also becomes totally implausible when we compare the texts and see that E, the text written by the early Mushite priests that is presumably closest to the religion of Moses, is far more advanced than what we would expect from such a primitive people. E has a monotheistic religion, an idea of God that is far from anthropomorphic, and a strong moral element. It represents a huge, sudden leap beyond primitive religions.

Likewise, many scholars claim that Moses did not exist and was just a legend of the early Israelites. But it is not plausible that a people as primitive as the early Israelites could have invented the monotheism of the E text. It is much more plausible that it was invented by someone who grew up in the Egyptian court, as Moses is said to have done. The Egyptian Pharaoh Akhenaten adopted a semi-monotheistic religion about a century before the time of Moses, based on exclusive worship of the sun god Aten, but the monotheism of the E text is less primitive than this worship of a force of nature. The most plausible explanation for the sudden appearance of monotheism in the E text is that Moses was influenced by Egyptian ideas and went even further in rejecting primitive religious thinking.

Thus, the documentary hypothesis takes us a long way around to bring us back to an idea that many people have believed all along. The most plausible explanation for the E text is that the early Israelite priesthood carried on the religion of Moses, who had broken decisively with primitive religion. Moses was a religious innovator whose ideas are the source of the monotheistic religions that now are followed by half of the world's people. His ideas were passed down by the Mushite priests, who distorted and mythologized them over time, but who still preserved many of them in the E text.

If you are secular, you can say that Moses was a genius who anticipated the religious needs that humanity would have thousands of years after his time. If you are religious, you can call it revelation.

# Judge for Yourself

During most of the twentieth century, academic Biblical scholars generally supported the documentary hypothesis, which says the Torah was edited together from the E, J, P, and D texts—though, of course, there have always been many traditionalists who continued to believe it is a single text written by Moses.

More recently, the documentary hypothesis has been challenged by other academic theories. The most prominent is called the supplementary hypothesis, because it claims that the Torah was created by a series of authors supplementing earlier texts rather than by redactors editing together independent documents. According to this theory, there was no separate E text; instead J drew on many earlier written and oral sources in addition to writing material herself, and scholars mistakenly considered these earlier sources to be a single E text. Likewise, P is not unified because it was never a separate text; P incorporated the JE text into what he wrote. This theory makes the J text much later than it is according to the documentary hypothesis, dating it to the time of the exile, so that D is the earliest text, then J and then P.[118]

This edition lets you judge for yourself whether the first four books of the Torah were created by editing together the E, J, and P source texts, as the documentary hypothesis says. You can read across the columns to see the differences between the same story in different texts—and to see which stories each text leaves out. You can read down the columns to read each text from beginning to end. This edition includes the complete J and E texts. It abridges some of the long and repetitive portions of the P text that have no parallel in J and E. After these three texts, it has a section with other texts that the redactor included though they are not from J, E or P.

When the texts are separated so you can compare the same stories in different texts, the contradictions become so clear that the traditional view that they were written by one author is no longer tenable. The Notes column highlights many of these contradictions.

As an experiment to test whether each text is unified, this edition uses the principle that the texts should be as consecutive and as coherent as possible as one of the criteria used to decide what should be included in each text. For example, some scholars say the genealogies that follow P's stories of Noah and of Abraham are from an earlier document and were added by a later redactor to make the text more continuous; but if these genealogies were added later, then the P text itself would not be continuous. This edition recognizes that these genealogies are from an earlier work, but in order to make the P text continuous, it assumes that P included them in his text.

This might seem like circular reasoning: this edition shows that the texts are continuous and unified by assuming that the texts are continuous and unified when it decides which passages to include in them. But it is actually an experiment to test whether it is possible to break up the Torah into cohesive texts. The real proof of the documentary hypothesis comes when you read the three texts and see that each text is consistent within itself but that the three texts repeatedly contradict each other and have authors with different personalities, different interests, and different ideas about religion. A book by a single author could not possibly be divided into separate books written by authors who are so different from each other.

The texts are not completely cohesive, as we have seen, because they were worked over by other editors and writers—particularly the P text. In addition, the texts are not completely continuous because the redactors omitted material, so you sometimes have to fill the gaps in one by looking at the same story in the other; because J was a more dramatic writer, most of these gaps are in E.

After reading the three texts, you can decide for yourself whether you agree with the documentary hypothesis. Did each text begin as a unified document with a continuous narrative and a consistent view of religion that contrasts with the views of the other texts? Read them, and judge for yourself.

# Part II:
# The E, J, and P Texts

# The Authors at a Glance

The E text was written by a Mushite priest—the group of priests who believed they were descended from Moses, who controlled Israel's early religious center at Shiloh, and who were displaced when Solomon built the Temple in Jerusalem. It has only stories that are specific to Israel, beginning with Abraham and continuing through Moses.

The J text was written by a member of the Judean court, which had many members from other nations. In addition to Israelite stories, it includes stories based on earlier myths from other nations. It also has an anthropomorphic view of God influenced by other nations. Since J was not a priest, she might have been a woman.

The P text was written by an Aaronid priest, the group of priests who believed they were descended from Aaron and who controlled the Temple in Jerusalem. It is later than the other two texts and is influenced by them. Its author emphasized what he considered the four key events of history, the creation, the covenant of Noah, the covenant of Abraham, and the covenant of Moses and Aaron. Apart from these key events, he often gives a very brief summary of history.

A redactor (editor) whom we call RJE combined the J and E texts to form what is called the JE text. RJE often included only one text's version of a story, leaving gaps in what survives of the J and E texts.

A redactor whom we call R combined this JE text with the P text, with the D text that is the basis of the book of Deuteronomy, and with some other shorter texts to form the Torah that has come down to us. Unlike RJE, R was very hesitant to remove material from his source texts.

For more information about the source texts and their authors, see the first section of this book.

In cases where there is not general agreement among scholars, the Notes column explains why this edition assigns a passage to a specific text.

This edition uses the Jewish Publication Society (JPS) translation of 1917, so its numbering of chapters and verses comes from the Masoretic text of the Bible (used by Jews). In the texts used by Christians, there are sometimes minor differences in numbering.

# Conventions

This edition of the E, J, and P texts uses the following conventions:

**{problematic}** Curly brackets indicate that a text is problematic. There is some significant question about whether it should be in the text where it is placed. The problem is explained in the Notes column.

**"quoted"** Quotation marks are used for material that the texts quote from earlier works.

Example: P quoted the genealogy that connects Adam with Noah from an earlier source, so this genealogy is in quotation marks.

**(added by a redactor)** Parentheses are used for material added by a redactor.

Example: RJE added statements in the form (These are the generations of) in many locations to make the combined text seem more consistent, so these statements are in parentheses. If you are reading to understand the meaning of the original source text, ignore the text in parentheses.

**[text used more than once]** Square brackets are used for text from the Bible that is used more than once in the source texts.

Example: The Bible says "And Moses said x and y." Statement x is in the J text and statement y is in the E text. The J text of this edition says, "[And Moses said] x." The E text of this edition says, "[And Moses said] y."

The assumption is that both of the original texts included "Moses said" and that a redactor included only one "Moses said" to avoid repetition. The exact wording may have been different in the two source texts, but the substance is presumably the same.

**[additions]** Square brackets and italics are used for text added in this edition.
Example: ***[Gap in the E text]***

**Section Headers** Section headers added in this edition are bold, centered, in a larger font.

In some cases, this edition changes the JPS translation. The new translation is an accurate rendering of the original Hebrew and is explained in the Notes column.

| E | J |
|---|---|
| | **Creation** |

**Creation**

(<sup>GEN 2:4</sup>These are the generations of the heaven and of the earth when they were created,) In the day that the Lord (God) made earth and heaven, ⁵No shrub of the field was yet in the earth, and no herb of the field had yet sprung up; for the Lord (God) had not caused it to rain upon the earth, and there was not a man to till the ground; ⁶but there went up a mist from the earth, and watered the whole face of the ground. ⁷Then the Lord (God) formed man of the dust of the ground, and breathed into his nostrils the breath of life; and man became a living soul.

⁸And the Lord (God) planted a garden eastward, in Eden; and there He put the man whom He had formed. ⁹And out of the ground made the Lord (God) to grow every tree that is pleasant to the sight, and good for food; the tree of life also in the midst of the garden, and the tree of the knowledge of good and evil.

¹⁰And a river went out of Eden to water the garden; and from thence it was parted, and became four heads. ¹¹The name of the first is Pishon; that is it which compasseth the whole land of Havilah, where there is gold; ¹²and the gold of that land is good; there is bdellium and the onyx stone. ¹³And the name of the second river is Gihon; the same is it that compasseth the whole land of Cush. ¹⁴And the name of the third river is Tigris; that is it which goeth toward the east of Asshur. And the fourth river is the Euphrates.

¹⁵And the Lord (God) took the man, and put him into the garden of Eden to dress it and to keep it. ¹⁶And the Lord (God) commanded the man, saying: 'Of every tree of the garden thou mayest freely eat; ¹⁷but of the tree of the knowledge of good and evil, thou shalt not eat of it; for in the day that thou eatest thereof thou shalt surely die.'

¹⁸And the Lord (God) said: 'It is not good that the man should be alone; I will make him a help meet for him.' ¹⁹And out of the ground the Lord (God)

*[Begins on p. 82]*

( added by redactor )                    { problematic }

| P | Notes |
|---|---|

### Creation

GEN 1:1In the beginning God created the heaven and the earth. ²Now the earth was unformed and void, and darkness was upon the face of the deep; and the spirit of God hovered over the face of the waters.

³And God said: 'Let there be light.' And there was light. ⁴And God saw the light, that it was good; and God divided the light from the darkness. ⁵And God called the light Day, and the darkness He called Night. And there was evening and there was morning, one day.

⁶And God said: 'Let there be a firmament in the midst of the waters, and let it divide the waters from the waters.' ⁷And God made the firmament, and divided the waters which were under the firmament from the waters which were above the firmament; and it was so. ⁸And God called the firmament Heaven. And there was evening and there was morning, a second day.

⁹And God said: 'Let the waters under the heaven be gathered together unto one place, and let the dry land appear.' And it was so. ¹⁰And God called the dry land Earth, and the gathering together of the waters called He Seas; and God saw that it was good. ¹¹And God said: 'Let the earth put forth grass, herb yielding seed, and fruit-tree bearing fruit after its kind, wherein is the seed thereof, upon the earth.' And it was so. ¹²And the earth brought forth grass, herb yielding seed af-

### Creation

**E Text**

The E text begins with the story of Abraham and contains only Israelite myths. The J text includes earlier myths derived from pagan sources; see Appendix 5. The P text adapts two of these earlier myths (the creation and the flood) to its own religious purposes; see page 34.

**J Text**

In many locations in all three texts, R added sentences beginning with "These are the generations" to make the three texts seem more consistent. The Hebrew can also be translated as "these are the records" or "this is the history." See Appendix 2.

The narrator in J uses the name YHWH, translated as "the Lord" throughout the text, while P and E use the word "God" before the time of Moses. In the J text here, R presumably changed "the Lord" to "the Lord God" to make the two texts more consistent by showing at the beginning that "the Lord" means the same thing as "God."

**J versus P Text**

The order of creation is different in the two texts. In J, God creates man (Gen. 2:7), creates the trees (Gen. 2:9), creates the animals and birds (Gen. 2:19), and then creates woman (Gen. 2:22). In P, God creates the birds (Gen. 1:20), creates the animals (Gen. 1:24), then creates both man and woman (Gen. 1:27).

J's God is more anthropomorphic

| [ used more than once ] | " quoting older text " |
|---|---|

| **E** | **J** |
|---|---|
| | formed every beast of the field, and every fowl of the air; and brought them unto the man to see what he would call them; and whatsoever the man would call every living creature, that was to be the name thereof. [20]And the man gave names to all cattle, and to the fowl of the air, and to every beast of the field; but for Adam there was not found a help meet for him. |
| | [21]And the Lord (God) caused a deep sleep to fall upon the man, and he slept; and He took one of his ribs, and closed up the place with flesh instead thereof. [22]And the rib, which the Lord (God) had taken from the man, made He a woman, and brought her unto the man. [23]And the man said: 'This is now bone of my bones, and flesh of my flesh; she shall be called Woman, because she was taken out of Man.' [24]Therefore shall a man leave his father and his mother, and shall cleave unto his wife, and they shall be one flesh. [25]And they were both naked, the man and his wife, and were not ashamed. |
| *[Begins on p. 82]* | **Loss of Eden** |
| | GEN 3:1Now the serpent was more subtle than any beast of the field which the Lord (God) had made. And he said unto the woman: 'Yea, hath God said: Ye shall not eat of any tree of the garden?' [2]And the woman said unto the serpent: 'Of the fruit of the trees of the garden we may eat; [3]but of the fruit of the tree which is in the midst of the garden, God hath said: Ye shall not eat of it, neither shall ye touch it, lest ye die.' [4]And the serpent said unto the woman: 'Ye shall not surely die; [5]for God doth know that in the day ye eat thereof, then your eyes shall be opened, and ye shall be as God, knowing good and evil.' |
| | [6]And when the woman saw that the tree was good for food, and that it was a delight to the eyes, and that the tree was to be desired to make one wise, she took of the fruit thereof, and did eat; and she gave also unto her husband with her, and he did eat. [7]And the eyes of them both were opened, and they knew that they were naked; and they sewed fig-leaves together, and made themselves girdles. |
| ( added by redactor ) | { problematic } |

| **P** | **Notes** |
|---|---|

ter its kind, and tree bearing fruit, wherein is the seed thereof, after its kind; and God saw that it was good. ¹³And there was evening and there was morning, a third day.

¹⁴And God said: 'Let there be lights in the firmament of the heaven to divide the day from the night; and let them be for signs, and for seasons, and for days and years; ¹⁵and let them be for lights in the firmament of the heaven to give light upon the earth.' And it was so. ¹⁶And God made the two great lights: the greater light to rule the day, and the lesser light to rule the night; and the stars. ¹⁷And God set them in the firmament of the heaven to give light upon the earth, ¹⁸and to rule over the day and over the night, and to divide the light from the darkness; and God saw that it was good. ¹⁹And there was evening and there was morning, a fourth day.

²⁰And God said: 'Let the waters swarm with swarms of living creatures, and let fowl fly above the earth in the open firmament of heaven.' ²¹And God created the great sea-monsters, and every living creature that creepeth, wherewith the waters swarmed, after its kind, and every winged fowl after its kind; and God saw that it was good. ²²And God blessed them, saying: 'Be fruitful, and multiply, and fill the waters in the seas, and let fowl multiply in the earth.' ²³And there was evening and there was morning, a fifth day.

²⁴And God said: 'Let the earth bring forth the living creature after its kind, cattle, and creeping thing,

and creates man by molding clay, like a human craftsman. P's God creates purely by speaking.

In the J text, there is a forbidden fruit: "ᴳᴱᴺ ²:¹⁷...but of the tree of the knowledge of good and evil, thou shalt not eat of it....'" In the P text, there is no forbidden fruit: "ᴳᴱᴺ ¹:²⁹And God said: 'Behold, I have given you every herb yielding seed, which is upon the face of all the earth, and every tree, in which is the fruit of a tree yielding seed—to you it shall be for food."

### Loss of Eden

**J Text**

J, a member of the multi-cultural Judean court, incorporates non-Israelite myths from a variety of sources in her writing. The myth of Eden seems to come from an early farming society. See Appendix 5.

The Hebrew word *adam* means "man" or "human" as well as being a name. In English translation, it seems there is no preparation for J's use of "Adam" in Genesis 2:20, but in the original Hebrew, the word *adam* is also used for all the earlier mentions of "man" in the English translation.

| [ used more than once ] | " quoting older text " |
|---|---|

| E | J |
|---|---|
| | ⁸And they heard the voice of the Lord (God) walking in the garden toward the cool of the day; and the man and his wife hid themselves from the presence of the Lord (God) amongst the trees of the garden. ⁹And the Lord (God) called unto the man, and said unto him: 'Where art thou?' ¹⁰And he said: 'I heard Thy voice in the garden, and I was afraid, because I was naked; and I hid myself.' ¹¹And He said: 'Who told thee that thou wast naked? Hast thou eaten of the tree, whereof I commanded thee that thou shouldest not eat?' ¹²And the man said: 'The woman whom Thou gavest to be with me, she gave me of the tree, and I did eat.' ¹³And the Lord (God) said unto the woman: 'What is this thou hast done?' And the woman said: 'The serpent beguiled me, and I did eat.'<br><br>¹⁴And the Lord (God) said unto the serpent: 'Because thou hast done this, cursed art thou from among all cattle, and from among all beasts of the field; upon thy belly shalt thou go, and dust shalt thou eat all the days of thy life. ¹⁵And I will put enmity between thee and the woman, and between thy seed and her seed; they shall bruise thy head, and thou shalt bruise their heel.'<br><br>¹⁶Unto the woman He said: 'I will greatly multiply thy pain and thy travail; in pain thou shalt bring forth children; and thy desire shall be to thy husband, and he shall rule over thee.'<br><br>¹⁷And unto Adam He said: 'Because thou hast hearkened unto the voice of thy wife, and hast eaten of the tree, of which I commanded thee, saying: Thou shalt not eat of it; cursed is the ground for thy sake; in toil shalt thou eat of it all the days of thy life. ¹⁸Thorns also and thistles shall it bring forth to thee; and thou shalt eat the herb of the field. ¹⁹In the sweat of thy face shalt thou eat bread, till thou return unto the ground; for out of it wast thou taken; for dust thou art, and unto dust shalt thou return.'<br><br>²⁰And the man called his wife's name Eve; because she was the mother of all living. ²¹And the Lord (God) made for Adam and for his wife garments of skins, and clothed them.<br><br>²²And the Lord (God) said: 'Behold, the man is be- |

*[Begins on p. 82]* is in the left (E) column.

| ( added by redactor ) | { problematic } |
|---|---|

| P | Notes |
|---|---|

and beast of the earth after its kind.' And it was so. [25]And God made the beast of the earth after its kind, and the cattle after their kind, and every thing that creepeth upon the ground after its kind; and God saw that it was good. [26]And God said: 'Let us make man in our image, after our likeness; and let them have dominion over the fish of the sea, and over the fowl of the air, and over the cattle, and over all the earth, and over every creeping thing that creepeth upon the earth.' [27]And God created man in His own image, in the image of God created He him; male and female created He them. [28]And God blessed them; and God said unto them: 'Be fruitful, and multiply, and replenish the earth, and subdue it; and have dominion over the fish of the sea, and over the fowl of the air, and over every living thing that creepeth upon the earth.' [29]And God said: 'Behold, I have given you every herb yielding seed, which is upon the face of all the earth, and every tree, in which is the fruit of a tree yielding seed—to you it shall be for food; [30]and to every beast of the earth, and to every fowl of the air, and to every thing that creepeth upon the earth, wherein there is a living soul, I have given every green herb for food.' And it was so. [31]And God saw every thing that He had made, and, behold, it was very good. And there was evening and there was morning, the sixth day.

GEN 2:1And the heaven and the earth were finished, and all the host of them. [2]And on the seventh day God

*[Continued on p. 53]*

| [ used more than once ] | " quoting older text " |
|---|---|

| **E** | **J** |
| --- | --- |
| | come as one of us, to know good and evil; and now, lest he put forth his hand, and take also of the tree of life, and eat, and live for ever.' ²³Therefore the Lord (God) sent him forth from the garden of Eden, to till the ground from whence he was taken. ²⁴So He drove out the man; and He placed at the east of the garden of Eden the cherubim, and the flaming sword which turned every way, to keep the way to the tree of life. |

### Cain and Abel

GEN 4:1And the man knew Eve his wife; and she conceived and bore Cain, and said: 'I have gotten a man with the help of the Lord.' ²And again she bore his brother Abel. And Abel was a keeper of sheep, but Cain was a tiller of the ground. ³And in process of time it came to pass, that Cain brought of the fruit of the ground an offering unto the Lord. ⁴And Abel, he also brought of the firstlings of his flock and of the fat thereof. And the Lord had respect unto Abel and to his offering; ⁵but unto Cain and to his offering He had not respect.

*[Begins on p. 82]*

And Cain was very wroth, and his countenance fell. ⁶And the Lord said unto Cain: 'Why art thou wroth? and why is thy countenance fallen? ⁷If thou doest well, shall it not be lifted up? and if thou doest not well, sin coucheth at the door; and unto thee is its desire, but thou mayest rule over it.' ⁸And Cain spoke unto Abel his brother. And it came to pass, when they were in the field, that Cain rose up against Abel his brother, and slew him.

⁹And the Lord said unto Cain: 'Where is Abel thy brother?' And he said: 'I know not; am I my brother's keeper?' ¹⁰And He said: 'What hast thou done? the voice of thy brother's blood crieth unto Me from the ground. ¹¹And now cursed art thou from the ground, which hath opened her mouth to receive thy brother's blood from thy hand. ¹²When thou tillest the ground, it shall not henceforth yield unto thee her strength; a fugitive and a wanderer shalt thou be in the earth.'

¹³And Cain said unto the Lord: 'My punishment is greater than I can bear. ¹⁴Behold, Thou hast driven

| ( added by redactor ) | { problematic } |

| P | Notes |
|---|---|
| finished His work which He had made; and He rested on the seventh day from all His work which He had made. ³And God blessed the seventh day, and hallowed it; because that in it He rested from all His work which God in creating had made. | |

**Cain and Abel**

**J Text**

   This is another early myth included by J. It seems to date to the early days of food production, when farming societies were expanding their territories and displacing herding societies because their populations grew more quickly. It is told from the point of view of the herders. See Appendix 5.

| [ used more than once ] | " quoting older text " |
|---|---|

| E | J |
|---|---|
| | me out this day from the face of the land; and from Thy face shall I be hid; and I shall be a fugitive and a wanderer in the earth; and it will come to pass, that whosoever findeth me will slay me.' [15]And the Lord said unto him: 'Therefore whosoever slayeth Cain, vengeance shall be taken on him sevenfold.' And the Lord set a sign for Cain, lest any finding him should smite him.<br><br>[16]And Cain went out from the presence of the Lord, and dwelt in the land of Nod, on the east of Eden.<br><br>**Pre-Flood Genealogy**<br>GEN 4:17And Cain knew his wife; and she conceived, and bore Enoch; and he builded a city, and called the name of the city after the name of his son Enoch. [18]And unto Enoch was born Irad; and Irad begot Mehujael; and Mehujael begot Methushael; and Methushael begot Lamech. [19]And Lamech took unto him two wives; the name of one was Adah, and the name of the other Zillah. [20]And Adah bore Jabal; he was the father of such as dwell in tents and have cattle. [21]And his brother's name was Jubal; he was the father of all such as handle the harp and pipe. [22]And Zillah, she also bore Tubal-cain, the forger of every cutting instrument of brass and iron; and the sister of Tubal-cain was Naamah. [23]And Lamech said unto his wives:<br><br>"Adah and Zillah, hear my voice; Ye wives of Lamech, hearken unto my speech; |
| *[Begins on p. 82]* | |
| ( added by redactor ) | { problematic } |

| P | Notes |
|---|---|

### Pre-Flood Genealogy

"<sup>GEN 5:1</sup>This is the book of the generations of Adam. In the day that God created man, in the likeness of God made He him; <sup>2</sup>male and female created He them, and blessed them, and called their name Adam, in the day when they were created. <sup>3</sup>And Adam lived a hundred and thirty years, and begot a son in his own likeness, after his image; and called his name Seth. <sup>4</sup>And the days of Adam after he begot Seth were eight hundred years; and he begot sons and daughters. <sup>5</sup>And all the days that Adam lived were nine hundred and thirty years; and he died.

<sup>6</sup>And Seth lived a hundred and five years, and begot Enosh. <sup>7</sup>And Seth lived after he begot Enosh eight hundred and seven years, and begot sons and daughters. <sup>8</sup>And all the days of Seth were nine hundred and twelve years; and he died.

<sup>9</sup>And Enosh lived ninety years, and

### Pre-Flood Genealogy

**P text**

As we have seen in the note to J's story of the Creation, the Hebrew word *adam* is a name and also a word that means "man" or "human." In P's creation story, in "<sup>GEN 1: 27</sup>And God created man," the word "man" translates "*ha'adam*," which means "the human" or "the man." Thus P's generations of Adam follow naturally from P's creation of man/Adam and God's command that he should be fruitful and multiply.

P's initial genealogies are taken from an earlier work whose name is provided: "<sup>GEN 5:1</sup>This is the book of the generations of Adam." The Hebrew word *sefer* is usually translated as "book," but in this case it would probably be better to translate it as "document," because "the document of the generations of Adam" is clearly less than book length.

Some scholars suggest that R added text from the book of the

---

| [ used more than once ] | " quoting older text " |

| E | J |
|---|---|
| | For I have slain a man for wounding me, And a young man for bruising me; 24If Cain shall be avenged sevenfold, Truly Lamech seventy and sevenfold." 25And Adam knew his wife again; and she bore a son, and called his name Seth: 'for God hath appointed me another seed instead of Abel; for Cain slew him.' 26And to Seth, to him also there was born a son; and he called his name Enosh; then began men to call upon the name of the Lord. |
| *[Begins on p. 82]* | ***[Gap in J: Son of Enoch to Birth of Noah]*** |
| ( added by redactor ) | { problematic } |

| P | Notes |
|---|---|

begot Kenan. [10]And Enosh lived after he begot Kenan eight hundred and fifteen years, and begot sons and daughters. [11]And all the days of Enosh were nine hundred and five years; and he died.

[12]And Kenan lived seventy years, and begot Mahalalel. [13]And Kenan lived after he begot Mahalalel eight hundred and forty years, and begot sons and daughters. [14]And all the days of Kenan were nine hundred and ten years; and he died.

[15]And Mahalalel lived sixty and five years, and begot Jared. [16]And Mahalalel lived after he begot Jared eight hundred and thirty years, and begot sons and daughters. [17]And all the days of Mahalalel were eight hundred ninety and five years; and he died.

[18]And Jared lived a hundred sixty and two years, and begot Enoch. [19]And Jared lived after he begot Enoch eight hundred years, and begot sons and daughters. [20]And all the days of Jared were nine hundred sixty and two years; and he died.

[21]And Enoch lived sixty and five years, and begot Methuselah. [22]And Enoch walked with God after he begot Methuselah three hundred years, and begot sons and daughters. [23]And all the days of Enoch were three hundred sixty and five years. [24]And Enoch walked with God, and he was not; for God took him.

[25]And Methuselah lived a hundred eighty and seven years, and begot Lamech. [26]And Methuselah lived after he begot Lamech seven hundred eighty and two years, and be-

generations of Adam to make the combined text more cohesive. But without the text from this book, the P text itself would not be cohesive: there would be no relation between the stories of the creation and Noah or between the stories of Noah and Abraham. This edition tests the documentary hypothesis by assuming that the source texts are cohesive, so it assumes that P included these genealogies from an earlier work.

Including these genealogies shows that they are essential to the plan of P's work. P is trying to write a precise history by using genealogies to establish a timeline that begins at creation and extends through the P text until the arrival in Canaan. P includes only the early genealogies that are needed for this timeline, from Seth to Noah and from Noah to Abraham. The timeline continues throughout the P text. For the complete timeline, see Appendix 1.

**J text**

The J text originally included the generations of both Cain and Seth, though you might think the line of Cain was not important because it died out when the flood occurred and only Noah, Seth's descendent, was saved. In the surviving J text, we have the entire line of Cain but only have the first verse about the line of Seth: "[GEN 2:26]And to Seth, to him also there was born a son; and he called his name Enosh." The surviving text omits the rest of Seth's line of descendents.

Some scholars suggest that J included only the line of Cain and

| [ used more than once ] | " quoting older text " |
|---|---|

| **E** | **J** |
|---|---|
| | |
| *[Begins on p. 82]* | |
| | **Giants in the Earth**<br><br>"GEN 6:1And it came to pass, when men began to multiply on the face of the earth, and daughters were born unto them, that the {sons of |
| ( added by redactor ) | { problematic } |

| P | Notes |
|---|---|
| got sons and daughters. <sup>27</sup>And all the days of Methuselah were nine hundred sixty and nine years; and he died. | that R added this verse about Seth to create a connection between the genealogies from J and P. But J would have no reason to include the line of Cain, which died out, and to omit the line of Seth, which survived through the flood. It is much more plausible that R removed J's account of Seth's descendents because it was different from P's, and R did not want to include this blatant contradiction. He kept Seth's son Enosh because it was the same in J and P, so he removed the rest of J's genealogy because it was different from P's. Comparing the post-flood genealogies provides decisive evidence that R removed parts of J's genealogy. See Appendix 3. |

got sons and daughters. <sup>27</sup>And all the days of Methuselah were nine hundred sixty and nine years; and he died.

<sup>28</sup>And Lamech lived a hundred eighty and two years, and begot a son. <sup>29</sup>And he called his name Noah, saying: 'This same shall comfort us in our work and in the toil of our hands, which cometh from the ground which the Lord hath cursed.' <sup>30</sup>And Lamech lived after he begot Noah five hundred ninety and five years, and begot sons and daughters. <sup>31</sup>And all the days of Lamech were seven hundred seventy and seven years; and he died.

<sup>32</sup>And Noah was five hundred years old; and Noah begot Shem, Ham, and Japheth."

**Notes**

that R added this verse about Seth to create a connection between the genealogies from J and P. But J would have no reason to include the line of Cain, which died out, and to omit the line of Seth, which survived through the flood. It is much more plausible that R removed J's account of Seth's descendents because it was different from P's, and R did not want to include this blatant contradiction. He kept Seth's son Enosh because it was the same in J and P, so he removed the rest of J's genealogy because it was different from P's. Comparing the post-flood genealogies provides decisive evidence that R removed parts of J's genealogy. See Appendix 3.

J says: "<sup>GEN 4:26</sup>And to Seth, to him also there was born a son; and he called his name Enosh; then began men to call upon the name of the Lord *[=YHWH]*." Both P and E say that the name of the Lord was first revealed to Moses. J places it much earlier in history, which justifies her using the name of the Lord throughout her narrative, and justifies her willingness to include myths of other nations. See p. 29.

**J versus P**

P's genealogy includes only the father-to-first-son sequence, the main line of descent from Adam to Noah, with the ages needed to establish a timeline.

J genealogy is less precise and more likely to include interesting incidental information. The J text does not establish a timeline. It includes other lines of descent and also include bits of ancient myths, such as "<sup>GEN 4:21</sup>And his brother's name was Jubal; he was the father of all such as handle the harp and pipe."

**Giants in the Earth**

This passage is typical of J's syncretism of Israelite and pagan religion, like the other bits of pagan myth that she includes in her pre-flood genealogy. It refers to popular myths about demigods

| [ used more than once ] | " quoting older text " |

| E | J |
|---|---|
| | God} saw the daughters of men that they were fair; and they took them wives, whomsoever they chose. ⁴The Nephilim *[giants]* were in the earth in those days, and also after that, when the {sons of God} came in unto the daughters of men, and they bore children to them; the same were the mighty men that were of old, the men of renown. |
| *[Begins on p. 82]* | |
| | **Noah and the Flood**<br><br>GEN 6:3 And the Lord said: 'My spirit shall not abide in man for ever, for that he also is flesh; therefore shall his days be a hundred and twenty years.'<br>⁵And the Lord saw that the wickedness of man was great in the earth, and that every imagination of the thoughts of his heart was only evil continually. ⁶And it repented the Lord that He had made man on the earth, and it grieved Him at His heart. ⁷And the Lord said: 'I will blot out man whom I have created from the face of the earth; both man, and beast, and creeping thing, and fowl of the air; for it repenteth Me |
| ( added by redactor ) | { problematic } |

| P | Notes |
|---|---|
| | or heroes who were descendents of gods and mortal women, like the Greek and Roman myths about heros descended from gods or goddesses and mortals. |

or heroes who were descendents of gods and mortal women, like the Greek and Roman myths about heros descended from gods or goddesses and mortals.

We see the Nephilim again later in J, when the Israelite spies report that there were Nephilim in Canaan (Num. 13:33). Earlier translations of the Bible translate the Hebrew word *nephilim* as "giants," but they also translate the Hebrew word *rephaim* as "giants"; many recent translations use the original Hebrew words to keep the distinction between the two.

"Sons of God" is problematic because the narrator in J does not use the word "God" as a rule. The Hebrew word for God, *Elohim*, is in the plural and can also mean "gods." J may well be referring to Canaanite myths about heros descended from their gods, since the Nephilim were Canaanite. As a member of the multicultural Judean court, J would have known these myths.

## Noah and the Flood

(GEN6:9These are the generations of Noah.) Noah was in his generations a man righteous and whole-hearted; Noah walked with God. [10]And Noah begot three sons, Shem, Ham, and Japheth. [11]And the earth was corrupt before God, and the earth was filled with violence. [12]And God saw the earth, and, behold, it was corrupt; for all flesh had corrupted their way upon the earth.

[13]And God said unto Noah: 'The end of all flesh

## Noah and the Flood

**J Text**

Notice J's usual anthropomorphic view of God, who feels grief because He thinks He made a mistake by creating man.

Notice also the use of dramatic repetition that is typical of J, as Noah sends out a dove three times before the water has receded enough that the dove does not come back.

J sets a limit of 120 years on the length of human life beginning at the time of the flood (Gen. 6:3). This limit is observed later in J: for example, she says "DEUT 34:7And Moses was a hundred and twenty years old when he died: his eye was not dim, nor his natural force abated." It is not observed by P: everyone in P's post-flood genealogy (beginning at Genesis 11:10) lives more than 120

| [ used more than once ] | " quoting older text " |

| **E** | **J** |
|---|---|
| | that I have made them.' [8]But Noah found grace in the eyes of the Lord. GEN 7:1And the Lord said unto Noah: 'Come thou and all thy house into the ark; for thee have I seen righteous before Me in this generation. [2]Of every clean beast thou shalt take to thee seven and seven, each with his mate; and of the beasts that are not clean two and two, each with his mate; [3]of the fowl also of the air, seven and seven, male and female; to keep seed alive upon the face of all the earth. [4]For yet seven days, and I will cause it to rain upon the earth forty days and forty nights; and every living substance that I have made will I blot out from off the face of the earth.' |
| *[Begins on p. 82]* | [5]And Noah did according unto all that the Lord commanded him. [7]And Noah went in, and his sons, and his wife, and his sons' wives with him, into the ark, because of the waters of the flood. [10]And it came to pass after the seven days, that the waters of the flood were upon the earth. [12]And the rain was upon the earth forty days and forty nights. |
| | [16b]And the Lord shut him in. [17]And the flood was forty days upon the earth; and the waters increased, and bore up the ark, and it was lifted up above the earth. [19]And the waters prevailed exceedingly upon the earth; and all the high mountains that were under the whole heaven were covered. [22]All in whose nostrils was the breath of the spirit of life, whatsoever was in the dry land, died. [23]And He blotted out every living substance which was upon |
| ( added by redactor ) | { problematic } |

| P | Notes |
|---|---|

is come before Me; for the earth is filled with violence through them; and, behold, I will destroy them with the earth. ¹⁴Make thee an ark of gopher wood; with rooms shalt thou make the ark, and shalt pitch it within and without with pitch. ¹⁵And this is how thou shalt make it: the length of the ark three hundred cubits, the breadth of it fifty cubits, and the height of it thirty cubits. ¹⁶A light shalt thou make to the ark, and to a cubit shalt thou finish it upward; and the door of the ark shalt thou set in the side thereof; with lower, second, and third stories shalt thou make it. ¹⁷And I, behold, I do bring the flood of waters upon the earth, to destroy all flesh, wherein is the breath of life, from under heaven; every thing that is in the earth shall perish. ¹⁸But I will establish My covenant with thee; and thou shalt come into the ark, thou, and thy sons, and thy wife, and thy sons' wives with thee. ¹⁹And of every living thing of all flesh, two of every sort shalt thou bring into the ark, to keep them alive with thee; they shall be male and female. ²⁰Of the fowl after their kind, and of the cattle after their kind, of every creeping thing of the ground after its kind, two of every sort shall come unto thee, to keep them alive. ²¹And take thou unto thee of all food that is eaten, and gather it to thee; and it shall be for food for thee, and for them.' ²²Thus did Noah; according to all that God commanded him, so did he.

GEN7:6And Noah was six hundred

years. Also in P, Abraham lives 175 years (Gen. 25:7) and Sarah lives 127 years (Gen. 23:1). But P does seem to agree that Moses lives 120 years: he was 80 at the time of the exodus (Ex. 7:7) and then spent 40 years wandering in the wilderness.

There is a very similar flood myth in the *Epic of Gilgamesh*, but flood myths were so common in other societies that we cannot know which pagan source or sources influenced J. See Appendix 5.

**P Text**

The P version of the flood provides exact dates for events. For example, "GEN 7:11In the six hundredth year of Noah's life, in the second month, on the seventeenth day of the month, on the same day were all the fountains of the great deep broken up, and the windows of heaven were opened." This is a sign of how precise or even pedantic P was, wanting to give every historic detail that he had.

In the same precise manner, P also includes God's instructions for constructing the ark, including its exact measurements (Gen. 6:15).

**P versus J**

Notice the contradictions between the two texts.

In J, Noah sends a dove to see if the flood has receded (Gen. 7:6). In P, Noah sends a raven to see if the flood has receded (Gen. 8:7).

In J, the flood lasts 40 days (Gen. 8:6) plus another seven days before the water recedes (Gen. 8:10). In P, the flood lasts much longer: P tells us that the flood began "GEN 7:11In the six hundredth year of Noah's life,

| [ used more than once ] | " quoting older text " |
|---|---|

| **E** | **J** |
|---|---|
|  | the face of the ground, both man, and cattle, and creeping thing, and fowl of the heaven; and they were blotted out from the earth; and Noah only was left, and they that were with him in the ark. |
|  | GEN 8:2b And the rain from heaven was restrained. 3a And the waters returned from off the earth continually; |
|  | 6 And it came to pass at the end of forty days, that Noah opened the window of the ark which he had made. 8 And he sent forth a dove from him, to see if the waters were abated from off the face of the ground. 9 But the dove found no rest for the sole of her foot, and she returned unto him to the ark, for the waters were on the face of the whole earth; and he put forth his hand, and took her, and brought her in unto him into the ark. |
| *[Begins on p. 82]* | 10 And he stayed yet other seven days; and again he sent forth the dove out of the ark. 11 And the dove came in to him at eventide; and lo in her mouth an olive-leaf freshly plucked; so Noah knew that the waters were abated from off the earth. |
|  | 12 And he stayed yet other seven days; and sent forth the dove; and she returned not again unto him any more. |
|  | 13b And Noah removed the covering of the ark, and looked, and behold, the face of the ground was dried. 20 And Noah builded an altar unto the Lord; and took of every clean beast, and of every clean fowl, and offered burnt-offerings on the altar. 21 And the Lord smelled the sweet |
| ( added by redactor ) | { problematic } |

| P | Notes |
| --- | --- |

years old when the flood of waters was upon the earth. 8Of clean beasts, and of beasts that are not clean, and of fowls, and of every thing that creepeth upon the ground, 9there went in two and two unto Noah into the ark, male and female, as God commanded Noah.

11In the six hundredth year of Noah's life, in the second month, on the seventeenth day of the month, on the same day were all the fountains of the great deep broken up, and the windows of heaven were opened. 13In the selfsame day entered Noah, and Shem, and Ham, and Japheth, the sons of Noah, and Noah's wife, and the three wives of his sons with them, into the ark; 14they, and every beast after its kind, and all the cattle after their kind, and every creeping thing that creepeth upon the earth after its kind, and every fowl after its kind, every bird of every sort. 15And they went in unto Noah into the ark, two and two of all flesh wherein is the breath of life. 16And they that went in, went in male and female of all flesh, as God commanded him.

18And the waters prevailed, and increased greatly upon the earth; and the ark went upon the face of the waters. 20Fifteen cubits upward did the waters prevail; and the mountains were covered. 21And all flesh perished that moved upon the earth, both fowl, and cattle, and beast, and every swarming thing that swarmeth upon the earth, and every man. 24And the waters prevailed upon the earth a hundred and fifty days.

in the second month, on the seventeenth day of the month," and that it ended about ten and a half months later: "GEN 8:13... in the six hundred and first year, in the first month, the first day of the month, the waters were dried up from off the earth."

In J, God commands Noah to take seven pairs of clean animals and one pair of unclean animals: "GEN 7:2Of every clean beast thou shalt take to thee seven and seven, each with his mate; and of the beasts that are not clean two and two, each with his mate." In P, God commands Noah to take one pair of all animals: "GEN 6:19And of every living thing of all flesh, two of every sort shalt thou bring into the ark, to keep them alive with thee; they shall be male and female." J has Noah take extras of the clean animals—that is, animals that can be sacrificed—so Noah can build an altar and make sacrifices after the flood ends (Gen. 8:20). P, as an Aaronid priest, believed that sacrifices should only be performed by priests at the tabernacle or the Temple, so he did not give Noah extra clean animals to sacrifice. P also omits sacrifices in his stories of the patriarchs, though J and E mention these sacrifices.

**Documentary or Supplementary**

The contradictions in the flood story are good evidence against the supplementary hypothesis. This book is based on the documentary hypothesis, which says that the Torah is made up of separate documents that were combined by editors. By contrast, the supplementary

| [ used more than once ] | " quoting older text " |
| --- | --- |

| **E** | **J** |
|---|---|
| | savour; and the Lord said in His heart: 'I will not again curse the ground any more for man's sake; for the imagination of man's heart is evil from his youth; neither will I again smite any more every thing living, as I have done. [22]While the earth remaineth, seedtime and harvest, and cold and heat, and summer and winter, and day and night shall not cease.' |
| *[Begins on p. 82]* | **Noah Drunk** |
| | GEN 9:18 And the sons of Noah, that went forth from the ark, were Shem, and Ham, and Japheth; and Ham is the father of Canaan. [19]These three were the sons of Noah, and of these was the whole earth overspread. |
| | [20]And Noah the husbandman began, and planted a vineyard. [21]And he drank of the wine, and was drunken; and he was uncovered within his tent. [22]And Ham, the father of Canaan, saw the nakedness of his father, and told his two brethren without. [23]And Shem and Japheth took a garment, and laid it upon both their shoulders, and went backward, and covered the nakedness of their father; and their faces were backward, and they saw not their father's nakedness. |
| ( added by redactor ) | { problematic } |

## P

[GEN 8:1]And God remembered Noah, and every living thing, and all the cattle that were with him in the ark; and God made a wind to pass over the earth, And the waters assuaged; [2]the fountains also of the deep and the windows of heaven were stopped, [3b]And after the end of a hundred and fifty days the waters decreased. [4]And the ark rested in the seventh month, on the seventeenth day of the month, upon the mountains of Ararat. [5]And the waters decreased continually until the tenth month; in the tenth month, on the first day of the month, were the tops of the mountains seen.

[7]And he sent forth a raven, and it went forth to and fro, until the waters were dried up from off the earth. [13a]And it came to pass in the six hundred and first year, in the first month, the first day of the month, the waters were dried up from off the earth; [14]And in the second month, on the seven and twentieth day of the month, was the earth dry.

[15]And God spoke unto Noah, saying: [16]'Go forth from the ark, thou, and thy wife, and thy sons, and thy sons' wives with thee. [17]Bring forth with thee every living thing that is with thee of all flesh, both fowl, and cattle, and every creeping thing that creepeth upon the earth; that they may swarm in the earth, and be fruitful, and multiply upon the earth.' [18]And Noah went forth, and his sons, and his wife, and his sons' wives with him; [19]every beast, every creeping thing, and every fowl, whatsoever moveth upon the earth,

## Notes

hypothesis says that the P text was not an independent document, that its author just revised the J text by adding supplementary material to it. But someone revising the J text would not have added new contradictory details or would have removed the old contradictory details from the J text. The contradictions can only be explained by saying that there were two independent documents and that the editor who combined them had such respect for the source texts that he kept details from both even if they contradicted each other.

This same issue exists in many places but is most obvious in the flood myth.

### Noah Drunk

J uses the story of Noah's drunkenness to discredit Ham and his descendent Canaan, ancestor of the Canaanites. In her post-flood genealogy this discredit is extended to other descendents of Ham, who are the nations that were enemies of Israel.

[ used more than once ] “ quoting older text ”

| E | J |
|---|---|
| | [24]And Noah awoke from his wine, and knew what his youngest son had done unto him. [25]And he said: |
| | Cursed be Canaan; |
| | A servant of servants shall he be unto his brethren. |
| | [26]And he said: |
| | Blessed be the Lord, the God of Shem; |
| | And let Canaan be their servant. |
| | [27]God enlarge Japheth, |
| | And he shall dwell in the tents of Shem; |
| | And let Canaan be their servant. |
| *[Begins on p. 82]* | |
| ( added by redactor ) | { problematic } |

| P | Notes |
|---|---|

after their families; went forth out of the ark.

### Covenant of Noah

GEN 9:1 And God blessed Noah and his sons, and said unto them: 'Be fruitful and multiply, and replenish the earth. ²And the fear of you and the dread of you shall be upon every beast of the earth, and upon every fowl of the air, and upon all wherewith the ground teemeth, and upon all the fishes of the sea: into your hand are they delivered. ³Every moving thing that liveth shall be for food for you; as the green herb have I given you all.

⁴Only flesh with the life thereof, which is the blood thereof, shall ye not eat. ⁵And surely your blood of your lives will I require; at the hand of every beast will I require it; and at the hand of man, even at the hand of every man's brother, will I require the life of man. ⁶Whoso sheddeth man's blood, by man shall his blood be shed; for in the image of God made He man. ⁷And you, be ye fruitful, and multiply; swarm in the earth, and multiply therein.'

⁸And God spoke unto Noah, and to his sons with him, saying: ⁹'As for Me, behold, I establish My covenant with you, and with your seed after you; ¹⁰and with every living creature that is with you, the fowl, the cattle, and every beast of the earth with you; of all that go out of the ark, even every beast of the earth. ¹¹And I will establish My covenant with you; neither shall all flesh be cut off any more by the waters of the flood; neither shall there any more be a flood to destroy the earth.' ¹²And God said: 'This is the token of the covenant which I make between Me and you and every living creature that is with you, for perpetual generations: ¹³I have set My bow in the cloud, and it shall be for a token of a covenant between Me and the earth. ¹⁴And it shall come to pass, when I bring clouds over the earth, and the bow is seen in

### Covenant of Noah

**P Text**

P made Adam and Eve vegetarians (Gen. 1:29), but after the time of Noah, P says people were allowed to eat meat, However, the covenant of Noah forbids them from eating animals' blood or from shedding human blood.

This is the first of three covenants in P: the covenant of Noah, the covenant of Abraham, and the covenant of Moses and Aaron. The creation and the three covenants in P all contain the command to be fruitful and multiply, and P apparently considered them the four most important events in history. See page 34.

| [ used more than once ] | " quoting older text " |
|---|---|

| **E** | **J** |
|---|---|
| | |

*[Begins on p. 82]*

**Post-Flood Genealogy**

GEN 10:1Now these are the generations of the sons of Noah: Shem, Ham, and Japheth; and unto them were sons born after the flood.

2The sons of Japheth: Gomer, and Magog, and Madai, and Javan, and Tubal, and Meshech, and Tiras. 3And the sons of Gomer: Ashkenaz, and Riphath, and Togarmah. 4And the sons of Javan: Elishah, and Tarshish, Kittim, and Dodanim. 5Of these were the isles of the nations divided in their lands, every one after his tongue, after their families, in their nations.

6And the sons of Ham: Cush, and Mizraim, and Put, and Canaan. 7And the sons of Cush: Seba, and Havilah, and Sabtah, and Raamah, and Sabteca; and the sons of

( added by redactor )        { problematic }

| P | Notes |
|---|---|

the cloud, [15]that I will remember My covenant, which is between Me and you and every living creature of all flesh; and the waters shall no more become a flood to destroy all flesh. [16]And the bow shall be in the cloud; and I will look upon it, that I may remember the everlasting covenant between God and every living creature of all flesh that is upon the earth.' [17]And God said unto Noah: 'This is the token of the covenant which I have established between Me and all flesh that is upon the earth.'

[28]And Noah lived after the flood three hundred and fifty years. [29]And all the days of Noah were nine hundred and fifty years; and he died.

## Post-Flood Genealogy

GEN 11:10(These are the generations of Shem.) "Shem was a hundred years old, and begot Arpachshad two years after the flood. [11]And Shem lived after he begot Arpachshad five hundred years, and begot sons and daughters.

[12]And Arpachshad lived five and thirty years, and begot Shelah. [13]And Arpachshad lived after he begot Shelah four hundred and three years, and begot sons and daughters.

[14]And Shelah lived thirty years, and begot Eber. [15]And Shelah lived after he begot Eber four hundred and three years, and begot sons and daughters.

[16]And Eber lived four and thirty years, and begot Peleg. [17]And Eber

## Post-Flood Genealogy

Like the pre-flood genealogies, the two post-flood genealogies have different purposes. J, living in a multi-cultural Judean court that had to deal with its relations with neighboring nations, was interested in all the surrounding nations. P, as an Israelite priest, was interested in the line that led to Abraham and thence to Moses and Aaron, and he was interested in continuing his timeline.

**P Text**

This passage continues P's earlier quotation from the Book of the Generations of Adam. Notice that the verses in P's pre-flood and post-flood genealogies take the same form: "And a lived b years, and begot c. And a lived after he begot c d years, and begot sons and

---

| [ used more than once ] | " quoting older text " |

| **E** | **J** |
|---|---|
| | Raamah: Sheba, and Dedan. [8]And Cush begot Nimrod; he began to be a mighty one in the earth. [9]He was a mighty hunter before the Lord; wherefore it is said: 'Like Nimrod a mighty hunter before the Lord.' [10]And the beginning of his kingdom was Babel, and Erech, and Accad, and Calneh, in the land of Shinar. [11]Out of that land went forth Asshur, and builded Nineveh, and Rehoboth-ir, and Calah, [12]and Resen between Nineveh and Calah—the same is the great city. [13]And Mizraim begot Ludim, and Anamim, and Lehabim, and Naphtuhim, [14]and Pathrusim, and Casluhim—whence went forth the Philistines—and Caphtorim. |
| *[Begins on p. 82]* | [15]And Canaan begot Zidon his first-born, and Heth; [16]and the Jebusite, and the Amorite, and the Girgashite; [17]and the Hivite, and the Arkite, and the Sinite; [18]and the Arvadite, and the Zemarite, and the Hamathite; and afterward were the families of the Canaanite spread abroad. [19]And the border of the Canaanite was from Zidon, as thou goest toward Gerar, unto Gaza; as thou goest toward Sodom and Gomorrah and Admah and Zeboiim, unto Lasha. [20]These are the sons of Ham, after their families, after their tongues, in their lands, in their nations. |
| | [21]And unto Shem, the father of all the children of Eber, the elder brother of Japheth, to him also were children born. [22]The sons of Shem: Elam, and Asshur, and Arpachshad, and Lud, and Aram. [23]And the sons |
| ( added by redactor ) | { problematic } |

| P | Notes |
|---|---|
| lived after he begot Peleg four hundred and thirty years, and begot sons and daughters. <br> ¹⁸And Peleg lived thirty years, and begot Reu. ¹⁹And Peleg lived after he begot Reu two hundred and nine years, and begot sons and daughters. <br> ²⁰And Reu lived two and thirty years, and begot Serug. ²¹And Reu lived after he begot Serug two hundred and seven years, and begot sons and daughters. <br> ²²And Serug lived thirty years, and begot Nahor. ²³And Serug lived after he begot Nahor two hundred years, and begot sons and daughters. <br> ²⁴And Nahor lived nine and twenty years, and begot Terah. ²⁵And Nahor lived after he begot Terah a hundred and nineteen years, and begot sons and daughters." | daughters." <br> The post-flood genealogy also continues the timeline of the pre-flood genealogy. There were ten generations from Adam to Noah and ten generations from Shem to Abraham; in every generation, we know the age of the father when his first son was born. Abraham is the heir of Noah through a series of eldest sons, which means he is also the heir of Adam's only surviving line of descendents. <br> As the notes on the pre-flood genealogy said, some scholars claim that these genealogies were added by a later redactor, but the timeline that they establish is a key feature throughout the P text, showing that they were included by P himself. See Appendix 1. <br> **J Text** <br> Like the pre-flood genealogy, J's post-flood genealogy contains multiple lines of descent (while P's contains only the one needed to establish the timeline and genealogy leading to Abraham). In line with her habit of borrowing myths from pagan sources, it also includes bits of earlier myths, such as the mention of Nimrod. <br> The three lines of descent in J's post-flood genealogy follow up on J's story of Noah's drunkenness, where Noah blessed Shem and (to a lesser extent) Japhet but cursed Ham and Ham's descendent Canaan. Here, J lists all the nations descended from Shem, Japhet, and Ham, so we know which nations are blessed and cursed. Ham is said to the father of Babylon, Assyria (Assur), Egypt (Mizraim), the Philistines (erroneously believed to be descended from Egypt), Canaan, the Hittites (Heth) and other Canaanite peoples, all enemies of Israel. Shem is the father of the Semites and so ultimately of the Israelites. |
| [ used more than once ] | " quoting older text " |

**E**

**J**

of Aram: Uz, and Hul, and Gether, and Mash. <sup>24</sup>And Arpachshad begot Shelah; and Shelah begot Eber. <sup>25</sup>And unto Eber were born two sons; the name of the one was Peleg; for in his days was the earth divided; and his brother's name was Joktan.

***[Gap in J: Sons of Peleg to Terah]***

<sup>26</sup>And Joktan begot Almodad, and Sheleph, and Hazarmaveth, and Jerah; <sup>27</sup>and Hadoram, and Uzal, and Diklah; <sup>28</sup>and Obal, and Abimael, and Sheba; <sup>29</sup>and Ophir, and Havilah, and Jobab; all these were the sons of Joktan. <sup>30</sup>And their dwelling was from Mesha, as thou goest toward Sephar, unto the mountain of the east. <sup>31</sup>These are the sons of Shem, after their families, after their tongues, in their lands, after their nations.

<sup>32</sup>These are the families of the sons of Noah, after their generations, in their nations; and of these were the nations divided in the earth after the flood.

*[Begins on p. 82]*

**Tower of Babel**

GEN 11:1And the whole earth was of one language and of one speech. <sup>2</sup>And it came to pass, as they journeyed east, that they found a plain in the land of Shinar; and they dwelt

( added by redactor )　　　{ problematic }

| P | Notes |
|---|---|
| | J's post-flood genealogy provides decisive evidence that R removed some information from J's genealogies: it does not include the sons of Peleg, leaving an obvious gap in the J text. P gives the following line of descendents from Shem to Terah, who was Abraham's father: Shem, Arpachshad, Shelah, Eber, Peleg, Reu, Serug. Nahor, Terah. The surviving J text gives the following as one line of descendents from Shem: Shem, Arpachshad, Shelah, Eber, Peleg. But the J text does not continue this line after Peleg, though it does include the generations of Peleg's brother Joktan who are clearly less important because they are not ancestors of Abraham. |
| | Later J says, "(<sup>GEN 11:27a</sup>Now these are the generations of Terah.) Terah begot Abram, Nahor, and Haran." But there is no previous mention of Terah in J before this verse, indicating that there is a gap in the surviving J text, where an earlier mention of Terah was removed. |
| *[Continued on p. 77]* | There is one plausible explanation for this gap in J: originally, J's post-flood genealogy included the line of descent from Peleg to Terah, but R removed it because it contradicted the line from Peleg to Terah in P, just as he presumably removed the line of Seth from J's pre-flood genealogy because it contradicted the line of Seth in P. Originally, this descent from Peleg to Terah introduced Terah and prepared for his begetting Abram in Genesis 11:27, but because R removed it, Terah's begetting Abraham appears in J without any preparation, as does Lot. See Appendix 3. |
| | **Tower of Babel** |
| | This is another borrowing from pre-Israelite myth. It seems to be an origin myth told from the point of view of nomadic people who were trying to explain the tall buildings and multiple languages that existed in large cities. It comes |
| [ used more than once ] | " quoting older text " |

Later J says, "(<sup>GEN 11:27a</sup>Now these are the generations of Terah.) Terah begot Abram, Nahor, and Haran." But there is no previous mention of Terah in J before this verse, indicating that there is a gap in the surviving J text, where an earlier mention of Terah was removed.

| E | J |
|---|---|
| | there. ³And they said one to another: 'Come, let us make brick, and burn them thoroughly.' And they had brick for stone, and slime had they for mortar. ⁴And they said: 'Come, let us build us a city, and a tower, with its top in heaven, and let us make us a name; lest we be scattered abroad upon the face of the whole earth.' |
| | ⁵And the Lord came down to see the city and the tower, which the children of men builded. ⁶And the Lord said: 'Behold, they are one people, and they have all one language; and this is what they begin to do; and now nothing will be withholden from them, which they purpose to do. ⁷Come, let us go down, and there confound their language, that they may not understand one another's speech.' ⁸So the Lord scattered them abroad from thence upon the face of all the earth; and they left off to build the city. |
| *[Begins on p. 82]* | ⁹Therefore was the name of it called Babel; because the Lord did there confound the language of all the earth; and from thence did the Lord scatter them abroad upon the face of all the earth. |
| | **Abram Goes to Canaan** |
| | (ᴳᴱᴺ 11:27ᵃNow these are the generations of Terah.) Terah begot Abram, Nahor, and Haran |
| | ᴳᴱᴺ 12:1Now the Lord said unto Abram: 'Get thee out of thy country, and from thy kindred, and from thy father's house, unto the land that I will show thee. ²And I will make of thee a great nation, and I will bless thee, and make thy name great; and be thou a blessing. ³And I will bless them that bless |
| ( added by redactor ) | { problematic } |

| P | Notes |
|---|---|
|   | from an early nomadic society, like the story of Cain and Abel, See Appendix 5. |

from an early nomadic society, like the story of Cain and Abel, See Appendix 5.

Notice J's usual anthropomorphic view of God, who seems to be worried about humans becoming too powerful, as He worried about Adam and Eve eating from the tree of life. And rather than being omnipotent and acting just by speaking, God must "go down" to deal with them.

God is talking to companions when He says, "GEN 11:7'Come, let us go down, and there confound their language, that they may not understand one another's speech,'" as He was talking to companions earlier when he said: "GEN 3:22...'Behold, the man is become as one of us, to know good and evil; and now, lest he put forth his hand, and take also of the tree of life, and eat, and live for ever.' 23Therefore the Lord (God) sent him forth from the garden of Eden, to till the ground from whence he was taken." Soon, we will learn more about who these companions were.

### Abram Goes to Canaan

"GEN 11:26And Terah lived seventy years, and begot Abram, Nahor, and Haran." 27band Haran begot Lot. 28And Haran died in the presence of his father Terah in the land of his nativity, in Ur of the Chaldees.

29And Abram and Nahor took them wives: the name of Abram's wife was Sarai; and the name of Nahor's wife, Milcah, the daughter of Haran, the father of Milcah, and the

### Abram Goes to Canaan

**J Text**

Genesis 11:27a: As mentioned earlier, Terah appears unexpectedly here without ever appearing before this point in J, presumably because R removed Terah from J's postflood genealogy.

In addition, Lot is mentioned for the first time in the J text here: "GEN 12:4So Abram went, as the Lord had spoken unto him; and Lot went

| [ used more than once ] | " quoting older text " |

| **E** | **J** |
|---|---|
| | thee, and him that curseth thee will I curse; and in thee shall all the families of the earth be blessed.' |
| | 4So Abram went, as the Lord had spoken unto him; and Lot went with him; 6And Abram passed through the land unto the place of Shechem, unto the terebinth of Moreh. And the Canaanite was then in the land. 7And the Lord appeared unto Abram, and said: 'Unto thy seed will I give this land'; and he builded there an altar unto the Lord, who appeared unto him. |
| *[Begins on p. 82]* | 8And he removed from thence unto the mountain on the east of Beth-el, and pitched his tent, having Beth-el on the west, and Ai on the east; and he builded there an altar unto the Lord, and called upon the name of the Lord. 9And Abram journeyed, going on still toward the South. |
| | **Abram Goes to Egypt** |
| | GEN 12:10And there was a famine in the land; and Abram went down into Egypt to sojourn there; for the famine was sore in the land. 11And it came to pass, when he was come near to enter into Egypt, that he said unto Sarai his wife: 'Behold now, I know that thou art a fair woman to look upon. 12And it will come to pass, when the Egyptians shall see thee, that they will say: This is his |
| ( added by redactor ) | { problematic } |

| P | Notes |
|---|---|
| father of Iscah. ³⁰And Sarai was barren; she had no child. ³¹And Terah took Abram his son, and Lot the son of Haran, his son's son, and Sarai his daughter-in-law, his son Abram's wife; and they went forth with them from Ur of the Chaldees, to go into the land of Canaan; and they came unto Haran, and dwelt there. ³²And the days of Terah were two hundred and five years; and Terah died in Haran.<br><br>GEN 12:4b And Abram was seventy and five years old when he departed out of Haran. ⁵And Abram took Sarai his wife, and Lot his brother's son, and all their substance that they had gathered, and the souls that they had gotten in Haran; and they went forth to go into the land of Canaan; and into the land of Canaan they came. | with him." There is presumably a gap in the J text where Lot was introduced. The simplest explanation is that Lot was also in the post flood genealogy, like Terah.<br>**P Text**<br>"GEN 11:26And Terah lived seventy years, and begot Abram, Nahor, and Haran" is a continuation of P's post-flood genealogy, with the same format: "And a lived b years and begot c." It also continues P's timeline. But it departs from the format of the genealogy by going on to tell stories about Terah's children.<br>**P versus E and J**<br>In the P text, Abram's family came from Ur of the Chaldees then moved to Haran before Abraham went to Canaan.<br><br>The J and E text do not mention Ur of the Chaldees and just say that Abraham came from Haran. Some scholars suggest that R added mentions of Haran to P's story to make it consistent with J and E, but it does not seem possible to make P's story continuous if all the references to Haran are removed; this edition assumes that the original P text included the references to Haran, in line with its principle of making the original texts as continuous as possible.<br><br>**Abram Goes to Egypt**<br>There are two other stories where a patriarch leaves Canaan and says that his wife is his sister, another story in J and one story in E. This edition tries to put doublets next to each other, so the reader can compare them easily, but in this case, it is impossible. To compare the stories, see J's other story in Genesis 26:1-17 and E's story in Genesis 20:1-18. |
| [ used more than once ] | " quoting older text " |

| **E** | **J** |
|---|---|
| | wife; and they will kill me, but thee they will keep alive. [13]Say, I pray thee, thou art my sister; that it may be well with me for thy sake, and that my soul may live because of thee.' |
| | [14]And it came to pass, that, when Abram was come into Egypt, the Egyptians beheld the woman that she was very fair. [15]And the princes of Pharaoh saw her, and praised her to Pharaoh; and the woman was taken into Pharaoh's house. [16]And he dealt well with Abram for her sake; and he had sheep, and oxen, and he-asses, and men-servants, and maid-servants, and she-asses, and camels. |
| | [17]And the Lord plagued Pharaoh and his house with great plagues because of Sarai Abram's wife. [18]And Pharaoh called Abram, and said: 'What is this that thou hast done unto me? why didst thou not tell me that she was thy wife? [19]Why saidst thou: She is my sister? so that I took her to be my wife; now therefore behold thy wife, take her, and go thy way.' [20]And Pharaoh gave men charge concerning him; and they brought him on the way, and his wife, and all that he had. |
| *[Begins on p. 82]* | |
| | **Abram and Lot Separate** |
| | GEN13:1And Abram went up out of Egypt, he, and his wife, and all that he had, and Lot with him, into the South. [2]And Abram was very rich in cattle, in silver, and in gold. [3]And he went on his journeys from the South even to Beth-el, unto the place where his tent had been at the beginning, between Beth-el and Ai; [4]unto the place of the altar, which he had made there at the first; and Abram called there on the name of the Lord. |
| | [5]And Lot also, who went with Abram, had flocks, and herds, and tents. [7]And there was a strife between the herdmen of Abram's cattle and the herdmen of Lot's cattle. And the Canaanite and the Perizzite dwelt then in the land. [8]And Abram said unto Lot: 'Let there be no strife, I pray thee, between me and thee, and between my herdmen and thy herdmen; for we are brethren. [9]Is not the whole land be- |
| ( added by redactor ) | { problematic } |

| P | Notes |
|---|---|
| **Abram and Lot Separate**<br><br>GEN 13:6And the land was not able to bear them, that they might dwell together; for their substance was great, so that they could not dwell together. 11bAnd Lot journeyed east; and they separated themselves the one from the other. 12aAbram dwelt in the land of Canaan, and Lot dwelt in the cities of the Plain. | **Abram and Lot Separate**<br>**J Text**<br>As we will learn soon, Lot is the ancestor of the nations of Moab and Ammon, which are east of the Jordan, while Abraham's Israelite descendents are promised Canaan, which is west of the Jordan. In the J text, Lot chooses to go east to the plain of the Jordan, where the land is more fertile, not knowing that this land will be degraded when Sodom is destroyed.<br>**P Text**<br>This is the sort of very brief summary history that is common in P. |
| [ used more than once ] | " quoting older text " |

| **E** | **J** |
|---|---|
| | fore thee? separate thyself, I pray thee, from me; if thou wilt take the left hand, then I will go to the right; or if thou take the right hand, then I will go to the left.' ¹⁰And Lot lifted up his eyes, and beheld all the plain of the Jordan, that it was well watered every where, before the Lord destroyed Sodom and Gomorrah, like the garden of the Lord, like the land of Egypt, as thou goest unto Zoar. ¹¹ᵃSo Lot chose him all the plain of the Jordan; ¹²ᵇAnd moved his tent as far as Sodom. ¹³Now the men of Sodom were wicked and sinners against the Lord exceedingly. ¹⁸And Abram moved his tent, and came and dwelt by the terebinths of Mamre, which are in Hebron, and built there an altar unto the Lord. |
| *[Gaps in E: Story of Abraham]* | |
| | **Birth and Casting Out of Ismael**<br><br>GEN 16:1Now Sarai Abram's wife bore him no children; and she had a handmaid, an Egyptian, whose name was Hagar. ²And Sarai said unto Abram: 'Behold now, the Lord hath restrained me from bearing; go in, I pray thee, unto my handmaid; it may be that I shall be builded up through her.' And Abram hearkened to the voice of Sarai. ⁴And he went in unto Hagar, and she conceived; and when she saw that she had conceived, her mistress was despised in her eyes. |
| *[Gap in E: Birth of Ishmael]* | |
| | ⁵And Sarai said unto Abram: 'My wrong be upon thee: I gave my handmaid into thy bosom; and when she saw that she had conceived, I was despised in her eyes: the Lord judge between me and thee.' ⁶But Abram said unto Sarai: 'Behold, thy maid is in thy hand; do to her that which is good in thine eyes.' |
| ( added by redactor ) | { problematic } |

| **P** | **Notes** |
|---|---|
| | **Gaps in E: Story of Abraham:** |
| | There are large gaps in the E text stories of the patriarchs, presumably because RJE chose to use sections from J which told similar stories. |
| | Despite the many gaps, the surviving fragments of the E text tell a coherent story. It begins with God's promise to Abraham. Then Abraham goes to Gerar, where he becomes rich. Then Isaac is born. Then Abraham is shown as wealthy and powerful, making a covenant with Abimelech at Beersheba. Then comes the story of the binding of Isaac. |
| **Birth of Ishmael** | **Birth/Casting Out of Ishmael** |
| GEN 16:3 And Sarai Abram's wife took Hagar the Egyptian, her handmaid, after Abram had dwelt ten years in the land of Canaan, and gave her to Abram her husband to be his wife. ¹⁵And Hagar bore Abram a son; and Abram called the name of his son, whom Hagar bore, Ishmael. ¹⁶And Abram was fourscore and six years old, when Hagar bore Ishmael to Abram. | This edition tries to place doublets next to each other, so readers can easily compare them, but it is not possible to do this for the casting out of Ishmael because many events occurred between the casting out of Ishmael in the J and in the E texts. To compare the two versions of the story of casting out Ishmael, look at J's text in Genesis 16, which is here, and E's text beginning with Genesis 21:9, which is below. |
| | **E Text** |
| | In the E text, Sarah does not ask Abraham to cast out Hagar until after Isaac is born, because she wants Isaac to be the only heir of Abraham (Gen. 21:9 ff.). Presumably, there must have been an earlier story in the E text about the birth of Ishmael, which RJE removed because he preferred J's story. |
| | **J Text** |
| | In the J text, Sarai asks Abram to cast out |
| [ used more than once ] | " quoting older text " |

| **E** | **J** |
|---|---|
| | And Sarai dealt harshly with her, and she fled from her face. |
| | <sup>7</sup>And the angel of the Lord found her by a fountain of water in the wilderness, by the fountain in the way to Shur. <sup>8</sup>And he said: 'Hagar, Sarai's handmaid, whence camest thou? and whither goest thou?' And she said: 'I flee from the face of my mistress Sarai.' (<sup>9</sup>And the angel of the Lord said unto her: 'Return to thy mistress, and submit thyself under her hands.') <sup>10</sup>And the angel of the Lord said unto her: 'I will greatly multiply thy seed, that it shall not be numbered for multitude. <sup>11</sup>(And the angel of the Lord said unto her:} 'Behold, thou art with child, and shalt bear a son; and thou shalt call his name Ishmael, because the Lord hath heard thy affliction. <sup>12</sup>And he shall be a wild ass of a man: his hand shall be against every man, and every man's hand against him; and he shall dwell in the face of all his brethren.' |
| | <sup>13</sup>And she called the name of the Lord that spoke unto her, Thou art a God of seeing; for she said: 'Have I even here seen Him that seeth Me?' <sup>14</sup>Wherefore the well was called Beer-lahai-roi; behold, it is between Kadesh and Bered. |
| **Promise to Abram** | **Covenant with Abram** |
| GEN 15:12And it came to pass, that, when the sun was going down, a deep sleep fell upon Abram; and, lo, a dread, even a great darkness, fell upon him. | GEN 13:14And the Lord said unto Abram, after that Lot was separated from him: 'Lift up now thine eyes, and look from the place where thou art, northward and southward and eastward and westward; <sup>15</sup>for all the land which thou seest, to thee will I give it, and to thy seed for ever. <sup>16</sup>And I will make thy seed as the dust of the earth; so that if a man can number the dust of the earth, then shall thy seed also be numbered. <sup>17</sup>Arise, walk through the land in the length of it and in the breadth of it; for unto thee will I give it.' |
| ( added by redactor ) | { problematic } |

| P | Notes |
|---|---|
| | |

Ishmael immediately after Ishmael is born, because Hagar despises Sarai after she has borne Abram a child while Sarai remains barren.

Presumably, a redactor added the verse "GEN 16:9And the angel of the Lord said unto her: 'Return to thy mistress, and submit thyself under her hands'" to make this J story consistent with the E story, where Hagar is with Sarah and Abraham when Isaac is born. In the J text, there is nothing about Hagar being with them after this point. The repetition of "And the angel of the Lord said unto her" is a hint that a redactor has altered this passage; the original writer would not include this phrase before each sentence that the angel said.

**P Text**

This is another brief summary history. It includes Abram's age, which is typical of P and another example of his precision.

### Hagar and Ishmael, Covenant with/ Promise to Abraham - Relocated

In the P text, the story of Hagar and Ishmael comes before the Covenant of Abraham, but in the J text, the Promise to Abraham comes before the story of Hagar and Ishmael. Because the goal of this edition is to show parallel passages next to each other, it reverses the order of these two stories in the J text.

**Covenant with Abram**

GEN 17:1And when Abram was ninety years old and nine, the Lord appeared to Abram, and said unto him: 'I am God Almighty; walk before Me, and be thou whole-hearted. ²And I

### Promise to/Covenant with Abram

**E Text**

There is no preparation in the E text for the verse, "GEN 15:3And Abram said: 'Behold, to me Thou hast given no seed."

Presumably, God must have appeared to Abram in a dream or vision before Abram made this reply (because God appears directly only to Moses in E). Therefore, this edition has moved Genesis 15:12 (where Abram is about to have a dream or vision) before Genesis 15:3.

In the received version of the Bible, Genesis 15:12 is in the middle of the covenant ceremony in J, but

| [ used more than once ] | " quoting older text " |
|---|---|

| **E** | **J** |
|---|---|
| *[Gap in E: God speaks to Abram in a dream]* | GEN 15:1(After these things the word of the Lord came unto Abram in a vision, saying:)'Fear not, Abram, I am thy shield, thy reward shall be exceeding great.' |
| GEN 15:3And Abram said: 'Behold, to me Thou hast given no seed, and, lo, one born in my house is to be mine heir.' 13And He said unto Abram: 'Know of a surety that thy seed shall be a stranger in a land that is not theirs, and shall serve them; and they shall afflict them four hundred years; 14and also that nation, whom they shall serve, will I judge; and afterward shall they come out with great substance. 15But thou shalt go to thy fathers in peace; thou shalt be buried in a good old age. 16And in the fourth generation they shall come back hither; for the iniquity of the Amorite is not yet full.' | 2And Abram said: 'O Lord God, what wilt Thou give me, seeing I go hence childless, and he that shall be possessor of my house is Eliezer of Damascus?' 4And, behold, the word of the Lord came unto him, saying: 'This man shall not be thine heir; but he that shall come forth out of thine own bowels shall be thine heir.' 5And He brought him forth abroad, and said: 'Look now toward heaven, and count the stars, if thou be able to count them'; and He said unto him: 'So shall thy seed be.'6And he believed in the Lord; and He counted it to him for righteousness. |
| | 7And He said unto him: 'I am the Lord that brought thee out (of Ur of the Chaldees,) to give thee this land to inherit it.' 8And he said: 'O Lord God, whereby shall I know that I shall inherit it?' 9And He said unto him: 'Take Me a heifer of three years old, and a ram of three years old, and a turtle-dove, and a young pigeon.' 10And he took him all these, and divided them in the midst, and laid each half over against the other; but the birds divided he not. 11And the birds of prey came down upon the carcasses, and Abram drove them away. 17And it came to pass, that, when the sun went down, and there was thick darkness, behold a smoking furnace, and a flaming torch that passed between these pieces. |
| ( added by redactor ) | { problematic } |

| P | Notes |
|---|---|

will make My covenant between Me and thee, and will multiply thee exceedingly.' ³And Abram fell on his face; And God talked with him, saying: ⁴'As for Me, behold, My covenant is with thee, and thou shalt be the father of a multitude of nations. ⁵Neither shall thy name any more be called Abram, but thy name shall be Abraham; for the father of a multitude of nations have I made thee. ⁶And I will make thee exceeding fruitful, and I will make nations of thee, and kings shall come out of thee. ⁷And I will establish My covenant between Me and thee and thy seed after thee throughout their generations for an everlasting covenant, to be a God unto thee and to thy seed after thee. ⁸And I will give unto thee, and to thy seed after thee, the land of thy sojournings, all the land of Canaan, for an everlasting possession; and I will be their God.'

⁹And God said unto Abraham: 'And as for thee, thou shalt keep My covenant, thou, and thy seed after thee throughout their generations. ¹⁰This is My covenant, which ye shall keep, between Me and you and thy seed after thee: every male among you shall be circumcised. ¹¹And ye shall be circumcised in the flesh of your foreskin; and it shall be a token of a covenant betwixt Me and you. ¹²And he that is eight days old shall be circumcised among you, every male throughout your generations, he that is born in the house, or bought with money of any foreigner, that is not of thy seed. ¹³He that is born in thy house, and

it is clearly out of place there and interrupts the narrative. Though this verse does not make sense in J, it does make sense in this new location in E.

**J Text**

A redactor interrupted the J passage describing God's promise to Abram in Genesis 13 and Genesis 15 by inserting Genesis 14, which scholars agree is not by J, E or P. Thus, this redactor had to add "After these things the word of the Lord came unto Abram in a vision" at the beginning of Genesis 15. This is not characteristic of J, where the Lord speaks directly to people rather than appearing in a vision.

In Genesis 15:7, R added "(of Ur of the Chaldees)" to make this text consistent with P's version saying Abraham came from Ur of the Chaldees.

J says, "ᴳᴱᴺ ¹⁵:¹⁸In that day the Lord made a covenant with Abram," but this covenant is more like a promise because it is one-sided: God asks nothing in return for his promise to Abram.

**P Text**

J places this event on his timeline, telling us it happened when Abram was 90 years old.

In P, there is really a covenant: God makes a promise to Abraham and makes a demand in return (circumcision). This is one of three covenants in P, the covenant of Noah, of Abraham, and of Moses and Aaron. In each covenant, God makes a promise and makes a demand in return. See page 35.

| [ used more than once ] | " quoting older text " |
|---|---|

| E | J |
|---|---|
| | [18]In that day the Lord made a covenant with Abram, saying: 'Unto thy seed have I given this land, from the river of Egypt unto the great river, the river Euphrates; [19]the Kenite, and the Kenizzite, and the Kadmonite, [20]and the Hittite, and the Perizzite, and the Rephaim, [21]and the Amorite, and the Canaanite, and the Girgashite, and the Jebusite.' |
| *[Continued on p. 96]* | **The Lord Visits Abraham's Tent**<br><br>GEN 18:1And the Lord appeared unto him by the terebinths of Mamre, as he sat in the tent door in the heat of the day; [2]and he lifted up his eyes and looked, and, lo, three men stood over against him; and when he saw them, he ran to meet them from the tent door, and bowed down to the earth, [3]and said: 'My lord, if now I have found favour in thy sight, pass not away, I pray thee, from thy servant. [4]Let now a little water be fetched, and wash your feet, and recline yourselves under the tree. [5]And I will fetch a morsel of bread, and stay ye your heart; after that ye shall pass on; forasmuch as ye are come to your servant.' And they said: 'So do, as thou hast said.'<br><br>[6]And Abraham hastened into the tent unto Sarah, and said: 'Make ready quickly three measures of fine meal, knead it, and make cakes.' [7]And Abraham ran unto the herd, and fetched a calf tender and good, and |
| ( added by redactor ) | { problematic } |

| **P** | **Notes** |
|---|---|

he that is bought with thy money, must needs be circumcised; and My covenant shall be in your flesh for an everlasting covenant. ¹⁴And the uncircumcised male who is not circumcised in the flesh of his foreskin, that soul shall be cut off from his people; he hath broken My covenant.'

¹⁵And God said unto Abraham: 'As for Sarai thy wife, thou shalt not call her name Sarai, but Sarah shall her name be. ¹⁶And I will bless her, and moreover I will give thee a son of her; yea, I will bless her, and she shall be a mother of nations; kings of peoples shall be of her.'

¹⁷Then Abraham fell upon his face, and laughed, and said in his heart: 'Shall a child be born unto him that is a hundred years old? and shall Sarah, that is ninety years old, bear?' ¹⁸And Abraham said unto God: 'Oh that Ishmael might live before Thee! '

¹⁹And God said: 'Nay, but Sarah thy wife shall bear thee a son; and thou shalt call his name Isaac; and I will establish My covenant with him for an everlasting covenant for his seed after him. ²⁰And as for Ishmael, I have heard thee; behold, I have blessed him, and will make him fruitful, and will multiply him exceedingly; twelve princes shall he beget, and I will make him a great nation. ²¹But My covenant will I establish with Isaac, whom Sarah shall bear unto thee at this set time in the next year.'

²²And He left off talking with him, and God went up from Abra-

### Abram Becomes Abraham

In the P text God changes Abram's name to Abraham (Gen. 17:5) as part of the covenant. In the J text, the name changes without notice from Abram in Genesis 15 to Abraham in Genesis 18, and in the E text, the name changes without notice from Abram in Genesis 15 to Abraham in Genesis 20. It is possible that there are gaps in the J and E texts describing this name change. It is also possible that J and E each used just one of the two names and that R changed the name to make it Abram before Genesis 17 and Abraham after Genesis 17, in order to make it consistent with the P text.

### The Lord Visits Abraham's Tent
**J Text**

This is the most extreme example of J's anthropomorphism. The Lord [=YHWH] walks right up to Abram's tent with two companions and stays for dinner.

This text explains the name of Isaac based on Sarah's reaction to the Lord's prediction before Isaac was born: "ᴳᴱᴺ ¹⁸:¹²And Sarah laughed within herself, saying: 'After I am waxed old shall I have pleasure, my lord being old also?'"

The E text explains the name a bit differently, basing it on Sarah's reaction after Isaac is born: "ᴳᴱᴺ ²¹: ⁶And Sarah said: 'God hath made laughter for me; every one that heareth will laugh on account of me.'"

| [ used more than once ] | " quoting older text " |
|---|---|

| E | J |
|---|---|
| | gave it unto the servant; and he hastened to dress it. [8]And he took curd, and milk, and the calf which he had dressed, and set it before them; and he stood by them under the tree, and they did eat. |
| | [9]And they said unto him: 'Where is Sarah thy wife?' And he said: 'Behold, in the tent.' [10]And He said: 'I will certainly return unto thee when the season cometh round; and, lo, Sarah thy wife shall have a son.' And Sarah heard in the tent door, which was behind him.—[11]Now Abraham and Sarah were old, and well stricken in age; it had ceased to be with Sarah after the manner of women.—[12]And Sarah laughed within herself, saying: 'After I am waxed old shall I have pleasure, my lord being old also?' |
| | [13]And the Lord said unto Abraham: 'Wherefore did Sarah laugh, saying: Shall I of a surety bear a child, who am old? [14]Is any thing too hard for the Lord. At the set time I will return unto thee, when the season cometh round, and Sarah shall have a son.' [15]Then Sarah denied, saying: 'I laughed not'; for she was afraid. And He said: 'Nay; but thou didst laugh.' |

*[Continued on p. 96]*

**Abraham Pleads for Sodom**

GEN 18:16And the men rose up from thence, and looked out toward Sodom; and Abraham went with them to bring them on the way.

[17]And the Lord said: 'Shall I hide from Abraham that which I am doing; [18]seeing that Abraham shall surely become a great and mighty nation, and all the nations of the earth shall be blessed in him? [19]For I have known him, to the end that he may command his children and his household after him, that they may keep the way of the Lord, to do righteousness and justice; to the end that the Lord may bring upon Abraham that which He hath spoken of him.' [20]And the Lord said: 'Verily, the cry of Sodom and Gomorrah is great, and, verily, their sin is exceeding grievous. [21]I will go down now, and see whether they have done altogether according to the cry of it, which is come unto Me; and if not, I will know.'

[22]And the men turned from thence, and went toward

( added by redactor )          { problematic }

| P | Notes |
|---|---|
| ham. ²³And Abraham took Ishmael his son, and all that were born in his house, and all that were bought with his money, every male among the men of Abraham's house, and circumcised the flesh of their foreskin in the selfsame day, as God had said unto him. ²⁴And Abraham was ninety years old and nine, when he was circumcised in the flesh of his foreskin. ²⁵And Ishmael his son was thirteen years old, when he was circumcised in the flesh of his foreskin. ²⁶In the selfsame day was Abraham circumcised, and Ishmael his son. ²⁷And all the men of his house, those born in the house, and those bought with money of a foreigner, were circumcised with him. | **Abraham Pleads for Sodom**<br>**J Text**<br>This is another example of J's anthropomorphism. The Lord has heard rumors about Sodom's evil, but He has to go to see whether the rumors are true (Gen. 18:21). So much for omniscience.<br>Abraham's pleading is a good example of J's characteristic use of repetition to heighten drama: Abraham first asks the Lord to spare Sodom if it has fifty righteous men and, after six tries, gets it down to ten righteous men.<br>**Other Texts**<br>There is a much more realistic account of Abraham helping Sodom in Genesis 14. Scholars generally |
| [ used more than once ] | " quoting older text " |

| **E** | **J** |
|---|---|
| | Sodom; but Abraham stood yet before the Lord. [23]And Abraham drew near, and said: 'Wilt Thou indeed sweep away the righteous with the wicked? [24]Peradventure there are fifty righteous within the city; wilt Thou indeed sweep away and not forgive the place for the fifty righteous that are therein? [25]That be far from Thee to do after this manner, to slay the righteous with the wicked, that so the righteous should be as the wicked; that be far from Thee; shall not the judge of all the earth do justly?' [26]And the Lord said: 'If I find in Sodom fifty righteous within the city, then I will forgive all the place for their sake.' [27]And Abraham answered and said: 'Behold now, I have taken upon me to speak unto the Lord, who am but dust and ashes. [28]Peradventure there shall lack five of the fifty righteous; wilt Thou destroy all the city for lack of five?' And He said: 'I will not destroy it, if I find there forty and five.' [29]And he spoke unto Him yet again, and said: 'Peradventure there shall be forty found there.' And He said: 'I will not do it for the forty's sake.' [30]And he said: 'Oh, let not the Lord be angry, and I will speak. Peradventure there shall thirty be found there.' And He said: 'I will not do it, if I find thirty there.' [31]And he said: 'Behold now, I have taken upon me to speak unto the Lord. Peradventure there shall be twenty found there.' And He said: 'I will not destroy it for the twenty's sake.' [32]And he said: 'Oh, let not the Lord be angry, and I will speak yet but this once. Peradventure ten shall be found there.' And He said: 'I will not destroy it for the ten's sake.' [33]And the Lord went His way, as soon as He had left off speaking to Abraham; and Abraham returned unto his place. |
| *[Continued on p. 96]* | **Sodom** |
| | [GEN 19:1]And the two angels came to Sodom at even; and Lot sat in the gate of Sodom; and Lot saw them, and rose up to meet them; and he fell down on his face to the earth; [2]and he said: 'Behold now, my lords, turn aside, I pray you, into your servant's |
| ( added by redactor ) | { problematic } |

*[Continued on p. 96]*

| P | Notes |
|---|---|
| | agree that it is not by E, J, or P, so it is in the section of Other Texts. |

**Sodom**

GEN 19:29 And it came to pass, when God destroyed the cities of the Plain, that God remembered Abraham, and sent Lot out of the midst of the overthrow, when He over-

**Sodom**

**J text**

　Earlier, the Lord and two companions came to visit Abraham, and the companions went on to Sodom while the Lord stayed to continue

| [ used more than once ] | " quoting older text " |

| **E** | **J** |
|---|---|
| | house, and tarry all night, and wash your feet, and ye shall rise up early, and go on your way.' And they said: 'Nay; but we will abide in the broad place all night.' ³And he urged them greatly; and they turned in unto him, and entered into his house; and he made them a feast, and did bake unleavened bread, and they did eat. |
| | ⁴But before they lay down, the men of the city, even the men of Sodom, compassed the house round, both young and old, all the people from every quarter. ⁵And they called unto Lot, and said unto him: 'Where are the men that came in to thee this night? bring them out unto us, that we may know them.' ⁶And Lot went out unto them to the door, and shut the door after him. ⁷And he said: 'I pray you, my brethren, do not so wickedly. ⁸Behold now, I have two daughters that have not known man; let me, I pray you, bring them out unto you, and do ye to them as is good in your eyes; only unto these men do nothing; forasmuch as they are come under the shadow of my roof.' ⁹And they said: 'Stand back.' And they said: 'This one fellow came in to sojourn, and he will needs play the judge; now will we deal worse with thee, than with them.' And they pressed sore upon the man, even Lot, and drew near to break the door. |
| *[Continued on p. 96]* | ¹⁰But the men put forth their hand, and brought Lot into the house to them, and the door they shut. ¹¹And they smote the men that were at the door of the house with blindness, both small and great; so that they wearied themselves to find the door. |
| | ¹²And the men said unto Lot: 'Hast thou here any besides? son-in-law, and thy sons, and thy daughters, and whomsoever thou hast in the city; bring them out of the place; ¹³for we will destroy this place, because the cry of them is waxed great before the Lord; and the Lord hath sent us to destroy it.' ¹⁴And Lot went out, and spoke unto his sons-in-law, who married his daughters, and said: 'Up, get you out of this place; for the Lord will destroy the city.' But he seemed unto his sons-in-law as one that jested. |
| ( added by redactor ) | { problematic } |

*[Continued on p. 96]*

| P | Notes |
|---|---|
| threw the cities in which Lot dwelt. | talking with Abraham (Gen. 18:22). Now, we learn for the first time that the two companions are angels.<br><br>Earlier in J, the Lord talked to companions about Adam threatening them by eating from the tree of life (Gen. 3:22) and about the threat posed by the tower of Babel (Gen. 11:6). Apparently, J took it for granted that her audience would realize from the beginning that the Lord was talking to angels.<br><br>**P Text**<br><br>It is a bit puzzling that P tells us that Lot survives, even though there is no mention of Lot later in P.<br><br>Presumably, the story of Lot escaping Sodom was so well known that P mentioned it in the brief summary way that he generally uses for history that is not connected to the four events that he considers most important: creation, the covenant of Noah, the covenant of Abraham, and the covenant of Moses and Aaron. |
| [ used more than once ] | " quoting older text " |

| **E** | **J** |
|---|---|

### Abraham in Gerar - Wife, Sister

GEN 20:1And Abraham journeyed from thence toward the land of the South, and dwelt between Kadesh and Shur; and he sojourned in Gerar. 2And Abraham said of Sarah his wife: 'She is my sister.' And Abimelech king of Gerar sent, and took Sarah.

3But God came to Abimelech in a dream of the night, and said to him: 'Behold, thou shalt die, because of the woman whom thou hast taken; for she is a man's wife.' 4Now Abimelech had not come near her; and he said: 'Lord, wilt Thou slay even a righteous nation? 5Said he not himself unto me: She is my sister? and she, even she herself said: He is my brother. In the simplicity of my heart and the innocency of my hands have I done this.'

6And God said unto him in the dream: 'Yea, I know that in the simplicity of thy heart thou hast done this, and I also withheld thee from sinning against Me. Therefore suffered I thee not to touch her. 7Now therefore restore the man's wife; for he is a prophet, and he shall pray for thee, and thou shalt live; and if thou restore her not, know thou that thou shalt surely die, thou, and all that are thine.'

8And Abimelech rose early in the morning, and called all his servants, and told all these things in their ears; and the men were sore afraid. 9Then Abimelech called Abraham, and said unto him: 'What hast thou done unto us? and wherein have I sinned against thee, that thou hast

15And when the morning arose, then the angels hastened Lot, saying: 'Arise, take thy wife, and thy two daughters that are here; lest thou be swept away in the iniquity of the city.' 16But he lingered; and the men laid hold upon his hand, and upon the hand of his wife, and upon the hand of his two daughters; the Lord being merciful unto him. And they brought him forth, and set him without the city.

17And it came to pass, when they had brought them forth abroad, that he said: 'Escape for thy life; look not behind thee, neither stay thou in all the Plain; escape to the mountain, lest thou be swept away.' 18And Lot said unto them: 'Oh, not so, my lord; 19behold now, thy servant hath found grace in thy sight, and thou hast magnified thy mercy, which thou hast shown unto me in saving my life; and I cannot escape to the mountain, lest the evil overtake me, and I die. 20Behold now, this city is near to flee unto, and it is a little one; oh, let me escape thither—is it not a little one?—and my soul shall live.' 21And he said unto him: 'See, I have accepted thee concerning this thing also, that I will not overthrow the city of which thou hast spoken. 22Hasten thou, escape thither; for I cannot do any thing till thou be come thither.'—Therefore the name of the city was called Zoar.—

23The sun was risen upon the earth when Lot came unto Zoar. 24Then the Lord caused to rain upon Sodom and upon Gomorrah brimstone and fire from the Lord out of heaven;

| ( added by redactor ) | { problematic } |
|---|---|

| P | Notes |
|---|---|
| | **Abraham in Gerar - Wife, Sister** |

**Abraham in Gerar - Wife, Sister**

This story is a very close doublet of J's story about Isaac going to Gerar in Genesis 26. In both stories, the patriarch goes to Gerar and claims that his wife is his sister. In both, the king of Gerar is named Abimelech, and when he learns that the supposed wife is actually his sister, he blames the patriarch for leading his people into possible sin. In both, the patriarch becomes wealthy in Gerar.

In general, this book places doublets next to each other so readers can compare them easily, but it is impossible in this case because the two versions of the story are a generation apart. To compare the stories, readers should look at the E story here in Genesis 20 and the J story in Genesis 26.

**E text**

"GEN 20:4Now Abimelech said: 'Lord, wilt Thou slay even a righteous nation?" In the original Hebrew, the word translated "Lord" is not YHWH. It is *ADNI*. This Hebrew word can be pronounced *Adonai*, which is a euphemism used instead of pronouncing the name of God, and that is why it is translated as "Lord," But it can also be pronounced *Adoni*, which simply means "sir" or "my lord." Thus, this verse is consistent with the fact that E does not use the name of the Lord before the time of Moses.

There is a lack of continuity in E, as the name has suddenly changed from Abram to Abraham. As mentioned earlier, it could be that a redactor dropped the E text's version

*[Continued on p. 101]*

[ used more than once ]     " quoting older text "

|       **E**       |       **J**       |
| --- | --- |

brought on me and on my kingdom a great sin? thou hast done deeds unto me that ought not to be done.' ¹⁰And Abimelech said unto Abraham: 'What sawest thou, that thou hast done this thing?'

¹¹And Abraham said: 'Because I thought: Surely the fear of God is not in this place; and they will slay me for my wife's sake. ¹²And moreover she is indeed my sister, the daughter of my father, but not the daughter of my mother; and so she became my wife. ¹³And it came to pass, when God caused me to wander from my father's house, that I said unto her: This is thy kindness which thou shalt show unto me; at every place whither we shall come, say of me: He is my brother.'

¹⁴And Abimelech took sheep and oxen, and men-servants and women-servants, and gave them unto Abraham, and restored him Sarah his wife. ¹⁵And Abimelech said: 'Behold, my land is before thee: dwell where it pleaseth thee.' ¹⁶And unto Sarah he said: 'Behold, I have given thy brother a thousand pieces of silver; behold, it is for thee a covering of the eyes to all that are with thee; and before all men thou art righted.'

¹⁷And Abraham prayed unto God; and God healed Abimelech, and his wife, and his maid-servants; and they bore children. ¹⁸For the Lord had fast closed up all the wombs of the house of Abimelech, because of Sarah Abraham's wife.

²⁵and He overthrow those cities, and all the Plain, and all the inhabitants of the cities, and that which grew upon the ground. ²⁶But his wife looked back from behind him, and she became a pillar of salt.

²⁷And Abraham got up early in the morning to the place where he had stood before the Lord. ²⁸And he looked out toward Sodom and Gomorrah, and toward all the land of the Plain, and beheld, and, lo, the smoke of the land went up as the smoke of a furnace.

### Lot and His Daughters

GEN 19:30And Lot went up out of Zoar, and dwelt in the mountain, and his two daughters with him; for he feared to dwell in Zoar; and he dwelt in a cave, he and his two daughters.

³¹And the first-born said unto the younger: 'Our father is old, and there is not a man in the earth to come in unto us after the manner of all the earth. ³²Come, let us make our father drink wine, and we will lie with him, that we may preserve seed of our father.' ³³And they made their father drink wine that night. And the first-born went in, and lay with her father; and he knew not when she lay down, nor when she arose. ³⁴And it came to pass on the morrow, that the first-born said unto the younger: 'Behold, I lay yesternight with my father. Let us make him drink wine this night also; and go thou in, and lie with him, that we may preserve seed of our father.'

| ( added by redactor ) | { problematic } |
| --- | --- |

| P | Notes |
|---|---|
| | of the change from Abram to Abraham, or it could be that it was always Abraham in E but a redactor changed it to Abram in the earlier passage to make it consistent with the other texts. |
| | |
| | **Lot and His Daughters** |
| | **J Text** |
| *[Continued on p. 101]* | Earlier, J included the story of Noah's drunkenness (beginning at Genesis 9:20) to discredit Ham and the nations descended from him, who were Israel's enemies. Likewise, she includes the story of Lot and his daughters to discredit the nations Moab and Ammon by saying that they were products of incest. |
| [ used more than once ] | " quoting older text " |

*[Continued on p. 101]*

| **E** | **J** |
|---|---|
| | [35]And they made their father drink wine that night also. And the younger arose, and lay with him; and he knew not when she lay down, nor when she arose. |
| | [36]Thus were both the daughters of Lot with child by their father. [37]And the first-born bore a son, and called his name Moab—the same is the father of the Moabites unto this day. [38]And the younger, she also bore a son, and called his name Benammi—the same is the father of the children of Ammon unto this day. |
| **Birth and Naming of Isaac** | **Birth and Naming of Isaac** |
| | GEN 21:1And the Lord remembered Sarah as He had said, and the Lord did unto Sarah as He had spoken. [2]And Sarah conceived, and bore Abraham a son in his old age, [7]And she said: 'Who would have said unto Abraham, that Sarah should give children suck? for I have borne him a son in his old age.' |
| *[Gap in E: Birth of Isaac]* | |
| GEN 21:6And Sarah said: 'God hath made laughter for me; every one that heareth will laugh on account of me.' | |
| | *[Gap in J: Naming of Isaac]* |
| [8]And the child grew, and was weaned. And Abraham made a great feast on the day that Isaac was weaned. | |
| **Casting Out Ishmael** | |
| GEN 21:9And Sarah saw the son of Hagar the Egyptian, whom she had borne unto Abraham, | |
| ( added by redactor ) | { problematic } |

| P | Notes |
|---|---|

**Birth and Naming
of Isaac**

GEN 21:2And Sarah con-
ceived, and bore Abraham
a son in his old age, at the
set time of which God
had spoken to him. ³And
Abraham called the name
of his son that was born
unto him, whom Sarah
bore to him, Isaac. ⁴And
Abraham circumcised his
son Isaac when he was
eight days old, as God had
commanded him. ⁵And
Abraham was a hundred
years old, when his son
Isaac was born unto him.

**Birth and Naming of Isaac**

**E text**

There are obvious gaps in the E text, which
just includes the explanation for the name
Isaac (which comes from the word meaning
"laugh") and the festival on the day he was
weaned and nothing else about the birth.

There is a different explanation of the name
Isaac in the J text: "GEN 18:12...Sarah laughed
within herself" when the Lord visited Abraham's tent and promised him children."

**J Text**

J just mentions the birth and not the naming
of Isaac here, as E mentions the naming but
not the birth. RJE obviously patched together
the combined story using pieces of the E and
J text.

**P text**

P continues his timeline by giving Abraham's age when Isaac was born, and he continues providing the very brief summary history that he commonly uses for events other
than the creation and the three covenants.

**Casting Out Ishmael**

This edition tries to place doublets next to
each other, so readers can easily compare
them, but it is not possible to do in this case,
because many events occurred between the

| [ used more than once ] | " quoting older text " |
|---|---|

| **E** | **J** |
|---|---|
| making sport. [10]Wherefore she said unto Abraham: 'Cast out this bondwoman and her son; for the son of this bondwoman shall not be heir with my son, even with Isaac.'

[11]And the thing was very grievous in Abraham's sight on account of his son. [12]And God said unto Abraham: 'Let it not be grievous in thy sight because of the lad, and because of thy bondwoman; in all that Sarah saith unto thee, hearken unto her voice; for in Isaac shall seed be called to thee. [13]And also of the son of the bondwoman will I make a nation, because he is thy seed.'

[14]And Abraham arose up early in the morning, and took bread and a bottle of water, and gave it unto Hagar, putting it on her shoulder, and the child, and sent her away; and she departed, and strayed in the wilderness of Beer-sheba. [15]And the water in the bottle was spent, and she cast the child under one of the shrubs. [16]And she went, and sat her down over against him a good way off, as it were a bowshot; for she said: 'Let me not look upon the death of the child.' And she sat over against him, and lifted up her voice, and wept.

[17]And God heard the voice of the lad; and the angel of God called to Hagar out of heaven, and said unto her: 'What aileth thee, Hagar? fear not; for God hath heard the voice of the lad where he is. [18]Arise, lift up the lad, and hold him fast by thy hand; for I will make him a great nation.' [19]And God opened her eyes, and she saw a well of water; and she went, and filled the bottle with water, and gave the lad drink.

[20]And God was with the lad, and he grew; and he dwelt in the wilderness, and became an archer. [21]And he dwelt in the wilderness of Paran; and his mother took him a wife out of the land of Egypt.

### Abraham's Oath at Beersheba

GEN 21:22And it came to pass at that time, that Abimelech and Phicol the captain of his host spoke unto Abraham, saying: 'God is with thee in all that thou doest. [23]Now therefore swear unto me here by God | *[Continued on p. 104]* |

| ( added by redactor ) | { problematic } |

| P | Notes |
|---|---|
| | casting out of Ishmael in the E and J texts. To compare the two versions of the story of casting out Ishmael, look at the J text in Genesis 16 above and the E's text in Genesis 21 here. |
| | The two stories are inconsistent. In the J text, Sarai asks Abram to cast out Ishmael immediately after he is born because Sarai is angry that Hagar despises her after having Abram's child. In the E text, Sarah asks Abraham to cast out Hagar after Isaac is born because she wants Isaac to be the only heir of Abraham. |
| *[Continued on p. 107]* | |
| | **Abraham's Oath at Beersheba** |
| | This text is a very close doublet of J's story about Isaac's oath at Beersheba beginning at Genesis 26:23. In both, Abimelech king of Gerar |
| [ used more than once ] | " quoting older text " |

| **E** | **J** |
|---|---|
| that thou wilt not deal falsely with me, nor with my son, nor with my son's son; but according to the kindness that I have done unto thee, thou shalt do unto me, and to the land wherein thou hast sojourned.' <br><br> [24]And Abraham said: 'I will swear.' [25]And Abraham reproved Abimelech because of the well of water, which Abimelech's servants had violently taken away. [26]And Abimelech said: 'I know not who hath done this thing; neither didst thou tell me, neither yet heard I of it, but to-day.' <br><br> [27]And Abraham took sheep and oxen, and gave them unto Abimelech; and they two made a covenant. [28]And Abraham set seven ewe-lambs of the flock by themselves. [29]And Abimelech said unto Abraham: 'What mean these seven ewe-lambs which thou hast set by themselves?' [30]And he said: 'Verily, these seven ewe-lambs shalt thou take of my hand, that it may be a witness unto me, that I have digged this well.' [31]Wherefore that place was called Beer-sheba; because there they swore both of them. <br><br> [32]So they made a covenant at Beer-sheba; and Abimelech rose up, and Phicol the captain of his host, and they returned into the land of the Philistines. [33]And Abraham planted a tamarisk-tree in Beer-sheba, {and called there on the name of the Lord, the Everlasting God.} [34]And Abraham sojourned in the land of the Philistines many days. | **Generations of Nahor** <br><br> GEN 22:20And it came to pass after these things, that it was told Abraham, saying: 'Behold, Milcah, she also hath borne children unto thy brother Nahor: [21]Uz his first-born, and Buz his brother, and Kemuel the father of Aram; [22]and Chesed, and Hazo, and Pildash, and Jid- |
| ( added by redactor ) | { problematic } |

| **P** | **Notes** |
|---|---|
| | and his captain Phicol come to see the patriarch in Beersheba and swear an oath of non-aggression with the patriarch. Both follow up the story of the patriarch's stay in Gerar (E's story of Abraham in Gerar in Genesis 20 and J's story of Isaac in Gerar in Genesis 26), which are also very close doublets. |
| | In general, this book places doublets next to each other so readers can compare them easily, but it is impossible in this case because the two versions of the story are a generation apart. To compare the stories, readers should look at the E story beginning at Genesis 21:20 here and the J story beginning at Genesis 26:23 below. |
| | **E Text** |
| | The Hebrew word *shiva* means both seven and oath. In J, Beersheba (Hebrew for "well of shiva") gets its name from the oath that Isaac swore. Here in E, there is a more elaborate story of Abraham sacrificing seven ewes and also swearing an oath. |
| *[Continued on p. 107]* | This half-verse is problematic: "<sup>GEN 21:33b</sup>called there on the name of the Lord, the Everlasting God" because it uses the name Lord (=YHWH), which E does not use before the time of Moses. Perhaps RJE added this word to make this verse more consistent with the J text, or perhaps RJE pulled in this half-verse from J's version of this story. |
| | Incidentally, the Philistines (Gen. 21:34) were not in Canaan in patriarchal times. This anachronism is found in both J and E. |
| | **Generations of Nahor** |
| | This passage is about the origin of a number of Aramean tribes. J tells us twelve Aramean tribes are descended from Nahor, as twelve Israelite tribes are descended from Nahor's brother Abraham. As we saw in the post-flood genealogy, J is interested in surrounding nations, not just in the Israelites. |
| | Of course, this genealogy also sets the stage for the appearance of Rebekah. R put Genesis 23 from P between the two J texts that introduce Rebekah: Genesis 22:20-24 describes Rebekah's ancestry, and Genesis 24 |
| [ used more than once ] | " quoting older text " |

| **E** | **J** |
|---|---|
| | laph, and Bethuel.' ²³And Bethuel begot Rebekah; these eight did Milcah bear to Nahor, Abraham's brother. ²⁴And his concubine, whose name was Reumah, she also bore Tebah, and Gaham, and Tahash, and Maacah. |

### Isaac and Rebekah

GEN 24:1And Abraham was old, well stricken in age; and the Lord had blessed Abraham in all things. ²And Abraham said unto his servant, the elder of his house, that ruled over all that he had: 'Put, I pray thee, thy hand under my thigh. ³And I will make thee swear by the Lord, the God of heaven and the God of the earth, that thou shalt not take a wife for my son of the daughters of the Canaanites, among whom I dwell. ⁴But thou shalt go unto my country, and to my kindred, and take a wife for my son, even for Isaac.'

⁵And the servant said unto him: 'Peradventure the woman will not be willing to follow me unto this land; must I needs bring thy son back unto the land from whence thou camest?'

*[Continued on p. 108]*

⁶And Abraham said unto him: 'Beware thou that thou bring not my son back thither. ⁷The Lord, the God of heaven, who took me from my father's house, and from the land of my nativity, and who spoke unto me, and who swore unto me, saying: Unto thy seed will I give this land; He will send His angel before thee, and thou shalt take a wife for my son from thence. ⁸And if the woman be not willing to follow thee, then thou shalt be clear from this my oath; only thou shalt not bring my son back thither.'

⁹And the servant put his hand under the thigh of Abraham his master, and swore to him concerning this matter. ¹⁰And the servant took ten camels, of the camels of his master, and departed; having all goodly things of his master's in his hand; and he arose, and went to Aram-naharaim, unto the city of Nahor. ¹¹And he made the camels to kneel down without the city by the well of water at the time of evening, the time that women go out to draw water.

( added by redactor )   { problematic }

| P | Notes |
|---|---|
| | describes Abraham's servant meeting Rebekah. When we separate the texts, these two passages from J form a connected narrative, which is interrupted in the received version of the Bible by Genesis 23. |

**Isaac and Rebecca**

The final verse of this passage is, "GEN 24:67And Isaac (brought her into his mother Sarah's tent, and) took Rebekah, and she became his wife; and he loved her. (And Isaac was comforted for his mother.)"

The death of Sarah is immediately before this in the Bible, but it is from the P text and is not mentioned in the J text. Therefore, R presumably added these references to Sarah to give more continuity to the edited-together stories.

**Death and Burial of Sarah**

GEN 23:1And the life of Sarah was a hundred and seven and twenty years; these were the years of the life of Sarah. 2And Sarah died in Kiriath-arba—the same is Hebron—in the land of Canaan; and Abraham came to mourn for Sarah, and to weep for her.

3And Abraham rose up from before his dead, and spoke unto the children of Heth, saying: 4'I am a stranger and a sojourner with you: give me a possession of a burying-place with you, that I may bury my dead out of my sight.' 5And the children of Heth answered Abraham, saying unto him: 6'Hear us, my lord: thou art a mighty prince among us;

**Death and Burial of Sarah**

**P Text**

Until this point, P has generally skimmed over events, except for those he considers critical turning points of history: the creation, the flood and covenant of Noah, and the covenant of Abraham.

Now, he breaks with this practice by including this long section about the burial of Sarah, which shows that Abraham and his descendents purchased the tomb of the patriarchs in Hebron and so have a right to it and that there were many witnesses to the purchase, since "GEN 23:10Ephron was sitting in the midst of the children of Heth" when it happened. Later, P will tell us that Abraham,

| [ used more than once ] | " quoting older text " |

| **E** | **J** |
|---|---|
| | $^{12}$And he said: 'O Lord, the God of my master Abraham, send me, I pray Thee, good speed this day, and show kindness unto my master Abraham. $^{13}$Behold, I stand by the fountain of water; and the daughters of the men of the city come out to draw water. $^{14}$So let it come to pass, that the damsel to whom I shall say: Let down thy pitcher, I pray thee, that I may drink; and she shall say: Drink, and I will give thy camels drink also; let the same be she that Thou hast appointed for Thy servant, even for Isaac; and thereby shall I know that Thou hast shown kindness unto my master.' |
| **Binding of Isaac**<br><br>GEN 22:1 And it came to pass after these things, that God did prove Abraham, and said unto him: 'Abraham'; and he said: 'Here am I.' $^{2}$And He said: 'Take now thy son, thine only son, whom thou lovest, even Isaac, and get thee into the land of Moriah; and offer him there for a burnt-offering upon one of the mountains which I will tell thee of.' $^{3}$And Abraham rose early in the morning, and saddled his ass, and took two of his young men with him, and Isaac his son; and he cleaved the wood for the burnt-offering, and rose up, and went unto the place of which God had told him. $^{4}$On the third day Abraham lifted up his eyes, and saw the place afar off. $^{5}$And Abraham said unto his young men: 'Abide ye here with the ass, and I and the lad will go yonder; and we will worship, and come back to you.' $^{6}$And Abraham took the wood of | $^{15}$And it came to pass, before he had done speaking, that, behold, Rebekah came out, who was born to Bethuel the son of Milcah, the wife of Nahor, Abraham's brother, with her pitcher upon her shoulder. $^{16}$And the damsel was very fair to look upon, a virgin, neither had any man known her; and she went down to the fountain, and filled her pitcher, and came up. $^{17}$And the servant ran to meet her, and said: 'Give me to drink, I pray thee, a little water of thy pitcher.' $^{18}$And she said: 'Drink, my lord'; and she hastened, and let down her pitcher upon her hand, and gave him drink. $^{19}$And when she had done giving him drink, she said: 'I will draw for thy camels also, until they have done drinking.' $^{20}$And she hastened, and emptied her pitcher into the trough, and ran again unto the well to draw, and drew for all his camels.<br><br>$^{21}$And the man looked stedfastly on her; holding his peace, to know |
| ( added by redactor ) | { problematic } |

| **P** | **Notes** |
|---|---|
| in the choice of our sepulchres bury thy dead; none of us shall withhold from thee his sepulchre, but that thou mayest bury thy dead.'<br><br>⁷And Abraham rose up, and bowed down to the people of the land, even to the children of Heth. ⁸And he spoke with them, saying: 'If it be your mind that I should bury my dead out of my sight, hear me, and entreat for me to Ephron the son of Zohar, ⁹that he may give me the cave of Machpelah, which he hath, which is in the end of his field; for the full price let him give it to me in the midst of you for a possession of a burying-place.'<br><br>¹⁰Now Ephron was sitting in the midst of the children of Heth; and Ephron the Hittite answered Abraham in the hearing of the children of Heth, even of all that went in at the gate of his city, saying: ¹¹'Nay, my lord, hear me: the field give I thee, and the cave that is therein, I give it thee; in the presence of the sons of my people give I it thee; bury thy dead.'<br><br>¹²And Abraham bowed down before the people of the land. ¹³And he spoke unto Ephron in the hearing of the people of the land, saying: 'But if thou wilt, I pray thee, hear me: I will give the price of the field; take it of me, and I will bury my dead there.'<br><br>¹⁴And Ephron answered Abraham, saying unto him: ¹⁵'My lord, hearken unto me: a piece of land worth four hundred shekels of silver, what is that betwixt me and thee? bury therefore thy dead.' ¹⁶And Abraham | Isaac, Rebekah, Leah, and Jacob are also buried in this cave (Gen. 49:27). The E and J texts do not mention this cave. For information about why P might have given more than his usual summary history here, see page 36.<br><br>There is a good realistic picture of polite bargaining in Genesis 23:13-16, where Ephron says that the price is four hundred shekels but Abraham does not have to pay it, and Abraham immediately pays the four hundred shekels.<br><br>**Binding of Isaac**<br>**E Text**<br>All of the mentions of the Lord in this passage clearly are not from the E text, where the name of the Lord is not used before it is revealed to Moses.<br><br>There is a problematic passage beginning at Genesis 22:19 that explains the place name Adonai-jireh. In Hebrew, this name is YH-WHjireh, but this JPS translation uses Adonai, which is the common euphemism for the name of the Lord. It is problematic that this passage uses the name of the Lord, which J would use but E would not use in stories of the patriarchs, but it also has God speaking through an angel, which is typical of E while J typically has the Lord appear Himself to speak.<br><br>One plausible explanation is that RJE created this problematic passage by combining the E text with small snippets of the J text, so small that we cannot untangle them. Then, |
| [ used more than once ] | " quoting older text " |

| E | J |
|---|---|
| the burnt-offering, and laid it upon Isaac his son; and he took in his hand the fire and the knife; and they went both of them together. [7]And Isaac spoke unto Abraham his father, and said: 'My father.' And he said: 'Here am I, my son.' And he said: 'Behold the fire and the wood; but where is the lamb for a burnt-offering?' [8]And Abraham said: 'God will provide Himself the lamb for a burnt-offering, my son.' So they went both of them together.<br>[9]And they came to the place which God had told him of; and Abraham built the altar there, and laid the wood in order, and bound Isaac his son, and laid him on the altar, upon the wood. [10]And Abraham stretched forth his hand, and took the knife to slay his son. [11]And the angel (of the Lord) called unto him out of heaven, and said: 'Abraham, Abraham.' And he said: 'Here am I.' [12]And he said: 'Lay not thy hand upon the lad, neither do thou any thing unto him; for now I know that thou art a God-fearing man, seeing thou hast not withheld thy son, thine only son, from Me.'<br>[13]And Abraham lifted up his eyes, and looked, and behold behind him a ram caught in the thicket by his horns. And Abraham went and took the ram, and offered him up for a burnt-offering in the stead of his son. {[14]And Abraham called the name of that place Adonaijireh; as it is said to this day: 'In the mount where the Lord is seen.' [15]And the angel of the Lord called unto Abraham a second time out of heaven, | whether the Lord had made his journey prosperous or not. [22]And it came to pass, as the camels had done drinking, that the man took a golden ring of half a shekel weight, and two bracelets for her hands of ten shekels weight of gold; [23]and said: 'Whose daughter art thou? tell me, I pray thee. Is there room in thy father's house for us to lodge in?'<br>[24]And she said unto him: 'I am the daughter of Bethuel the son of Milcah, whom she bore unto Nahor.' [25]She said moreover unto him: 'We have both straw and provender enough, and room to lodge in.' [26]And the man bowed his head, and prostrated himself before the Lord. [27]And he said: 'Blessed be the Lord, the God of my master Abraham, who hath not forsaken His mercy and His truth toward my master; as for me, the Lord hath led me in the way to the house of my master's brethren.' [28]And the damsel ran, and told her mother's house according to these words.<br>[29]And Rebekah had a brother, and his name was Laban; and Laban ran out unto the man, unto the fountain. [30]And it came to pass, when he saw the ring, and the bracelets upon his sister's hands, and when he heard the words of Rebekah his sister, saying: 'Thus spoke the man unto me,' that he came unto the man; and, behold, he stood by the camels at the fountain. [31]And he said: 'Come in, thou blessed of the Lord; wherefore standest thou without? for I have cleared the house, and made room for the camels.' |
| ( added by redactor ) | { problematic } |

| P | Notes |
|---|---|

hearkened unto Ephron; and Abraham weighed to Ephron the silver, which he had named in the hearing of the children of Heth, four hundred shekels of silver, current money with the merchant.

[17]So the field of Ephron, which was in Machpelah, which was before Mamre, the field, and the cave which was therein, and all the trees that were in the field, that were in all the border thereof round about, were made sure [18]unto Abraham for a possession in the presence of the children of Heth, before all that went in at the gate of his city. [19]And after this, Abraham buried Sarah his wife in the cave of the field of Machpelah before Mamre—the same is Hebron—in the land of Canaan. [20]And the field, and the cave that is therein, were made sure unto Abraham for a possession of a burying-place by the children of Heth.

to make the entire story of the binding of Isaac more consistent, RJE added the name of the Lord in other places in the story.

The myth of the binding of Isaac is an origin myth explaining the Israelites' use of animal sacrifice rather than human sacrifice. In the Covenant Code, E says that the requirement that first-born animals be sacrificed and that first-born children be redeemed by sacrifice commemorates the plague of the slaying of the first born:

"[EX 13:12]... thou shalt set apart unto the Lord all that openeth the womb; every firstling that is a male, which thou hast coming of a beast, shall be the Lord's. [13]And every firstling of an ass thou shalt redeem with a lamb; and if thou wilt not redeem it, then thou shalt break its neck; and all the first-born of man among thy sons shalt thou redeem. [14]And it shall be when thy son asketh thee in time to come, saying: What is this? that thou shalt say unto him: By strength of hand the Lord brought us out from Egypt, from the house of bondage; [15]and it came to pass, when Pharaoh would hardly let us go that the Lord slew all the first-born in the land of Egypt, both the first-born of man, and the first-born of beast; therefore I sacrifice to the Lord all that openeth the womb, being males; but all the first-born of my sons I redeem."

Here, he gives another origin myth for the custom of sacrificing an animal to redeem your first-born son, tracing it to Abraham.

| [ used more than once ] | " quoting older text " |
|---|---|

| E | J |
|---|---|
| [16]and said: 'By Myself have I sworn, saith the Lord, because thou hast done this thing, and hast not withheld thy son, thine only son, [17]that in blessing I will bless thee, and in multiplying I will multiply thy seed as the stars of the heaven, and as the sand which is upon the sea-shore; and thy seed shall possess the gate of his enemies; [18]and in thy seed shall all the nations of the earth be blessed; because thou hast hearkened to My voice.'} [19]So Abraham returned unto his young men, and they rose up and went together to Beer-sheba; and Abraham dwelt at Beer-sheba.<br><br><br><br>*[Gap in E: Abraham to Jacob]* | [32]And the man came into the house, and he ungirded the camels; and he gave straw and provender for the camels, and water to wash his feet and the feet of the men that were with him. [33]And there was set food before him to eat; but he said: 'I will not eat, until I have told mine errand.' And he said: 'Speak on.' [34]And he said: 'I am Abraham's servant. [35]And the Lord hath blessed my master greatly; and he is become great; and He hath given him flocks and herds, and silver and gold, and men-servants and maid-servants, and camels and asses. [36]And Sarah my master's wife bore a son to my master when she was old; and unto him hath he given all that he hath. [37]And my master made me swear, saying: Thou shalt not take a wife for my son of the daughters of the Canaanites, in whose land I dwell. [38]But thou shalt go unto my father's house, and to my kindred, and take a wife for my son. [39]And I said unto my master: Peradventure the woman will not follow me. [40]And he said unto me: The Lord, before whom I walk, will send His angel with thee, and prosper thy way; and thou shalt take a wife for my son of my kindred, and of my father's house; [41]then shalt thou be clear from my oath, when thou comest to my kindred; and if they give her not to thee, thou shalt be clear from my oath. [42]And I came this day unto the fountain, and said: O Lord, the God of my master Abraham, if now Thou do prosper my way which I go: [43]behold, I stand by the fountain |
| ( added by redactor ) | { problematic } |

| P | Notes |
|---|---|
| | |

*[Continued on p. 117]*

### Gap in E: Abraham to Jacob

There is a long gap in the E text, from the Binding of Isaac (Gen. 22) to Jacob's Vision in Bethel (beginning at Genesis 28:11). E has no story of the marriage of Isaac, of the birth of Jacob and Esau, of Jacob getting Esau's birthright, or of Jacob leaving Canaan to go to Haran and see Laban. The E text jumps from Isaac's childhood to Jacob's vision at Bethel while he is on his way to see Laban. Presumably, RJE preferred J's stories about these events.

| [ used more than once ] | " quoting older text " |
|---|---|

| **E** | **J** |
|---|---|
| | of water; and let it come to pass, that the maiden that cometh forth to draw, to whom I shall say: Give me, I pray thee, a little water from thy pitcher to drink; ⁴⁴and she shall say to me: Both drink thou, and I will also draw for thy camels; let the same be the woman whom the Lord hath appointed for my master's son. ⁴⁵And before I had done speaking to my heart, behold, Rebekah came forth with her pitcher on her shoulder; and she went down unto the fountain, and drew. And I said unto her: Let me drink, I pray thee. ⁴⁶And she made haste, and let down her pitcher from her shoulder, and said: Drink, and I will give thy camels drink also. So I drank, and she made the camels drink also. ⁴⁷And I asked her, and said: Whose daughter art thou? And she said: The daughter of Bethuel, Nahor's son, whom Milcah bore unto him. And I put the ring upon her nose, and the bracelets upon her hands. ⁴⁸And I bowed my head, and prostrated myself before the Lord, and blessed the Lord, the God of my master Abraham, who had led me in the right way to take my master's brother's daughter for his son. ⁴⁹And now if ye will deal kindly and truly with my master, tell me; and if not, tell me; that I may turn to the right hand, or to the left.' |

**Sons of Keturah**

GEN 25:1And Abraham took another wife *[=concubine]*, and her name was Keturah. ²And she bore him Zimran, and Jokshan, and Medan, and Midian, and Ishbak, and Shuah. ³And Jokshan begot Sheba, and Dedan. And the sons of Dedan were Asshurim, and Letushim, and Leummim. ⁴And the sons of Midian: Ephah, and Epher, and Hanoch, and Abida, and Eldaah. All these were the children of Keturah. ⁵And Abraham gave all that he had unto Isaac. ⁶But unto the sons of the concubine(s), that Abraham had, Abraham gave gifts; and he sent them away from Isaac his son, while he yet lived, eastward, unto the east country.

⁵⁰Then Laban and Bethuel answered and said: 'The thing proceedeth from the Lord; we cannot speak unto thee bad or good. ⁵¹Behold, Rebekah is before thee, take her, and go, and let her be thy master's son's wife, as the Lord hath

| ( added by redactor ) | { problematic } |
|---|---|

| P | Notes |
|---|---|
| *[Continued on p. 117]* | **Sons of Keturah**<br>**E Text**<br>There is a problem in the received Biblical text, which does not result from separating source texts.<br>At first glance, this passage seems to be about several women, Abraham's second wife and his concubines, since "another wife" is in the singular and concubines is in the plural.<br>If Abraham had a second wife, her children would normally have inherited his property. Genesis 25:5-6 says that Abraham gave his property to Isaac and gave gifts to the sons of the concubines and sent them away, but this says nothing about property given to the sons of his wife Keturah.<br>Here is a possible explanation: in Hebrew, *isha* means woman as well as wife, so Genesis 25:1 could be |
| [ used more than once ] | " quoting older text " |

*[Continued on p. 117]*

| **E** | **J** |
|---|---|
| | spoken.' [52]And it came to pass, that, when Abraham's servant heard their words, he bowed himself down to the earth unto the Lord. [53]And the servant brought forth jewels of silver, and jewels of gold, and raiment, and gave them to Rebekah; he gave also to her brother and to her mother precious things. [54]And they did eat and drink, he and the men that were with him, and tarried all night; and they rose up in the morning, and he said: 'Send me away unto my master.' [55]And her brother and her mother said: 'Let the damsel abide with us a few days, at the least ten; after that she shall go.' [56]And he said unto them: 'Delay me not, seeing the Lord hath prospered my way; send me away that I may go to my master.' [57]And they said: 'We will call the damsel, and inquire at her mouth.' [58]And they called Rebekah, and said unto her: 'Wilt thou go with this man?' And she said: 'I will go.' |
| *[Continued on p. 130]* | [59]And they sent away Rebekah their sister, and her nurse, and Abraham's servant, and his men. [60]And they blessed Rebekah, and said unto her: 'Our sister, be thou the mother of thousands of ten thousands, and let thy seed possess the gate of those that hate them.' [61]And Rebekah arose, and her damsels, and they rode upon the camels, and followed the man. And the servant took Rebekah, and went his way. |
| | [62]And Isaac came from the way of Beer-lahai-roi; for he dwelt in the land of the South. [63]And Isaac went out to meditate in the field at the eventide; and he lifted up his eyes, and saw, and, behold, there were camels coming. [64]And Rebekah lifted up her eyes, and when she saw Isaac, she alighted from the camel. [65]And she said unto the servant: 'What man is this that walketh in the field to meet us?' And the servant said: 'It is my master.' And she took her veil, and covered herself. [66]And the servant told Isaac all the things that he had done. [67]And Isaac (brought her into his mother Sarah's tent, and) took Rebekah, and she became his wife; and he loved her. (And Isaac was comforted for his mother.) |
| ( added by redactor ) | { problematic } |

| P | Notes |
|---|---|
| | |

### P

#### Death of Abraham

GEN 25:7And these are the days of the years of Abraham's life which he lived, a hundred threescore and fifteen years. 8And Abraham expired, and died in a good old age, an old man, and full of years; and was gathered to his people. 9And Isaac and Ishmael his sons buried him in the cave of Machpelah, in the field of Ephron the son of Zohar the Hittite, which is before Mamre; 10the field which Abraham purchased of the children of Heth; there was Abraham buried, and Sarah his wife. 11And it came to pass after the death of Abraham, that God blessed Isaac his son; and Isaac dwelt by Beer-lahai-roi.

### Notes

translated "Abraham took another woman," which could refer to a concubine as well as a wife.

This edition puts the final s of concubines in parentheses in Genesis 25:6, assuming that Keturah was a concubine and that a redactor or copyist made concubine plural, not realizing that *isha* was used here to refer to a concubine. This is the only interpretation that makes the passage coherent, rather than leaving the issue of Keturah's children unresolved.

In another location, the P text uses a form of the word *isha* to refer to concubines, and it is translated as wives: "GEN 37:2bJoseph, being seventeen years old, was feeding the flock with his brethren, being still a lad even with the sons of Bilhah, and with the sons of Zilpah, his father's wives," Yet we know that Bilhah and Zilpah were actually Jacob's concubines and Rachel and Leah were his wives. Thus it is plausible that *isha* was also used in this story of Abraham to refer to Abraham's concubine.

It is hard to decide whether to attribute this passage to J or E. Both J and E have Moses go to Midian and learn from his Midianite father-in-law, so both have a motive for this genealogy showing that the Midianites were also descended from Abraham. J is generally interested in genealogies of surrounding peoples, not just of the Israelites, so she had some motive to include this. However, E was a Mushite priest who believed he was descended from Moses and thus also from Moses' Midianite wife, so he had an even stronger motive for saying that the Midianites were descended from Abraham.

| [ used more than once ] | " quoting older text " |
|---|---|

| **E** | **J** |
|---|---|
| | **Generations of Ishmael**<br><br>(GEN 25:12Now these are the generations of Ishmael, Abraham's son, whom Hagar the Egyptian, Sarah's handmaid, bore unto Abraham.) 13And these are the names of the sons of Ishmael, by their names, according to their generations: the first-born of Ishmael, Nebaioth; and Kedar, and Adbeel, and Mibsam, 14and Mishma, and Dumah, and Massa; 15Hadad, and Tema, Jetur, Naphish, and Kedem; 16these are the sons of Ishmael, and these are their names, by their villages, and by their encampments; twelve princes according to their nations.<br><br>18And they dwelt from Havilah unto Shur that is before Egypt, as thou goest toward Asshur: over against all his brethren he did settle. |
| *[Continued on p. 130]* | **Birth of Jacob and Esau**<br><br>GEN 25:21And Isaac entreated the Lord for his wife, because she was barren; and the Lord let Himself be entreated of him, and Rebekah his wife conceived. 22And the children struggled together within her; and she said: 'If it be so, wherefore do I live?' And she went to inquire of the Lord. 23And the Lord said unto her:<br>"Two nations are in thy womb,<br>And two peoples shall be separated from thy bowels;<br>And the one people shall be stronger than the other people;<br>And the elder shall serve the younger."<br>24And when her days to be delivered were fulfilled, behold, there were twins in her womb. 25And the first came forth ruddy, all over like a hairy mantle; and they called his name Esau. 26aAnd after that came forth his brother, and his hand had hold on Esau's heel; and his name was called Jacob. |
| ( added by redactor ) | { problematic } |

*[Continued on p. 130]*

| **P** | **Notes** |
|---|---|
| **Life of Ishmael** | **Generations/Life of Ishmael** |

### Life of Ishmael

GEN 25:17And these are the years of the life of Ishmael, a hundred and thirty and seven years; and he expired and died; and was gathered unto his people.

### Generations/Life of Ishmael

**J Text**

Many scholars attribute this passage to P. This edition assigns it to J because in this edition, P gives only the mainline genealogy that leads from Adam to the patriarchs, while J gives genealogies of surrounding people. This distinction goes back to the pre-flood and post-flood genealogies of these two texts.

R added the introduction "(GEN 25:12Now these are the generations of Ishmael, Abraham's son, whom Hagar the Egyptian, Sarah's handmaid, bore unto Abraham.)," as R added many introductions beginning with "These are the generations of."

**P Text**

The one verse Genesis 25:17 is clearly from P and is typical of P's summary histories. J does not give age at death, and P does. J does not use the word that is translated as "expired," and P does.

### Birth of Jacob and Esau

GEN 25:19And these are the generations of Isaac, Abraham's son: Abraham begot Isaac. 20And Isaac was forty years old when he took Rebekah, the daughter of Bethuel the Aramean, of Paddan-aram, the sister of Laban the Aramean, to be his wife. 26bAnd Isaac was threescore years old when she bore (them) *[Jacob and Esau]*.

### Birth of Jacob and Esau

**J Text**

J apparently quotes an earlier poem about Jacob and Esau, which refers to the fact that Israel (descended from Jacob) conquered Edom (descended from Esau).

**P Text**

Genesis 25:26b is sometimes attributed to J and sometimes to P, but it is clearly needed to fill a gap in the timeline genealogy that P has maintained since Adam, and it is typical of P's habit of summarizing many historical events, rather than narrating them in detail. To avoid repetition when he combined it with J, R changed P's "Jacob and Esau" to "them."

J does not typically give the age of the father at the time a child is born, and P does.

| [ used more than once ] | " quoting older text " |

| **E** | **J** |
|---|---|
| | **Esau Sells His Birthright** |
| | GEN 25:27And the boys grew; and Esau was a cunning hunter, a man of the field; and Jacob was a quiet man, dwelling in tents. 28Now Isaac loved Esau, because he did eat of his venison; and Rebekah loved Jacob. 29And Jacob sod pottage; and Esau came in from the field, and he was faint. 30And Esau said to Jacob: 'Let me swallow, I pray thee, some of this red, red pottage; for I am faint.' Therefore was his name called Edom. 31And Jacob said: 'Sell me first thy birthright.' 32And Esau said: 'Behold, I am at the point to die; and what profit shall the birthright do to me?' 33And Jacob said: 'Swear to me first'; and he swore unto him; and he sold his birthright unto Jacob. 34And Jacob gave Esau bread and pottage of lentils; and he did eat and drink, and rose up, and went his way. So Esau despised his birthright. |
| *[Continued on p. 130]* | **Isaac in Gerar - Wife, Sister** |
| | GEN 26:1And there was a famine in the land, beside the first famine that was in the days of Abraham. And Isaac went unto Abimelech king of the Philistines unto Gerar. |
| | 2And the Lord appeared unto him, and said: 'Go not down unto Egypt; dwell in the land which I shall tell thee of. 3Sojourn in this land, and I will be with thee, and will bless thee; for unto thee, and unto thy seed, I will give all these lands, and I will establish the oath which I swore unto Abraham thy father; 4and I will multiply thy seed as the stars of heaven, and will give unto thy seed all these lands; and by thy seed shall all the nations of the earth bless themselves; 5because that Abraham hearkened to My voice, and kept My charge, My commandments, My statutes, and My laws.' |
| | 6And Isaac dwelt in Gerar. 7And the men of the place asked him of his wife; and he said: 'She is my sister'; for he feared to say: 'My wife'; 'lest the men of the place should kill me for Rebekah, because she is fair to look upon.' 8And it came to pass, when he had been there a long time, that Abimelech king of |
| ( added by redactor ) | { problematic } |

*[Continued on p. 130]*

| P | Notes |
|---|-------|

## Esau Sells His Birthright

**J Text**

In this passage, Genesis 25:27-34, Esau is a hunter and Jacob is a farmer. Esau sells his birthright to Jacob because he is starving and Jacob has food, a myth about agriculture displacing hunting and gathering because it could produce food more reliably.

The later passage in J (Gen. 27:1-40), where Jacob steals Esau's blessing by getting two kids from the flock more quickly than Esau could hunt venison, is a myth about herding displacing hunting and gathering.

These seem to be two more cases of J using pre-Israelite myths, like those in Genesis 2 through Genesis 11, though in these two cases the earlier myths have been turned into myths about Israelite patriarchs.

*[Continued on p. 131]*

## Isaac in Gerar - Wife, Sister

**J Text**

This story is a very close doublet of E's story about Abraham going to Gerar in Genesis 20. In both stories, the patriarch goes to Gerar and claims that his wife is his sister. In both, the king of Gerar is named Abimelech, and when he learns that the supposed sister is actually his wife, he blames the patriarch for leading his people into possible sin. In both, the patriarch becomes wealthy in Gerar.

In general, this book places doublets next to each other so readers can compare them easily, but it is impossible in this case because the two versions of the story are a generation apart. To compare the stories, readers should look at the E story in Genesis 20 and the J story here in Genesis 26.

**E Text versus J Text**

Though the similarities are striking, there are some differences between the stories in E and J. In E, God appears to Abimelech in a dream (God's typical way of communicating in E) to tell him that Sarah is Abraham's wife. In J, the Lord appears to Isaac to tell him directly that he should go to Gerar (God's

| [ used more than once ] | " quoting older text " |
|---|---|

| E | J |
|---|---|
| | the Philistines looked out at a window, and saw, and, behold, Isaac was sporting with Rebekah his wife. |

the Philistines looked out at a window, and saw, and, behold, Isaac was sporting with Rebekah his wife.

[9]And Abimelech called Isaac, and said: 'Behold, of a surety she is thy wife; and how saidst thou: She is my sister?' And Isaac said unto him: 'Because I said: Lest I die because of her.' [10]And Abimelech said: 'What is this thou hast done unto us? one of the people might easily have lain with thy wife, and thou wouldest have brought guiltiness upon us.' [11]And Abimelech charged all the people, saying: 'He that toucheth this man or his wife shall surely be put to death.'

[12]And Isaac sowed in that land, and found in the same year a hundredfold; and the Lord blessed him. [13]And the man waxed great, and grew more and more until he became very great. [14]And he had possessions of flocks, and possessions of herds, and a great household; and the Philistines envied him. [15]Now all the wells which his father's servants had digged in the days of Abraham his father, the Philistines had stopped them, and filled them with earth.

*[Continued on p. 130]*

[16]And Abimelech said unto Isaac: 'Go from us; for thou art much mightier than we.' [17]And Isaac departed thence, and encamped in the valley of Gerar, and dwelt there. [18]And Isaac digged again the wells of water, which they had digged in the days of Abraham his father; for the Philistines had stopped them after the death of Abraham; and he called their names after the names by which his father had called them.

[19]And Isaac's servants digged in the valley, and found there a well of living water. [20]And the herdmen of Gerar strove with Isaac's herdmen, saying: 'The water is ours.' And he called the name of the well Esek; because they contended with him. [21]And they digged another well, and they strove for that also. And he called the name of it Sitnah. [22]And he removed from thence, and digged another well; and for that they strove not. And he called the name of it Rehoboth; and he said: 'For now the Lord hath made room for us, and we shall be fruitful in the land.'

| ( added by redactor ) | { problematic } |

| P | Notes |
|---|---|
| | typical way of communicating in J), and God does not appear to Abimelech; instead, he happens to see Isaac and Rebekah "sporting." In E, Abimelech is simply king of Gerar; in J, Abimelech is a Philistine king, though the Philistines were not actually in Canaan at the time of the patriarchs. |
| *[Continued on p. 131]* | |
| [ used more than once ] | " quoting older text " |

*[Continued on p. 131]*

| **E** | **J** |
|---|---|
| | ### Isaac's Oath at Beersheba |
| | GEN 26:23 And he went up from thence to Beer-sheba. 24And the Lord appeared unto him the same night, and said: 'I am the God of Abraham thy father. Fear not, for I am with thee, and will bless thee, and multiply thy seed for My servant Abraham's sake.' 25And he builded an altar there, and called upon the name of the Lord, and pitched his tent there; and there Isaac's servants digged a well. |
| | 26Then Abimelech went to him from Gerar, and Ahuzzath his friend, and Phicol the captain of his host. 27And Isaac said unto them: 'Wherefore are ye come unto me, seeing ye hate me, and have sent me away from you?' 28And they said: 'We saw plainly that the Lord was with thee; and we said: Let there now be an oath betwixt us, even betwixt us and thee, and let us make a covenant with thee; 29that thou wilt do us no hurt, as we have not touched thee, and as we have done unto thee nothing but good, and have sent thee away in peace; thou art now the blessed of the Lord.' 30And he made them a feast, and they did eat and drink. 31And they rose up betimes in the morning, and swore one to another; and Isaac sent them away, and they departed from him in peace. |
| *[Continued on p. 130]* | 32And it came to pass the same day, that Isaac's servants came, and told him concerning the well which they had digged, and said unto him: 'We have found water.' 33And he called it Shibah. Therefore the name of the city is Beer-sheba unto this day. |
| | ### Jacob Steals Esau's Blessing |
| | GEN 27:1 And it came to pass, that when Isaac was old, and his eyes were dim, so that he could not see, he called Esau his elder son, and said unto him: 'My son'; and he said unto him: 'Here am I.' 2And he said: 'Behold now, I am old, I know not the day of my death. 3Now therefore take, I pray thee, thy weapons, thy quiver and thy bow, and go out to the field, and take me venison; 4and make me savoury food, such as I love, and bring it to me, that I may eat; that my soul may bless thee before I die.' |
| | 5And Rebekah heard when Isaac spoke to Esau his |
| ( added by redactor ) | { problematic } |

*[Continued on p. 130]*

| P | Notes |
|---|---|

### Isaac's Oath at Beersheba

**J Text**

This story is a very close doublet of E's story about Abraham's oath at Beersheba in Genesis 21:22. Both follow up the story of the patriarch's stay in Gerar (J's story of Abraham in Gerar in Genesis 20 and E's story of Isaac in Gerar in Genesis 26), which are also close doublets. In both, Abimelech king of Gerar and his captain Phicol come to see the patriarch in Beersheba and swear an oath of non-aggression.

In general, this book places doublets next to each other so readers can compare them easily, but it is impossible in this case because the two versions of the story are a generation apart. To compare the stories, readers should look at the E story beginning at Genesis 21:20 and the J story beginning at Genesis 26:23.

**E Text versus J Text**

The Hebrew word *shiva* (or *shibah*, as this translation spells it) means both seven and oath. Here in J, Beersheba gets its name from the oath that Isaac swore there. In E, there is a more elaborate story of Abraham sacrificing seven ewes and also swearing an oath.

*[Continued on p. 131]*

### Jacob Steals Esau's Blessing

J uses her typical technique of heightening drama through repetition. Isaac asks Jacob twice whether he is Esau, and then he tests it again by smelling his clothes.

In this passage (Gen. 27:1-40) Esau is a hunter and Jacob is a herder. Jacob can steal the blessing because he can get food more quickly than Esau, a myth about herding displacing hunting and gathering.

The earlier passage in J, where Jacob buys Esau's birthright by feeding him lentils (Gen. 25:27-34) is

| [ used more than once ] | " quoting older text " |
|---|---|

| **E** | **J** |
|---|---|
|  | son. And Esau went to the field to hunt for venison, and to bring it. [6]And Rebekah spoke unto Jacob her son, saying: 'Behold, I heard thy father speak unto Esau thy brother, saying: [7]Bring me venison, and make me savoury food, that I may eat, and bless thee before the Lord before my death. [8]Now therefore, my son, hearken to my voice according to that which I command thee. [9]Go now to the flock, and fetch me from thence two good kids of the goats; and I will make them savoury food for thy father, such as he loveth; [10]and thou shalt bring it to thy father, that he may eat, so that he may bless thee before his death.' |
|  | [11]And Jacob said to Rebekah his mother: 'Behold, Esau my brother is a hairy man, and I am a smooth man. [12]My father peradventure will feel me, and I shall seem to him as a mocker; and I shall bring a curse upon me, and not a blessing.' [13]And his mother said unto him: 'Upon me be thy curse, my son; only hearken to my voice, and go fetch me them.' |
| *[Continued on p. 130]* | [14]And he went, and fetched, and brought them to his mother; and his mother made savoury food, such as his father loved. [15]And Rebekah took the choicest garments of Esau her elder son, which were with her in the house, and put them upon Jacob her younger son. [16]And she put the skins of the kids of the goats upon his hands, and upon the smooth of his neck. [17]And she gave the savoury food and the bread, which she had prepared, into the hand of her son Jacob. |
|  | [18]And he came unto his father, and said: 'My father'; and he said: 'Here am I; who art thou, my son?' [19]And Jacob said unto his father: 'I am Esau thy first-born; I have done according as thou badest me. Arise, I pray thee, sit and eat of my venison, that thy soul may bless me.' [20]And Isaac said unto his son: 'How is it that thou hast found it so quickly, my son?' And he said: 'Because the Lord thy God sent me good speed.' |
|  | [21]And Isaac said unto Jacob: 'Come near, I pray thee, that I may feel thee, my son, whether thou be my very son Esau or not.' [22]And Jacob went near unto Isaac his father; and he felt him, and said: 'The voice is the voice of Jacob, but the hands are the hands of |
| ( added by redactor ) | { problematic } |

*[Continued on p. 130]*

| P | Notes |
|---|---|
| | a myth about agriculture displacing hunting and gathering. |
| | These seem to be two more cases of J using pre-Israelite myths, like those in Genesis 2 through Genesis 11, though in these cases the earlier myths have been turned into myths about Israelite patriarchs. |
| *[Continued on p. 131]* | |
| [ used more than once ] | " quoting older text " |

*[Continued on p. 131]*

| E | J |
|---|---|
| | Esau.' [23]And he discerned him not, because his hands were hairy, as his brother Esau's hands; so he blessed him. [24]And he said: 'Art thou my very son Esau?' And he said: 'I am.' [25]And he said: 'Bring it near to me, and I will eat of my son's venison, that my soul may bless thee.' And he brought it near to him, and he did eat; and he brought him wine, and he drank. |
| | [26]And his father Isaac said unto him: 'Come near now, and kiss me, my son.' [27]And he came near, and kissed him. And he smelled the smell of his raiment, and blessed him, and said: |
| | See, the smell of my son |
| | Is as the smell of a field which the Lord hath blessed. |
| | [28]So God give thee of the dew of heaven, |
| | And of the fat places of the earth, |
| | And plenty of corn and wine. |
| | [29]Let peoples serve thee, |
| | And nations bow down to thee. |
| *[Continued on p. 130]* | Be lord over thy brethren, |
| | And let thy mother's sons bow down to thee. |
| | Cursed be every one that curseth thee, |
| | And blessed be every one that blesseth thee. |
| | [30]And it came to pass, as soon as Isaac had made an end of blessing Jacob, and Jacob was yet scarce gone out from the presence of Isaac his father, that Esau his brother came in from his hunting. [31]And he also made savoury food, and brought it unto his father; and he said unto his father: 'Let my father arise, and eat of his son's venison, that thy soul may bless me.' [32]And Isaac his father said unto him: 'Who art thou?' And he said: 'I am thy son, thy first-born, Esau.' [33]And Isaac trembled very exceedingly, and said: 'Who then is he that hath taken venison, and brought it me, and I have eaten of all before thou camest, and have blessed him? yea, and he shall be blessed.' |
| | [34]When Esau heard the words of his father, he cried with an exceeding great and bitter cry, and said unto his father: 'Bless me, even me also, O my father.' [35]And he said: 'Thy brother came with guile, and hath taken away thy blessing.' [36]And he said: 'Is not he rightly named Jacob? for he hath supplanted me |
| ( added by redactor ) | { problematic } |

*[Continued on p. 130]*

| P | Notes |
|---|---|
| | |
| *[Continued on p. 131]* | *[Continued on p. 131]* |
| | |
| [ used more than once ] | " quoting older text " |

*[Continued on p. 131]* *[Continued on p. 131]*

| E | J |
|---|---|
| | these two times: he took away my birthright; and, behold, now he hath taken away my blessing.' And he said: 'Hast thou not reserved a blessing for me?' [37]And Isaac answered and said unto Esau: 'Behold, I have made him thy lord, and all his brethren have I given to him for servants; and with corn and wine have I sustained him; and what then shall I do for thee, my son?' [38]And Esau said unto his father: 'Hast thou but one blessing, my father? bless me, even me also, O my father.' And Esau lifted up his voice, and wept. |
| | [39]And Isaac his father answered and said unto him: Behold, of the fat places of the earth shall be thy dwelling, And of the dew of heaven from above; [40]And by thy sword shalt thou live, And thou shalt serve thy brother; And it shall come to pass when thou shalt break loose, That thou shalt shake his yoke from off thy neck. |
| *[Gap in E: Jacob Goes to Laban]* | **Jacob Goes to Laban** GEN 27:41 And Esau hated Jacob because of the blessing wherewith his father blessed him. And Esau said in his heart: 'Let the days of mourning for my father be at hand; then will I slay my brother Jacob.' [42]And the words of Esau her elder son were told to Rebekah; and she sent and called Jacob her younger son, and said unto him: 'Behold, thy brother Esau, as touching thee, doth comfort himself, purposing to kill thee. [43]Now therefore, my son, hearken to my voice; and arise, flee thou to Laban my brother to Haran; [44]and tarry with him a few days, until thy brother's fury turn away; [45]until thy brother's anger turn away from thee, and he forget that which thou hast done to him; then I will send, and fetch thee from thence; why should I be bereaved of you both in one day?' |
| ( added by redactor ) | { problematic } |

| P | Notes |
|---|---|

### Jacob Goes to Laban

GEN 26:34And when Esau was forty years old, he took to wife Judith the daughter of Beeri the Hittite, and Basemath the daughter of Elon the Hittite. 35And they were a bitterness of spirit unto Isaac and to Rebekah.

GEN 27:46And Rebekah said to Isaac: 'I am weary of my life because of the daughters of Heth. If Jacob take a wife of the daughters of Heth, such as these, of the daughters of the land, what good shall my life do me?'

GEN 28:1And Isaac called Jacob, and blessed him, and charged him, and said unto him: 'Thou shalt not take a wife of the daughters of Canaan. 2Arise, go to Paddan-aram, to the house of Bethuel thy mother's fa-

### Jacob Goes to Laban

**P Text Versus J Text**

The P and J texts contradict each other in many ways. In J, Jacob leaves because he is afraid of Esau; in P, he leaves because Isaac and Rebekah want him to find a wife. In J, Isaac is old and feeble; in P (which comes afterwards in our text of the Bible), Isaac is apparently healthy. In J, Isaac favors Esau; over Jacob; in P, he seems to favor Jacob over Esau. In J, Laban lives in Haran; in P, he lives in Paddan-aram. The combined story in the received text of the Bible is inconsistent and confusing, but when we separate the source texts, each story is consistent.

**E Text**

Though we do not have the E text

| [ used more than once ] | " quoting older text " |
|---|---|

| E | J |
|---|---|
| *[Continued on p. 134]* | *[Continued on p. 134]* |
| ( added by redactor ) | { problematic } |

| P | Notes |
|---|---|

ther; and take thee a wife from thence of the daughters of Laban thy mother's brother. ³And God Almighty bless thee, and make thee fruitful, and multiply thee, that thou mayest be a congregation of peoples; ⁴and give thee the blessing of Abraham, to thee, and to thy seed with thee; that thou mayest inherit the land of thy sojournings, which God gave unto Abraham.'

⁵And Isaac sent away Jacob; and he went to Paddan-aram unto Laban, son of Bethuel the Aramean, the brother of Rebekah, Jacob's and Esau's mother.

⁶Now Esau saw that Isaac had blessed Jacob and sent him away to Paddan-aram, to take him a wife from thence; and that as he blessed him he gave him a charge, saying: 'Thou shalt not take a wife of the daughters of Canaan'; ⁷and that Jacob hearkened to his father and his mother, and was gone to Paddan-aram; ⁸and Esau saw that the daughters of Canaan pleased not Isaac his father; ⁹so Esau went unto Ishmael, and took unto the wives that he had Mahalath the daughter of Ishmael Abraham's son, the sister of Nebaioth, to be his wife.

of this story, we know that Jacob fled from Esau in the original E text, as in J, because the E text refers to it later: "GEN 35:1And God said unto Jacob: 'Arise, go up to Beth-el, and dwell there; and make there an altar unto God, who appeared unto thee when thou didst flee from the face of Esau thy brother.'"

**P Text**

The beginning of P's story is a good example of inept editing. P's story begins in Genesis 26:34-35 and concludes in Genesis 27:46-28:9, but R interrupted it by inserting the entire J story of Jacob stealing Isaac's blessing in Genesis 27:1-45. It is particularly hard for modern readers to see that this P story is continuous: you have to know that the Hittites are the same as the sons and daughters of Heth. See Appendix 4.

We have to wonder why P includes this long story. In general, P gives most of the history in very brief outline form and only elaborates on what he considers the four key events of history: the creation, covenant of Noah, covenant of Abraham, and Covenant of Moses and Aaron. But there are exceptions in the P text. We have seen that it elaborates on the story of Abraham's purchasing Sarah's burial place in order to have a very firm legal basis for the Israelites owning the tomb of the patriarch.

Why does it elaborate on this story? It seems to be emphasizing the importance of racial purity. Unlike J and E, P was writing after the religious reforms that followed the conquest of the northern kingdom of Israel by Syria, which was blamed on Israel marrying pagan wives and worshipping pagan gods. Notice that Esau makes up for marrying a Canaanite wife by marrying an Ishmaelite wife, which is still in the family, since Ishmael is a son of Abraham by Hagar.

| [ used more than once ] | " quoting older text " |
|---|---|

| E | J |
|---|---|

### Jacob's Vision at Beth-El

GEN 28:11And he *[Jacob]* lighted upon the place, and tarried there all night, because the sun was set; and he took one of the stones of the place, and put it under his head, and lay down in that place to sleep. 12And he dreamed, and behold a ladder set up on the earth, and the top of it reached to heaven; and behold the angels of God ascending and descending on it.

16:aAnd Jacob awaked out of his sleep, 17And he was afraid, and said: 'How full of awe is this place! this is none other than the house of God, and this is the gate of heaven.' 18And Jacob rose up early in the morning, and took the stone that he had put under his head, and set it up for a pillar, and poured oil upon the top of it. 19And he called the name of that place Beth-el, but the name of the city was Luz at the first.

20And Jacob vowed a vow, saying: 'If God will be with me, and will keep me in this way that I go, and will give me bread to eat, and raiment to put on, 21so that I come back to my father's house in peace, then 22(and) this stone, which I have set up for a pillar, shall be God's house; and of all that Thou shalt give me I will surely give the tenth unto Thee.'

### Jacob's Vision at Beth-El

GEN 28:10And Jacob went out from Beer-sheba, and went toward Haran. 13And, behold, the Lord stood beside him, and said: 'I am the Lord, the God of Abraham thy father, and the God of Isaac. The land whereon thou liest, to thee will I give it, and to thy seed. 14And thy seed shall be as the dust of the earth, and thou shalt spread abroad to the west, and to the east, and to the north, and to the south. And in thee and in thy seed shall all the families of the earth be blessed. 15And, behold, I am with thee, and will keep thee whithersoever thou goest, and will bring thee back into this land; for I will not leave thee, until I have done that which I have spoken to thee of.'

16bAnd he said: 'Surely the Lord is in this place; and I knew it not. 21bThe Lord shall be my God."

| ( added by redactor ) | { problematic } |

| P | Notes |
|---|---|
| | For more information on these exceptions to the overall pattern of the P text, see pages 36-38. |
| | **Jacob's Vision at Beth-El** |
| | **E Text** |
| | As is usual in E, God appears to Jacob in a dream. E includes the name Bethel and an explanation for the name, which means "house of God" and which probably originally meant "house of El," reading El as the name of the Canaanite father god rather than as a word meaning God. |
| | **J Text** |
| | As usual in J, God is anthropomorphic and stands right next to Jacob. God's blessing of Jacob here is similar to the blessing of Abraham in J: "GEN 12:3bAnd in thee shall all the families of the earth be blessed." |
| *[Continued on p. 155]* | **P Text** |
| | P leaves out Jacob's vision at Bethel. Perhaps, as a Aaronid priest, a group of priests centered in the Temple in Jerusalem, he does not want to give any religious credibility to Bethel, which is where the northern kingdom of Israel set up one of its religious centers that were rivals to the temple in Jerusalem. More generally, P focuses on the covenant of Abraham as one of the four key events of history and tends to skim over the other patriarchs. |
| | **Translation** |
| | J Text: In the JPS translation, Genesis 28:21b is translated "shall the Lord be my God" but the Hebrew can just as well be translated "the Lord shall be my God." |
| [ used more than once ] | " quoting older text " |

*[Continued on p. 155]*

| E | J |
|---|---|
| *[gap in E: Jacob Marries Leah and Rachel]* | **Jacob Marries Leah and Rachel**<br><br>GEN 29:1Then Jacob went on his journey, and came to the land of the children of the east. 2And he looked, and behold a well in the field, and, lo, three flocks of sheep lying there by it.—For out of that well they watered the flocks. And the stone upon the well's mouth was great. 3And thither were all the flocks gathered; and they rolled the stone from the well's mouth, and watered the sheep, and put the stone back upon the well's mouth in its place.—<br><br>4And Jacob said unto them: 'My brethren, whence are ye?' And they said: 'Of Haran are we.' 5And he said unto them: 'Know ye Laban the son of Nahor?' And they said: 'We know him.' 6And he said unto them: 'Is it well with him?' And they said: 'It is well; and, behold, Rachel his daughter cometh with the sheep.' 7And he said: 'Lo, it is yet high day, neither is it time that the cattle should be gathered together; water ye the sheep, and go and feed them.' 8And they said: 'We cannot, until all the flocks be gathered together, and they roll the stone from the well's mouth; then we water the sheep.' 9While he was yet speaking with them, Rachel came with her father's sheep; for she tended them.<br><br>10And it came to pass, when Jacob saw Rachel the daughter of Laban his mother's brother, and the sheep of Laban his mother's brother, that Jacob went near, and rolled the stone from the well's mouth, and watered the flock of Laban his mother's brother. 11And Jacob kissed Rachel, and lifted up his voice, and wept. 12And Jacob told Rachel that he was her father's brother, and that he was Rebekah's son; and she ran and told her father. 13And it came to pass, when Laban heard the tidings of Jacob his sister's son, that he ran |
| ( added by redactor ) | { problematic } |

| P | Notes |
|---|---|
| | **Jacob Marries Leah and Rachel** **E Text** There are later sections in the E text about Jacob's children, so there must have been something in the original E text about his marriages. RJE presumably removed this because he preferred J's story. |
| *[Continued on p. 155]* | |
| [ used more than once ] | " quoting older text " |

| E | J |
|---|---|
| | to meet him, and embraced him, and kissed him, and brought him to his house. And he told Laban all these things. [14]And Laban said to him: 'Surely thou art my bone and my flesh.' And he abode with him the space of a month. |

[15]And Laban said unto Jacob: 'Because thou art my brother, shouldest thou therefore serve me for nought? tell me, what shall thy wages be?' [16]Now Laban had two daughters: the name of the elder was Leah, and the name of the younger was Rachel. [17]And Leah's eyes were weak; but Rachel was of beautiful form and fair to look upon. [18]And Jacob loved Rachel; and he said: 'I will serve thee seven years for Rachel thy younger daughter.' [19]And Laban said: 'It is better that I give her to thee, than that I should give her to another man; abide with me.' [20]And Jacob served seven years for Rachel; and they seemed unto him but a few days, for the love he had to her.

*[Continued on p. 140]*

[21]And Jacob said unto Laban: 'Give me my wife, for my days are filled, that I may go in unto her.' [22]And Laban gathered together all the men of the place, and made a feast. [23]And it came to pass in the evening, that he took Leah his daughter, and brought her to him; and he went in unto her. [24]And Laban gave Zilpah his handmaid unto his daughter Leah for a handmaid. [25]And it came to pass in the morning that, behold, it was Leah; and he said to Laban: 'What is this thou hast done unto me? did not I serve with thee for Rachel? wherefore then hast thou beguiled me?'

[26]And Laban said: 'It is not so done in our place, to give the younger before the first-born. [27]Fulfil the week of this one, and we will give thee the other also for the service which thou shalt serve with me yet seven other years.' [28]And Jacob did so, and fulfilled her week; and he gave him Rachel his daughter to wife. [29]And Laban gave to Rachel his daughter Bilhah his handmaid to be her handmaid. [30]And he went in also unto Rachel, and he loved Rachel more than Leah, and served with him yet seven other years.

( added by redactor )        { problematic }

| P | Notes |
|---|---|
| *[Continued on p. 155]* | *[Continued on p. 141]* |
| [ used more than once ] | " quoting older text " |

| **E** | **J** |
|---|---|
| **Jacob's Children** | **Jacob's Children** |
|  | GEN 29:31And the Lord saw that Leah was hated, and he opened her womb; but Rachel was barren. 32And Leah conceived, and bore a son, and she called his name Reuben; for she said: 'Because the Lord hath looked upon my affliction; for now my husband will love me.' 33And she conceived again, and bore a son; and said: 'Because the Lord hath heard that I am hated, He hath therefore given me this son also.' And she called his name Simeon. 34And she conceived again, and bore a son; and said: 'Now this time will my husband be joined unto me, because I have borne him three sons.' Therefore was his name called Levi. 35And she conceived again, and bore a son; and she said: 'This time will I praise the Lord.' Therefore she called his name Judah; and she left off bearing. |
| *[Gap in E: see J]* |  |
| GEN 30:1bRachel envied her sister; and she said unto Jacob: 'Give me children, or else I die.' 2And Jacob's anger was kindled against Rachel; and he said: 'Am I in God's stead, who hath withheld from thee the fruit of the womb?' 3And she said: 'Behold my maid Bilhah, go in unto her; that she may bear upon my knees, and I also may be builded up through her.' | GEN 30:1aAnd Rachel saw that she bore Jacob no children, 4And she gave him Bilhah her handmaid to wife; and Jacob went in unto her. |
|  | *[Gap in J: see E]* |
| 5And Bilhah conceived, and bore Jacob a son. 6And Rachel said: 'God hath judged me, and hath also heard my voice, and hath given me a son.' Therefore called she his name Dan. | 7And Bilhah Rachel's handmaid conceived again, and bore Jacob a second son. 8And Rachel said: 'With mighty wrestlings have I wrestled with my sister, and have prevailed.' And she called his name Naphtali. 9When Leah saw that she |
| ( added by redactor ) | { problematic } |

| P | Notes |
|---|---|

### Jacob's Children

**J and E Texts**

It seems that RJE put together this section by alternating passages from J and E, so you have to read back and forth between the texts to get the whole story. In some cases, we can attribute passages to E or J easily because they use the words "God" or "Lord." In other cases, the attribution is more speculative, though we have a bit of a clue with the story of the mandrakes, which sounds like the sort of dramatic flourish that J likes to add.

There are several cases where RJE kept different etymologies from the two different texts.

The name Issachar comes from the root *SKhR*, meaning to hire. One text explains the name origin with "GEN 30:16'I have surely hired thee with my son's mandrakes,'" while the other text explains it with "GEN 30:18And Leah said: 'God hath given me my hire, because I gave my handmaid to my husband.'"

The name Zebulun seems to be explained using two different roots. *ZBD* is the root of *zebed*, meaning dowry and of *zabad*, meaning to endow with a dowry, and one text explains the name based on this root "GEN 30:20God hath endowed me with a good dowry." The root *ZBL* means to dwell, and the other text explains the name by saying "GEN 30:20now will my husband dwell with me."

The name Joseph is also explained using two different roots. The root *YSF* means to add, and J explains the name when Rachel

*[Continued on p. 155]*

| [ used more than once ] | " quoting older text " |
|---|---|

| **E** | **J** |
|---|---|
| | had left off bearing, she took Zilpah her handmaid, and gave her to Jacob to wife. [10]And Zilpah Leah's handmaid bore Jacob a son. [11]And Leah said: 'Fortune is come!' And she called his name Gad. [12]And Zilpah Leah's handmaid bore Jacob a second son. [13]And Leah said: 'Happy am I! for the daughters will call me happy.' And she called his name Asher. |
| *[Gap in E: see J]* | [14]And Reuben went in the days of wheat harvest, and found mandrakes in the field, and brought them unto his mother Leah. Then Rachel said to Leah: 'Give me, I pray thee, of thy son's mandrakes.' [15]And she said unto her: 'Is it a small matter that thou hast taken away my husband? and wouldest thou take away my son's mandrakes also?' And Rachel said: 'Therefore |
| [17]And God hearkened unto Leah, and she conceived, and bore Jacob a fifth son. [18]And Leah said: 'God hath given me my hire, because I gave my handmaid to my husband. And she called his name Issachar. | he shall lie with thee to-night for thy son's mandrakes.' [16]And Jacob came from the field in the evening, and Leah went out to meet him, and said: 'Thou must come in unto me; for I have surely hired thee with my son's mandrakes.' And he lay with her that night. |
| [19]And Leah conceived again, and bore a sixth son to Jacob. [20][And Leah said:] 'God hath endowed me with a good dowry; [And she called his name Zebulun.] | *[Gap in J: see E]* |
| [21]And afterwards she bore a daughter, and called her name Dinah. | [20][And Leah said:] ... now will my husband dwell with me, because I have borne him six sons.' [And she called his name Zebulun.] |
| [22]And God remembered Rachel, and God hearkened to her, and opened her womb. [23]And she conceived, and bore a son, and said: 'God hath taken away my reproach.' [24a]And she called his name Joseph, | *[Gap in J: see E]*

[24b]Saying: 'The Lord add to me another son.' |
| ( added by redactor ) | { problematic } |

| P | Notes |
|---|---|
| | says, "<sup>GEN 30:24</sup>The Lord add to me another son." The root *ASF* means to gather or to take away, and E explains the name when Rachel says "<sup>GEN 30:23</sup>God hath taken away my reproach." In this case, we can identify which text had which explanation because one uses "the Lord" and one uses "God." |
| | Presumably, RJE kept both etymologies when they were different in order to preserve more information, implying that the other sons' names had the same etymology in both texts. |
| | **P Text** |
| | P lists the sons of Jacob in a passage that begins with Genesis 35:22b. Though the goal of this edition is to place doublets next to each other, it is not possible to move P's passage about the Sons of Israel next to J's and E's description of the sons of Israel here. |
| *[Continued on p. 155]* | **Translation** |
| | J Text: The JPS translation says "<sup>GEN 30:1a</sup>And when Rachel saw that she bore Jacob no children,...." However, the word "when" is not in the Hebrew, so this edition leaves it out, making the J text a grammatical English sentence. |

| [ used more than once ] | " quoting older text " |

| E | J |
|---|---|
| *[Gap in E: Jacob's Wages]* | **Jacob's Wages** |

GEN 30:25 And it came to pass, when Rachel had borne Joseph, that Jacob said unto Laban: 'Send me away, that I may go unto mine own place, and to my country. 26Give me my wives and my children for whom I have served thee, and let me go; for thou knowest my service wherewith I have served thee.'

27And Laban said unto him: 'If now I have found favour in thine eyes—I have observed the signs, and the Lord hath blessed me for thy sake.' 28And he said: 'Appoint me thy wages, and I will give it.'

29And he said unto him: 'Thou knowest how I have served thee, and how thy cattle have fared with me. 30For it was little which thou hadst before I came, and it hath increased abundantly; and the Lord hath blessed thee whithersoever I turned. And now when shall I provide for mine own house also?'

31And he said: 'What shall I give thee?' And Jacob said: 'Thou shalt not give me aught; if thou wilt do this thing for me, I will again feed thy flock and keep it. 32I will pass through all thy flock to-day, removing from thence every speckled and spotted one, and every dark one among the sheep, and the spotted and speckled among the goats; and of such shall be my hire. 33So shall my righteousness witness against me hereafter, when thou shalt come to look over my hire that is before thee: every one that is not speckled and spotted among the goats, and dark among the sheep, that if found with me shall be counted stolen.'

34And Laban said: 'Behold, would it might be according to thy word.' 35And he removed that day the he-goats that

| ( added by redactor ) | { problematic } |

| P | Notes |
|---|---|
| | **Jacob's Wages** |

**J Text**

J depicts Jacob as a trickster who steals Esau's blessing and outwits Laban to get his wages. There are many other stories where J admires tricksters, such as the story of Rebekah deceiving Laban after she steals his teraphim (Gen. 31:34-35), and Tamar tricking Judah by posing as a harlot (Gen. 38). adding to the evidence that her religion is ritualistic and is not connected with morality. Likewise, her version of the Ten Commandments (Ex. 34:12-26) has ritual commandments and does not have the familiar moral commandments, such as "Thou shalt not steal." See page 29-30.

*[Continued on p. 155]*

**E Text**

Though we do not have the E text about Jacob getting his wages from Laban, this slightly later passage from E shows that E's Jacob was not a trickster:

"GEN 31:6And ye know that with all my power I have served your father. 7And your father hath mocked me, and changed my wages ten times; but God suffered him not to hurt me. 8If he said thus: The speckled shall be thy wages; then all the flock bore speckled; and if he said thus: The streaked shall be thy wages; then bore all the flock streaked. 9Thus God hath taken away the cattle of your father, and given them to me. 10And it came to pass at the time that the flock conceived, that I lifted up mine eyes, and saw in a dream, and, behold, the he-goats which leaped upon the flock were streaked, speck-

| [ used more than once ] | " quoting older text " |

| **E** | **J** |
|---|---|
| | were streaked and spotted, and all the she-goats that were speckled and spotted, every one that had white in it, and all the dark ones among the sheep, and gave them into the hand of his sons. [36]And he set three days' journey betwixt himself and Jacob. And Jacob fed the rest of Laban's flocks. [37]And Jacob took him rods of fresh poplar, and of the almond and of the plane-tree; and peeled white streaks in them, making the white appear which was in the rods. [38]And he set the rods which he had peeled over against the flocks in the gutters in the watering-troughs where the flocks came to drink; and they conceived when they came to drink. [39]And the flocks conceived at the sight of the rods, and the flocks brought forth streaked, speckled, and spotted. [40]And Jacob separated the lambs—he also set the faces of the flocks toward the streaked and all the dark in the flock of Laban— and put his own droves apart, and put them not unto Laban's flock. [41]And it came to pass, whensoever the stronger of the flock did conceive, that Jacob laid the rods before the eyes of the flock in the gutters, that they might conceive among the rods; [42]but when the flock were feeble, he put them not in; so the feebler were Laban's, and the stronger Jacob's. [43]And the man increased exceedingly, and had large flocks, and maid-servants and men-servants, and camels and asses. |
| **Covenant of Jacob and Laban**<br><br>GEN ³¹:¹And he [Jacob] heard the words of Laban's sons, saying: 'Jacob hath taken away all that was our father's; and of that which was our father's hath he gotten all this wealth.' | **Covenant of Jacob and Laban**<br><br>GEN 31:3And the Lord said unto Jacob: 'Return unto the land of thy fathers, and to thy kindred; and I will be with thee.'<br><br>[[17]Then Jacob rose up, and set his sons and his wives upon the camels; [18a]And he carried away] all his cattle, and all his substance which he had gathered, [19b]And Rachel stole the teraphim that were her father's.<br><br>[21]So he fled with all that he had; and he rose up, and passed over the River, and set his face toward the mountain of Gilead. [25b]Now Jacob had pitched his tent in the mountain; and Laban with his brethren |
| ( added by redactor ) | { problematic } |

| P | Notes |
|---|---|
| | led, and grizzled. [11]And the angel of God said unto me in the dream: Jacob; and I said: Here am I. [12]And he said: Lift up now thine eyes, and see, all the he-goats which leap upon the flock are streaked, speckled, and grizzled; for I have seen all that Laban doeth unto thee." |
| | In J, Jacob out-tricks Laban by using rods of poplar, almond and plane trees to control which lambs were streaked, speckled and spotted. |
| | In E, God makes the goats streaked, speckled, or grizzled because He sees that Laban is trying to cheat Jacob. In E, God does not like tricksters and cheaters like Laban, so He sees that justice is done. E's religion has a moral element, unlike J's |
| | Notice that J talks about Laban's lambs and E about his goats. |
| *[Continued on p. 155]* | |
| | **Covenant of Jacob and Laban.** |
| | **Separating the Texts** |
| | This passage clearly comes from more than one source, because it uses both "God" and "Lord," and it has repetitions, such as the double explanation for the place name and the setting up of both a pile of stones and a pillar of stone. |
| | Many scholars think Genesis 31:18 is from P, since it mentions Paddan-aram, but attributing it to P would create large gaps in the P text, which does not have the story of the conflict between Jacob and Laban. This edition's goal is to create continuous texts to the extent possible (taking into account that RJE |
| [ used more than once ] | " quoting older text " |

| **E** | **J** |
|---|---|
| ²And Jacob beheld the countenance of Laban, and, behold, it was not toward him as beforetime. ⁴And Jacob sent and called Rachel and Leah to the field unto his flock, ⁵and said unto them: 'I see your father's countenance, that it is not toward me as beforetime; but the God of my father hath been with me. ⁶And ye know that with all my power I have served your father. ⁷And your father hath mocked me, and changed my wages ten times; but God suffered him not to hurt me. ⁸If he said thus: The speckled shall be thy wages; then all the flock bore speckled; and if he said thus: The streaked shall be thy wages; then bore all the flock streaked. ⁹Thus God hath taken away the cattle of your father, and given them to me.<br><br>¹⁰And it came to pass at the time that the flock conceived, that I lifted up mine eyes, and saw in a dream, and, behold, the he-goats which leaped upon the flock were streaked, speckled, and grizzled. ¹¹And the angel of God said unto me in the dream: Jacob; and I said: Here am I. ¹²And he said: Lift up now thine eyes, and see, all the he-goats which leap upon the flock are streaked, speckled, and grizzled; for I have seen all that Laban doeth unto thee. ¹³I am the God of Beth-el, where thou didst anoint a pillar, where thou didst vow a vow unto Me. Now arise, get thee out from this land, and return unto the land of thy nativity.'<br><br>¹⁴And Rachel and Leah answered and said unto him: 'Is there yet any portion or inheritance for us in our father's house? ¹⁵Are we not accounted by him strangers? for he hath sold us, and hath also quite devoured our price. ¹⁶For all the riches which God hath taken away from our father, that is ours and our children's. Now then, whatsoever God hath said unto thee, do.'<br><br>[¹⁷Then Jacob rose up, and set his sons and | pitched in the mountain of Gilead.<br><br>[²⁶And Laban said to Jacob] ³⁰And now that thou art surely gone, because thou sore longest after thy father's house, wherefore hast thou stolen my gods?'<br><br>³¹ᵇAnd he said to Laban: ³²With whomsoever thou findest thy gods, he shall not live; before our brethren discern thou what is thine with me, and take it to thee.'— For Jacob knew not that Rachel had stolen them.— ³³And Laban went into Jacob's tent, and into Leah's tent, and into the tent of the two maid-servants; but he found them not. And he went out of Leah's tent, and entered into Rachel's tent. ³⁴Now Rachel had taken the teraphim, and put them in the saddle of the camel, and sat upon them. And Laban felt about all the tent, but found them not. ³⁵And she said to her father: 'Let not my lord be angry that I cannot rise up before thee; for the manner of women is upon me.' And he searched, but found not the teraphim.<br><br>³⁶ᵇAnd Jacob (answered and) said to Laban: 'What is my trespass? what is my sin, that thou hast hotly pursued after me? ³⁷Whereas thou hast felt about all |
| ( added by redactor ) | { problematic } |

| P | Notes |
|---|---|
| | often removed parts of J and E but R rarely removed parts of JE or P). To avoid creating a large gap in P, this edition assumes that the mention of Paddan-aram was added by R to make this story more consistent with the P text. |

often removed parts of J and E but R rarely removed parts of JE or P). To avoid creating a large gap in P, this edition assumes that the mention of Paddan-aram was added by R to make this story more consistent with the P text.

In the division in this edition, J uses the word "heap" and E uses the word "pillar." J and P do not have people set up pillars in any other location, while E does: In the E text, Jacob sets up a pillar in Bethel and pours oil on it (Gen. 28:18), Jacob sets up a pillar on Rachel's grave (Gen. 35:20), Moses sets up twelve pillars when Israel accepts the covenant (Ex. 24:4).

Galeed means "heap of witness," so the name makes sense in J but not in E, where there is a pillar not a heap. It seems that RJE added Galeed to the following verse of E to make it consistent with J, "[GEN 31:47]And Laban called it Jegar-sahadutha; but Jacob called it (Galeed [49]and) Mizpah, for he said: 'The Lord watch between me and thee, when we are absent one from another.'" RJE added "Galeed" to smooth over the difference between E and J, which is why Jacob is said to have given it two names.

There are two explanations of the covenant between Laban and Jacob: "[GEN 31:50]If thou shalt afflict my daughters, and if thou shalt take wives beside my daughters, no man being with us; see, God is witness betwixt me and thee" and "[GEN 31:52]This heap be witness, (and the pillar be witness,) that I will not pass over this heap to thee, and that thou shalt not pass over this heap (and this pillar) unto me, for harm." It seems most plausible that the witness that Jacob will not take any other wives comes from E, and the witness that Jacob and Laban will not pass over the heap to harm each other comes from J, with RJE adding the mentions of "pillar" to Genesis 31:52 to reconcile it with the story in E. Notice that the

*[Continued on p. 155]*

| [ used more than once ] | " quoting older text " |

| **E** | **J** |
|---|---|
| his wives upon the camels; [18a]and he carried away ... the cattle of his getting, which he had gathered] (in Paddan-aram,) to go to Isaac his father unto the land of Canaan. | my stuff, what hast thou found of all thy household stuff? Set it here before my brethren and thy brethren, that they may judge betwixt us two. |
| [19a]Now Laban was gone to shear his sheep. [20]And Jacob outwitted Laban the Aramean, in that he told him not that he fled. [22]And it was told Laban on the third day that Jacob was fled. [23]And he took his brethren with him, and pursued after him seven days' journey; and he overtook him in the mountain of Gilead. [24]And God came to Laban the Aramean in a dream of the night, and said unto him: 'Take heed to thyself that thou speak not to Jacob either good or bad.' [25a]And Laban came up with Jacob. | [[43]And Laban answered and said unto Jacob: '[44a]Now come, let us make a covenant, I and thou;] and let it be for a witness between me and thee.' |
| [[26]And Laban said to Jacob:] 'What hast thou done, that thou hast outwitted me, and carried away my daughters as though captives of the sword? [27]Wherefore didst thou flee secretly, and outwit me; and didst not tell me, that I might have sent thee away with mirth and with songs, with tabret and with harp; [28]and didst not suffer me to kiss my sons and my daughters? now hast thou done foolishly. [29]It is in the power of my hand to do you hurt; but the God of your father spoke unto me yesternight, saying: Take heed to thyself that thou speak not to Jacob either good or bad. | [46]And Jacob said unto his brethren: 'Gather stones'; and they took stones, and made a heap. And they did eat there by the heap. [48]And Laban said: 'This heap is witness between me and thee this day.' Therefore was the name of it called Galeed; |
| [31]And Jacob answered 'Because I was afraid; for I said: Lest thou shouldest take thy daughters from me by force. [36a]And Jacob was wroth, and strove with Laban *[and said]* [38]These twenty years have I been with thee; thy ewes and thy she-goats have not cast their young, and the rams of thy flocks have I not eaten. [39]That which was torn of beasts I brought not unto thee; I bore the loss of it; of my hand didst thou require it, whether stolen by day or stolen by night. [40]Thus I was: in the day the drought consumed me, and the frost by night; and my sleep fled from mine eyes. [41]These twenty years have I been in thy house: I served thee fourteen years | [51]And Laban said to Jacob: 'Behold this heap, (and behold the pillar,) which I have set up betwixt me and thee. [52]This heap be witness, (and the pillar be witness,) that I will not pass over this heap to thee, and that thou shalt not pass over this heap (and this pillar) unto me, for harm. [53a]The God of Abraham, and the God of Nahor, the God of their father, judge betwixt us.' |

| ( added by redactor ) | { problematic } |

| P | Notes |
|---|---|
| | verse says "I will not pass over this heap to thee," so it looks as if RJE added "pillar" in the other cases in this verse but neglected to add it and kept just "heap" in this case, giving us a clue to the original text. |
| | The division here attributes the talk about the God of Abraham and god of Nahor to J. This sort of syncretism is characteristic of J, who has the worship of the Lord [=YHWH] begin only a couple of generations after creation (Gen. 4:26). J does not think that Abraham began to worship a new God whose name was later revealed to Moses, as P and E do; she thinks that Abraham worshipped the same god that Nahor did, a god that people have worshipped since before the flood. |
| *[Continued on p. 155]* | The division between J and E here leaves a few minor gaps, which can be filled by using several phrases in both J and E. These duplicated phrases are indicated by square brackets in the J text. As in other passages edited together by RJE, the duplicated phrases here occur when the substance of what J and E say is the same, though there were probably minor differences in wording that are lost. |
| | One minor problem with any division of the text of this passage is the inconsistency between two verses in the received text of the Bible. First the text says that Jacob set up a pillar and heap: "GEN 31:45 And Jacob took a stone, and set it up for a pillar. 46 And Jacob said unto his brethren: 'Gather stones'; and they took stones, and made a heap." Then Laban claims that he set up the pillar and heap: "GEN 31:' 51 And Laban said to Jacob: 'Behold this heap, and behold the pillar, which I have set up betwixt me and thee." Why does Laban say that he set up the pillar and the heap, though Jacob did the work? Maybe Laban means that he established the covenant that the heap and pillar represent rather than that he set up the physical heap and pillar. |
| [ used more than once ] | " quoting older text " |

*[Continued on p. 155]*

| **E** | **J** |
|---|---|
| for thy two daughters, and six years for thy flock; and thou hast changed my wages ten times. ⁴²Except the God of my father, the God of Abraham, and the Fear of Isaac, had been on my side, surely now hadst thou sent me away empty. God hath seen mine affliction and the labour of my hands, and gave judgment yesternight.' | |
| | **Jacob Reconciles with Esau** |
| [⁴³And Laban answered and said unto Jacob:] 'The daughters are my daughters, and the children are my children, and the flocks are my flocks, and all that thou seest is mine; and what can I do this day for these my daughters, or for their children whom they have borne? ⁴⁴And [now come, let us make a covenant, I and thou.'] | GEN 32:4And Jacob sent messengers before him to Esau his brother unto the land of Seir, the field of Edom. ⁵And he commanded them, saying: 'Thus shall ye say unto my lord Esau: Thus saith thy servant Jacob: I have sojourned with Laban, and stayed until now. ⁶And I have oxen, and asses and flocks, and men-servants and maid-servants; and I have sent to tell my lord, that I may find favour in thy sight.' ⁷And the messengers returned to Jacob, saying: 'We came to thy brother Esau, and moreover he cometh to meet thee, and four hundred men with him.' ⁸Then Jacob was greatly afraid and was distressed. And he divided the people that was with him, and the flocks, and the herds, |
| ⁴⁵And Jacob took a stone, and set it up for a pillar. | |
| ⁴⁷And Laban called it Jegar-sahadutha; but Jacob called it (Galeed ⁴⁹and) Mizpah, for he *[Laban]* said: 'The Lord watch between me and thee, when we are absent one from another. | |
| ⁵⁰If thou shalt afflict my daughters, and if thou shalt take wives beside my daughters, no man being with us; see, God is witness betwixt me and thee.' | |
| ⁵³ᵇAnd Jacob swore by the Fear of his father Isaac. ⁵⁴And Jacob offered a sacrifice in the mountain, and called his brethren to eat bread; and they did eat bread, and tarried all night in the mountain. | |
| GEN 32:1And early in the morning Laban rose up, and kissed his sons and his daughters, and blessed them. And Laban departed, and returned unto his place. | |
| ²And Jacob went on his way, and the angels of God met him. ³And Jacob said when he saw them: 'This is God's camp.' And he called the name of that place Mahanaim. | |

| ( added by redactor ) | { problematic } |
|---|---|

| P | Notes |
|---|---|

**Translation**

J Text: The JPS translation says "[GEN 31:31b]And said to Laban." This edition translates it as "And he said to Laban." Hebrew does not use the pronoun, so this translation is equally accurate.

### Jacob Reconciles with Esau:
### Separating the Texts

When RJE edited the story of how Jacob reconciled with Esau in Genesis 32:4-33:20, he alternated long passages from J and E, leaving out the equivalent passages in the other text.

The beginning is clearly J, because when Jacob says "[GEN 32:10]O God of my father Abraham, and God of my father Isaac, O Lord, who saidst unto me: Return unto thy country, and to thy kindred...," he is referring back to this earlier passage in J: "[GEN 31:3]And the Lord said unto Jacob: 'Return unto the land of thy fathers, and to thy kindred; and I will be with thee.'"

The second passage is from E, the famous story of Jacob wrestling with "a man" that begins at Genesis 32:23.

The third passage, which begins at Genesis 33:1, is from J. It refers back to Esau's 400 men, mentioned in the first passage. Jacob's wives and children were sent to the other side of the river in the second passage (from E), but are suddenly back with him in the third passage (from J). The third passage also gives an alternate explanation of the place name Peniel, which means "face of God": Jacob says to Esau, "[GEN 33:10]I have seen thy face, as one seeth the face of God, and thou wast pleased with me." Though it does not explicitly mention the place name, this was obviously originally an alternative explanation for the name Peniel. This place name was explained differently in the sec-

*[Continued on p. 155]*

*[Continued on p. 155]*

| [ used more than once ] | " quoting older text " |
|---|---|

| E | J |
|---|---|
| | and the camels, into two camps. [9]And he said: 'If Esau come to the one camp, and smite it, then the camp which is left shall escape.' |
| | [10]And Jacob said: 'O God of my father Abraham, and God of my father Isaac, O Lord, who saidst unto me: Return unto thy country, and to thy kindred, and I will do thee good; [11]I am not worthy of all the mercies, and of all the truth, which Thou hast shown unto Thy servant; for with my staff I passed over this Jordan; and now I am become two camps. [12]Deliver me, I pray Thee, from the hand of my brother, from the hand of Esau; for I fear him, lest he come and smite me, the mother with the children. [13]And Thou saidst: I will surely do thee good, and make thy seed as the sand of the sea, which cannot be numbered for multitude.' |
| *[Gap in E: Jacob Travels to see Esau]* | [14]And he lodged there that night; and took of that which he had with him a present for Esau his brother: [15]two hundred she-goats and twenty he-goats, two hundred ewes and twenty rams, [16]thirty milch camels and their colts, forty kine and ten bulls, twenty she-asses and ten foals. [17]And he delivered them into the hand of his servants, every drove by itself; and said unto his servants: 'Pass over before me, and put a space betwixt drove and drove.' [18]And he commanded the foremost, saying: 'When Esau my brother meeteth thee, and asketh thee, saying: Whose art thou? and whither goest thou? and whose are these before thee? [19]then thou shalt say: They are thy servant Jacob's; it is a present sent unto my lord, even unto Esau; and, behold, he also is behind us.' [20]And he commanded also the second, and the third, and all that followed the droves, saying: 'In this manner shall ye speak unto Esau, when ye find him; [21]and ye shall say: Moreover, behold, thy servant Jacob is behind us.' For he said: 'I will appease him with the present that goeth before me, and afterward I will see his face; peradventure he will accept me.' [22]So the present passed over |
| **Jacob Is Renamed Israel** | |
| GEN 32:23And he rose up that night, and took his two wives, and his two handmaids, and his eleven children, and passed over the ford of the Jabbok. [24]And he took them, and sent them over the stream, and sent over that which he had. [25]And Jacob was left alone; and there wrestled a man with him until the breaking of the day. [26]And when he saw that he prevailed not against | |
| ( added by redactor ) | { problematic } |

| P | Notes |
|---|---|

ond passage (from E), which says after the wrestling match, "ᴳᴱᴺ 32:31And Jacob called the name of the place Peniel: 'for I have seen God face to face.'"

Genesis 33:12-17 may be from either J or E. This edition assigns it to J but puts it in curly brackets to indicate that it is problematic whether it is from J or E.

### Gap in E: Jacob Travels to see Esau
**E Text**

In this passage, E describe how Jacob camped for the night, moving his wives and children so they would not be with him if Esau attacked. Thus, the original E text must have had an earlier section where Jacob traveled to see Esau and a later section where Jacob reconciled with Esau. Presumably, RJE removed these sections because he preferred J's story.

### Jacob Is Renamed Israel

ᴳᴱᴺ 35:9And God appeared unto Jacob (again), when he came from Paddan-aram, and blessed him. ¹⁰And God said unto him: 'Thy name is Jacob: thy name shall not be called any more Jacob, but Israel shall be thy name'; and He called his name Israel. ¹¹And God said unto him: 'I am God Almighty.

### Jacob Is Renamed Israel

This seems to be a very ancient Israelite myth, which shows that the Israelites had an extremely anthropomorphic view of God in patriarchal times, with El unable even to outwrestle a human.
**E Text**

In the E text, Jacob is renamed Israel in Peniel (which means Face of El). E is obviously embarrassed by this story's anthropomorphic view of God, and so he says that Jacob "wrestled a man" who refused to tell Jacob his name, and he explains away the name Israel as "you have striven with God and with men." But the identity of this "man" is given away in the place-name Peniel (with Jacob's explanation that the place name means he saw God [=El] face-to-face) and in Jacob's new name Israel (which actually means "he strove with El" or "he overcame El" and does not say anything about "and man"). Though he was embarrassed by the story, E did not alter these names.

| [ used more than once ] | " quoting older text " |
|---|---|

| **E** | **J** |
|---|---|
| him, he touched the hollow of his thigh; and the hollow of Jacob's thigh was strained, as he wrestled with him. | before him; and he himself lodged that night in the camp. |
| ²⁷And he said: 'Let me go, for the day breaketh.' And he said: 'I will not let thee go, except thou bless me.' ²⁸And he said unto him: 'What is thy name?' And be said: 'Jacob.' ²⁹And he said: 'Thy name shall be called no more Jacob, but Israel; for thou hast striven with God and with men, and hast prevailed.' ³⁰And Jacob asked him, and said: 'Tell me, I pray thee, thy name.' And he said: 'Wherefore is it that thou dost ask after my name?' And he blessed him there. | GEN 33:1And Jacob lifted up his eyes and looked, and, behold, Esau came, and with him four hundred men. And he divided the children unto Leah, and unto Rachel, and unto the two handmaids. ²And he put the handmaids and their children foremost, and Leah and her children after, and Rachel and Joseph hindermost. ³And he himself passed over before them, and bowed himself to the ground seven times, until he came near to his brother. |
| ³¹And Jacob called the name of the place Peniel: 'for I have seen God face to face, and my life is preserved.' ³²And the sun rose upon him as he passed over Peniel, and he limped upon his thigh. ³³Therefore the children of Israel eat not the sinew of the thigh-vein which is upon the hollow of the thigh, unto this day; because he touched the hollow | ⁴And Esau ran to meet him, and embraced him, and fell on his neck, and kissed him; and they wept. ⁵And he lifted up his eyes, and saw the women and the children; and said: 'Who are these with thee?' And he said: 'The children whom God hath graciously given thy servant.' ⁶Then the handmaids came near, they and their children, and they bowed down. ⁷And Leah also and her children came near, and bowed down; and after came Joseph near and Rachel, and they bowed down. |
| | ⁸And he said: 'What meanest thou by all this camp which I met?' And he said: 'To find favour in the sight of my lord.' ⁹And Esau said: 'I have enough; my brother, let that which thou hast be thine.' ¹⁰And Jacob said: 'Nay, I pray thee, if now I have found favour in thy sight, then receive my present at my hand; forasmuch as I have seen thy face, as one seeth the face of God, and thou wast pleased with me. ¹¹Take, I pray thee, my gift that is brought to thee; because God hath dealt graciously with me, and because I have enough.' And he urged him, and he took it. |
| | {¹²And he said: 'Let us take our journey, and let us go, and I will go before thee.' ¹³And he said unto him: 'My lord knoweth that the children are tender, and that the flocks and herds giving suck are a care to me; and if they overdrive them one day, all the flocks will die. ¹⁴Let |
| ( added by redactor ) | { problematic } |

| P | Notes |
|---|---|
| Be fruitful and multiply; a nation and a company of nations shall be of thee, and kings shall come out of thy loins; [12]and the land which I gave unto Abraham and Isaac, to thee I will give it, and to thy seed after thee will I give the land.' [13]And God went up from him in the place where He spoke with him. [15]And Jacob called the name of the place where God spoke with him, Beth-el. | Many scholars attribute the following verse to P because it is next to the rest of P's account: { [GEN] [35:14]And Jacob set up a pillar in the place where He spoke with him, a pillar of stone, and he poured out a drink-offering thereon, and poured oil thereon.} Though the verse is distant from E's account in Chapter 32, this edition attributes it to E. Nowhere else in P does someone set up a pillar to worship at, in keeping with P's belief that the only legitimate place for offerings is at the tabernacle or the temple. E has pillars set up in a number of cases: Jacob sets up a pillar in Bethel and pours oil on it (Gen. 28:18), Jacob sets up a pillar to mark his covenant with Laban (Gen. 31:45), Jacob sets up a pillar on Rachel's grave (Gen. 35:20), Moses sets up twelve pillars when Israel accepts the covenant (Ex. 24:4). **J Text** The J text does not have the story about renaming Jacob, which RJE presumably removed because he preferred E's story. It would have been interesting to see how J, with her anthropomorphic view of God, handled this incident. In one hint, J gives a different and very far-fetched explanation for the name Peniel: when Jacob saw that Esau was no longer angry at him, "[GEN 33:10]Jacob said: '... I have seen thy face, as one seeth the face of God, and thou wast pleased with me." Since J tried to explain away the place name, she probably also |
| [ used more than once ] | " quoting older text " |

| E | J |
|---|---|
| of Jacob's thigh, even in the sinew of the thigh-vein.<br><br>{ GEN 35:14And Jacob set up a pillar in the place where He spoke with him, a pillar of stone, and he poured out a drink-offering thereon, and poured oil thereon.} | my lord, I pray thee, pass over before his servant; and I will journey on gently, according to the pace of the cattle that are before me and according to the pace of the children, until I come unto my lord unto Seir.' 15And Esau said: 'Let me now leave with thee some of the folk that are with me.' And he said: 'What needeth it? let me find favour in the sight of my lord.'<br><br>16So Esau returned that day on his way unto Seir. 17And Jacob journeyed to Succoth, and built him a house, and made booths for his cattle. Therefore the name of the place is called Succoth.} |

### Jacob Builds an Altar in Shechem

GEN 33:18[And Jacob came] in peace [to] the city of [Shechem], which is in the land of Canaan, (when he came from Paddan-aram); and encamped before the city. 19And he bought the parcel of ground, where he had spread his tent, at the hand of the children of Hamor, Shechem's father, for a hundred pieces of money. 20And he erected there an altar, and called it El-elohe-Israel.

### Jacob Builds Altar in Bethel

GEN 35:1And God said

### The Rape of Dinah in Shechem

[GEN 33:18And Jacob came to Shechem,] GEN 34:1And Dinah the daughter of Leah, whom she had borne unto Jacob, went out to see the daughters of the land. 2And Shechem the son of Hamor the Hivite, the prince of the land, saw her; and he took her, and lay with her, and humbled her. 3And his soul did cleave unto Dinah the daughter of Jacob, and he loved the damsel, and spoke comfortingly unto the damsel. 4And Shechem spoke unto his father Hamor, saying: 'Get me this damsel to wife.'

5Now Jacob heard that he had defiled Dinah his daughter; and his sons were with his cattle in the field; and Jacob held his peace until they came. 6And Hamor the father of Shechem went out unto Jacob to speak with him. 7And the sons of Jacob came in from the field when they heard it; and the men were grieved, and they were very wroth, because he had wrought a vile deed in Israel in lying with Jacob's daughter; which thing ought not to be done.

8And Hamor spoke with them, saying 'The soul of my son Shechem longeth for your daughter. I pray you give her unto him to wife. 9And make ye marriages with us; give your daughters unto us, and take our daughters unto you. 10And ye shall dwell with us; and the land shall be before you; dwell and trade ye therein, and get you posses-

( added by redactor )     { problematic }

| P | Notes |
|---|---|
| | was embarrassed by this story because it was too anthropomorphic even for her.<br>**P Text**<br>In the P text, Jacob is renamed Israel in Beth-el (which means House of El) and not in Peniel (a name that implies that he saw the face of El). P does not say anything about the meaning of the name Israel or about the wrestling match, which might show that he too is embarrassed by the anthropomorphic view of God in this ancient myth.<br><br>**Altar and Rape in Shechem**<br>**E Text**<br>The mention of Paddan-aram in Genesis 33:18, was added by R, trying to make this story consistent with the stories in P.<br>**J Text**<br>This is one of three passages that J (who was a member of the Judean court) uses to legitimize the dominance of the tribe of Judah.<br>The blessing of Jacob in Genesis 49 says that Reuben, the first born, defiled his father's bed. Simeon and Levi, the second and third born, are angry and violent. Therefore Judah, the fourth born, will become the ruler.<br>The story of Reuben defiling his father's bed is in Genesis 35:21. The story of Simeon and Levi being violent is here in Genesis 34, in the story of the rape of Dinah.<br>The blessing of Jacob is an earlier text that J quotes. The stories of Reuben, Simeon and Levi were presumably written by J to substantiate this earlier text, drawing on traditions of the tribe of Judah.<br>**J versus E Text**<br>Presumably, both the E and J texts mentioned the arrival in Shechem, and RJE removed one of these mentions to avoid duplication. This edition places this passage in both texts, and |

*[Continued on p. 161]*

[ used more than once ]                    " quoting older text "

| **E** | **J** |
|---|---|
| unto Jacob: 'Arise, go up to Beth-el, and dwell there; and make there an altar unto God, who appeared unto thee when thou didst flee from the face of Esau thy brother.' ²Then Jacob said unto his household, and to all that were with him: 'Put away the strange gods that are among you, and purify yourselves, and change your garments; ³and let us arise, and go up to Beth-el; and I will make there an altar unto God, who answered me in the day of my distress, and was with me in the way which I went.' ⁴And they gave unto Jacob all the foreign gods which were in their hand, and the rings which were in their ears; and Jacob hid them under the terebinth which was by Shechem. ⁵And they journeyed; and a terror of God was upon the cities that were round about them, and they did not pursue after the sons of Jacob. ⁶So Jacob came to Luz, which is in the land of Canaan—the same is Bethel—he and all the people that were with him. ⁷And he built there an altar, and called the place El-bethel, because there God | sions therein.' ¹¹And Shechem said unto her father and unto her brethren: 'Let me find favour in your eyes, and what ye shall say unto me I will give. ¹²Ask me never so much dowry and gift, and I will give according as ye shall say unto me; but give me the damsel to wife.' ¹³And the sons of Jacob answered Shechem and Hamor his father with guile, and spoke, because he had defiled Dinah their sister, ¹⁴and said unto them: 'We cannot do this thing, to give our sister to one that is uncircumcised; for that were a reproach unto us. ¹⁵Only on this condition will we consent unto you: if ye will be as we are, that every male of you be circumcised; ¹⁶then will we give our daughters unto you, and we will take your daughters to us, and we will dwell with you, and we will become one people. ¹⁷But if ye will not hearken unto us, to be circumcised; then will we take our daughter, and we will be gone.' ¹⁸And their words pleased Hamor, and Shechem Hamor's son. ¹⁹And the young man deferred not to do the thing, because he had delight in Jacob's daughter. And he was honoured above all the house of his father. ²⁰And Hamor and Shechem his son came unto the gate of their city, and spoke with the men of their city, saying: ²¹'These men are peaceable with us; therefore let them dwell in the land, and trade therein; for, behold, the land is large enough for them; let us take their daughters to us for wives, and let us give them our daughters. ²²Only on this condition will the men consent unto us to dwell with us, to become one people, if every male among us be circumcised, as they are circumcised. ²³Shall not their cattle and their substance and all their beasts be ours? only let us consent unto them, and they will dwell with us.' ²⁴And unto Hamor and unto Shechem his son hearkened all that went out of the gate of his city; and every male was circumcised, all that went out |
| ( added by redactor ) | { problematic } |

| P | Notes |
|---|---|
| | puts the duplicate text in square brackets. |

puts the duplicate text in square brackets.

In E's story of Jacob building an altar in Shechem, Jacob comes "in peace" to Shechem, buys land to build an altar there, and leaves when God tells him to go to Bethel.

In J's story of the rape of Dinah, Jacob leaves Shechem because he is afraid the inhabitants will revenge the killings.

Shechem was capital of the northern kingdom of Israel. Perhaps E, as a northerner, wanted to give the Israelite's settlement at Shechem a legitimate history, based on Jacob buying land there, while J, as a Judean, wanted to give Shechem a more shameful history.

### Jacob's Sons

GEN 35:22bNow the sons of Jacob were twelve: 23the sons of Leah: Reuben, Jacob's first-born, and Simeon, and Levi, and Judah, and Issachar, and Zebulun; 24the sons of Rachel: Joseph and Benjamin; 25and the sons of Bilhah, Rachel's handmaid: Dan and Naphtali; 26and the sons of Zilpah, Leah's handmaid: Gad and Asher. These are the sons of Jacob, that were born to him in Paddan-aram.

### Jacob's Sons

In his usual way, P just gives a summary list of Jacob's sons. J and E give longer stories about the births of these sons and the origin of their names (Gen. 29:31-30:24).

This book tries to put parallel passages in the three texts next to each other, but in this case, it is impossible to put P's list of Jacob's sons next to J and E's accounts of the birth of Jacob's children.

[ used more than once ]     " quoting older text "

| **E** | **J** |
|---|---|
| was revealed unto him, when he fled from the face of his brother. [8]And Deborah Rebekah's nurse died, and she was buried below Beth-el under the oak; and the name of it was called Allon-bacuth. | of the gate of his city. |

**J** (continued):

[25]And it came to pass on the third day, when they were in pain, that two of the sons of Jacob, Simeon and Levi, Dinah's brethren, took each man his sword, and came upon the city unawares, and slew all the males. [26]And they slew Hamor and Shechem his son with the edge of the sword, and took Dinah out of Shechem's house, and went forth. [27]The sons of Jacob came upon the slain, and spoiled the city, because they had defiled their sister. [28]They took their flocks and their herds and their asses, and that which was in the city and that which was in the field; [29]and all their wealth, and all their little ones and their wives, took they captive and spoiled, even all that was in the house.

[30]And Jacob said to Simeon and Levi: 'Ye have troubled me, to make me odious unto the inhabitants of the land, even unto the Canaanites and the Perizzites; and, I being few in number, they will gather themselves together against me and smite me; and I shall be destroyed, I and my house.' [31]And they said: 'Should one deal with our sister as with a harlot?'

**E** (continued):

### Death of Rachel, Birth of Benjamin

GEN 35:16And they journeyed from Beth-el; and there was still some way to come to Ephrath; and Rachel travailed, and she had hard labour. [17]And it came to pass, when she was in hard labour, that the midwife said unto her: 'Fear not; for this also is a son for thee.' [18]And it came to pass, as her soul was in departing—for she died—that she called his name Ben-oni; but his father called him Benjamin. [19]And Rachel died, and was

**J** (continued):

### Reuben Lies with Israel's Concubine

GEN 35:21And Israel journeyed, and spread his tent beyond Migdal-eder. [22]And it came to pass, while Israel dwelt in that land, that Reuben went and lay with Bilhah his father's concubine; and Israel heard of it.

### Generations of Esau

GEN 36:1(Now these are the generations of Esau—the same is Edom.) [2]Esau took his wives of the

| ( added by redactor ) | { problematic } |
|---|---|

| **P** | **Notes** |

### Death of Isaac

GEN 35:27And Jacob came unto Isaac his father to Mamre, to Kiriath-arba—the same is Hebron—where Abraham and Isaac sojourned.

28And the days of Isaac were a hundred and fourscore years. 29And Isaac expired, and died, and was gathered unto his people, old and full of days; and Esau and Jacob his sons buried him.

GEN 37:1And Jacob dwelt in the land of his father's sojournings, in the land of Canaan.

### Death of Isaac

In J, Isaac seemed to be on his death bed when he was tricked into blessing Jacob rather than Esau (Gen. 27). Here in P, he dies much later. P gives his usual summary account of the death and, with his typical precision, mentions Isaac's age. P often uses the word translated as "expired," which is not used in the other texts.

### Reuben Lies with Israel's Concubine

This passage is one of three passages that J uses to legitimize the dominance of Judah, her tribe.

The blessing of Jacob in Genesis 49 says that Reuben, the first born, defiled his father's bed. Simeon and Levi, the second and third born, are angry and violent. Therefore Judah, the fourth born will become the ruler.

The story of Reuben defiling his father's bed is here, in Genesis 35:21-22. The story of Simeon and Levi being violent is in Genesis 34.

### Generations of Esau

Many scholars attribute this passage to P, but this edition attributes it to J for several reasons.

| [ used more than once ] | " quoting older text " |

| **E** | **J** |
|---|---|
| buried in the way to Ephrath—the same is Beth-le-hem. [20]And Jacob set up a pillar upon her grave; the same is the pillar of Rachel's grave unto this day. | daughters of Canaan; Adah the daughter of Elon the Hittite, and Oholibamah the daughter of Anah, the daughter of Zibeon the Hivite, [3]and Basemath Ishmael's daughter, sister of Nebaioth. [4]And Adah bore to Esau Eliphaz; and Basemath bore Reuel; [5]and Oholibamah bore Jeush, and Jalam, and Korah. These are the sons of Esau, that were born unto him in the land of Canaan.<br><br>[6]And Esau took his wives, and his sons, and his daughters, and all the souls of his house, and his cattle, and all his beasts, and all his possessions, which he had gathered in the land of Canaan; and went into a land away from his brother Jacob. [7]For their substance was too great for them to dwell together; and the land of their sojournings could not bear them because of their cattle. [8]And Esau dwelt in the mountain-land of Seir—Esau is Edom.<br><br>([9]And these are the generations of Esau the father of the Edomites in the mountain-land of Seir.) [10]These are the names of Esau's sons: Eliphaz the son of Adah the wife of Esau, Reuel the son of Basemath the wife of Esau. [11]And the sons of Eliphaz were Teman, Omar, Zepho, and Gatam, and Kenaz. [12]And Timna was concubine to Eliphaz Esau's son; and she bore to Eliphaz Amalek. These are the sons of Adah Esau's wife. [13]And these are the sons of Reuel: Nahath, and Zerah, Shammah, and Mizzah. These were the sons of Basemath Esau's wife. [14]And these were the sons of Oholibamah the daughter of Anah, the daughter of Zibeon, Esau's wife; and she bore to Esau Jeush, and Jalam, and Korah. |
| ( added by redactor ) | { problematic } |

| P | Notes |
|---|---|
| | |

P focuses on the mainline genealogy leading to the Israelites, while J often includes genealogies of other nations, as we have seen beginning with the pre-flood and post-flood genealogies of the two texts. J lives in a multi-national court and so is interested in the surrounding nations.

P has already had a story about the children of Esau, which contradicts this story. For example, the earlier P story said: "[GEN 26:34]And when Esau was forty years old, he took to wife Judith the daughter of Beeri the Hittite, and Basemath the daughter of Elon the Hittite." This genealogy gives different names for these Canaanite wives: "[GEN 36:2]Esau took his wives of the daughters of Canaan; Adah the daughter of Elon the Hittite, and Oholibamah the daughter of Anah, the daughter of Zibeon the Hivite."

J is likely to includes the generations of Esau because she is clearly sympathetic to Esau: in her story of Jacob stealing Esau's blessing, Esau is an innocent victim, and in her story of Esau meeting Jacob when he returns from Haran, Esau magnanimously forgives the brother who stole his blessing. In other traditions, Esau is not so sympathetic: in E, Esau disappoints Isaac and Rebekah by marrying Canaanites. J's sympathetic portrayal of Esau raises the possibility that perhaps she had some Edomite ancestry.

For these reasons, J is more likely than P to have written this list of Esau's descendents.

### Edomite Chiefs - Relocated

Following the generations of Esau in Genesis 36:1-14 is a list of Edomite chiefs or kings in Genesis 36:15-43. This list of is made up of several later texts that a redactor added here to follow up the list of Esau's descendents, so this edition has relocated it to the section of Other Texts that are not from J, E, or P.

*[Continued on p. 167]*

| [ used more than once ] | " quoting older text " |
|---|---|

| **E** | **J** |
|---|---|
| **Joseph and His Brothers** | **Joseph and His Brothers** |
| GEN 37:5And Joseph dreamed a dream, and he told it to his brethren; and they hated him (yet the more). 6And he said unto them: 'Hear, I pray you, this dream which I have dreamed: 7for, behold, we were binding sheaves in the field, and, lo, my sheaf arose, and also stood upright; and, behold, your sheaves came round about, and bowed down to my sheaf.' 8And his brethren said to him: 'Shalt thou indeed reign over us? or shalt thou indeed have dominion over us?' And they hated him (yet the more) for his dreams, and for his words. | GEN 37:3Now Israel loved Joseph more than all his children, because he was the son of his old age; and he made him a coat of many colours. 4And when his brethren saw that their father loved him more than all his brethren, they hated him, and could not speak peaceably unto him. |
| 9And he dreamed yet another dream, and told it to his brethren, and said: 'Behold, I have dreamed yet a dream: and, behold, the sun and the moon and eleven stars bowed down to me.' 10And he told it to his father, and to his brethren; and his father rebuked him, and said unto him: 'What is this dream that thou hast dreamed? Shall I and thy mother and thy brethren indeed come to bow down to thee to the earth?' 11And his brethren envied him; but his father kept the saying in mind. | 14aAnd he *[Israel]* said to him: 'Go now, see whether it is well with thy brethren, and well with the flock; and bring me back word.' |
| | 15And a certain man found him, and, behold, he was wandering in the field. And the man asked him, saying: 'What seekest thou?' 16And he said: 'I seek my brethren. Tell me, I pray thee, where they are feeding the flock.' 17And the man said: 'They are departed hence; for I heard them say: Let us go to Dothan.' And Joseph went after his brethren, and found them in Dothan. 18And they saw him afar off, and before he came near unto them, they conspired against him to slay him. |
| 12And his brethren went to feed their father's flock in Shechem. 13And Israel said unto Joseph: 'Do not thy brethren feed the flock in Shechem? come, and I will send thee unto them.' And he said to him: 'Here am I. | 23And it came to pass, when Joseph was come unto his brethren, that they stripped Joseph of his coat, the coat of many colours that was on him; And they lifted up their eyes and looked, and, behold, a caravan of Ishmaelites came from Gilead, with their camels bearing spicery and balm and ladanum, going to carry it down to Egypt. 26And Judah said unto his brethren: 'What profit is it if we slay our brother and conceal his blood? 27Come, and let us sell him to the Ishmaelites, and let not our hand be upon him; for |
| 14bSo he sent him out of the vale of Hebron, and he came to Shechem. 19And they said one to another: 'Be- | |
| ( added by redactor ) | { problematic } |

| **P** | **Notes** |
|---|---|
| **Joseph and His Brothers** <br><br> GEN 37:2(These are the generations of Jacob.) Joseph, being seventeen years old, was feeding the flock with his brethren, being still a lad even with the sons of Bilhah, and with the sons of Zilpah, his father's wives; and Joseph brought evil report of them unto their father. <br><br><br><br> *[Gap in P]* | **Joseph and His Brothers** <br> The tribes supposedly descended from Joseph, Ephraim and Manasseh, were the most powerful and prosperous tribes in the early days of settlement in Canaan. The Joseph stories justify their superiority over the other tribes. <br> **Separating the Texts** <br> There are clearly contradictions in the story of Joseph that show it is made up of more than one text, but there are differences among scholars about how to assign the story to the E and J texts. <br> This edition uses the following criteria to distinguish between texts: <br> E uses the word "God" and J uses "the Lord." This is the easiest way to distinguish between texts, but there are relatively few uses of these words in this story, and none in its earliest parts. <br> In E, Reuben saves Joseph's life. In J, Judah saves Joseph's life. Scholars agree that J gave this sympathetic role to Judah because she is from the kingdom of Judah. <br> In E, the brothers put Joseph in a pit, and while they are not watching, Midianite slave traders take him from the pit. We assign this story to E because Reuben finds that the pit is empty. In J, the brothers deliberately sell Joseph to Ishmaelite slave traders. <br> In E, the brothers are angry because of Joseph's dream that they bowed down to him and in J because Jacob has given him the coat of many colors. Though many scholars would disagree, this edition assigns Joseph's dreams to E because dreams are important throughout the E text, and because Joseph's dream turns out to be prophetic, like the other dreams in the E version of this story. The text itself points out that this dream was prophetic: "GEN 42:6And Joseph was the governor over the land; he it was that sold to all the people of the land. And Joseph's brethren came, and bowed down to him with their faces to the earth. 9And Joseph remembered the dreams which he dreamed of them." This edition assigns the coat of many colors to J, because there are two reasons in JE for the brothers being angry at Joseph, so it is most plausible that one reason comes from each of the two texts, and we know that dreams are emphasized throughout E. |
| [ used more than once ] | " quoting older text " |

| E | J |
|---|---|
| hold, this dreamer cometh. [20]Come now therefore, and let us slay him, and cast him into one of the pits, and we will say: An evil beast hath devoured him; and we shall see what will become of his dreams.' [21]And Reuben heard it, and delivered him out of their hand; and said: 'Let us not take his life.' [22]And Reuben said unto them: 'Shed no blood; cast him into this pit that is in the wilderness, but lay no hand upon him'—that he might deliver him out of their hand, to restore him to his father. <br><br> [24]And they took him, and cast him into the pit—and the pit was empty, there was no water in it. [25]And they sat down to eat bread. [28a]And there passed by Midianites, merchantmen; and they drew and lifted up Joseph out of the pit, [28c]And they brought Joseph into Egypt. [29]And Reuben returned unto the pit; and, behold, Joseph was not in the pit; and he rent his clothes. [30]And he returned unto his brethren, and said: 'The child is not; and as for me, whither shall I go?' | he is our brother, our flesh.' And his brethren hearkened unto him [28b]And sold Joseph to the Ishmaelites for twenty shekels of silver. <br><br> [31]And they took Joseph's coat, and killed a he-goat, and dipped the coat in the blood; [32]and they sent the coat of many colours, and they brought it to their father; and said: 'This have we found. Know now whether it is thy son's coat or not.' [33]And he knew it, and said: 'It is my son's coat; an evil beast hath devoured him; Joseph is without doubt torn in pieces.' [34]And Jacob rent his garments, and put sackcloth upon his loins, and mourned for his son many days. [35]And all his sons and all his daughters rose up to comfort him; but he refused to be comforted; and he said: 'Nay, but I will go down to the grave to my son mourning.' And his father wept for him. |
| ( added by redactor ) | { problematic } |

| **P** | **Notes** |
|---|---|
| | This edition does not use the following criteria to distinguish between the E and J texts: |
| | It does not try to distinguish between these two source texts on the grounds that one uses the name Jacob and one uses Israel. Both names are used by both sources in later stories, and at the end of this story, we have the following passage from E that uses both names: "<sup>GEN 46:2</sup>And God spoke unto Israel in the visions of the night, and said: 'Jacob, Jacob.'" |
| | It does not try to distinguish between the two source texts on the grounds that the story uses two Hebrew words that are translated "sack," *amtahat* and *saq*. It is possible that one author would use these two words, just as someone writing a story today might use the two words "bag" and "sack" interchangeably. Instead of assigning the two Hebrew words to two different texts, this edition puts the story of Benjamin and the sacks in the J text, because they involve J's typical device of using repetition to build dramatic tension, and it puts the story that Simeon is held hostage in the E text. To let readers judge about this issue for themselves, this edition includes the original Hebrew when the word "sack" is used in the translation. |
| *[Continued on p. 177]* | **E Text** |
| | The Joseph stories are one of the most elaborate myths in the E text. E emphasized these stories because he was a Mushite priest, the group of priests who had been in charge of the religious center at Shiloh, which was in the territory of the tribe Ephraim, which believed it was descended from Joseph's son Ephraim. This myth establishes Joseph's superiority over the other brothers and thus his descendents' superiority over the other tribes. |
| | Note that in the E text story, the brothers do not violate the following commandment in E's code of law: "<sup>EX 21:16</sup>And he that stealeth a man, and selleth him, or if he be found in his hand, he shall surely be put to death." In the J story, the brothers sell Joseph, violating this commandment, but in the E story, they just leave Joseph in a pit and the Midianites find him there. |
| | **J Text** |
| | The story in J becomes very melodramatic, with |
| [ used more than once ] | " quoting older text " |

| E | J |
|---|---|
| *[Continued on p. 176]* | |
| | **Tamar Lies with Judah**<br>GEN 38:1(And it came to pass at that time, that) Judah went down |
| ( added by redactor ) | { problematic } |

*[Continued on p. 176]*

| P | Notes |
|---|---|
| | Joseph unable to restrain his tears. It is a good example of J's tendency to dramatize the traditional stories that she works with. |
| | **P text** |
| | Though it is not always recognized, Genesis 37:2 is clearly from the P text. It gives Joseph's age at the time of the event, as P commonly does. Most important, it gives a different account of the quarrel than the other two texts. In the other texts, the quarrel is with all the sons, but in P, the quarrel is only with the sons of the Jacob's concubines, who (P has told us a bit earlier) are "GEN 35:25... the sons of Bilhah, Rachel's handmaid: Dan and Naphtali; 26and the sons of Zilpah, Leah's handmaid: Gad and Asher." |
| | The cause of the quarrel is different in P than in other two texts: In P, Joseph brings back a bad report of some of his brothers to Jacob. In the other texts, all of his brothers are resentful and jealous because of his coat of many colors or because of his dream. |
| *[Continued on p. 177]* | We only have a few sentences from the P text of the Joseph story. Presumably, the P text must have contradicted the JE text so blatantly that R removed it. It probably was a brief summary story, of the sort that P usually provides. |
| | The two texts from P that we do have (Gen. 37:2 and Genesis 41:46) both mention Joseph's age. Presumably, R kept them to preserve this extra information about Joseph's age, but in an example of inept editing, R kept all of Genesis 37:2, including the part that contradicts the other texts by saying the quarrel was just with the sons of Jacob's two concubines. This intriguing hint at P's story makes us wonder why P wanted to blame Dan, Naphtali, Gad and Asher for quarreling with Joseph and not the other tribes. |
| | R added a phrase beginning with "These are the generations of" at the beginning of P's version of this story, as he did in many locations, to make the combined text appear unified. See Appendix 2. |
| | **Tamar Lies with Judah** |
| | This story explains the origin of two subgroups within the tribe of Judah. The fact that Zerah came out first gave |
| [ used more than once ] | " quoting older text " |

| **E** | **J** |
|---|---|
| | from his brethren, and turned in to a certain Adullamite, whose name was Hirah. [2]And Judah saw there a daughter of a certain Canaanite whose name was Shua; and he took her, and went in unto her. [3]And she conceived, and bore a son; and he called his name Er. [4]And she conceived again, and bore a son; and she called his name Onan. [5]And she yet again bore a son, and called his name Shelah; and he was at Chezib, when she bore him. |

from his brethren, and turned in to a certain Adullamite, whose name was Hirah. [2]And Judah saw there a daughter of a certain Canaanite whose name was Shua; and he took her, and went in unto her. [3]And she conceived, and bore a son; and he called his name Er. [4]And she conceived again, and bore a son; and she called his name Onan. [5]And she yet again bore a son, and called his name Shelah; and he was at Chezib, when she bore him.

[6]And Judah took a wife for Er his first-born, and her name was Tamar. [7]And Er, Judah's first-born, was wicked in the sight of the Lord; and the Lord slew him. [8]And Judah said unto Onan: 'Go in unto thy brother's wife, and perform the duty of a husband's brother unto her, and raise up seed to thy brother.' [9]And Onan knew that the seed would not be his; and it came to pass when he went in unto his brother's wife, that he spilled it on the ground, lest he should give seed to his brother. [10]And the thing which he did was evil in the sight of the Lord; and He slew him also.

*[Continued on p. 176]*

[11]Then said Judah to Tamar his daughter-in-law: 'Remain a widow in thy father's house, till Shelah my son be grown up'; for he said: 'Lest he also die, like his brethren.' And Tamar went and dwelt in her father's house. [12]And in process of time Shua's daughter, the wife of Judah, died; and Judah was comforted, and went up unto his sheep-shearers to Timnah, he and his friend Hirah the Adullamite.

[13]And it was told Tamar, saying: 'Behold, thy father-in-law goeth up to Timnah to shear his sheep.' [14]And she put off from her the garments of her widowhood, and covered herself with her veil, and wrapped herself, and sat in the entrance of Enaim, which is by the way to Timnah; for she saw that Shelah was grown up, and she was not given unto him to wife. [15]When Judah saw her, he thought her to be a harlot; for she had covered her face.

[16]And he turned unto her by the way, and said: 'Come, I pray thee, let me come in unto thee'; for he knew not that she was his daughter-in-law. And she said: 'What wilt thou give me, that thou mayest come

( added by redactor )                    { problematic }

| P | Notes |
|---|---|
| | his descendents birthright over the descendents of Perez.<br><br>This story is probably by J, who is Judean and who is interested in the status of the tribes of Judah: J also has other stories where women manipulate the action in similar ways: Lot's daughters get him drunk so they can have children by him (Gen. 19:30-38). Rebekah controls Jacob and manipulates Isaac to make Isaac steal Esau's blessing (Gen. 27). Rachel tricks her father Laban after stealing his teraphim (Gen. 31:35).<br><br>If this story is from J, however, it seems likely that a redactor changed its location. J is usually such an effective story-teller that it is hard to believe she would interrupt the story of Joseph by putting this unrelated story right in its midst. Presumably, The redactor tried to make this story fit in at this location by adding "<sup>GEN 38:1</sup>And it came to pass at that time, that..." at its beginning. |
| *[Continued on p. 177]* | |
| [ used more than once ] | " quoting older text " |

*[Continued on p. 177]*

| **E** | **J** |
|---|---|
| | in unto me?' [17]And he said: 'I will send thee a kid of the goats from the flock.' And she said: 'Wilt thou give me a pledge, till thou send it?' [18]And he said: 'What pledge shall I give thee?' And she said: 'Thy signet and thy cord, and thy staff that is in thy hand.' And he gave them to her, and came in unto her, and she conceived by him. |
| | [19]And she arose, and went away, and put off her veil from her, and put on the garments of her widowhood. [20]And Judah sent the kid of the goats by the hand of his friend the Adullamite, to receive the pledge from the woman's hand; but he found her not. [21]Then he asked the men of her place, saying: 'Where is the harlot, that was at Enaim by the wayside?' And they said: 'There hath been no harlot here.' [22]And he returned to Judah, and said: 'I have not found her; and also the men of the place said: There hath been no harlot here.' [23]And Judah said: 'Let her take it, lest we be put to shame; behold, I sent this kid, and thou hast not found her.' |
| *[Continued on p. 176]* | [24]And it came to pass about three months after, that it was told Judah, saying: 'Tamar thy daughter-in-law hath played the harlot; and moreover, behold, she is with child by harlotry.' And Judah said: 'Bring her forth, and let her be burnt.' [25]When she was brought forth, she sent to her father-in-law, saying: 'By the man, whose these are, am I with child'; and she said: 'Discern, I pray thee, whose are these, the signet, and the cords, and the staff.' [26]And Judah acknowledged them, and said: 'She is more righteous than I; forasmuch as I gave her not to Shelah my son.' And he knew her again no more. |
| | [27]And it came to pass in the time of her travail, that, behold, twins were in her womb. [28]And it came to pass, when she travailed, that one put out a hand; and the midwife took and bound upon his hand a scarlet thread, saying: 'This came out first.' [29]And it came to pass, as he drew back his hand, that, behold his brother came out; and she said: 'Wherefore hast thou made a breach for thyself?' Therefore his name was called Perez. [30]And afterward came out his brother, that had the scarlet thread upon his hand; and his name was called Zerah. |
| ( added by redactor ) | { problematic } |

*[Continued on p. 176]*

| P | Notes |
|---|---|
| | |
| *[Continued on p. 177]* | *[Continued on p. 177]* |
| | |
| [ used more than once ] | " quoting older text " |

*[Continued on p. 177]*

| E | J |
|---|---|
| **Joseph and His Master** | **Joseph and His Master** |

**Joseph and His Master**

GEN 39:2b And he [Joseph] was in the house of his master the Egyptian. ⁴And Joseph found favour in his sight, and he ministered unto him. And he appointed him overseer over his house, and all that he had he put into his hand.

⁶ᵇAnd Joseph was of beautiful form, and fair to look upon. ⁷And it came to pass (after these things,) that his master's wife cast her eyes upon Joseph; and she said: 'Lie with me.' ⁸But he refused, and said unto his master's wife: 'Behold, my master, having me, knoweth not what is in the house, and he hath put all that he hath into my hand; ⁹he is not greater in this house than I; neither hath he kept back any thing from me but thee, because thou art his wife. How then can I do this great wickedness, and sin against God?' ¹⁰And it came to pass, as she spoke to Joseph day by day, that he hearkened not unto her, to lie by her, or to be with her.

¹¹And it came to pass on a certain day, when he went into the house to do his work, and there was none of the men of the house there within, ¹²that she caught him by his garment, saying: 'Lie with me.' And he left his garment in her hand, and fled, and got him out. ¹³And it came to pass, when she saw that he had left his garment in her hand, and was fled forth, ¹⁴that she called unto the men of her house, and spoke unto them, saying: 'See, he hath brought in a Hebrew unto us to mock us; he came in unto me to lie with me, and I cried with a loud voice. ¹⁵And it came to pass, when he heard that I lifted up my voice and cried, that he left his garment by me, and fled, and got him out.'

¹⁶And she laid up his garment by her, until his master came home. ¹⁷And she spoke unto him according to these words, saying: 'The Hebrew servant, whom thou hast brought unto us, came in unto me to mock me. ¹⁸And it came to pass, as I lifted up my voice and cried, that he left his garment by me, and fled out.' ¹⁹And it came to pass, when his master heard the words of his wife,

**Joseph and His Master**

GEN 39:1 And Joseph was brought down to Egypt; and Potiphar, an officer of Pharaoh's, the captain of the guard, an Egyptian, bought him of the hand of the Ishmaelites, that had brought him down thither.

²ᵃAnd the Lord was with Joseph, and he was a prosperous man; ³And his master saw that the Lord was with him, and that the Lord made all that he did to prosper in his hand.

⁵And it came to pass from the time that he appointed him overseer in his house, and over all that he had, that the Lord blessed the Egyptian's house for Joseph's sake; and the blessing of the Lord was upon all that he had, in the house and in the field. ⁶ᵃAnd he left all that he had in Joseph's hand; and, having him, he knew not aught save the bread which he did eat.

| ( added by redactor ) | { problematic } |

| P | Notes |
|---|---|
| | **Joseph and His Master** |
| | **Separating the Texts** |
| | In the early parts of this section, it is difficult to separate the J text from the E text This edition gives one possible division, which is speculative. |
| | **E Text** |
| | E does not give any name for the Egyptian who bought Joseph and just refers to "his master." We know from Genesis 39:8 that Joseph became overseer of his master's house before he was disgraced and jailed when his master's wife accused him of sexually molesting her. He became influential with Pharaoh because he interpreted dreams in jail, typical of the importance that E gives to dreams. |
| *[Gap in P: Joseph Becomes Influential in Egypt]* | Notice that, in E, Joseph recoils from the sexual irregularity when his master's wife approaches him (Gen. 39:9), while J has stories elsewhere that condone sexual irregularity, such as Lot offering his daughters to the men of Sodom (Gen. 19:8) and Tamar posing as a harlot to get Judah to impregnate her (Gen. 38). Here, again, we see E's more moralistic approach. |
| | **J Text** |
| | J tells us that Joseph was sold to Potiphar. Joseph becomes overseer because he does such a good job of managing Potiphar's household. In J, we do not know why Joseph is sent to jail, and we do not know how Joseph becomes influential with Pharaoh, since dream interpretation is a focus of E, not of J. |
| | Note the use of "the Lord" in the |
| [ used more than once ] | " quoting older text " |

| **E** | **J** |
|---|---|
| which she spoke unto him, saying: 'After this manner did thy servant to me'; that his wrath was kindled. [20]And Joseph's master took him, and put him into the prison, the place where the king's prisoners were bound; and he was there in the prison. GEN 40:1And it came to pass after these things, that the butler of the king of Egypt and his baker offended their lord the king of Egypt. [2]And Pharaoh was wroth against his two officers, against the chief of the butlers, and against the chief of the bakers. [3]And he put them in ward in the house of the captain of the guard, into the prison, the place where Joseph was bound. [4]And the captain of the guard charged Joseph to be with them, and he ministered unto them; and they continued a season in ward.<br><br>[5]And they dreamed a dream both of them, each man his dream, in one night, each man according to the interpretation of his dream, the butler and the baker of the king of Egypt, who were bound in the prison. [6]And Joseph came in unto them in the morning, and saw them, and, behold, they were sad. [7]And he asked Pharaoh's officers that were with him in the ward of his master's house, saying: 'Wherefore look ye so sad to-day?' [8]And they said unto him: 'We have dreamed a dream, and there is none that can interpret it.' And Joseph said unto them: 'Do not interpretations belong to God? tell it me, I pray you.'<br><br>[9]And the chief butler told his dream to Joseph, and said to him: 'In my dream, behold, a vine was before me; [10]and in the vine were three branches; and as it was budding, its blossoms shot forth, and the clusters thereof brought forth ripe grapes, [11]and Pharaoh's cup was in my hand; and I took the grapes, and pressed them into Pharaoh's cup, and I gave the cup into Pharaoh's hand.' [12]And Joseph said unto him: 'This is the interpretation of it: the three branches are three days; [13]within yet three days shall Pharaoh lift up thy head, and restore thee unto thine office; and thou shalt give Pharaoh's cup into his hand, after the former manner when thou wast his butler. [14]But have me in thy remembrance when it shall be well with thee, and show kindness, I pray thee, unto me, | *[Gap in J: Joseph put in prison]*<br><br><br><br><br><br><br><br><br><br><br>GEN 39:21But the Lord was with Joseph, and showed kindness unto him, and gave him favour in the sight of the keeper of the prison. [22]And the keeper of the prison committed to Joseph's hand all the prisoners that were in the prison; and what- |

| ( added by redactor ) | { problematic } |
|---|---|

| P | Notes |
|---|---|
| | J text, and note the similar wording in "GEN 39: 3And his master saw that the Lord was with him, and that the Lord made all that he did to prosper in his hand" and "GEN 39:23bbecause the Lord was with him; and that which he did, the Lord made it to prosper," which are both in the J text. |

**P Text**

P tells us later, "GEN 41:46aAnd Joseph was thirty years old when he stood before Pharaoh king of Egypt." Joseph must have done something in P to become influential enough to stand before Pharaoh, but we cannot guess what because we have lost almost all of the P text of this story.

*[Continued on p. 181]*

| [ used more than once ] | " quoting older text " |
|---|---|

| **E** | **J** |
|---|---|
| and make mention of me unto Pharaoh, and bring me out of this house. [15]For indeed I was stolen away out of the land of the Hebrews; and here also have I done nothing that they should put me into the dungeon.' | soever they did there, he was the doer of it. [23]The keeper of the prison looked not to any thing that was under his hand, because the Lord was with him; and that which he did, the Lord made it to prosper. |
| [16]When the chief baker saw that the interpretation was good, he said unto Joseph: 'I also saw in my dream, and, behold, three baskets of white bread were on my head; [17]and in the uppermost basket there was of all manner of baked food for Pharaoh; and the birds did eat them out of the basket upon my head.' [18]And Joseph answered and said: 'This is the interpretation thereof: the three baskets are three days; [19]within yet three days shall Pharaoh lift up thy head from off thee, and shall hang thee on a tree; and the birds shall eat thy flesh from off thee.' | |
| [20]And it came to pass the third day, which was Pharaoh's birthday, that he made a feast unto all his servants; and he lifted up the head of the chief butler and the head of the chief baker among his servants. [21]And he restored the chief butler back unto his butlership; and he gave the cup into Pharaoh's hand. [22]But he hanged the chief baker, as Joseph had interpreted to them. [23]Yet did not the chief butler remember Joseph, but forgot him. | |
| **Joseph Counsels Pharaoh** | *[Gap in J: Joseph Counsels Pharaoh]* |
| GEN 41:1And it came to pass at the end of two full years, that Pharaoh dreamed: and, behold, he stood by the river. [2]And, behold, there came up out of the river seven kine, well-favoured and fat-fleshed; and they fed in the reed-grass. [3]And, behold, seven other kine came up after them out of the river, ill-favoured and lean-fleshed; and stood by the other kine upon the brink of the river. [4]And the ill-favoured and lean-fleshed kine did eat up the seven well-favoured and fat kine. So Pharaoh awoke. | |
| [5]And he slept and dreamed a second time: and, behold, seven ears of corn came up upon one stalk, rank and good. [6]And, behold, seven ears, thin and blasted with the east wind, sprung up after them. [7]And the thin ears swallowed up the seven rank and full ears. | |

| ( added by redactor ) | { problematic } |

| P | Notes |
|---|---|
| **Joseph Counsels Pharaoh**<br><br>GEN 41:46aAnd Joseph was thirty years old when he stood before Pharaoh king of Egypt. | **Joseph Counsels Pharaoh**<br>**E Text**<br>"GEN 41:45b(And Joseph went out over the land of Egypt)" repeats "GEN 41:46bAnd Joseph went out from the presence of Pharaoh, and went throughout all the land of Egypt." Presumably, R added it to make the narrative seem continuous after inserting the P text's "GEN 41:46aAnd Joseph was thirty years old when he stood before Pharaoh king of Egypt." It is common for R to add this sort of repetition around inserted passages.<br>**J Text**<br>There is a gap in the J text, which |
| [ used more than once ] | " quoting older text " |

| **E** | **J** |
|---|---|
| And Pharaoh awoke, and, behold, it was a dream. | |

And Pharaoh awoke, and, behold, it was a dream.

[8]And it came to pass in the morning that his spirit was troubled; and he sent and called for all the magicians of Egypt, and all the wise men thereof; and Pharaoh told them his dream; but there was none that could interpret them unto Pharaoh.

[9]Then spoke the chief butler unto Pharaoh, saying: 'I make mention of my faults this day: [10]Pharaoh was wroth with his servants, and put me in the ward of the house of the captain of the guard, me and the chief baker. [11]And we dreamed a dream in one night, I and he; we dreamed each man according to the interpretation of his dream. [12]And there was with us there a young man, a Hebrew, servant to the captain of the guard; and we told him, and he interpreted to us our dreams; to each man according to his dream he did interpret. [13]And it came to pass, as he interpreted to us, so it was: I was restored unto mine office, and he was hanged.'

[14]Then Pharaoh sent and called Joseph, and they brought him hastily out of the dungeon. And he shaved himself, and changed his raiment, and came in unto Pharaoh. [15]And Pharaoh said unto Joseph: 'I have dreamed a dream, and there is none that can interpret it; and I have heard say of thee, that when thou hearest a dream thou canst interpret it.' [16]And Joseph answered Pharaoh, saying: 'It is not in me; God will give Pharaoh an answer of peace.'

[17]And Pharaoh spoke unto Joseph: 'In my dream, behold, I stood upon the brink of the river. [18]And, behold, there came up out of the river seven kine, fat-fleshed and well-favoured; and they fed in the reed-grass. [19]And, behold, seven other kine came up after them, poor and very ill-favoured and lean-fleshed, such as I never saw in all the land of Egypt for badness. [20]And the lean and ill-favoured kine did eat up the first seven fat kine. [21]And when they had eaten them up, it could not be known that they had eaten them; but they were still ill-favoured as at the beginning. So I awoke. [22]And I saw in my dream, and, behold, seven ears came up upon one stalk, full and good. [23]And, behold, seven ears, withered, thin,

*[Continued on p. 188]*

| ( added by redactor ) | { problematic } |
|---|---|

| P | Notes |
|---|---|
| | must have originally described Joseph counseling Pharaoh. From what comes before in J, Potiphar must have recommended Joseph to Pharaoh as a manager because of Joseph's success in managing his household. From what comes after in J, Joseph must have managed the distribution of food during the famine in J, as in E. |
| ***[Gap in P: Joseph Brings His Father and Brothers to Egypt]*** | Presumably, RJE left out J's version of this story because he preferred E's version. |
| | **E Text versus P Text** |
| | Notice the difference in the timeline in E and P. |
| | In E, Joseph presumably was thrown in prison shortly after being bought by Potiphar, and he remained in prison "GEN 41:1... two full years..." before he counseled Pharaoh. |
| | In P, Joseph was 17 years old when he quarreled with his brothers (Gen. 37:2) and was 30 years old when he counseled Pharaoh (Gen. 41:46)— thirteen years rather than two. |
| [ used more than once ] | " quoting older text " |

*The Bible Untangled*

| **E** | **J** |
|---|---|
| and blasted with the east wind, sprung up after them. [24]And the thin ears swallowed up the seven good ears. And I told it unto the magicians; but there was none that could declare it to me.' | |

[25]And Joseph said unto Pharaoh: 'The dream of Pharaoh is one; what God is about to do He hath declared unto Pharaoh. [26]The seven good kine are seven years; and the seven good ears are seven years: the dream is one. [27]And the seven lean and ill-favoured kine that came up after them are seven years, and also the seven empty ears blasted with the east wind; they shall be seven years of famine. [28]That is the thing which I spoke unto Pharaoh: what God is about to do He hath shown unto Pharaoh. [29]Behold, there come seven years of great plenty throughout all the land of Egypt. [30]And there shall arise after them seven years of famine; and all the plenty shall be forgotten in the land of Egypt; and the famine shall consume the land; [31]and the plenty shall not be known in the land by reason of that famine which followeth; for it shall be very grievous. [32]And for that the dream was doubled unto Pharaoh twice, it is because the thing is established by God, and God will shortly bring it to pass. [33]Now therefore let Pharaoh look out a man discreet and wise, and set him over the land of Egypt. [34]Let Pharaoh do this, and let him appoint overseers over the land, and take up the fifth part of the land of Egypt in the seven years of plenty. [35]And let them gather all the food of these good years that come, and lay up corn under the hand of Pharaoh for food in the cities, and let them keep it. [36]And the food shall be for a store to the land against the seven years of famine, which shall be in the land of Egypt; that the land perish not through the famine.'

[37]And the thing was good in the eyes of Pharaoh, and in the eyes of all his servants. [38]And Pharaoh said unto his servants: 'Can we find such a one as this, a man in whom the spirit of God is?' [39]And Pharaoh said unto Joseph: 'Forasmuch as God hath shown thee all this, there is none so discreet and wise as thou. [40]Thou shalt be over my house, and according unto thy word shall all my people be ruled; only in

*[Continued on p. 188]*

( added by redactor )          { problematic }

| **P** | **Notes** |
|---|---|
| *[Continued on p. 203]* | *[Continued on p. 189]* |
| [ used more than once ] | " quoting older text " |

| **E** | **J** |
|---|---|
| the throne will I be greater than thou.' <sup></sup>⁴¹And Pharaoh said unto Joseph: 'See, I have set thee over all the land of Egypt.' ⁴²And Pharaoh took off his signet ring from his hand, and put it upon Joseph's hand, and arrayed him in vestures of fine linen, and put a gold chain about his neck. ⁴³And he made him to ride in the second chariot which he had; and they cried before him: 'Abrech'; and he set him over all the land of Egypt. ⁴⁴And Pharaoh said unto Joseph: 'I am Pharaoh, and without thee shall no man lift up his hand or his foot in all the land of Egypt.' ⁴⁵And Pharaoh called Joseph's name Zaphenath-paneah; and he gave him to wife Asenath the daughter of Poti-phera priest of On. (And Joseph went out over the land of Egypt.) ⁴⁶ᵇAnd Joseph went out from the presence of Pharaoh, and went throughout all the land of Egypt. ⁴⁷And in the seven years of plenty the earth brought forth in heaps. ⁴⁸And he gathered up all the food of the seven years which were in the land of Egypt, and laid up the food in the cities; the food of the field, which was round about every city, laid he up in the same. ⁴⁹And Joseph laid up corn as the sand of the sea, very much, until they left off numbering; for it was without number. ⁵⁰And unto Joseph were born two sons before the year of famine came, whom Asenath the daughter of Poti-phera priest of On bore unto him. ⁵¹And Joseph called the name of the first-born Manasseh: 'for God hath made me forget all my toil, and all my father's house.' ⁵²And the name of the second called he Ephraim: 'for God hath made me fruitful in the land of my affliction.' ⁵³And the seven years of plenty, that was in the land of Egypt, came to an end. ⁵⁴And the seven years of famine began to come, according as Joseph had said; and there was famine in all lands; but in all the land of Egypt there was bread. ⁵⁵And when all the land of Egypt was famished, the people cried to Pharaoh for bread; and Pharaoh said unto all the Egyptians: 'Go unto Joseph; what he saith to you, do.' ⁵⁶And the famine was over all the face of the earth; and Jo- | *[Continued on p. 188]* |
| ( added by redactor ) | { problematic } |

| P | Notes |
|---|---|
| | |
| *[Continued on p. 203]* | *[Continued on p. 189]* |
| | |
| [ used more than once ] | " quoting older text " |

*[Continued on p. 203]*

*[Continued on p. 189]*

| **E** | **J** |
|---|---|

seph opened all the store-houses, and sold unto the Egyptians; and the famine was sore in the land of Egypt. [57]And all countries came into Egypt to Joseph to buy corn; because the famine was sore in all the earth.

### Joseph's Brothers Buy Grain

GEN 42:2And he *[Jacob]* said: 'Behold, I have heard that there is corn in Egypt. Get you down thither, and buy for us from thence; that we may live, and not die.'

[5]And the sons of Israel came to buy among those that came; for the famine was in the land of Caanan. [6]And Joseph was the governor over the land; he it was that sold to all the people of the land. And Joseph's brethren came, and bowed down to him with their faces to the earth. [7b]and he spoke roughly with them; [8]And Joseph knew his brethren, but they knew him not. [9a]And Joseph remembered the dreams which he dreamed of them,

[17]And he put them all together into ward three days. [18]And Joseph said unto them the third day.' This do, and live; for I fear God: [19]if ye be upright men, let one of your brethren be bound in your prison-house; but go ye, carry corn for the famine of your houses; [20b]And they did so. [21]And they said one to another: 'We are verily guilty concerning our brother, in that we saw the distress of his soul, when he besought us, and we would not hear; therefore is this distress come upon us.'

### Joseph's Brothers Buy Grain

GEN 42:1Now Jacob saw that there was corn in Egypt, and Jacob said unto his sons: 'Why do ye look one upon another?' [3]And Joseph's ten brethren went down to buy corn from Egypt. [4]But Benjamin, Joseph's brother, Jacob sent not with his brethren; for he said: 'Lest peradventure harm befall him.'

[7a]And Joseph saw his brethren, and he knew them, but made himself strange unto them, [7c]And he said unto them: 'Whence come ye?' And they said: 'From the land of Canaan to buy food.'

[9b]And he said unto them: 'Ye are spies; to see the nakedness of the land ye are come.' [10]And they said unto him: 'Nay, my lord, but to buy food are thy servants come. [11]We are all one man's sons; we are upright men, thy servants are no spies.' [12]And he said unto them: 'Nay, but to see the nakedness of the land ye are come.' [13]And they said: 'We thy servants are twelve brethren, the sons of one man in the land of Canaan; and, behold, the youngest is this day with our father, and one is not.' [14]And Joseph said unto them: 'That is it that I spoke unto you, saying: Ye are spies. [15]Hereby

| ( added by redactor ) | { problematic } |
|---|---|

| P | Notes |
|---|---|
| | |

**Notes**

**Joseph's Brothers Buy Grain**
**Separating the Texts**

This edition divides this story into two texts.

In the E text, there is a more matter-of-fact story: Joseph takes Simeon as hostage when his brothers come to buy grain. His brothers bring Joseph presents. Joseph reveals his identity, forgives them, and says it was God's will that he go to Egypt to save the family, rather than being their fault. He repeats this theological explanation later in the E text (Gen. 50:19).

In the J text, there is a more melodramatic story. Joseph makes it look like his brothers cheated him and demands that they bring Benjamin. This story includes J's characteristic technique of heightening the suspense through repetition: Joseph pulls a similar trick by putting silver in his brothers' bags twice, with the second time worse than the first because he also puts a silver goblet in Benjamin's bag.

This story obviously came from two texts, because it has repetitions, which the division in this edition resolve. For example, the received text tells us twice that Joseph knew his brothers but they did not know

*[Continued on p. 203]*

| [ used more than once ] | " quoting older text " |
|---|---|

| **E** | **J** |
|---|---|
| [22]And Reuben answered them, saying: 'Spoke I not unto you, saying: Do not sin against the child; and ye would not hear? therefore also, behold, his blood is required.' [23]And they knew not that Joseph understood them; for the interpreter was between them. [24]And he turned himself about from them, and wept; and he returned to them, and spoke to them, and took Simeon from among them, and bound him before their eyes.<br><br>[28b]And they turned trembling one to another, saying: 'What is this that God hath done unto us?' [[29]And they came unto Jacob their father unto the land of Canaan, and told him all that had befallen them, saying: [30]'The man, the lord of the land,] spoke roughly with us, and [said unto us:] [33b]leave one of | ye shall be proved, as Pharaoh liveth, ye shall not go forth hence, except your youngest brother come hither. [16]Send one of you, and let him fetch your brother, and ye shall be bound, that your words may be proved, whether there be truth in you; or else, as Pharaoh liveth, surely ye are spies. [20a]And bring your youngest brother unto me; so shall your words be verified, and ye shall not die.'<br>[25]Then Joseph commanded to fill their vessels with corn, and to restore every man's money into his sack *[saq]*, and to give them provision for the way; and thus was it done unto them. [26]And they laded their asses with their corn, and departed thence. [27]And as one of them opened his sack *[saq]* to give his ass provender in the lodging-place, he espied his money; and, behold, it was in the mouth of his sack *[amtahat]*. [28a]And he said unto his brethren: 'My money is restored; and, lo, it is even in my sack *[amtahat]*.' And their heart failed them,<br>[[29]And they came unto Jacob their father unto the land of Canaan, and told him all that had befallen them, saying: [30]'The man, the lord of the land,] took us for spies of the country. [31]And we said unto him: We are upright men; we are no spies. [32]We are twelve brethren, sons of our father; one is not, and the youngest is this day with our father in the land of Canaan. [33]And the man, the lord of the land, [said unto us:] Hereby shall I know that ye are upright men: [take corn for the famine of your houses, and go your way.] [34]And bring your youngest brother unto me; then shall I know that ye are no spies, but that ye are upright men; so (will I deliver you your brother, and) ye shall traffic in the land.'<br>[35]And it came to pass as they emptied their sacks *[saq]*, that, behold, every man's bundle of money was in his sack *[saq]*; and when they and their father saw their bundles of money, they were afraid.<br>[[36a]And Jacob their father said unto them: 'Me have ye bereaved of my children: Joseph is not,] [36c]And ye will take Benjamin away; upon me are all these things come.' [37]And (Reuben) *[Judah]* spoke unto his father, saying: 'Thou shalt slay my two sons, if I |
| ( added by redactor ) | { problematic } |

| P | Notes |
|---|---|
| *[Continued on p. 203]* | him, that Joseph tells his brothers he is Joseph, and that Joseph asks about how their father is. To resolve the repetition, this edition puts the following in E: <br> GEN 42:7And Joseph saw his brethren, and he knew them, but made himself strange unto them, ... <br> GEN 45:3And Joseph said unto his brethren: 'I am Joseph; doth my father yet live?' <br> And it puts the following in J: <br> GEN 42:8And Joseph knew his brethren, but they knew him not. GEN 45:27And he asked them of their welfare, and said: 'Is your father well, the old man of whom ye spoke? Is he yet alive?' <br> GEN 45:4And he [Joseph] said: 'I am Joseph your brother, whom ye sold into Egypt. <br> This division assumes that, in some cases, RJE removed some brief passages from one of the text because it was repetitious, and so it duplicates some brief passages in both texts, putting them in square brackets. <br> However, this division has a few problems. <br> At one point, this division makes Reuben is a hero among the brothers in J: "GEN 42:37And {Reuben} spoke unto his father, saying: 'Thou shalt slay my two sons, if I bring him not to thee; deliver him into my hand, and I will bring him back to thee.'" Generally, Reuben is the hero in E and Judah in the J version of this story. The only way to eliminate this problem is to put the story of Joseph demanding Benjamin in E, which does not seem possible. For |
| [ used more than once ] | " quoting older text " |

*[Continued on p. 203]*

| E | J |
|---|---|
| your brethren with me, and [take corn for the famine of your houses, and go your way.]<br><br>[³⁶ᵃAnd Jacob their father said unto them: 'Me have ye bereaved of my children: Joseph is not,] ³⁶ᵇAnd Simeon is not.<br><br>[ᴳᴱᴺ ⁴³ˑ¹And the famine was sore in the land. ²And it came to pass, when they had eaten up the corn which they had brought out of Egypt, that their father said unto them: 'Go again, buy us a little food.'] ¹¹ᵇTake of the choice fruits of the land in your vessels, and carry down the man a present, a little balm, and a little honey, spicery and ladanum, nuts, and almonds; ¹⁴ᵃAnd God Almighty give you mercy before the man, that he may release unto you your other brother (and Benjamin). | bring him not to thee; deliver him into my hand, and I will bring him back to thee.' ³⁸And he said: 'My son shall not go down with you; for his brother is dead, and he only is left; if harm befall him by the way in which ye go, then will ye bring down my gray hairs with sorrow to the grave.<br><br>[ᴳᴱᴺ ⁴³ˑ¹And the famine was sore in the land. ²And it came to pass, when they had eaten up the corn which they had brought out of Egypt, that their father said unto them: 'Go again, buy us a little food.'] ³And Judah spoke unto him, saying: 'The man did earnestly forewarn us, saying: Ye shall not see my face, except your brother be with you. ⁴If thou wilt send our brother with us, we will go down and buy thee food; ⁵But if thou wilt not send him, we will not go down, for the man said unto us: Ye shall not see my face, except your brother be with you.' ⁶And Israel said: 'Wherefore dealt ye so ill with me, as to tell the man whether ye had yet a brother?' ⁷And they said: 'The man asked straitly concerning ourselves, and concerning our kindred, saying: Is your father yet alive? have ye another brother? and we told him according to the tenor of these words; could we in any wise know that he would say: Bring your brother down?' ⁸And Judah said unto Israel his father: 'Send the lad with me, and we will arise and go, that we may live, and not die, both we, and thou, and also our little ones. ⁹I will be surety for him; of my hand shalt thou require him; if I bring him not unto thee, and set him before thee, then let me bear the blame for ever. ¹⁰For except we had lingered, surely we had now returned a second time.'<br><br>¹¹ᵃAnd their father Israel said unto them: 'If it be so now, do this: ¹²(and) take double money in your hand; and the money that was returned in the mouth of your sacks *[amtahat]* carry back in your hand; peradventure it was an oversight; ¹³take also your brother, and arise, go again unto the man; ¹⁴ᵇAnd as for me, if I be bereaved of my children, I am bereaved.'<br><br>¹⁵... They took double money in their hand, and Benjamin; and rose up, and [went down to Egypt] and stood before Joseph.<br><br>[¹⁶And] when [Joseph] saw Benjamin with them, |

| ( added by redactor ) | { problematic } |
|---|---|

| P | Notes |
|---|---|

example, Genesis 46:3, which we just looked at, is part of the story of Joseph demanding Benjamin, and it is clearly from the J text because it makes Judah the hero.

In the J text, "GEN 42:34will I deliver you your brother" seems to refer to the E story, where a brother is left as hostage. We have to assume that RJE added this to make the J story more consistent with the E story.

In the E text, this division also forces us to move "GEN 43:23bAnd he brought Simeon out unto them" so it is after Genesis 45:3, in order to make the E text coherent.

There are also problems in the received text of the Bible:

There is no previous mention of the brothers giving money before "GEN 42:25Then Joseph commanded to fill their vessels with corn, and to restore every man's money into his sack."

There is no previous mention of Joseph asking these questions before the brothers tell Jacob: "GEN 43:7... The man asked straitly concerning ourselves, and concerning our kindred, saying: Is your father yet alive? have ye another brother?"

These problems in the received text seem to indicate that RJE made extensive changes to reconcile the J and E texts, which may also have caused the problems in this edition's division of the two texts as well as the problems in the received text.

**Translation**

E text: the JPS translation says, "GEN 42:7band spoke roughly with them." This edition changes it to

*[Continued on p. 203]*
*[Continued on p. 203]*

| [ used more than once ] | " quoting older text " |
|---|---|

| **E** | **J** |
|---|---|
| [¹⁵And the men took] that present, and [went down to Egypt,] [¹⁶And ... Joseph ... said to the steward of his house: 'Bring the men into the house,] | he [said to the steward of his house: 'Bring the men into the house,] and kill the beasts, and prepare the meat; for the men shall dine with me at noon.' ¹⁷And the man did as Joseph bade; and the man brought the men into Joseph's house. |
| ²⁴And the man brought the men into Joseph's house, and gave them water, and they washed their feet; and he gave their asses provender. ²⁵And they made ready the present against Joseph's coming at noon; for they heard that they should eat bread there. ²⁶And when Joseph came home, they brought him the present which was in their hand into the house, and bowed down to him to the earth. ²³ᵇAnd he brought Simeon out unto them. [ᴳᴱᴺ ⁴⁵:⁴And Joseph said .... 'I am Joseph your brother, whom ye sold into Egypt.] ⁵And now be not grieved, nor angry | ¹⁸And the men were afraid, because they were brought into Joseph's house; and they said: 'Because of the money that was returned in our sacks *[amtahat]* at the first time are we brought in; that he may seek occasion against us, and fall upon us, and take us for bondmen, and our asses.' ¹⁹And they came near to the steward of Joseph's house, and they spoke unto him at the door of the house, ²⁰and said: 'Oh my lord, we came indeed down at the first time to buy food. ²¹And it came to pass, when we came to the lodging-place, that we opened our sacks *[amtahat]*, and, behold, every man's money was in the mouth of his sack *[amtahat]*, our money in full weight; and we have brought it back in our hand. ²²And other money have we brought down in our hand to buy food. We know not who put our money in our sacks *[amtahat]*.' ²³And he said: 'Peace be to you, fear not; your God, and the God of your father, hath given you treasure in your sacks *[amtahat]*; I had your money.' ²⁷And [Joseph] he asked them of their welfare, and said: 'Is your father well, the old man of whom ye spoke?' ²⁸And they said: 'Thy servant our father is well, he is yet alive.' And they bowed the head, and made obeisance. ²⁹And he lifted up his eyes, and saw Benjamin his brother, his mother's son, and said: 'Is this your youngest brother of whom ye spoke unto me?' And he said: 'God be gracious unto thee, my son.' ³⁰And Joseph made haste; for his heart yearned toward his brother; and he sought where to weep; and he entered into his chamber, and wept there. ³¹And he washed his face, and came out; and he refrained himself, and said: 'Set on bread.' ³²And they set on for him by himself, and for them by themselves, and for the Egyptians, that did eat with him, by themselves; because the Egyptians might not eat bread with the Hebrews; for that is an abomination unto the Egyptians. ³³And they sat before him, the |
| ( added by redactor ) | { problematic } |

| P | Notes |
|---|---|
| | [7b]and he spoke roughly with them." Biblical Hebrew does not use the pronoun, so this translation is just as accurate. |
| | J Text: The JPS translation says "[GEN 42:9b]And said unto them: 'Ye are spies;'" This edition translates it as "And he said unto them: 'Ye are spies;'" Again, Biblical Hebrew does not use the pronoun, so this translation is just as accurate. |
| *[Continued on p. 203]* | |
| [ used more than once ] | " quoting older text " |

*[Continued on p. 203]*

| **E** | **J** |
|---|---|
| with yourselves, that ye sold me hither; for God did send me before you to preserve life. ⁶For these two years hath the famine been in the land; and there are yet five years, in which there shall be neither plowing nor harvest. ⁷And God sent me before you to give you a remnant on the earth, and to save you alive for a great deliverance. ⁸So now it was not you that sent me hither, but God; and He hath made me a father to Pharaoh, and lord of all his house, and ruler over all the land of Egypt. ⁹Hasten ye, and go up to my father, and say unto him: Thus saith thy son Joseph: God hath made me lord of all Egypt; come down unto me, tarry not. ¹⁰And thou shalt dwell in the land of Goshen, and thou shalt be near unto me, thou, and thy chil- | first-born according to his birthright, and the youngest according to his youth; and the men marvelled one with another. ³⁴And portions were taken unto them from before him; but Benjamin's portion was five times so much as any of theirs. And they drank, and were merry with him. <br><br> GEN 44:1 And he commanded the steward of his house, saying: 'Fill the men's sacks *[amtahat]* with food, as much as they can carry, and put every man's money in his sack's *[amtahat]* mouth. ²And put my goblet, the silver goblet, in the sack's *[amtahat]* mouth of the youngest, and his corn money.' And he did according to the word that Joseph had spoken. ³As soon as the morning was light, the men were sent away, they and their asses. <br><br> ⁴And when they were gone out of the city, and were not yet far off, Joseph said unto his steward: 'Up, follow after the men; and when thou dost overtake them, say unto them: Wherefore have ye rewarded evil for good? ⁵Is not this it in which my lord drinketh, and whereby he indeed divineth? ye have done evil in so doing.' ⁶And he overtook them, and he spoke unto them these words. <br><br> ⁷And they said unto him: 'Wherefore speaketh my lord such words as these? Far be it from thy servants that they should do such a thing. ⁸Behold, the money, which we found in our sacks' *[amtahat]* mouths, we brought back unto thee out of the land of Canaan; how then should we steal out of thy lord's house silver or gold? ⁹With whomsoever of thy servants it be found, let him die, and we also will be my lord's bondmen.' <br><br> ¹⁰And he said: 'Now also let it be according unto your words: he with whom it is found shall be my bondman; and ye shall be blameless.' ¹¹Then they hastened, and took down every man his sack *[amtahat]* to the ground, and opened every man his sack *[amtahat]*. ¹²And he searched, beginning at the eldest, and leaving off at the youngest; and the goblet was found in Benjamin's sack *[amtahat]*. ¹³And they rent their clothes, and laded every man his ass, and returned to the city. |

( added by redactor )                                    { problematic }

| P | Notes |
|---|---|
| *[Continued on p. 203]* | *[Continued on p. 203]* |
| [ used more than once ] | " quoting older text " |

| **E** | **J** |
|---|---|
| dren, and thy children's children, and thy flocks, and thy herds, and all that thou hast; [11]and there will I sustain thee; for there are yet five years of famine; lest thou come to poverty, thou, and thy household, and all that thou hast. | [14]And Judah and his brethren came to Joseph's house, and he was yet there; and they fell before him on the ground. [15]And Joseph said unto them: 'What deed is this that ye have done? know ye not that such a man as I will indeed divine?' [16]And Judah said: 'What shall we say unto my lord? what shall we speak? or how shall we clear ourselves? God hath found out the iniquity of thy servants; behold, we are my lord's bondmen, both we, and he also in whose hand the cup is found.' [17]And he said: 'Far be it from me that I should do so; the man in whose hand the goblet is found, he shall be my bondman; but as for you, get you up in peace unto your father.' [18]Then Judah came near unto him, and said: 'Oh my lord, let thy servant, I pray thee, speak a word in my lord's ears, and let not thine anger burn against thy servant; for thou art even as Pharaoh. [19]My lord asked his servants, saying: Have ye a father, or a brother? [20]And we said unto my lord: We have a father, an old man, and a child of his old age, a little one; and his brother is dead, and he alone is left of his mother, and his father loveth him. [21]And thou saidst unto thy servants: Bring him down unto me, that I may set mine eyes upon him. [22]And we said unto my lord: The lad cannot leave his father; for if he should leave his father, his father would die. [23]And thou saidst unto thy servants: Except your youngest brother come down with you, ye shall see my face no more. [24]And it came to pass when we came up unto thy servant my father, we told him the words of my lord. [25]And our father said: Go again, buy us a little food. [26]And we said: We cannot go down; if our youngest brother be with us, then will we go down; for we may not see the man's face, except our youngest brother be with us. [27]And thy servant my father said unto us: Ye know that my wife bore me two sons; [28]and the one went out from me, and I said: Surely he is torn in pieces; and I have not seen him since; [29]and if ye take this one also from me, and harm befall him, ye will bring down my gray hairs with sorrow to the grave. [30]Now therefore when I come to thy servant my father, and the lad is not |

( added by redactor )                              { problematic }

| P | Notes |
|---|---|
| | |
| *[Continued on p. 203]* | *[Continued on p. 203]* |
| | |
| [ used more than once ] | " quoting older text " |

| **E** | **J** |
|---|---|
| | with us; seeing that his soul is bound up with the lad's soul; [31]it will come to pass, when he seeth that the lad is not with us, that he will die; and thy servants will bring down the gray hairs of thy servant our father with sorrow to the grave. [32]For thy servant became surety for the lad unto my father, saying: If I bring him not unto thee, then shall I bear the blame to my father for ever. [33]Now therefore, let thy servant, I pray thee, abide instead of the lad a bondman to my lord; and let the lad go up with his brethren. [34]For how shall I go up to my father, if the lad be not with me? lest I look upon the evil that shall come on my father.'|
| | GEN 45:1Then Joseph could not refrain himself before all them that stood by him; and he cried: 'Cause every man to go out from me.' And there stood no man with him, while Joseph made himself known unto his brethren. [2]And he wept aloud; and the Egyptians heard, and the house of Pharaoh heard. [[4]And Joseph said] unto his brethren: 'Come near to me, I pray you.' And they came near. And he said: ['I am Joseph your brother, whom ye sold into Egypt.] [12]And, behold, your eyes see, and the eyes of my brother Benjamin, that it is my mouth that speaketh unto you. [13]And ye shall tell my father of all my glory in Egypt, and of all that ye have seen; and ye shall hasten and bring down my father hither.' [14]And he fell upon his brother Benjamin's neck, and wept; and Benjamin wept upon his neck. [15]And he kissed all his brethren, and wept upon them; and after that his brethren talked with him. |
| *[Continued on p. 202]* | [16]And the report thereof was heard in Pharaoh's house, saying: 'Joseph's brethren are come'; and it pleased Pharaoh well, and his servants. [17]And Pharaoh said unto Joseph: 'Say unto thy brethren: This do ye: lade your beasts, and go, get you unto the land of Canaan; [18]and take your father and your households, and come unto me; and I will give you the good of the land of Egypt, and ye shall eat the fat of the land. [19]Now thou art commanded, this do ye: take you wagons out of the land of Egypt for your little ones, and for your wives, and bring your father, and come. [20]Also regard not your stuff; for the good things of all the land of Egypt are yours.' |
| ( added by redactor ) | { problematic } |

*[Continued on p. 202]*

| P | Notes |
|---|---|
| | |
| *[Continued on p. 203]* | *[Continued on p. 203]* |
| | |
| [ used more than once ] | " quoting older text " |

| **E** | **J** |
|---|---|
| | [21]And the sons of Israel did so; and Joseph gave them wagons, according to the commandment of Pharaoh, and gave them provision for the way. [22]To all of them he gave each man changes of raiment; but to Benjamin he gave three hundred shekels of silver, and five changes of raiment. [23]And to his father he sent in like manner ten asses laden with the good things of Egypt, and ten she-asses laden with corn and bread and victual for his father by the way. [24]So he sent his brethren away, and they departed; and he said unto them: 'See that ye fall not out by the way.' |
| | [25]And they went up out of Egypt, and came into the land of Canaan unto Jacob their father. [26]And they told him, saying: 'Joseph is yet alive, and he is ruler over all the land of Egypt.' And his heart fainted, for he believed them not. [27]And they told him all the words of Joseph, which he had said unto them; and when he saw the wagons which Joseph had sent to carry him, the spirit of Jacob their father revived. [28]And Israel said: 'It is enough; Joseph my son is yet alive; I will go and see him before I die.' |
| **Israel Goes to Egypt** | **Israel Goes to Egypt** |
| GEN 46:1 And Israel took his journey with all that he had, and came to Beer-sheba, and offered sacrifices unto the God of his father Isaac. [2]And God spoke unto Israel in the visions of the night, and said: 'Jacob, Jacob.' And he said: 'Here am I.' [3]And He said: 'I am God, the God of thy father; fear not | GEN 46:5b And the sons of Israel carried Jacob their father, and their little ones, and their wives, in the wagons which Pharaoh had sent to carry him. [6a]And they took their cattle, and their goods, which they had gotten in the land of Canaan, |
| | [28]And he sent Judah before him unto Joseph, to show the way before him unto Goshen; and they came into the land of Goshen. [29]And Joseph made ready his chariot, and went up to meet Israel his father, to Goshen; and he presented himself unto him, and fell on his neck, and wept on his neck a good while. [30]And Israel said unto Joseph: 'Now let me die, since I have seen thy face, that thou art yet alive.' |
| | [31]And Joseph said unto his brethren, and unto his father's house: 'I will go up, and tell Pharaoh, and will say unto him: My brethren, and my father's house, who were in the land of Canaan, are come unto me; [32]and the men are shepherds, for they have been keep- |
| ( added by redactor ) | { problematic } |

| P | Notes |
|---|---|
| **Israel Goes to Egypt** | **Israel Goes to Egypt** |

**P**

### Israel Goes to Egypt

GEN 46:8And these are the names of the children of Israel, who came into Egypt, Jacob and his sons: Reuben, Jacob's first-born. ⁹And the sons of Reuben: Hanoch, and Pallu, and Hezron, and Carmi. ¹⁰And the sons of Simeon: Jemuel, and Jamin, and Ohad, and Jachin, and Zohar, and Shaul the son of a Canaanitish woman. ¹¹And the sons of Levi: Gershon, Kohath, and Merari. ¹²And the sons of Judah: Er, and Onan, and Shelah, and Perez, and Zerah; but Er and Onan died in the land of Canaan. And the sons of Perez were Hezron and Hamul. ¹³And the sons of Issachar: Tola, and Puvah, and Iob, and Shimron. ¹⁴And the

**Notes**

### Israel Goes to Egypt

**E Text**

"GEN 46:2And God spoke unto Israel in the visions of the night." Presumably, "visions of the night" is another way of referring to dreams. As usual in E, God appears to everyone except Moses in visions or dreams.

**J Text**

Genesis 47:13 ff., J adds an origin myth that makes Joseph's efficient management the origin of serfdom in Egypt.

**P Text**

P continues the timeline by giving Jacob's age when he came to Egypt. In P, the only question that Pharaoh asks Jacob is his age. It is unlikely that this would actually be the one

[ used more than once ]     " quoting older text "

| **E** | **J** |
|---|---|

to go down into Egypt; for I will there make of thee a great nation. ⁴I will go down with thee into Egypt; and I will also surely bring thee up again; and Joseph shall put his hand upon thine eyes.'

⁵ᵃAnd Jacob rose up from Beersheba; ⁶ᵇAnd came into Egypt, Jacob, and all his seed with him; ⁷his sons, and his sons' sons with him, his daughters, and his sons' daughters, and all his seed brought he with him into Egypt.

ers of cattle; and they have brought their flocks, and their herds, and all that they have. ³³And it shall come to pass, when Pharaoh shall call you, and shall say: What is your occupation? ³⁴that ye shall say: Thy servants have been keepers of cattle from our youth even until now, both we, and our fathers; that ye may dwell in the land of Goshen; for every shepherd is an abomination unto the Egyptians.'

GEN 47:1Then Joseph went in and told Pharaoh, and said: 'My father and my brethren, and their flocks, and their herds, and all that they have, are come out of the land of Canaan; and, behold, they are in the land of Goshen.' ²And from among his brethren he took five men, and presented them unto Pharaoh. ³And Pharaoh said unto his brethren: 'What is your occupation?' And they said unto Pharaoh: 'Thy servants are shepherds, both we, and our fathers.' ⁴And they said unto Pharaoh: 'To sojourn in the land are we come; for there is no pasture for thy servants' flocks; for the famine is sore in the land of Canaan. Now therefore, we pray thee, let thy servants dwell in the land of Goshen.' ⁵And Pharaoh spoke unto Joseph, saying: 'Thy father and thy brethren are come unto thee; ⁶the land of Egypt is before thee; in the best of the land make thy father and thy brethren to dwell; in the land of Goshen let them dwell. And if thou knowest any able men among them, then make them rulers over my cattle.

¹³And there was no bread in all the land; for the famine was very sore, so that the land of Egypt and the land of Canaan languished by reason of the famine. ¹⁴And Joseph gathered up all the money that was found in the land of Egypt, and in the land of Canaan, for the corn which they bought; and Joseph brought the money into Pharaoh's house. ¹⁵And when the money was all spent in the land of Egypt, and in the land of Canaan, all the Egyptians came unto Joseph, and said: 'Give us bread; for why should we die in thy presence? for our money faileth.' ¹⁶And Joseph said: 'Give your cattle, and I will give you bread for your cattle, if money fail.' ¹⁷And they brought their cattle unto Joseph. And Joseph gave them bread in

| ( added by redactor ) | { problematic } |

| P | Notes |
|---|---|

sons of Zebulun: Sered, and Elon, and Jahleel. [15]These are the sons of Leah, whom she bore unto Jacob in Paddan-aram, with his daughter Dinah; all the souls of his sons and his daughters were thirty and three.

[16]And the sons of Gad: Ziphion, and Haggi, Shuni, and Ezbon, Eri, and Arodi, and Areli. [17]And the sons of Asher: Imnah, and Ishvah, and Ishvi, and Beriah, and Serah their sister; and the sons of Beriah: Heber, and Malchiel. [18]These are the sons of Zilpah, whom Laban gave to Leah his daughter, and these she bore unto Jacob, even sixteen souls.

[19]The sons of Rachel Jacob's wife: Joseph and Benjamin. [20]And unto Joseph in the land of Egypt were born Manasseh and Ephraim, whom Asenath the daughter of Poti-phera priest of On bore unto him. [21]And the sons of Benjamin: Bela, and Becher, and Ashbel, Gera, and Naaman, Ehi, and Rosh, Muppim, and Huppim, and Ard. [22]These are the sons of Rachel, who were born to Jacob; all the souls were fourteen.

[23]And the sons of Dan: Hushim. [24]And the sons of Naphtali: Jahzeel, and Guni, and Jezer, and Shillem. [25]These are the sons of Bilhah, whom Laban gave unto Rachel his daughter, and these she bore unto Jacob; all the souls were seven.

[26]All the souls belonging to Jacob that came into Egypt, that came out of his loins, besides Jacob's sons' wives, all the souls were threescore and six. [27]And the sons of Joseph, who were born to him in Egypt, were two souls; all the souls of

thing Pharaoh would discuss when he sees Jacob, but it is essential to P's timeline. At this point, the timeline changes: previously, it was based on the age of fathers when their eldest sons were born, but from now on, it is based on the time Israel is in Egypt and is in the desert, connected with the earlier part of the timeline by Jacob's age when he came to Egypt. See Appendix 1.

With his usual pedantic attention to detail, P lists the names of all those who went to Egypt with Israel.

**E and J versus P**

Pharaoh has Israel dwell in the land of Goshen according to E (Gen. 45:10) and J (Gen. 47:6), but Pharaoh has them dwell in the land of Ramses according to P (Gen. 47:11).

| [ used more than once ] | " quoting older text " |
|---|---|

| **E** | **J** |
|---|---|
| | exchange for the horses, and for the flocks, and for the herds, and for the asses; and he fed them with bread in exchange for all their cattle for that year. [18]And when that year was ended, they came unto him the second year, and said unto him: 'We will not hide from my lord, how that our money is all spent; and the herds of cattle are my lord's; there is nought left in the sight of my lord, but our bodies, and our lands. [19]Wherefore should we die before thine eyes, both we and our land? buy us and our land for bread, and we and our land will be bondmen unto Pharaoh; and give us seed, that we may live, and not die, and that the land be not desolate.' [20]So Joseph bought all the land of Egypt for Pharaoh; for the Egyptians sold every man his field, because the famine was sore upon them; and the land became Pharaoh's. [21]And as for the people, he removed them city by city, from one end of the border of Egypt even to the other end thereof. [22]Only the land of the priests bought he not, for the priests had a portion from Pharaoh, and did eat their portion which Pharaoh gave them; wherefore they sold not their land. |
| *[Continued on p. 208]* | [23]Then Joseph said unto the people: 'Behold, I have bought you this day and your land for Pharaoh. Lo, here is seed for you, and ye shall sow the land. [24]And it shall come to pass at the ingatherings, that ye shall give a fifth unto Pharaoh, and four parts shall be your own, for seed of the field, and for your food, and for them of your households, and for food for your little ones.' [25]And they said: 'Thou hast saved our lives. Let us find favour in the sight of my lord, and we will be Pharaoh's bondmen.' [26]And Joseph made it a statute concerning the land of Egypt unto this day, that Pharaoh should have the fifth; only the land of the priests alone became not Pharaoh's. |
| | [27]And Israel dwelt in the land of Egypt, in the land of Goshen; and they got them possessions therein, and were fruitful, and multiplied exceedingly. |
| | [29]And the time drew near that Israel must die; and he called his son Joseph, and said unto him: 'If now I have found favour in thy sight, put, I pray thee, thy hand under my thigh, and deal kindly and truly |
| ( added by redactor ) | { problematic } |

| P | Notes |
|---|---|
| the house of Jacob, that came into Egypt, were threescore and ten.<br><sup></sup>GEN 47:7And Joseph brought in Jacob his father, and set him before Pharaoh. And Jacob blessed Pharaoh. 8And Pharaoh said unto Jacob: 'How many are the days of the years of thy life?' 9And Jacob said unto Pharaoh: 'The days of the years of my sojournings are a hundred and thirty years; few and evil have been the days of the years of my life, and they have not attained unto the days of the years of the life of my fathers in the days of their sojournings.' 10And Jacob blessed Pharaoh, and went out from the presence of Pharaoh.<br>11And Joseph placed his father and his brethren, and gave them a possession in the land of Egypt, in the best of the land, in the land of Rameses, as Pharaoh had commanded. 12And Joseph sustained his father, and his brethren, and all his father's household, with bread, according to the want of their little ones.<br>28And Jacob lived in the land of Egypt seventeen years; so the days of Jacob, the years of his life, were a hundred forty and seven years. | *[Continued on p. 209]* |
| [ used more than once ] | " quoting older text " |

| **E** | **J** |
|---|---|
| | with me; bury me not, I pray thee, in Egypt. [30]But when I sleep with my fathers, thou shalt carry me out of Egypt, and bury me in their burying-place.' And he said: 'I will do as thou hast said.' [31]And he said: 'Swear unto me.' And he swore unto him. And Israel bowed down upon the bed's head. |
| **Jacob Blesses Ephraim and Menasseh** | **Jacob's Blesses His Sons** |
| GEN 48:1And it came to pass after these things, that one said to Joseph: 'Behold, thy father is sick.' And he took with him his two sons, Manasseh and Ephraim. [2]And one told Jacob, and said: 'Behold, thy son Joseph cometh unto thee.' And Israel strengthened himself, and sat upon the bed. [8]And Israel beheld Joseph's sons, and said: 'Who are these?' [9]And Joseph said unto his father: 'They are my sons, whom God hath given me here.' And he said: 'Bring them, I pray thee, unto me, and I will bless them.' [10]Now the eyes of Israel were dim for age, so that he could not see. And he brought them near unto him; and he kissed them, and embraced them. | GEN 49:1And Jacob called unto his sons, and said: 'Gather yourselves together, that I may tell you that which shall befall you in the end of days. "[2]Assemble yourselves, and hear, ye sons of Jacob; And hearken unto Israel your father. [3]Reuben, thou art my first-born, My might, and the first-fruits of my strength; The excellency of dignity, and the excellency of power. [4]Unstable as water, have not thou the excellency; Because thou wentest up to thy father's bed; Then defiledst thou it—he went up to my couch. [5]Simeon and Levi are brethren; Weapons of violence their kinship. [6]Let my soul not come into their council; Unto their assembly let my glory not be not united; For in their anger they slew men, And in their self-will they houghed oxen. [7]Cursed be their anger, for it was fierce, And their wrath, for it was cruel; I will divide them in Jacob, And scatter them in Israel. [8]Judah, thee shall thy brethren praise; Thy hand shall be on the neck of thine enemies; Thy father's sons shall bow down before thee. [9]Judah is a lion's whelp; From the prey, my son, thou art gone up. He stooped down, he couched as a lion, And as a lioness; who shall rouse him up? [10]The sceptre shall not depart from Judah, |
| ( added by redactor ) | { problematic } |

| P | Notes |
|---|---|
| **Jacob Legitimizes Ephraim and Menasseh** | **Jacob Blesses/Legitimizes** |

### Jacob Legitimizes Ephraim and Menasseh

" {GEN 48:3 And Jacob said unto Joseph: 'God Almighty appeared unto me at Luz in the land of Canaan, and blessed me, 4and said unto me: Behold, I will make thee fruitful, and multiply thee, and I will make of thee a company of peoples; and will give this land to thy seed after thee for an everlasting possession. 5And now thy two sons, who were born unto thee in the land of Egypt before I came unto thee into Egypt, are mine; Ephraim and Manasseh, even as Reuben and Simeon, shall be mine. 6And thy issue, that thou begettest after them, shall be thine; they shall be called after the name of their brethren in their inheritance. 7And as for me, when I came from Paddan, Rachel died unto me in the land of Canaan in the way, when there was still some way to come unto Ephrath; and I buried her there in the way to Ephrath—the same is Beth-lehem.'

GEN 49:29 And be charged them, and said unto them: 'I am to be gathered unto my people; bury me with my fathers in the cave that is in the field of Ephron the Hittite, 30in the cave that is in the field of Machpelah, which is before Mamre, in the land

### Jacob Blesses/Legitimizes

**E Text:**

Though Manasseh is the first born son of Joseph, this blessing of makes Ephraim the more powerful tribe of the two. E is particularly interested in these tribes because he is one of the Mushite priests who had controlled the religious center at Shiloh before the time of Solomon, and Shiloh was in the territory of Ephraim.

**J Text**

J seems to imply that Jacob is buried in Abel-Mizraim, on the other side of the Jordan: "GEN 50:10 And they came to the threshing-floor of Atad, which is beyond the Jordan, and there they wailed with a very great and sore wailing; and he made a mourning for his father seven days. 11And when the inhabitants of the land, the Canaanites, saw the mourning in the floor of Atad, they said: 'This is a grievous mourning to the Egyptians.' Wherefore the name of it was called Abel-mizraim, which is beyond the Jordan." {14And Joseph returned into Egypt, he, and his brethren, and all that went up with him to bury his father, after he had buried his father.} Genesis 50:14 is flagged as problematic, because it implies that Joseph did not go any further than Abel-mizraim to bury

---

| [ used more than once ] | " quoting older text " |

| E | J |
|---|---|

[11]And Israel said unto Joseph: 'I had not thought to see thy face; and, lo, God hath let me see thy seed also.' [12]And Joseph brought them out from between his knees; and he fell down on his face to the earth. [13]And Joseph took them both, Ephraim in his right hand toward Israel's left hand, and Manasseh in his left hand toward Israel's right hand, and brought them near unto him. [14]And Israel stretched out his right hand, and laid it upon Ephraim's head, who was the younger, and his left hand upon Manasseh's head, guiding his hands wittingly; for Manasseh was the first-born.

[15]And he blessed Joseph, and said: 'The God before whom my fathers Abraham and Isaac did walk, the God who hath been my shepherd all my life long unto this day, [16]the angel who hath redeemed me from all evil, bless the lads; and let my name be named in them, and the name of my fathers Abraham and Isaac; and let them grow into a multitude in the midst of the earth.'

[17]And when Joseph saw that his father was laying his right hand upon the head of Ephraim, it displeased him, and he held up his father's hand, to remove it from Ephraim's head unto Manasseh's head. [18]And Jo-

Nor the ruler's staff from between his feet,
As long as men come to Shiloh;
And unto him shall the obedience of the peoples be.
[11]Binding his foal unto the vine,
And his ass's colt unto the choice vine;
He washeth his garments in wine,
And his vesture in the blood of grapes;
[12]His eyes shall be red with wine,
And his teeth white with milk.
[13]Zebulun shall dwell at the shore of the sea,
And he shall be a shore for ships,
And his flank shall be upon Zidon.
[14]Issachar is a large-boned ass,
Couching down between the sheep-folds.
[15]For he saw a resting-place that it was good,
And the land that it was pleasant;
And he bowed his shoulder to bear,
And became a servant under taskwork.
[16]Dan shall judge his people,
As one of the tribes of Israel.
[17]Dan shall be a serpent in the way,
A horned snake in the path,
That biteth the horse's heels,
So that his rider falleth backward.
[18]I wait for Thy salvation, O Lord.
[19]Gad, a troop shall troop upon him;
But he shall troop upon their heel.
[20]As for Asher, his bread shall be fat,
And he shall yield royal dainties.
[21]Naphtali is a hind let loose:
He giveth goodly words.
[22]Joseph is a fruitful vine,
A fruitful vine by a fountain;
Its branches run over the wall.
[23]The archers have dealt bitterly with him,
And shot at him, and hated him;

| ( added by redactor ) | { problematic } |

| P | Notes |
|---|---|

of Canaan, which Abraham bought with the field from Ephron the Hittite for a possession of a burying-place. ³¹There they buried Abraham and Sarah his wife; there they buried Isaac and Rebekah his wife; and there I buried Leah. ³²The field and the cave that is therein, which was purchased from the children of Heth.' ³³And when Jacob made an end of charging his sons, he gathered up his feet into the bed, and expired, and was gathered unto his people.

GEN 50:12And his sons did unto him according as he commanded them. ¹³For his sons carried him into the land of Canaan, and buried him in the cave of the field of Machpelah, which Abraham bought with the field, for a possession of a burying-place, of Ephron the Hittite, in front of Mamre.}

Jacob before returning to Egypt.

It is hard to believe that J said Jacob was buried on the other side of the Jordan, not in Canaan, but the only intervening verses in the received text of the Bible are: "GEN 50:12And his sons did unto him according as he commanded them. ¹³For his sons carried him into the land of Canaan, and buried him in the cave of the field of Machpelah, which Abraham bought with the field, for a possession of a burying-place, of Ephron the Hittite, in front of Mamre." The part of this about the field of Machpelah is clearly from P, since it refers back to the passage in P about Abraham purchasing the field. The rest also seems to be from P rather than J, since it talks about Jacob's "sons" carrying him, while J talks about Joseph's brothers.

Perhaps there was a passage in J similar to "GEN 50:13For his sons carried him into the land of Canaan, and buried him," which R eliminated to avoid duplication.

**P Text**

The P text is problematic because the P text said earlier that Jacob died: "GEN 47:28And Jacob lived in the land of Egypt seventeen years; so the days of Jacob, the years of his life, were a hundred forty and seven years." But here, beginning in Genesis 48:3, the P text says that Jacob is alive again to legitimize Ephraim and Manasseh.

This passage is also problematic, like a number of other passages in P, because it is a lengthy narrative about something that is not one of

| [ used more than once ] | " quoting older text " |
|---|---|

| **E** | **J** |
|---|---|
| seph said unto his father: 'Not so, my father, for this is the first-born; put thy right hand upon his head.' [19]And his father refused, and said: 'I know it, my son, I know it; he also shall become a people, and he also shall be great; howbeit his younger brother shall be greater than he, and his seed shall become a multitude of nations.' | [24]But his bow abode firm, |
| | And the arms of his hands were made supple, |
| | By the hands of the Mighty One of Jacob, |
| | From thence, from the Shepherd, the Stone of Israel, |
| | [25]Even by the God of thy father, who shall help thee, |
| | And by the Almighty, who shall bless thee, |
| | With blessings of heaven above, |
| [20]And he blessed them that day, saying: 'By thee shall Israel bless, saying: God make thee as Ephraim and as Manasseh.' And he set Ephraim before Manasseh. [21]And Israel said unto Joseph: 'Behold, I die; but God will be with you, and bring you back unto the land of your fathers. [22]Moreover I have given to thee one portion above thy brethren, which I took out of the hand of the Amorite with my sword and with my bow.' | Blessings of the deep that coucheth beneath, |
| | Blessings of the breasts, and of the womb. |
| | [26]The blessings of thy father |
| | Are mighty beyond the blessings of my progenitors |
| | Unto the utmost bound of the everlasting hills; |
| | They shall be on the head of Joseph, |
| | And on the crown of the head of the prince among his brethren. |
| | [27]Benjamin is a wolf that raveneth; |
| | In the morning he devoureth the prey, |
| | And at even he divideth the spoil." |
| GEN 50:15And when Joseph's brethren saw that their father was dead, they said: 'It may be that Joseph will hate us, and will fully requite us all the evil which we did unto him.' [16]And they sent a message unto Joseph, saying: 'Thy father did command before he died, saying: [17]So shall ye say unto Joseph: Forgive, I pray thee now, the transgression of thy brethren, and their sin, for that they did unto thee evil. And now, we pray thee, for- | ([28]All these are the twelve tribes of Israel, and this is it that their father spoke unto them and blessed them; every one according to his blessing he blessed them.) |
| | GEN 50:1And Joseph fell upon his father's face, and wept upon him, and kissed him. [2]And Joseph commanded his servants the physicians to embalm his father. And the physicians embalmed Israel. [3]And forty days were fulfilled for him; for so are fulfilled the days of embalming. And the Egyptians wept for him threescore and ten days. |
| | [4]And when the days of weeping for him were past, Joseph spoke unto the house |

( added by redactor )                    { problematic }

| P | Notes |
|---|---|
| | the four key events of the P text (creation, covenant of Noah, covenant of Abraham, covenant of Moses and Aaron). In general, P just gives summary accounts of history outside of these four key events. |
| | For both these reasons, it is plausible that this was not part of the original plan of the P text and was added because it was considered important legally that the tribes of Ephraim and Manasseh be legitimate. |
| | For more about the original unified plan of P and passages that are not part of this plan, see page 34-37. |
| *[Continued on p. 217]* | |
| [ used more than once ] | " quoting older text " |

*[Continued on p. 217]*

| E | J |
|---|---|
| give the transgression of the servants of the God of thy father.' And Joseph wept when they spoke unto him. [18]And his brethren also went and fell down before his face; and they said: 'Behold, we are thy bondmen.' [19]And Joseph said unto them: 'Fear not; for am I in the place of God? [20]And as for you, ye meant evil against me; but God meant it for good, to bring to pass, as it is this day, to save much people alive. [21]Now therefore fear ye not; I will sustain you, and your little ones.' And he comforted them, and spoke kindly unto them. | of Pharaoh, saying: 'If now I have found favour in your eyes, speak, I pray you, in the ears of Pharaoh, saying: [5]My father made me swear, saying: Lo, I die; in my grave which I have digged for me in the land of Canaan, there shalt thou bury me. Now therefore let me go up, I pray thee, and bury my father, and I will come back.' [6]And Pharaoh said: 'Go up, and bury thy father, according as he made thee swear.' [7]And Joseph went up to bury his father; and with him went up all the servants of Pharaoh, the elders of his house, and all the elders of the land of Egypt, [8]and all the house of Joseph, and his brethren, and his father's house; only their little ones, and their flocks, and their herds, they left in the land of Goshen. [9]And there went up with him both chariots and horsemen; and it was a very great company. |
| [23]And Joseph saw Ephraim's children of the third generation; the children also of Machir the son of Manasseh were born upon Joseph's knees. [24]And Joseph said unto his brethren: 'I die; but God will surely remember you, and bring you up out of this land unto the land which He swore to Abraham, to Isaac, and to Jacob.' [25]And Joseph took an oath of the children of Israel, saying: 'God will surely remember you, and ye shall carry up my bones from hence.' [26]So Joseph died, being a hundred and ten years old. And they embalmed him, and he was put in a coffin in Egypt. | [10]And they came to the threshing-floor of Atad, which is beyond the Jordan, and there they wailed with a very great and sore wailing; and he made a mourning for his father seven days. [11]And when the inhabitants of the land, the Canaanites, saw the mourning in the floor of Atad, they said: 'This is a grievous mourning to the Egyptians.' Wherefore the name of it was called Abel-mizraim, which is beyond the Jordan. |
| | {[14]And Joseph returned into Egypt, he, and his brethren, and all that went up with him to bury his father, after he had buried his father.} [22]And Joseph dwelt in Egypt, he, and his father's house; and Joseph lived a hundred and ten years. |
| ( added by redactor ) | { problematic } |

| P | Notes |
|---|---|
| *[Continued on p. 217]* | *[Continued on p. 217]* |
| [ used more than once ] | " quoting older text " |

| **E** | **J** |
|---|---|
| **Pharaoh Oppresses the Israelites** | **Pharaoh Oppresses the Israelites** |

### E

*[Gap in E: the Israelites multiplied and the Egyptians were afraid of them.]*

EX 1:11Therefore they did set over them taskmasters to afflict them with their burdens. And they built for Pharaoh store-cities, Pithom and Raamses. 12But the more they afflicted them, the more they multiplied and the more they spread abroad. And they were adread because of the children of Israel.

15And the king of Egypt spoke to the Hebrew midwives, of whom the name of the one was Shiphrah, and the name of the other Puah; 16and he said: 'When ye do the office of a midwife to the Hebrew women, ye shall look upon the birthstool: if it be a son, then ye shall kill him; but if it be a daughter, then she shall live.' 17But the midwives feared God, and did not as the king of Egypt commanded them, but saved the men-children alive. 18And the king of Egypt called for the midwives, and said unto them: 'Why have ye done this thing, and have saved the men-children alive?' 19And the midwives said unto Pharaoh: 'Because the Hebrew women are not as the Egyptian women; for they are lively, and are delivered ere the midwife come unto them.' 20aAnd God dealt well with the midwives; 21And it came to pass, because the midwives feared God, that He made them houses.

*[Gap in E: Early Life of Moses.]*

### J

{EX 1:6And Joseph died, and all his brethren, and all that generation. 8Now there arose a new king over Egypt, who knew not Joseph. 9And he said unto his people: 'Behold, the people of the children of Israel are too many and too mighty for us; 10come, let us deal wisely with them, lest they multiply, and it come to pass, that, when there befalleth us any war, they also join themselves unto our enemies, and fight against us, and get them up out of the land.'}

22And Pharaoh charged all his people, saying: 'Every son that is born ye shall cast into the river, and every daughter ye shall save alive.'

**Early Life of Moses**

EX 2:1And there went a man of the house of Levi, and took to

| ( added by redactor ) | { problematic } |
|---|---|

| P | Notes |
|---|---|

**Pharaoh Oppresses the Israelites**

EX 1:1Now these are the names of the sons of Israel, who came into Egypt with Jacob; every man came with his household: 2Reuben, Simeon, Levi, and Judah; 3Issachar, Zebulun, and Benjamin; 4Dan and Naphtali, Gad and Asher. 5And all the souls that came out of the loins of Jacob were seventy souls; and Joseph was in Egypt already.

7And the children of Israel were fruitful, and increased abundantly, and multiplied, and waxed exceeding mighty; and the land was filled with them.

13And the Egyptians made the children of Israel to serve with rigour. 14And they made their lives bitter with hard service, in mortar and in brick, and in all manner of service in the field; in all their service, wherein they made them serve with rigour.

20bAnd the people multiplied, and waxed very mighty.

**Pharaoh Oppresses the Israelites**

**Separating the Texts**

Exodus 1:6 and 8-10 are problematic because It is hard to say whether they come from E or J.

There does not seem to be anything in the language that helps us decide. Either the E or J text would be continuous with this passage, since both continue with Pharaoh's plan to kill new-born males to prevent Israelites from multiplying.

This edition puts these verses at the beginning of J speculatively, but it is also possible that the passage is from the beginning of E and there is a gap at the beginning of J.

**P Text**

P is summarizing to get back to the thread of his narrative after Jacob legitimizes Ephraim and Manasseh. He gave more details about the sons of Israel who came to Egypt in Genesis 46. Here, he repeats it without the details. He also repeats the fact that seventy people came to Egypt. This repetition in Exodus 1 is another sign that the previous passage was inserted in the P text. See page 37.

**God Remembers Israel**

GEN 2:23And it came to pass in the course of those many days that the king of Egypt died; and the children of Israel sighed by reason of the bondage, and they cried, and their cry came up unto God by reason of the bondage. 24And God heard their

**Early Life of Moses**

**E Text**

Based on what comes later, we can

| [ used more than once ] | " quoting older text " |
|---|---|

| **E** | **J** |
|---|---|
| | wife a daughter of Levi. ²And the woman conceived, and bore a son; and when she saw him that he was a goodly child, she hid him three months. ³And when she could not longer hide him, she took for him an ark of bulrushes, and daubed it with slime and with pitch; and she put the child therein, and laid it in the flags by the river's brink. ⁴And his sister stood afar off, to know what would be done to him. |
| | ⁵And the daughter of Pharaoh came down to bathe in the river; and her maidens walked along by the river-side; and she saw the ark among the flags, and sent her handmaid to fetch it. ⁶And she opened it, and saw it, even the child; and behold a boy that wept. And she had compassion on him, and said: 'This is one of the Hebrews' children.' ⁷Then said his sister to Pharaoh's daughter: 'Shall I go and call thee a nurse of the Hebrew women, that she may nurse the child for thee?' ⁸And Pharaoh's daughter said to her: 'Go.' And the maiden went and called the child's mother. ⁹And Pharaoh's daughter said unto her: 'Take this child away, and nurse it for me, and I will give thee thy wages.' And the woman took the child, and nursed it. ¹⁰And the child grew, and she brought him unto Pharaoh's daughter, and he became her son. And she called his name Moses, and said: 'Because I drew him out of the water.' |
| *[Continued on p. 220]* | ¹¹And it came to pass in those days, when Moses was grown up, that he went out unto his brethren, and looked on their burdens; and he saw an Egyptian smiting a Hebrew, one of his brethren. ¹²And he looked this way and that way, and when he saw that there was no man, he smote the Egyptian, and hid him in the sand. ¹³And he went out the second day, and, behold, two men of the Hebrews were striving together; and he said to him that did the wrong: 'Wherefore smitest thou thy fellow?' ¹⁴And he said: 'Who made thee a ruler and a judge over us? thinkest thou to kill me, as thou didst kill the Egyptian?' And Moses feared, and said: 'Surely the thing is known.' |
| | ¹⁵Now when Pharaoh heard this thing, he sought to slay Moses. But Moses fled from the face of |
| ( added by redactor ) | { problematic } |

[Continued on p. 220]

| P | Notes |
|---|---|
| groaning, and God remembered His covenant with Abraham, with Isaac, and with Jacob. ²⁵And God saw the children of Israel, and God took cognizance of them. | guess that the gap in the E text may have described the birth of Moses and certainly described his leaving Egypt to escape a threat to his life and marrying in Midian. RJE presumably removed this because it he preferred the J text. |
| [ used more than once ] | " quoting older text " |

| **E** | **J** |
|---|---|
| | Pharaoh, and dwelt in the land of Midian; and he sat down by a well. ¹⁶Now the priest of Midian had seven daughters; and they came and drew water, and filled the troughs to water their father's flock. ¹⁷And the shepherds came and drove them away; but Moses stood up and helped them, and watered their flock. ¹⁸And when they came to Reuel their father, he said: 'How is it that ye are come so soon to-day?' ¹⁹And they said: 'An Egyptian delivered us out of the hand of the shepherds, and moreover he drew water for us, and watered the flock.' ²⁰And he said unto his daughters: 'And where is he? Why is it that ye have left the man? call him, that he may eat bread.' |
| | ²¹And Moses was content to dwell with the man; and he gave Moses Zipporah his daughter. ²²And she bore a son, and he called his name Gershom; for he said: 'I have been a stranger in a strange land.' |

| **The Calling of Moses** | **The Calling of Moses** |
|---|---|
| EX 3:1Now Moses was keeping the flock of Jethro his father-in-law, the priest of Midian; and he led the flock to the farthest end of the wilderness, and came to the mountain of God, unto Horeb. ²ᵇAnd he looked, and, behold, (the) a bush burned with fire, and the bush was not consumed. | ***[Gap in J: Moses Was Out with His Flock]*** |
| | EX 3:2aAnd the angel of the Lord appeared unto him in a flame of fire out of the midst of a bush; ³And Moses said: 'I will turn aside now, and see this great sight, why the bush is not burnt.' ⁴aAnd (when) the Lord saw that he turned aside to see. ⁷And the Lord said: 'I have surely seen the affliction of My people that are in Egypt, and have heard their cry by reason of their taskmasters; for I know their pains; ⁸and I am come down to deliver them out of the hand of the Egyptians, and to bring them up out of that land unto a good land and a large, unto a land flowing with milk and honey; unto the place of the Canaanite, and the Hittite, and the Amorite, and the Perizzite, and the Hivite, and the Jebusite. |
| ⁴ᵇGod called unto him out of the midst of the bush, and said: 'Moses, | ¹⁶Go, and gather the elders of Israel together, and say unto them: The Lord, the God of your fathers, the God of Abraham, of Isaac, and of Jacob, hath appeared unto me, saying: I have surely remembered you, and seen that which is done to you in Egypt. |

| ( added by redactor ) | { problematic } |

| P | Notes |
|---|---|

**The Calling of Moses**

EX 6:2And God spoke unto Moses, and said unto him: 'I am the Lord; ³and I appeared unto Abraham, unto Isaac, and unto Jacob, as God Almighty, but by My name YHWH I made Me not known to them. ⁴And I have also established My covenant with them, to give them the land of Canaan, the land of their sojournings, wherein they sojourned. ⁵And moreover I have heard the groaning of the

**The Calling of Moses**

**Separating the Texts**

This is a key location in the E and P texts because God reveals his name to Moses here. Up to this point, theses texts have used the word "God." After this point, they will use both God and the Lord (=YHWH).

Both E and P say that this is the event when the Lord revealed his name to Moses, though P says it in summary form (Ex. 6:2) while E tells a story about it: (Ex. 3:13-15).

As we have seen, J has used this name throughout, and she believed it was revealed before the flood (Gen. 4:26).

It becomes more difficult to separate the texts after this point, because use of "the Lord" is no longer enough to assign a passage to the J text.

Note that Moses' father-in-law is named Jethro in E and Reuel in J. Reuel means shepherd of El.

**E Text**

Moses receives the ten commandments on Mt. Sinai in J and P and on Mt. Horeb in E and D. The

| [ used more than once ] | " quoting older text " |
|---|---|

| **E** | **J** |
|---|---|
| Moses.' And he said: 'Here am I.' 5And He said: 'Draw not nigh hither; put off thy shoes from off thy feet, for the place whereon thou standest is holy ground.' 6Moreover He said: 'I am the God of thy father, the God of Abraham, the God of Isaac, and the God of Jacob.' And Moses hid his face; for he was afraid to look upon God. 9And *[God said]* 'now, behold, the cry of the children of Israel is come unto Me; moreover I have seen the oppression wherewith the Egyptians oppress them. 10Come now therefore, and I will send thee unto Pharaoh, that thou mayest bring forth My people the children of Israel out of Egypt.' <br> 11And Moses said unto God: 'Who am I, that I should go unto Pharaoh, and that I should bring forth the children of Israel out of Egypt?' 12And He said: 'Certainly I will be with thee; and this shall be the token unto thee, that I have sent thee: when thou hast brought forth the people out of Egypt, ye shall serve God upon this mountain.' <br> 13And Moses said unto God: 'Behold, when I come unto the children of Israel, and shall say unto them: The God of your fathers hath sent me unto you; and they shall say to me: What is His name? what shall I say unto them?' 14And God said unto Moses: 'I am that I am'; and He said: 'Thus shalt thou say unto the children of Israel: I am hath sent me unto you.' 15And God said moreover unto Moses: 'Thus shalt thou say unto the children of Israel: The Lord *[=YHWH]*, the God of your fathers, the God of Abraham, the God of Isaac, and the God of Jacob, hath sent me unto you; this is My name for ever, and this is My memorial unto all generations. | 17And I have said: I will bring you up out of the affliction of Egypt unto the land of the Canaanite, and the Hittite, and the Amorite, and the Perizzite, and the Hivite, and the Jebusite, unto a land flowing with milk and honey. <br> 18And they shall hearken to thy voice. And thou shalt come, thou and the elders of Israel, unto the king of Egypt, and ye shall say unto him: The Lord, the God of the Hebrews, hath met with us. And now let us go, we pray thee, three days' journey into the wilderness, that we may sacrifice to the Lord our God. 19And I know that the king of Egypt will not give you leave to go, except by a mighty hand. 20And I will put forth My hand, and smite Egypt with all My wonders which I will do in the midst thereof. And after that he will let you go. 21And I will give this people favour in the sight of the Egyptians. And it shall come to pass, that, when ye go, ye shall not go empty; 22but every woman shall ask of her neighbour, and of her that sojourneth in her house, jewels of silver, and jewels of gold, and raiment; and ye shall put them upon your sons, and upon your daughters; and ye shall spoil the Egyptians.' |
| ( added by redactor ) | { problematic } |

| P | Notes |
|---|---|
| children of Israel, whom the Egyptians keep in bondage; and I have remembered My covenant. <sup>6</sup>Wherefore say unto the children of Israel: I am the Lord, and I will bring you out from under the burdens of the Egyptians, and I will deliver you from their bondage, and I will redeem you with an outstretched arm, and with great judgments; <sup>7</sup>and I will take you to Me for a people, and I will be to you a God; and ye shall know that I am the Lord your God, who brought you out from under the burdens of the Egyptians. <sup>8</sup>And I will bring you in unto the land, concerning which I lifted up My hand to give it to Abraham, to Isaac, and to Jacob; and I will give it you for a heritage: I am the Lord.' <sup>9</sup>And Moses spoke so unto the children of Israel; but they hearkened | E text is anticipating the E revelation on Mt. Horeb when it says that Moses "<sup>EX 3:1</sup>came to the mountain of God, unto Horeb" and adds "<sup>EX 3:12</sup>when thou hast brought forth the people out of Egypt, ye shall serve God upon this mountain." <br><br> But when they come to the mountain, the received text does not mention Horeb, presumably because a redactor removed it to eliminate the contradiction. <br><br>**J Text** <br> "Three days' journey" is used repeatedly in the J text but not in the E text or P text. <br><br>**P Text** <br> P continues to give a sort of summary history: he gives very little background about Moses' life and does not even mention the burning bush, but he does give an account of the conversation between Moses and God, which is essential to the covenant that P considers one of the four key events of history. <br><br>**Translation** <br> E Text: The JPS translation says "<sup>EX 3:2b</sup>And he looked, and, behold, the bush burned with fire." This edition changes it to "<sup>EX 3:2b</sup>And he looked, and, behold, (the) a bush burned with fire." Hebrew does not use an indefinite article. The same word means either "bush" or "a bush." This is the first mention of the burning bush in E, and we assume that a redactor changed it from "bush" to "the bush" when he inserted an earlier mention of it from the J text. <br><br> J text: The JPS translation say "<sup>EX 3:4a</sup>And when the Lord saw that he turned aside to see," but the word "when" that is in the translation is not in the original Hebrew. |
| [ used more than once ] | " quoting older text " |

| **E** | **J** |
|---|---|
| **Moses Questions His Capability** | **Moses Questions His Capability** |

## E

### Moses Questions His Capability

EX 4:1And Moses answered and said: 'But, behold, they will not believe me, nor hearken unto my voice; for they will say: The Lord hath not appeared unto thee.' ²And the Lord said unto him: 'What is that in thy hand?' And he said: 'A rod.' ³And He said: 'Cast it on the ground.' And he cast it on the ground, and it became a serpent; and Moses fled from before it. ⁴And the Lord said unto Moses: 'Put forth thy hand, and take it by the tail—and he put forth his hand, and laid hold of it, and it became a rod in his hand—⁵that they may believe that the Lord, the God of their fathers, the God of Abraham, the God of Isaac, and the God of Jacob, hath appeared unto thee.'

⁶And the Lord said furthermore unto him: 'Put now thy hand into thy bosom.' And he put his hand into his bosom; and when he took it out, behold, his hand was leprous, as white as snow. ⁷And He said: 'Put thy hand back into thy bosom.—And he put his hand back into his bosom; and when he took it out of his bosom, behold, it was turned again as his other flesh.—⁸And it shall come to pass, if they will not believe thee, neither hearken to the voice of the first sign, that they will believe the voice of the latter sign.

⁹And it shall come to pass, if they will not believe even these two

*( added by redactor )*

## J

### Moses Questions His Capability

[EX 4:10And Moses said unto the Lord: 'Oh Lord, I am not a man of words, neither heretofore, nor since Thou hast spoken unto Thy servant; for I am slow of speech, and of a slow tongue.'] ¹³And he said: 'Oh Lord, send, I pray Thee, by the hand of him whom Thou wilt send.' ¹⁴And the anger of the Lord was kindled against Moses, and He said: 'Is there not Aaron thy brother the Levite? I know that he can speak well. And also, behold, he cometh forth to meet thee; and when he seeth thee, he will be glad in his heart. ¹⁵And thou shalt speak unto him, and put the words in his mouth; and I will be with thy mouth, and with his mouth, and will teach you what ye shall do. ¹⁶And he shall be thy spokesman unto the people; and it shall come to pass, that he shall be to thee a mouth, and thou shalt be to him in God's stead.

¹⁹And the Lord said unto Moses in Midian: 'Go, return into Egypt; for all the men are dead that sought thy life.' ²⁰ᵃAnd Moses took his wife and his sons, and set them upon an ass, and he returned to the land of Egypt.

*{ problematic }*

| **P** | **Notes** |
|---|---|
| not unto Moses for impatience of spirit, and for cruel bondage.<br><br>**Moses Questions His Capability**<br><br>EX 6:10And the Lord spoke unto Moses, saying: 11'Go in, speak unto Pharaoh king of Egypt, that he let the children of Israel go out of his land.' 12And Moses spoke before the Lord, saying: 'Behold, the children of Israel have not hearkened unto me; how then shall Pharaoh hear me, who am of uncircumcised lips?' EX 7:1And the Lord said unto Moses: 'See, I have set thee in God's stead to Pharaoh; and Aaron thy brother shall be thy prophet. 2Thou shalt speak all that I command thee; and Aaron thy brother shall speak unto Pharaoh, that he let the children of Israel go out of his land. 3And I will harden *[QShH]* Pharaoh's heart, and multiply My signs and My wonders in the land of Egypt. 4But Pharaoh will not hearken unto you, and I will lay My hand upon Egypt, and bring forth My hosts, My people the children of Israel, out of the land of Egypt, by great judgments. 5And the Egyptians shall know that I am the Lord, when I stretch forth My hand upon Egypt, and bring out the children of Israel from among them.' | **Moses Questions His Capability**<br><br>Exodus 4:10, where Moses says he is not a man of words, is needed in both E and J. Presumably, these two texts both had a similar statement by Moses, and RJE removed one to eliminate repetition.<br>**E Text**<br>In E, when Moses says he is not a good speaker, God says that He will speak through him. E was one of the Mushite priests who believed they were descended from Moses, and he has Moses speak to Pharaoh and work the wonders without help from Aaron. Moses' use of the rod to work wonders is a continuing theme in E but not in the other texts,<br>**J Text**<br>In J, when Moses says he is not a good speaker, God tells him that Aaron will speak for him. J is in the court in Jerusalem and presumably she is influenced here by the Aaronid priests who control the Temple in Jerusalem.<br>**P Text**<br>In P, Aaron speaks for Moses and also uses the rod to perform magic. Aaron's use of the rod is a continuing theme in P. P was one of the Aaronid priests, who believed they were descended from Aaron, and he persistently tries to expand Aaron's role at the expense of Moses.<br>**Translation**<br>E text: For information about the root *HZQ* and the translation |
| [ used more than once ] | " quoting older text " |

| **E** | **J** |
|---|---|
| signs, neither hearken unto thy voice, that thou shalt take of the water of the river, and pour it upon the dry land; and the water which thou takest out of the river shall become blood upon the dry land.' | |
| [EX 4:10And Moses said unto the Lord: 'Oh Lord, I am not a man of words, neither heretofore, nor since Thou hast spoken unto Thy servant; for I am slow of speech, and of a slow tongue.'] 11And the Lord said unto him: 'Who hath made man's mouth? or who maketh a man dumb, or deaf, or seeing, or blind? is it not I the Lord? 12Now therefore go, and I will be with thy mouth, and teach thee what thou shalt speak.' 17And thou shalt take in thy hand this rod, wherewith thou shalt do the signs.' | **Moses Returns to Egypt** |
| | EX 4:24And it came to pass on the way at the lodging-place, that the Lord met him, and sought to kill him. 25Then Zipporah took a flint, and cut off the foreskin of her son, and cast it at his feet; and she said: 'Surely a bridegroom of blood art thou to me.' 26So He let him alone. Then she said: 'A bridegroom of blood in regard of the circumcision.' |
| 18And Moses went and returned to Jethro his father-in-law, and said unto him: 'Let me go, I pray thee, and unto my brethren that are in Egypt, and see whether they be yet alive.' And Jethro said to Moses: 'Go in peace.' 20bAnd Moses took the rod of God in his hand. | 27And the Lord said to Aaron: 'Go into the wilderness to meet Moses.' And he went, and met him in the mountain (of God), and kissed him. 28And Moses told Aaron all the words of the Lord wherewith He had sent him, and all the signs wherewith He had charged him. 29And Moses and Aaron went and gathered together all the elders of the children of Israel. 30And Aaron spoke all the words which the Lord had spoken unto Moses, and did the signs in the sight of the people. 31And the people believed; and when they heard that the Lord had remembered the children of Is- |
| EX 4:21And the Lord said unto Moses: 'When thou goest back into Egypt, see that thou do before Pharaoh all the wonders which I have put in thy hand; (but I will strengthen [HZQ] his heart, and he will not let the people go.) 22And thou shalt say unto Pharaoh: Thus saith the Lord: Israel is My son, My first-born. 23And I have said unto thee: Let My son go, that he may serve Me; and thou hast refused to let him go. Behold, I will slay thy son, thy first-born.' | |
| ( added by redactor ) | { problematic } |

| P | Notes |
|---|---|
| | "strengthen," see the section about the ten plagues below. Within the narrative of the ten plagues, R adds text using *HZQ* in many places to unify the different accounts, so it is reasonable to assume that R did the same here. |

### Catalog of Israelites - Relocated

Exodus 6:13-30 was inserted by a redactor, interrupting a passage from P. Because the goal of this edition is to place the J, E, and P texts in parallel columns, this passage has been relocated to the section of Other Texts.

### Moses Returns to Egypt

**J Text**

In a very strange passage (Ex. 4:24, 26), the Lord tries to kill Moses, his wife Zipporah circumcises their son to deal with the threat, and she then says Moses is a "bridegroom of blood."

*[Continued on p. 229]*

Notice the similarity with the Passover story, where the Lord passes through Egypt and kills the first born, and the Israelites must put blood on the doorposts to save themselves. This ritual may date back to patriarchal times, when seasonal nomads sacrificed a lamb to ward off death when they could no longer graze in the stubble of the farmland and had to graze their herds in the wilderness.

In these cases, the blood of circumcision or of the paschal lamb is needed to ward off the demonic aspect of God. We can speculate that J's primitive view of God may have let her preserve these demonic remnants of the patriarchal religion.

"EX 4:27bAnd he went, and met him in the mountain (of God), and kissed him" is one of the very few places where J uses the word "God" rather than "the Lord," so it is likely that this word was added by a later redactor. E calls it the mountain of God (Ex. 3:1) so it is plausible that RJE duplicated the phrase here to make the texts seem more unified.

| [ used more than once ] | " quoting older text " |
|---|---|

| E | J |
|---|---|
| | rael, and that He had seen their affliction, then they bowed their heads and worshipped. |
| **Let My People Go** | **Let My People Go** |
| | EX 5:1a And afterward Moses and Aaron came and said unto Pharaoh ³And they said: 'The God of the Hebrews hath met with us. Let us go, we pray thee, three days' journey into the wilderness, and sacrifice unto the Lord our God; lest He fall upon us with pestilence, or with the sword.' ⁴And the king of Egypt said unto them: 'Wherefore do ye, Moses and Aaron, cause the people to break loose from their work? get you unto your burdens.' |
| *[Gap in E; Moses Goes to Pharaoh]* | |
| EX 5:1b 'Thus saith the Lord, the God of Israel: Let My people go, that they may hold a feast unto Me in the wilderness.' ²And Pharaoh said: 'Who is the Lord, that I should hearken unto His voice to let Israel go? I know not the Lord, and moreover I will not let Israel go.' | |
| | ⁶And the same day Pharaoh commanded the taskmasters of the people, and their officers, saying: ⁷'Ye shall no more give the people straw to make brick, as heretofore. Let them go and gather straw for themselves. ⁸And the tale of the bricks, which they did make heretofore, ye shall lay upon them; ye shall not diminish aught thereof; for they are idle; therefore they cry, saying: Let us go and sacrifice to our God. ⁹Let heavier work be laid upon the men, that they may labour therein; and let them not regard lying words.' |
| ⁵And Pharaoh said: 'Behold, the people of the land are now many, and will ye make them rest from their burdens?' | ¹⁰And the taskmasters of the people went out, and their officers, and they spoke to the people, saying: 'Thus saith Pharaoh: I will not give you straw. ¹¹Go yourselves, get you straw where ye can find it; for nought of your work shall be diminished.' |
| | ¹²So the people were scattered abroad throughout all the land of Egypt to gather stubble for straw. ¹³And the taskmasters were urgent, saying: 'Fulfil your work, your daily task, as when there was straw.' ¹⁴And the officers of the children of Israel, whom Pharaoh's taskmasters had set over them, were beaten, saying: 'Wherefore have ye not fulfilled your appointed task in making brick both yesterday and to-day as heretofore?' ¹⁵Then the officers of the children of Israel came and cried unto Pharaoh, saying: 'Wherefore dealest thou thus with thy servants? ¹⁶There is no straw given unto thy servants, and they |
| *[Gap in E: see J]* | |
| ( added by redactor ) | { problematic } |

| P | Notes |
|---|---|

### Let My People Go

EX 7:6And Moses and Aaron did so; as the Lord commanded them, so did they. ⁷And Moses was fourscore years old, and Aaron fourscore and three years old, when they spoke unto Pharaoh.

⁸And the Lord spoke unto Moses and unto Aaron, saying: ⁹'When Pharaoh shall speak unto you, saying: Show a wonder for you; then thou shalt say unto Aaron: Take thy rod, and cast it down before Pharaoh, that it become a serpent.'

¹⁰And Moses and Aaron went in unto Pharaoh, and they did so, as the Lord had commanded; and Aaron cast down his rod before Pharaoh and before his servants, and it became a serpent. ¹¹Then Pharaoh also called for the wise men and the sorcerers; and they also, the magicians of Egypt, did in like manner with their secret arts. ¹²For they cast down every man his rod, and they became serpents; but Aaron's rod swallowed up their rods. ¹³And Pharaoh's heart was strengthened *[HZQ]*, and he hearkened not unto them; as the Lord had spoken.

### Let My People Go

**Separating the Texts**

In these sections, there is little reason to assign the Non-P account to J or E based on language, so we assign it based on content.

This edition assigns passages to J if they make both Moses and Aaron the spokesmen, as J said that Aaron should be the spokesman when Moses questioned his own capability (Ex. 4:14). In E, by contrast, God made Moses the spokesman after he questioned his own capability (Ex. 4:10-12).

There are two repetitions here: they ask twice to go and worship in the wilderness, and Pharaoh replies twice about the Israelites not putting down their burdens. The repetition probably comes from two texts. Exodus 5:1a seems to be from J because Moses and Aaron speak to Pharaoh. Exodus 5:3 is from J because God commands Moses to say these words in J (Ex. 1:18) and the three-day journey into the wilderness is also mentioned later in J (Ex. 6:23) but not in E. If we assign the repetitions of these two points to E and also assign Exodus 5:5 to E, we can eliminate the repetitions within each text and create consecutive texts for both J and E.

**E Text**

Notice that, earlier in the E text, God told Moses to cast down his rod to turn it into a serpent (Ex. 4:3) but in the P text, Aaron casts down his rod when they actually come before Pharaoh (Ex. 7:10). Undoubtedly, there is a gap in the E text where Moses casts down his rod, which R left out because it contradicts the P text.

| [ used more than once ] | " quoting older text " |
|---|---|

| **E** | **J** |
|---|---|
| | say to us: Make brick; and, behold, thy servants are beaten, but the fault is in thine own people.' [17]But he said: 'Ye are idle, ye are idle; therefore ye say: Let us go and sacrifice to the Lord. [18]Go therefore now, and work; for there shall no straw be given you, yet shall ye deliver the tale of bricks.' |
| | [19]And the officers of the children of Israel did see that they were set on mischief, when they said: 'Ye shall not diminish aught from your bricks, your daily task.' [20]And they met Moses and Aaron, who stood in the way, as they came forth from Pharaoh; [21]and they said unto them: 'The Lord look upon you, and judge; because ye have made our savour to be abhorred in the eyes of Pharaoh, and in the eyes of his servants, to put a sword in their hand to slay us.' |
| | [22]And Moses returned unto the Lord, and said: 'Lord, wherefore hast Thou dealt ill with this people? why is it that Thou hast sent me? [23]For since I came to Pharaoh to speak in Thy name, he hath dealt ill with this people; neither hast Thou delivered Thy people at all.' |
| | EX 6:1And the Lord said unto Moses: 'Now shalt thou see what I will do to Pharaoh; for by a strong hand shall he let them go, and by a strong hand shall he drive them out of his land.' |
| **The Plagues** | **The Plagues** |
| EX 7:14[And the Lord said unto Moses:] 'Pharaoh's heart is stubborn [KBD], he refuseth to let the people go. [15]Get thee unto Pharaoh in the morning; lo, he goeth out unto the water; and thou shalt stand by the river's brink to meet him; and the | *[Gap in J: see E]* |
| ( added by redactor ) | { problematic } |

| P | Notes |
|---|---|
| | |

**The Plagues**

EX 7:19And the Lord said unto Moses: 'Say unto Aaron: Take thy rod, and stretch out thy hand over the waters of Egypt, over their rivers, over their streams, and over their pools, and over all their ponds of water, that they may become blood; and there shall be blood throughout all the land of Egypt, both in vessels of wood and in vessels of stone.' 20aAnd Moses and Aaron did so, as the Lord commanded. 22And the magicians of Egypt did in like manner with their secret arts; and Pharaoh's heart was strengthened

**The Plagues**

**Separating the Texts**

Scholars find it hard to distinguish the E and J text here. This edition separates them based on Moses acting alone in E, in keeping with God's instructions to Moses in E (Ex. 4:11-12); Moses acting alone is part of E's general bias toward Moses, whom he considers his ancestor. This edition assigns the passages where Moses and Aaron act together to J if they are not in P, in keeping with God's instructions to Moses in J (Ex. 4:14-15).

This division implies that RJE

| [ used more than once ] | " quoting older text " |

| **E** | **J** |
|---|---|
| rod which was turned to a serpent shalt thou take in thy hand. ¹⁶And thou shalt say unto him: The Lord, the God of the Hebrews, hath sent me unto thee, saying: Let My people go, that they may serve Me in the wilderness; and, behold, hitherto thou hast not hearkened; ¹⁷thus saith the Lord: In this thou shalt know that I am the Lord—behold, I will smite with the rod that is in my hand upon the waters which are in the river, and they shall be turned to blood. ¹⁸And the fish that are in the river shall die, and the river shall become foul; and the Egyptians shall loathe to drink water from the river.' | EX 8:3bAnd they brought up frogs upon the land of Egypt. ⁴Then Pharaoh called for Moses and Aaron, and said: 'Entreat the Lord, |
| ²⁰bAnd he lifted up the rod, and smote the waters that were in the river, in the sight of Pharaoh, and in the sight of his servants; and all the waters that were in the river were turned to blood. ²¹And the fish that were in the river died; and the river became foul, and the Egyptians could not drink water from the river; and the blood was throughout all the land of Egypt. | that He take away the frogs from me, and from my people; and I will let the people go, that they may sacrifice unto the Lord.' ⁵And |
| ²³And Pharaoh turned and went into his house, neither did he lay even this to heart. ²⁴And all the Egyptians digged round about the river for water to drink; for they could not drink of the water of the river. ²⁵And seven days were fulfilled, after that the Lord had smitten the river. ²⁶And the Lord spoke unto Moses: 'Go in unto Pharaoh, and say unto him: Thus saith the Lord: Let My people go, that they may serve Me. ²⁷And if thou refuse to let them go, behold, I will smite all thy borders with frogs. ²⁸And the river shall swarm with frogs, which shall go up and come into thy house, and into thy bed-chamber, and upon thy bed, and into the house of thy servants, and upon thy people, and into thine ovens, and into thy kneading-troughs. ²⁹And the frogs shall come up both upon thee, and upon thy people, and upon all thy servants.' | Moses said unto Pharaoh: 'Have thou this glory over me; against what time shall I entreat for thee, and for thy servants, and for thy people, that the frogs be destroyed from thee and thy houses, and remain in the river only?' ⁶And he said: 'Against to-morrow.' And he said: 'Be it ac- |
| *[Gap in E: see J]* | |

| ( added by redactor ) | { problematic } |

| P | Notes |
|---|---|

*[HZQ]*, and he hearkened not unto them; as the Lord had spoken.

EX 8:1 And the Lord said unto Moses: 'Say unto Aaron: Stretch forth thy hand with thy rod over the rivers, over the canals, and over the pools, and cause frogs to come up upon the land of Egypt.' ²And Aaron stretched out his hand over the waters of Egypt; and the frogs came up, and covered the land of Egypt. ³aAnd the magicians did in like manner with their secret arts,

¹²And the Lord said unto Moses: 'Say unto Aaron: Stretch out thy rod, and smite the dust of the earth, that it may become gnats throughout all the land of Egypt.' ¹³And they did so; and Aaron stretched out his hand with his rod, and smote the dust of the earth, and there were gnats upon man, and upon beast; all the dust of the earth became gnats throughout all the land of Egypt. ¹⁴And the magicians did so with their secret arts to bring forth gnats, but they could not; and there were gnats upon man, and upon beast. ¹⁵Then the magicians said unto Pharaoh: 'This is the finger of God'; and Pharaoh's heart was strengthened *[HZQ]*, and he hearkened not unto them; as the Lord had spoken.

EX 9:8 And the Lord said unto Moses and unto Aaron: 'Take to you handfuls of soot of the furnace, and let Moses throw it heavenward in the sight of Pharaoh. ⁹And it shall become small dust over all the land of Egypt, and shall be a boil breaking forth with blains upon man and upon beast, throughout all the land

patched together the stories of some of the plagues out of passages from E and J, so you have to look back and forth between these two texts to get the whole story.

Confirming this division, there seems to be a discontinuity between the passage ending with Exodus 10:11a, which this edition assigns to J, and the passage beginning with Exodus 10:11b, which this edition assigns to E. In Exodus 10:11a, Pharaoh agrees that the Israelites can go and serve the Lord, but in Exodus 11b, Pharaoh drives Moses out and Moses must cause another plague to change his mind.

Confirming this division, also, notice the inconsistency in grammatical number in Exodus 10. In Exodus 10:3, Moses and Aaron go to Pharaoh. But Exodus 10:6 says "he turned" and left rather than "they turned" and left. Exodus 10:8 has Moses and Aaron again, and Exodus 10:11 uses the right pronoun for the two of them, saying "they are driven out." The use of the singular "he" in Exodus 10:6, and of the plural in the surrounding verses implies that RJE patched this passage together from the E text, where Moses acts alone, and the J text, where Moses and Aaron act together. (Note: Hebrew does not use the pronoun explicitly; it is implied by the form of the verb.)

The demands for a "three days's journey into the wilderness to sacrifice" (Ex. 3:18, Exodus 5:1a, Exodus 8:23) all seem to come from J.

**P Text**

It is easy to identify the P text's

| [ used more than once ] | " quoting older text " |
|---|---|

| **E** | **J** |
|---|---|
| | cording to thy word; that thou mayest know that there is none like unto the Lord our God. [7]And the frogs shall depart from thee, and from thy houses, and from thy servants, and from thy people; they shall remain in the river only.' [8]And Moses and Aaron went out from Pharaoh; and Moses cried unto the Lord concerning the frogs, which He had brought upon Pharaoh. |
| EX 8:9And the Lord did according to the word of Moses; and the frogs died out of the houses, out of the courts, and out of the fields. [10]And they gathered them together in heaps; and the land stank. [11]But when Pharaoh saw that there was respite, he made stubborn *[KBD]* his heart, (and hearkened not unto them; as the Lord had spoken.) | |
| [16]And the Lord said unto Moses: 'Rise up early in the morning, and stand before Pharaoh; lo, he cometh forth to the water; and say unto him: Thus saith the Lord: Let My people go, that they may serve Me. [17]Else, if thou wilt not let My people go, behold, I will send swarms of flies upon thee, and upon thy servants, and upon thy people, and into thy houses; and the houses of the Egyptians shall be full of swarms of flies, and also the ground whereon they are. [18]And I will set apart in that day the land of Goshen, in which My people dwell, that no swarms of flies shall be there; to the end that thou mayest know that I am the Lord in the midst of the earth. [19]And I will put a division between My people and thy people—by to-morrow shall this sign be.' [20]And the Lord did so; and there came grievous swarms of flies into the house of Pharaoh, and into his servants' houses; and in all the land of Egypt the land was ruined by reason of the swarms of flies. | *[Gap in J: see E]* |
| | [21]And Pharaoh called for Moses and for Aaron, and said: 'Go ye, sacrifice to your God in the land.' [22]And Moses said: 'It is not meet so to do; for we shall sacrifice the abomination of the Egyptians to the Lord our God; lo, if we sacrifice the abomination of the Egyptians before their eyes, will they not stone us? [23]We will go three days' journey into the wilderness, and sacrifice to the Lord our God, as He shall command us.' [24]And Pharaoh said: 'I |
| *[Gap in E: see J]* | |
| ( added by redactor ) | { problematic } |

| P | Notes |
|---|---|
| of Egypt.' ¹⁰And they took soot of the furnace, and stood before Pharaoh; and Moses threw it up heavenward; and it became a boil breaking forth with blains upon man and upon beast. ¹¹And the magicians could not stand before Moses because of the boils; for the boils were upon the magicians, and upon all the Egyptians. ¹²And the Lord strengthened *[HZQ]* the heart of Pharaoh, and he hearkened not unto them; as the Lord had spoken unto Moses. | story of the plagues. It begins with two plagues that are in the same form and that both begin with Moses telling Aaron what to do, in keeping with God's instruction to Moses in Exodus 7:1-2. Then it gives Aaron an even more prominent role, as God speaks to both Moses and Aaron. In P's account of the plagues, there is an ongoing competition of Moses and Aaron with the Egyptian magicians, as there was earlier in P, when Moses and Aaron first approached Pharaoh (Ex. 7:8-12). |

story of the plagues. It begins with two plagues that are in the same form and that both begin with Moses telling Aaron what to do, in keeping with God's instruction to Moses in Exodus 7:1-2. Then it gives Aaron an even more prominent role, as God speaks to both Moses and Aaron. In P's account of the plagues, there is an ongoing competition of Moses and Aaron with the Egyptian magicians, as there was earlier in P, when Moses and Aaron first approached Pharaoh (Ex. 7:8-12).

The P text continues at Exodus 12:1, in the section headed "Commandment to Keep Passover." This section also includes the final plague, death of the first born, which leads to the flight from Egypt, so the P text seems to be continuous and not to have any gaps.

One of the plagues in P is *kinim.* This edition keeps the JPS translation of this word as gnats, but it is also commonly translated as "lice" or "vermin," and readers may be more familiar with those words in other translations.

**Translation**

Giving us an important clue to separating the texts, P uses words based on the Hebrew root *HZQ* (which literally means "to be strong") to say that Pharaoh's heart was hardened, and JE uses the root *KBD* (which usually means "to be heavy" and can also mean "to be stubborn") to say that Pharaoh's heart was hardened. This edition attributes all the uses of *KBD* to E, but it is also possible that some are from J.

| [ used more than once ] | " quoting older text " |

| **E** | **J** |
|---|---|
| | will let you go, that ye may sacrifice to the Lord your God in the wilderness; only ye shall not go very far away; entreat for me.' |
| <sup>25</sup>And Moses said: 'Behold, I go out from thee, and I will entreat the Lord that the swarms of flies may depart from Pharaoh, from his servants, and from his people, to-morrow; only let not Pharaoh deal deceitfully any more in not letting the people go to sacrifice to the Lord.' <sup>26</sup>And Moses went out from Pharaoh, and entreated the Lord. <sup>27</sup>And the Lord did according to the word of Moses; and He removed the swarms of flies from Pharaoh, from his servants, and from his people; there remained not one. <sup>28</sup>And Pharaoh made stubborn *[KBD]* his heart this time also, and he did not let the people go. | |
| EX 9:1Then the Lord said unto Moses: 'Go in unto Pharaoh, and tell him: Thus saith the Lord, the God of the Hebrews: Let My people go, that they may serve Me. <sup>2</sup>For if thou refuse to let them go, and wilt hold them still, <sup>3</sup>behold, the hand of the Lord is upon thy cattle which are in the field, upon the horses, upon the asses, upon the camels, upon the herds, and upon the flocks; there shall be a very grievous murrain. <sup>4</sup>And the Lord shall make a division between the cattle of Israel and the cattle of Egypt; and there shall nothing die of all that belongeth to the children of Israel.' <sup>5</sup>And the Lord appointed a set time, saying: 'To-morrow the Lord shall do this thing in the land.' <sup>6</sup>And the Lord did that thing on the morrow, and all the cattle of Egypt died; but of the cattle of the children of Israel died not one. <sup>7</sup>And Pharaoh sent, and, behold, there was not so much as one of the cattle of the Israelites dead. But the heart of Pharaoh was stubborn *[KBD]*, and he did not let the people go. | *[Gap in J: see E]* |
| <sup>13</sup>And the Lord said unto Moses: 'Rise up early in the morning, and stand before Pharaoh, and say unto him: Thus saith the Lord, the God of the Hebrews: Let My people go, that they may serve Me. <sup>14</sup>For I will this time send all My plagues upon thy person, and upon thy servants, and upon thy people; that thou mayest know that there is none like Me in all the earth. <sup>15</sup>Surely now I had put forth My hand, and smitten | |

| ( added by redactor ) | { problematic } |

| P | Notes |
|---|---|
| | This clue is muddied by the fact that R apparently tried to make the text more continuous by adding the phrase "(And the heart of Pharaoh was strengthened *[HZQ]*, and he did not let the children of Israel go" in a number of locations in the JE text to make it more consistent with the P text. The best evidence that this phrase was added is: "EX 9:34And when Pharaoh saw that the rain and the hail and the thunders were ceased, he sinned yet more, and made stubborn *[KBD]* his heart, he and his servants. (35And the heart of Pharaoh was strengthened *[HZQ]*, and he did not let the children of Israel go; as the Lord had spoken by Moses.)" A single author would not be likely to repeat himself in this way: it seems that the author wrote Exodus 9:34 and a redactor added Exodus 9:35 here when he was adding it in many places. |
| *[Continued on p. 247]* | It seems that this phrase was originally in the P text, since that text would not be continuous without it, and that R added it to the JE text. |
| | At the end of the plagues, R added this phrase preceded with "And Moses and Aaron did all these wonders before Pharaoh" to tie the narrative together as it approached its climax. |
| | The difference between *HZQ* and *KBD* is very important to separating the texts, but the JPS translation translates these words inconsistently. It translates words based on *HZQ* as "hardened." It translates words based on *KBD* as "stubborn" when they just describe Pharaoh's heart but as "hardened" when they |
| [ used more than once ] | " quoting older text " |

| **E** | **J** |
|---|---|
| thee and thy people with pestilence, and thou hadst been cut off from the earth. ¹⁶But in very deed for this cause have I made thee to stand, to show thee My power, and that My name may be declared throughout all the earth. ¹⁷As yet exaltest thou thyself against My people, that thou wilt not let them go? ¹⁸Behold, to-morrow about this time I will cause it to rain a very grievous hail, such as hath not been in Egypt since the day it was founded even until now. ¹⁹Now there-fore send, hasten in thy cattle and all that thou hast in the field; for every man and beast that shall be found in the field, and shall not be brought home, the hail shall come down upon them, and they shall die.' ²⁰He that feared the word of the Lord among the servants of Pharaoh made his servants and his cattle flee into the houses; ²¹and he that regarded not the word of the Lord left his servants and his cattle in the field. | |
| ²²And the Lord said unto Moses: 'Stretch forth thy hand toward heaven, that there may be hail in all the land of Egypt, upon man, and upon beast, and upon every herb of the field, throughout the land of Egypt.' ²³And Moses stretched forth his rod toward heaven; and the Lord sent thunder and hail, and fire ran down unto the earth; and the Lord caused to hail upon the land of Egypt. ²⁴So there was hail, and fire flashing up amidst the hail, very grievous, such as had not been in all the land of Egypt since it became a nation. ²⁵And the hail smote throughout all the land of Egypt all that was in the field, both man and beast; and the hail smote every herb of the field, and broke every tree of the field. ²⁶Only in the land of Goshen, where the children of Israel were, was there no hail. | EX ⁹:²⁷And Pha-raoh sent, and called for Moses and Aaron, and said unto them: 'I have sinned this time; the Lord is righteous, and I and my people are wicked. ²⁸En-treat the Lord, and let there be enough of these mighty thunder-ings and hail; and I will let you go, and ye shall stay no longer.' |
| *[Gap in E: see J]* | |
| EX ⁹:²⁹And Moses said unto him: 'As soon as I am gone out of the city, I will spread forth my hands unto the Lord; the thunders shall cease, neither shall there be any more hail; that thou mayest know that the earth is the Lord's. ³⁰But as for thee and thy servants, I know that ye will not yet fear the Lord God.'— | |
| ( added by redactor ) | { problematic } |

| P | Notes |
|---|---|
| | describe what God did to Pharaoh's heart (presumably because "made stubborn" is a bit clumsy). To top it off, it also translates a third word in Exodus 7:3, with the root *QShH*, as "hardened." |
| | This edition alters the JPS translation to make the translation consistent with the original Hebrew. It always translates words with the root *HZQ* as "strengthened" or "strong." It always translated words with the root *KBD* as "made stubborn" or "stubborn." For the one case with the root *QShH*, it keeps the JPS translation of "hardened." It also includes the Hebrew roots *HZQ* and *KBD* in brackets when words based on these roots are used to describe Pharaoh's hard heart. |
| *[Continued on p. 247]* | J text: The JPS translation says "EX 8:3b And brought up frogs upon the land of Egypt." This edition translates it as "And they brought up frogs upon the land of Egypt." Hebrew does not use the pronoun, so this translation is just as accurate. |
| [ used more than once ] | " quoting older text " |

*[Continued on p. 247]*

| **E** | **J** |
|---|---|
| ³¹And the flax and the barley were smitten; for the barley was in the ear, and the flax was in bloom. ³²But the wheat and the spelt were not smitten; for they ripen late.— ³³And Moses went out of the city from Pharaoh, and spread forth his hands unto the Lord; and the thunders and hail ceased, and the rain was not poured upon the earth. ³⁴And when Pharaoh saw that the rain and the hail and the thunders were ceased, he sinned yet more, and made stubborn *[KBD]* his heart, he and his servants. (³⁵And the heart of Pharaoh was strengthened *[HZQ]*, and he did not let the children of Israel go; as the Lord had spoken by Moses.)<br>EX 10:1And the Lord said unto Moses: 'Go in unto Pharaoh; for I have made stubborn *[KBD]* his heart, and the heart of his servants, that I might show these My signs in the midst of them; ²and that thou mayest tell in the ears of thy son, and of thy son's son, what I have wrought upon Egypt, and My signs which I have done among them; that ye may know that I am the Lord.'<br><br><br><br><br>*[Gap in E: see J]*<br><br><br><br>EX 10:6bAnd he turned, and went out from Pharaoh. ⁷And Pharaoh's servants said unto him: 'How long shall this man be a snare unto us? let the men go, that they may serve the Lord their God, knowest thou not yet that Egypt is destroyed? | *[Gap in J: see E]*<br><br><br>EX 10:3And Moses and Aaron went in unto Pharaoh, and said unto him: 'Thus saith the Lord, the God of the Hebrews: How long wilt thou refuse to humble thyself before Me? let My people go, that they may serve Me. ⁴Else, if thou refuse to let My people go, behold, to-morrow will I bring locusts into thy border; ⁵and they shall cover the face of the earth, that one shall not be able to see the earth; and they shall eat the residue of that which is escaped, which remaineth unto you from the hail, and shall eat every tree which groweth for you out of the field; ⁶aAnd thy houses shall be filled, and the houses of all thy servants, and the houses of all the Egyptians; as neither thy fathers nor thy fathers' fathers have seen, since the day that they were upon the earth unto this day.'<br><br>*[Gap in J: see E]* |
| ( added by redactor ) | { problematic } |

| P | Notes |
|---|---|
| *[Continued on p. 247]* | *[Continued on p. 247]* |

| [ used more than once ] | " quoting older text " |

| **E** | **J** |
|---|---|
| | EX 10:8And Moses and Aaron were brought again unto Pharaoh; and he said unto them: 'Go, serve the Lord your God; but who are they that shall go?' 9And Moses said: 'We will go with our young and with our old, with our sons and with our daughters, with our flocks and with our herds we will go; for we must hold a feast unto the Lord.' 10And he said unto them: 'So be the Lord with you, as I will let you go, and your little ones; see ye that evil is before your face. 11Not so; go now ye that are men, and serve the Lord; for that is what ye desire.' And they were driven out from Pharaoh's presence. |
| *[Gap in E: see J]* | |
| EX 10:12And the Lord said unto Moses: 'Stretch out thy hand over the land of Egypt for the locusts, that they may come up upon the land of Egypt, and eat every herb of the land, even all that the hail hath left.' 13And Moses stretched forth his rod over the land of Egypt, and the Lord brought an east wind upon the land all that day, and all the night; and when it was morning, the east wind brought the locusts. 14And the locusts went up over all the land of Egypt, and rested in all the borders of Egypt; very grievous were they; before them there were no such locusts as they, neither after them shall be such. 15For they covered the face of the whole earth, so that the land was darkened; and they did eat every herb of the land, and all the fruit of the trees which the hail had left; and there remained not any green thing, either tree or herb of the field, through all the land of Egypt. | *[Gap in J: see E]* |
| | EX 10:16Then Pharaoh called for Moses and Aaron in haste; and he said: 'I have sinned against the Lord your God, and against you. 17Now therefore forgive, I pray thee, my sin only this once, and entreat the Lord your God, that He may take away from me this death only.' 18And |
| *[Gap in E: see J]* | |
| ( added by redactor ) | { problematic } |

| P | Notes |
|---|---|

*[Continued on p. 247]*

*[Continued on p. 247]*

| [ used more than once ] | " quoting older text " |
|---|---|

| E | J |
|---|---|
| EX 10:21 And the Lord said unto Moses: 'Stretch out thy hand toward heaven, that there may be darkness over the land of Egypt, even darkness which may be felt.' 22And Moses stretched forth his hand toward heaven; and there was a thick darkness in all the land of Egypt three days; 23they saw not one another, neither rose any from his place for three days; but all the children of Israel had light in their dwellings. 24And Pharaoh called unto Moses, and said: 'Go ye, serve the Lord; only let your flocks and your herds be stayed; let your little ones also go with you.' 25And Moses said: 'Thou must also give into our hand sacrifices and burnt-offerings, that we may sacrifice unto the Lord our God. 26Our cattle also shall go with us; there shall not a hoof be left behind; for thereof must we take to serve the Lord our God; and we know not with what we must serve the Lord, until we come thither.' (27But the Lord strengthened *[HZQ]* Pharaoh's heart, and he would not let them go.) 28And Pharaoh said unto him: 'Get thee from me, take heed to thyself, see my face no more; for in the day thou seest my face thou shalt die.' 29And Moses said: 'Thou hast spoken well; I will see thy face again no more.' | he went out from Pharaoh, and entreated the Lord. 19And the Lord turned an exceeding strong west wind, which took up the locusts, and drove them into the Red Sea; there remained not one locust in all the border of Egypt. (20But the Lord strengthened *[HZQ]* Pharaoh's heart, and he did not let the children of Israel go.) |
| EX 11:1 And the Lord said unto Moses: 'Yet one plague more will I bring upon Pharaoh, and upon Egypt; afterwards he will let you go hence; when he shall let you go, he shall surely thrust you out hence altogether. 2Speak now in the ears of the people, and let them ask every man of his neighbour, and every woman of her neighbour, jewels of silver, and jewels of gold.' 3And the Lord gave the people favour in the sight of the Egyptians. Moreover the man Moses was very great in the land of Egypt, in the sight of Pharaoh's servants, and in the sight of the people.\n\n4And Moses said: 'Thus saith the Lord: About midnight will I go out into the midst of Egypt; 5and all the first-born in the land of Egypt shall die, from the first-born of Pharaoh that sitteth upon his throne, even unto the first-born of the maid-servant that is behind the mill; and all the first-born of cattle. 6And there shall be a great cry throughout all the land of Egypt, | *[Gap in J: see E]* |
| ( added by redactor ) | { problematic } |

| P | Notes |
|---|---|

*[Continued on p. 247]*

*[Continued on p. 247]*

| [ used more than once ] | " quoting older text " |

| **E** | **J** |
|---|---|
| such as there hath been none like it, nor shall be like it any more. [7]But against any of the children of Israel shall not a dog whet his tongue, against man or beast; that ye may know how that the Lord doth put a difference between the Egyptians and Israel. [8]And all these thy servants shall come down unto me, and bow down unto me, saying: Get thee out, and all the people that follow thee; and after that I will go out.' And he went out from Pharaoh in hot anger. | |
| [9]And the Lord said unto Moses: 'Pharaoh will not hearken unto you; that My wonders may be multiplied in the land of Egypt.' ([10]And Moses and Aaron did all these wonders before Pharaoh; and the Lord strengthened *[HZQ]* Pharaoh's heart, and he did not let the children of Israel go out of his land.) | |

| **Passover Commandments and Sacrifice of First Born** | **Passover Commandments** |
|---|---|
| EX 13:1And the Lord spoke unto Moses, saying: [2]'Sanctify unto Me all the first-born, whatsoever openeth the womb among the children of Israel, both of man and of beast, it is Mine.' | EX 12:21Then Moses called for all the elders of Israel, and said unto them: 'Draw out, and take you lambs according to your families, and kill the passover lamb. [22]And ye shall |
| [3]And Moses said unto the people: 'Remember this day, in which ye came out from Egypt, out of the house of bondage; for by strength of hand the Lord brought you out from this place; there shall no leavened bread be eaten. [4]This day ye go forth in the month Abib. [5]And it shall be when the Lord shall bring thee into the land of the Canaanite, and the Hittite, and the Amorite, and the Hivite, and the Jebusite, which He swore unto thy fathers to give thee, a land flowing with milk and honey, that thou shalt keep this service in this month. [6]Seven days thou shalt eat unleavened bread, and in the seventh day shall be a feast to the Lord. [7]Unleavened bread shall be eaten throughout the seven days; and there shall no leavened bread be seen with thee, neither shall there be leaven seen with thee, in all thy | take a bunch of hyssop, and dip it in the blood that is in the basin, and strike the lintel and the two side-posts with the blood that is in the basin; and none of you shall go out of the door of his house until the morning. [23]For the Lord will pass through to smite the Egyptians; and when He seeth the |

| ( added by redactor ) | { problematic } |
|---|---|

| **P** | **Notes** |
|---|---|

### Passover Commandments

EX 12:1And the Lord spoke unto Moses and Aaron in the land of Egypt, saying: 2'This month shall be unto you the beginning of months; it shall be the first month of the year to you. 3Speak ye unto all the congregation of Israel, saying: In the tenth day of this month they shall take to them every man a lamb, according to their fathers' houses, a lamb for a household; 4and if the household be too little for a lamb, then shall he and his neighbour next unto his house take one according to the number of the souls; according to every man's eating ye shall make your count for the lamb. 5Your lamb shall be without blemish, a male of the first year; ye shall take it from the sheep, or from the goats; 6and ye shall keep it unto the fourteenth day of the same month; and the whole assembly of the congregation of Israel shall kill it at dusk. 7And they shall take of the blood, and put it on the two side-posts and on the lintel, upon the houses wherein they shall eat it. 8And they shall eat the flesh in that night, roast with fire, and unleavened bread; with bit-

### Passover Commandments

**E Text**

E includes the commandment to sacrifice all first born animals and to redeem all first born children with a sacrifice. E connects this sacrifice of the first born with the plague of slaying the first born when he describes the first celebration of Passover in Exodus 13. The other texts do not mention this practice in connection with Passover.

Because he is a priest, E has a much longer description of the rituals than J.

| [ used more than once ] | " quoting older text " |
|---|---|

| **E** | **J** |
|---|---|
| borders. [8]And thou shalt tell thy son in that day, saying: It is because of that which the Lord did for me when I came forth out of Egypt. [9]And it shall be for a sign unto thee upon thy hand, and for a memorial between thine eyes, that the law of the Lord may be in thy mouth; for with a strong hand hath the Lord brought thee out of Egypt. [10]Thou shalt therefore keep this ordinance in its season from year to year. | blood upon the lintel, and on the two side-posts, the Lord will pass over the door, and will not suffer the destroyer to come in unto your houses to smite you. |
| [11]And it shall be when the Lord shall bring thee into the land of the Canaanite, as He swore unto thee and to thy fathers, and shall give it thee, [12]that thou shalt set apart unto the Lord all that openeth the womb; every firstling that is a male, which thou hast coming of a beast, shall be the Lord's. [13]And every firstling of an ass thou shalt redeem with a lamb; and if thou wilt not redeem it, then thou shalt break its neck; and all the first-born of man among thy sons shalt thou redeem. [14]And it shall be when thy son asketh thee in time to come, saying: What is this? that thou shalt say unto him: By strength of hand the Lord brought us out from Egypt, from the house of bondage; [15]and it came to pass, when Pharaoh would hardly let us go that the Lord slew all the first-born in the land of Egypt, both the first-born of man, and the first-born of beast; therefore I sacrifice to the Lord all that openeth the womb, being males; but all the first-born of my sons I redeem. [16]And it shall be for a sign upon thy hand, and for frontlets between thine eyes; for by strength of hand the Lord brought us forth out of Egypt.' | [24]And ye shall observe this thing for an ordinance to thee and to thy sons for ever. [25]And it shall come to pass, when ye be come to the land which the Lord will give you, according as He hath promised, that ye shall keep this service. [26]And it shall come to pass, when your children shall say unto you: What mean ye by this service? [27]that ye shall say: It is the sacrifice of the Lord's passover, for that He passed over the houses of the children of Israel in Egypt, when He smote the Egyptians, and delivered our houses.' And the people bowed the head and worshipped. |
| ( added by redactor ) | { problematic } |

| P | Notes |
|---|---|

**P**

ter herbs they shall eat it. [9]Eat not of it raw, nor sodden at all with water, but roast with fire; its head with its legs and with the inwards thereof. [10]And ye shall let nothing of it remain until the morning; but that which remaineth of it until the morning ye shall burn with fire. [11]And thus shall ye eat it: with your loins girded, your shoes on your feet, and your staff in your hand; and ye shall eat it in haste—it is the Lord's passover.

[12]For I will go through the land of Egypt in that night, and will smite all the first-born in the land of Egypt, both man and beast; and against all the gods of Egypt I will execute judgments: I am the Lord. [13]And the blood shall be to you for a token upon the houses where ye are; and when I see the blood, I will pass over you, and there shall no plague be upon you to destroy you, when I smite the land of Egypt.

[14]And this day shall be unto you for a memorial, and ye shall keep it a feast to the Lord; throughout your generations ye shall keep it a feast by an ordinance for ever. [15]Seven days shall ye eat unleavened bread; howbeit the first day ye shall put away leaven out of your houses; for whosoever eateth leavened bread from the first day until the seventh day, that soul shall be cut off from Israel. [16]And in the first day there shall be to you a holy convocation, and in the seventh day a holy convocation; no manner of work shall be done in them, save that which every man must eat, that only may be done by you. [17]And ye shall observe the feast of unleavened bread; for in this selfsame day have I brought your hosts out of the land of Egypt; therefore shall ye observe this day throughout your generations by an ordinance for ever. [18]In the first month, on the fourteenth day of the month at even, ye shall eat unleavened bread, until the one and twentieth day of the month at even. [19]Seven days shall there be no leaven found in your houses; for whosoever eateth that which is leavened, that soul shall be cut off from the congregation of Israel, whether he

**Notes**

**J Text**

In this location, J includes only the sacrifice of the lamb, the most primitive Passover ritual. However, J's version of the Ten Commandments includes only the eating of unleavened bread: "[EX 34:18]The feast of unleavened bread shalt thou keep. Seven days thou shalt eat unleavened bread, as I commanded thee, at the time appointed in the month Abib, for in the month Abib thou camest out from Egypt."

**P Text**

P has a much longer description of the rituals than E or J.

The repetition in Exodus 12:28 and Exodus 13:50 is a typical device that the redactor uses to frame passages that he inserts. Thus, the extra details about observing Passover in Exodus 13:43-50 are probably a separate text added by R. Because it is so brief, this edition keeps it here rather than moving it to the section of Other Texts.

[ used more than once ]     " quoting older text "

| **E** | **J** |
|---|---|
| *[Gap in E: Pharaoh Lets Israel Go]* | |
| **Flight from Egypt** | **Flight from Egypt** |
| EX 13:17And it came to pass, when Pharaoh had let the people go, that God led them not by the way of the land of the Philistines, although that was near; for God said: 'Lest peradventure the people repent when they see war, and they return to Egypt.' 18But God led the people about, by the way of the wilderness by the Red Sea; and the children of Israel went up armed out of the land of Egypt. 19And Moses took the bones of Joseph with him; for he had straitly sworn the children of Israel, saying: 'God will surely remember you; and ye shall carry up my bones away hence with you.' | EX 12:29And it came to pass at midnight, that the Lord smote all the first-born in the land of Egypt, from the first-born of Pharaoh that sat on his throne unto the first-born of the captive that was in the dungeon; and all the first-born of cattle. 30And Pharaoh rose up in the night, he, and all his servants, and all the Egyptians; and there was a great cry in Egypt; for there was not a house where there was not one dead. 31And he called for Moses and Aaron by night and said: 'Rise up, get you forth from among my people, both ye and the children of Israel; and go, serve the Lord, as ye have said. 32Take both your flocks and your herds, as ye have said, and be gone; and bless me also.' |
| EX 14:5bAnd the heart of Pharaoh and of his servants was turned towards the people, and they said: 'What is this we have done, that we have let Israel go from serving us? | |
| 7And he took six hundred chosen chariots, and all the chariots of Egypt, and captains over all of them. | 33And the Egyptians were urgent upon the people, to send them out of the land in haste; for they said: 'We are all dead men.' 34And the people took their dough before it was leavened, their kneading-troughs being bound up in their clothes upon their shoulders. 35And the children of Israel did according to the word |
| 9aAnd the Egyptians pursued after them, all the horses and chariots of Pharaoh, and his horsemen, and his army. | |
| ( added by redactor ) | { problematic } |

| **P** | **Notes** |

be a sojourner, or one that is born in the land. [20]Ye shall eat nothing leavened; in all your habitations shall ye eat unleavened bread.'

EX 12:28And the children of Israel went and did so; as the Lord had commanded Moses and Aaron, so did they.

### Flight from Egypt

EX 12:40Now the time that the children of Israel dwelt in Egypt was four hundred and thirty years. [41]And it came to pass at the end of four hundred and thirty years, even the selfsame day it came to pass, that all the host of the Lord went out from the land of Egypt. [42]It was a night of watching unto the Lord for bringing them out from the land of Egypt; this same night is a night of watching unto the Lord for all the children of Israel throughout their generations.

(EX 12:43And the Lord said unto Moses and Aaron: 'This is the ordinance of the passover: there shall no alien eat thereof; [44]but every man's servant that is bought for money, when thou hast circumcised him, then shall he eat thereof. [45]A sojourner and a hired servant shall not eat thereof. [46]In one house shall it be eaten; thou shalt not carry forth aught of the flesh abroad out of the house; neither shall ye break a bone thereof. [47]All the congregation of Israel shall keep it. [48]And when a stranger shall sojourn with thee, and

### Gap in E - Pharaoh Lets Israel Go

E does not tell the story of Pharaoh letting Israel go, but he does look back on it in "EX 13:17And it came to pass, when Pharaoh had let the people go...."

Presumably, RJE preferred J's story of letting Israel go, leaving this gap in the E text.

### Flight from Egypt

**E Text**

In E, the Israelites are led by an angel (Ex. 14:19a), in keeping with E's general principle that God appears directly only to Moses and appears to others either in dreams or visions or through angels. In E, this angel moves from before to behind the Israelites to come between them and the Egyptians (Ex. 14:19a).

Our surviving E text does not describe the dividing of the red sea or drowning of the Egyptians, but what we have of E hints at more of his story. E's version of the Song of the Sea mentions the drowning of the Egyptians:

EX 15:1Then sang Moses and the children of Israel this song unto the Lord, and spoke, saying:

"I will sing unto the Lord, for He is highly exalted;
The horse and his rider hath He thrown into the sea.

There is also a hint later in E that Moses struck the water with his rod:

EX 17:5And the Lord said unto Moses: 'Pass on before the people, and take with thee of the elders

| [ used more than once ] | " quoting older text " |

| **E** | **J** |
|---|---|

**E**

[10b]And the children of Israel cried out unto the Lord. [11]And they said unto Moses: 'Because there were no graves in Egypt, hast thou taken us away to die in the wilderness? wherefore hast thou dealt thus with us, to bring us forth out of Egypt? [12]Is not this the word that we spoke unto thee in Egypt, saying: Let us alone, that we may serve the Egyptians? For it were better for us to serve the Egyptians, than that we should die in the wilderness.'

[13]And Moses said unto the people: 'Fear ye not, stand still, and see the salvation of the Lord, which He will work for you to-day; for whereas ye have seen the Egyptians to-day, ye shall see them again no more for ever. [14]The Lord will fight for you, and ye shall hold your peace.'

[19a]And the angel of God, who went before the camp of Israel, removed and went behind them; [20a]And it came between the camp of Egypt and the camp of Israel; [24b]And discomfited the host of the Egyptians. [28b]There remained not so much as one of them.

[31]And Israel saw the great work which the Lord did upon the Egyptians, and the people feared the Lord; and they believed in the Lord, and in His servant Moses.

**J**

of Moses; and they asked of the Egyptians jewels of silver, and jewels of gold, and raiment. [36]And the Lord gave the people favour in the sight of the Egyptians, so that they let them have what they asked. And they despoiled the Egyptians.

[37]And the children of Israel journeyed from Rameses to Succoth, about six hundred thousand men on foot, beside children. [38]And a mixed multitude went up also with them; and flocks, and herds, even very much cattle. [39]And they baked unleavened cakes of the dough which they brought forth out of Egypt, for it was not leavened; because they were thrust out of Egypt, and could not tarry, neither had they prepared for themselves any victual.

EX 13:21 And the Lord went before them by day in a pillar of cloud, to lead them the way; and by night in a pillar of fire, to give them light; that they might go by day and by night: [22]the pillar of cloud by day, and the pillar of fire by night, departed not from before the people.

EX14:5a And it was told the king of Egypt that the people were fled; [6]And he made ready his chariots, and took his people with him. [10a]And when Pharaoh drew nigh, the children of Israel lifted up their eyes, and, behold, the Egyptians were marching after them; and they were sore afraid;

[19b]And the pillar of cloud removed from before them, and stood behind them; [20b]And there was the cloud and the darkness here, yet gave it light by night there; and the one

| ( added by redactor ) | { problematic } |
|---|---|

| P | Notes |
|---|---|
| will keep the passover to the Lord, let all his males be circumcised, and then let him come near and keep it; and he shall be as one that is born in the land; but no uncircumcised person shall eat thereof. ⁴⁹One law shall be to him that is home-born, and unto the stranger that sojourneth among you.' ⁵⁰Thus did all the children of Israel; as the Lord commanded Moses and Aaron, so did they. ) | of Israel; and thy rod, wherewith thou smotest the river, take in thy hand, and go. |
| | These two hints imply that Moses used his rod to divide the water and let the Israelites pass, and then the water closed to drown the Egyptians—though it is odd that the second one talks about the Israelites crossing a river rather than the sea. |
| ⁵¹And it came to pass the selfsame day that the Lord did bring the children of Israel out of the land of Egypt by their hosts. | Notice also that only E mentions bringing the "bones of Joseph" back to Canaan. E was a Mushite priest, the group of priests who had been in charge of the religious center at Shiloh, which was in the territory of Ephraim, who was the son of Joseph. |
| EX 13:20And they took their journey from Succoth, and encamped in Etham, in the edge of the wilderness. | **J Text** |
| EX 14:1And the Lord spoke unto Moses, saying: ²'Speak unto the children of Israel, that they turn back and encamp before Pi-hahiroth, between Migdol and the sea, before Baal-zephon, over against it shall ye encamp by the sea. ³And Pharaoh will say of the children of Israel: They are entangled in the land, the wilderness hath shut them in. ⁴And I will strengthen *[HZQ]* Pharaoh's heart, and he shall follow after them; and I will get Me honour upon Pharaoh, and upon all his host; and the Egyptians shall know that I am the Lord.' And they did so. | In J, the Israelites are led by God as a pillar of cloud, in keeping with J's belief that God often appears directly. |
| | Notice the doublet in J and E. In E, the angel moves behind the Israelites, and in J, God as a pillar of cloud moves behind the Israelites to come between them and the Egyptians (Ex. 14:19b) |
| | Unlike the surviving portion of E, J explicitly describes the parting of the sea to let the Israelites pass and the closing of the sea to drown the Egyptians, but it is caused by the Lord sending a wind with no mention of Moses' rod. |
| | **P Text** |
| ⁸And the Lord strengthened *[HZQ]* the heart of Pharaoh king of Egypt, and he pursued after the children of Israel; for the children of Israel went out with a high hand. ⁹b And they overtook them encamping by the | In P, neither a pillar of cloud nor an angel leads the Israelites. |
| | Exodus 12:43-50 was probably inserted by a redactor. It includes supplementary commandments for observing Passover beyond the |

| [ used more than once ] | " quoting older text " |

| E | J |
|---|---|
| | came not near the other all the night. [21b]And the Lord caused the sea to go back by a strong east wind all the night, and made the sea dry land, and the waters were divided. [24a]And it came to pass in the morning watch, that the Lord looked forth upon the host of the Egyptians through the pillar of fire and of cloud, [25]And He took off their chariot wheels, and made them to drive heavily; so that the Egyptians said: 'Let us flee from the face of Israel; for the Lord fighteth for them against the Egyptians.' [27b]And the sea returned to its strength when the morning appeared; and the Egyptians fled against it; and the Lord overthrew the Egyptians in the midst of the sea. [30]Thus the Lord saved Israel that day out of the hand of the Egyptians; and Israel saw the Egyptians dead upon the sea-shore. |
| *[Continued on p. 256]* | |
| ( added by redactor ) | { problematic } |

| P | Notes |
|---|---|

sea, beside Pi-hahiroth, in front of Baal-zephon. [15]And the Lord said unto Moses: {'Wherefore criest thou unto Me?} speak unto the children of Israel, that they go forward. [16]And lift thou up thy rod, and stretch out thy hand over the sea, and divide it; and the children of Israel shall go into the midst of the sea on dry ground. [17]And I, behold, I will strengthen *[HZQ]* the hearts of the Egyptians, and they shall go in after them; and I will get Me honour upon Pharaoh, and upon all his host, upon his chariots, and upon his horsemen. [18]And the Egyptians shall know that I am the Lord, when I have gotten Me honour upon Pharaoh, upon his chariots, and upon his horsemen.'

[21a]And Moses stretched out his hand over the sea; [22]And the children of Israel went into the midst of the sea upon the dry ground; and the waters were a wall unto them on their right hand, and on their left. [23]And the Egyptians pursued, and went in after them into the midst of the sea, all Pharaoh's horses, his chariots, and his horsemen. [26]And the Lord said unto Moses: 'Stretch out thy hand over the sea, that the waters may come back upon the Egyptians, upon their chariots, and upon their horsemen.' [27a]And Moses stretched forth his hand over the sea, [28a]And the waters returned, and covered the chariots, and

commandments in Exodus 12:14-20, but these supplementary commandments are out of place, separated from P's main list of commandments by Exodus 12:28 and Exodus 12:40-42. In addition, it is framed by a repetition: the main list ended with "[EX 12:28]And the children of Israel went and did so; as the Lord had commanded Moses and Aaron, so did they," while this supplementary list ends with "[EX 12:50]Thus did all the children of Israel; as the Lord commanded Moses and Aaron, so did they." The separation and repetition are signs of a later insertion.

One verse in P seems problematic: "[EX 14:15]And the Lord said unto Moses: {'Wherefore criest thou unto Me?} speak unto the children of Israel." This verse seems out of place because Moses has not been crying out to the Lord. But this problem is not a result of this edition's division of texts. It is present in the received version of the Bible:

[EX 14:13]And Moses said unto the people: 'Fear ye not, stand still, and see the salvation of the Lord, which He will work for you to-day; for whereas ye have seen the Egyptians to-day, ye shall see them again no more for ever. [14]The Lord will fight for you, and ye shall hold your peace.' [15]And the Lord said unto Moses: 'Wherefore criest thou unto Me? speak unto the children of Israel, that they go forward.'

This problem is probably the result of a corrupt text.

**Translation**

P Text: The JPS translation says "[GEN 14:9b]And overtook them encamping by the sea...." This edition translates it as

| [ used more than once ] | " quoting older text " |
|---|---|

| **E** | **J** |
|---|---|
| | |

### Song of the Sea

EX 15:1Then sang Moses and the children of Israel this song unto the Lord, and spoke, saying:

"I will sing unto the Lord, for He is highly exalted;
The horse and his rider hath He thrown into the sea.
²The Lord is my strength and song,
And He is become my salvation;
This is my God, and I will glorify Him;
My father's God, and I will exalt Him.
³The Lord is a man of war,
The Lord is His name.
⁴Pharaoh's chariots and his host hath He cast into the sea,
And his chosen captains are sunk in the Red Sea.
⁵The deeps cover them—
They went down into the depths like a stone.
⁶Thy right hand, O Lord, glorious in power,
Thy right hand, O Lord, dasheth in pieces the enemy.
⁷And in the greatness of Thine excellency Thou overthrowest them that rise up against Thee;
Thou sendest forth Thy wrath, it consumeth them as stubble.
⁸And with the blast of Thy nostrils the waters were piled up—

### Song of the Sea

EX 15:20And Miriam the prophetess, the sister of Aaron, took a timbrel in her hand; and all the women went out after her with timbrels and with dances. ²¹And Miriam sang unto them:

"Sing ye to the Lord, for He is highly exalted:
The horse and his rider hath He thrown into the sea."

*[Gap in J: see E]*

( added by redactor )  { problematic }

| **P** | **Notes** |
|---|---|
| the horsemen, even all the host of Pharaoh that went in after them into the sea; ²⁹But the children of Israel walked upon dry land in the midst of the sea; and the waters were a wall unto them on their right hand, and on their left. | "And they overtook them encamping by the sea." Hebrew does not use the pronoun, so this translation is just as accurate. |

**Song of the Sea**

The Song of the Sea is an earlier text, apparently so well known that was quoted by both J and E. This edition assigns the version sung by Moses to the E text, because E is generally an admirer of Moses.

There is a minor difference in the lines quoted in both versions, "I will sing unto the Lord" in E and "Sing ye to the Lord" in J, so there were presumably also minor differences in other verses.

This song includes an indication of how ancient it is. It says "chiefs of Edom" (Ex. 15:15), showing that it was written when Edom was a chiefdom, before it became a monarchy. By contrast, the body of the E text says Moses sent messengers to the king of Edom (Num. 20:14), showing it was written later, after Edom became a monarchy. Unfortunately, it is not known exactly when Edom became a monarchy, so we can say that the Song of the Sea is earlier than the E text but cannot date it more precisely.

**Translation**

This JPS version has a misleading translation of "ᴱˣ ¹⁵˸¹¹Who is like unto Thee, O Lord, among the

| [ used more than once ] | " quoting older text " |

| **E** | **J** |
|---|---|
| The floods stood upright as a heap;<br>The deeps were congealed in the heart of the sea.<br>[9]The enemy said:<br>'I will pursue, I will overtake, I will divide the spoil;<br>My lust shall be satisfied upon them;<br>I will draw my sword, my hand shall destroy them.'<br>[10]Thou didst blow with Thy wind, the sea covered them;<br>They sank as lead in the mighty waters.<br>[11]Who is like unto Thee, O Lord, among the mighty?<br>Who is like unto Thee, glorious in holiness,<br>Fearful in praises, doing wonders?<br>[12]Thou stretchedst out Thy right hand—<br>The earth swallowed them.<br>[13]Thou in Thy love hast led the people that Thou hast redeemed;<br>Thou hast guided them in Thy strength to Thy holy habitation.<br>[14]The peoples have heard, they tremble;<br>Pangs have taken hold on the inhabitants of Philistia.<br>[15]Then were the chiefs of Edom affrighted;<br>The mighty men of Moab, trembling taketh hold upon them;<br>All the inhabitants of Canaan are melted away.<br>[16]Terror and dread falleth upon them;<br>By the greatness of Thine arm they are as still as a stone;<br>Till Thy people pass over, O Lord,<br>Till the people pass over that Thou hast gotten.<br>[17]Thou bringest them in, and plantest them in the mountain of Thine inheritance,<br>The place, O Lord, which Thou hast made for Thee to dwell in,<br>The sanctuary, O Lord, which Thy hands have established.<br>[18]The Lord shall reign for ever and ever."<br>([19]For the horses of Pharaoh went in with his chariots and with his horsemen into the sea, and the Lord | *[Continued on p. 260]* |
| ( added by redactor ) | { problematic } |

| P | Notes |
|---|---|
| | mighty?" It translates the Hebrew *elim* as "mighty," but the word actually means "gods" and the verse is commonly translated "Who is like unto Thee, O Lord, among the gods?" Presumably, the JPS changed the translation because the original Hebrew hints at polytheism.<br><br>This verse shows that, even at the early date of the Song of the Sea, the word "el" was used to mean "god" as well as being the name of a specific god. |
| *[Continued on p. 261]* | |
| [ used more than once ] | " quoting older text " |

| **E** | **J** |
|---|---|
| brought back the waters of the sea upon them; but the children of Israel walked on dry land in the midst of the sea.) | |

### Promise of No Diseases

EX 15:25bThere He made for them a statute and an ordinance, and there He proved them; 26and He said: 'If thou wilt diligently hearken to the voice of the Lord thy God, and wilt do that which is right in His eyes, and wilt give ear to His commandments, and keep all His statutes, I will put none of the diseases upon thee, which I have put upon the Egyptians; for I am the Lord that healeth thee.'

| **Water - Striking a Rock** | **Water - Sweet from Bitter** |
|---|---|
| EX 17:1And all the congregation of the children of Israel journeyed from the wilderness of Sin, by their stages, according to the commandment of the Lord, and encamped in Rephidim; and there was no water for the people to drink. 2Wherefore the people strove with Moses, and said: 'Give us water that we may drink.' And Moses said unto them: 'Why strive ye with me? wherefore do ye try the Lord?' 3And the people thirsted there for water; and the people murmured against Moses, and said: 'Wherefore hast thou brought us up out of Egypt, to kill us and our children and our cattle with thirst?' 4And Moses cried unto the Lord, saying: 'What shall I do unto this people? they are almost ready to stone me.' | EX 15:22And Moses led Israel onward from the Red Sea, and they went out into the wilderness of Shur; and they went three days in the wilderness, and found no water. 23And when they came to Marah, they could not drink of the waters of Marah, for they were bitter. Therefore the name of it was called Marah. 24And the people murmured against Moses, saying: 'What shall we drink?' 25aAnd he cried unto the Lord; and the Lord showed him a tree, and he cast it into the waters, and the waters were made sweet. |
| 5And the Lord said unto Moses: 'Pass on before the people, and take with thee of the elders of Israel; and thy rod, wherewith thou smotest the river, take in thy hand, and go. 6Behold, I will stand before thee there upon the rock in Horeb; and thou | 27And they came to Elim, where were twelve springs of water, and three score and ten palm-trees; and they encamped there by the waters. |
| ( added by redactor ) | { problematic } |

| **P** | **Notes** |
|---|---|
| **Water - Striking a Rock** | **Water** |
| NUM 20:1And the children of Israel, even the whole congregation, came into the wilderness of Zin in the first month; and the people abode in Kadesh; and Miriam died there, and was buried there. ²And there was no water for the congregation; and they assembled themselves together against Moses and against Aaron. ³And the people strove with Moses, and spoke, saying: 'Would that we had perished when our brethren perished before the Lord! ⁴And why have ye brought the assembly of the Lord into this wilderness, to die there, we and our cattle? ⁵And wherefore have ye made us to come up out of Egypt, to bring us in unto this evil place? it is no place of seed, or of figs, or of vines, or of pomegranates; neither is there any water to drink.'<br><br>⁶And Moses and Aaron went from the presence of the assembly unto | **Relocated Text**<br>There are three texts about providing water to the Israelites in the wilderness:<br>In Exodus 17:1-7 (E) the people complain about lack of water and Moses provides it by striking a rock.<br>In Numbers 20:1-29 (P) the people complain about lack of water and Moses provides it by striking a rock.<br>In Exodus 15:22-25 (J): the people cannot drink the bitter water and Moses makes the water sweet.<br>This edition is meant to allow readers to compare doublets by reading across columns, so it moves Numbers 21:1-29, placing it next to its doublet in Exodus to let readers compare the P text and E text about striking a rock to produce water.<br>**E Text**<br>E's version is favorable to Moses: he is commanded to strike the rock to produce water and he does so. E |
| [ used more than once ] | " quoting older text " |

| E | J |
|---|---|
| shalt smite the rock, and there shall come water out of it, that the people may drink.' And Moses did so in the sight of the elders of Israel. ⁷And the name of the place was called Massah, and Meribah, because of the striving of the children of Israel, and because they tried the Lord, saying: 'Is the Lord among us, or not?' | |

### Battle with Amalek in Rephidim

EX 17:8Then came Amalek, and fought with Israel in Rephidim. ⁹And Moses said unto Joshua: 'Choose us out men, and go out, fight with Amalek; to-morrow I will stand on the top of the hill with the rod of God in my hand.' ¹⁰So Joshua did as Moses had said to him, and fought with Amalek; and Moses, Aaron, and Hur went up to the top of the hill. ¹¹And it came to pass, when Moses held up his hand, that Israel prevailed; and when he let down his hand, Amalek prevailed. ¹²But Moses' hands were heavy; and they took a stone, and put it under him, and he sat thereon; and Aaron and Hur stayed up his hands, the one on the one side, and the other on the other side; and his hands were steady until the going down of the sun. ¹³And Joshua discomfited Amalek and his people with the edge of the sword.

¹⁴And the Lord said unto Moses: 'Write this for a memorial in the book, and re-

### Food - Manna

EX 16:1And they took their journey from Elim, and all the congregation of the children of Israel came unto the wilderness of Sin, which is

| ( added by redactor ) | { problematic } |
|---|---|

| P | Notes |
|---|---|

the door of the tent of meeting, and fell upon their faces; and the glory of the Lord appeared unto them. [7]And the Lord spoke unto Moses, saying: [8]'Take the rod, and assemble the congregation, thou, and Aaron thy brother, and speak ye unto the rock before their eyes, that it give forth its water; and thou shalt bring forth to them water out of the rock; so thou shalt give the congregation and their cattle drink.'

[9]And Moses took the rod from before the Lord, as He commanded him. [10]And Moses and Aaron gathered the assembly together before the rock, and he said unto them: 'Hear now, ye rebels; are we to bring you forth water out of this rock?' [11]And Moses lifted up his hand, and smote the rock with his rod twice; and water came forth abundantly, and the congregation drank, and their cattle.

[12]And the Lord said unto Moses and Aaron: 'Because ye believed not in Me, to sanctify Me in the eyes of the children of Israel, therefore ye shall not bring this assembly into the land which I have given them.' [13]These are the waters of Meribah, where the children of Israel strove with the Lord, and He was sanctified in them.

was a Mushite priest who believed he was descended from Moses, so the E text generally favors Moses.

**P Text**

P's version is unfavorable to Moses: he is commanded to speak to the rock to produce water and instead he strikes the rock. As a punishment, he and Aaron are both kept out of the promised land, with Aaron suffering as an innocent victim of Moses' disobedience. P was a Aaronid priest who believed he was descended from Aaron, and he generally favors Aaron, often at Moses' expense.

### Battle with Amalek in Rephidim

**E Text**

Exodus 17:9 is the first mention of Joshua in the E text, and it sounds like the readers are expected to know who Joshua is. Possibly, Joshua was introduced earlier in a passage that RJE removed.

### Food - Manna and Quails

EX 16:2And the whole congregation of the children of Israel murmured against Moses and against Aaron in the wilderness; [3]and the children of Israel said unto them: 'Would that

### Food - Manna, Quails

**Relocated Text**

The P text has one passage about food in the wilderness, which includes both manna and quails.

The J text has two passages about

| [ used more than once ] | " quoting older text " |
|---|---|

| **E** | **J** |
|---|---|
| hearse it in the ears of Joshua: for I will utterly blot out the remembrance of Amalek from under heaven.' ¹⁵And Moses built an altar, and called the name of it Adonai-nissi. ¹⁶And he said: 'The hand upon the throne of the Lord: the Lord will have war with Amalek from generation to generation.' | between Elim and Sinai, on the fifteenth day of the second month after their departing out of the land of Egypt. ⁴Then said the Lord unto Moses: 'Behold, I will cause to rain bread from heaven for you; and the people shall go out and gather a day's portion every day, that I may prove them, whether they will walk in My law, or not. ⁵And it shall come to pass on the sixth day that they shall prepare that which they bring in, and it shall be twice as much as they gather daily.' ³⁵And the children of Israel did eat the manna forty years, until they came to a land inhabited; they did eat the manna, until they came unto the borders of the land of Canaan. |

**Food - Quails**

ᴺᵁᴹ ¹¹:⁴And the mixed multitude that was among them fell a lusting; and the children of Israel also wept on their part, and said: 'Would that we were given flesh to eat! ⁵We remember the fish, which we were wont to eat in Egypt for nought; the cucumbers, and the melons, and the leeks, and the onions, and the garlic; ⁶but now our soul is dried away; there is nothing at all; we have nought save this manna to look to.'—

⁷Now the manna was like coriander seed, and the appearance thereof as the appearance of bdellium. ⁸The people went about, and gathered it, and ground it in mills, or beat it in mortars, and seethed it in pots, and made cakes of it; and the taste of it

| ( added by redactor ) | { problematic } |

| P | Notes |
|---|---|

we had died by the hand of the Lord in the land of Egypt, when we sat by the flesh-pots, when we did eat bread to the full; for ye have brought us forth into this wilderness, to kill this whole assembly with hunger.'

⁶And Moses and Aaron said unto all the children of Israel: 'At even, then ye shall know that the Lord hath brought you out from the land of Egypt; ⁷and in the morning, then ye shall see the glory of the Lord; for that He hath heard your murmurings against the Lord; and what are we, that ye murmur against us?'

⁸And Moses said: 'This shall be, when the Lord shall give you in the evening flesh to eat, and in the morning bread to the full; for that the Lord heareth your murmurings which ye murmur against Him; and what are we? your murmurings are not against us, but against the Lord.'

⁹And Moses said unto Aaron: 'Say unto all the congregation of the children of Israel: Come near before the Lord; for He hath heard your murmurings.' ¹⁰And it came to pass, as Aaron spoke unto the whole congregation of the children of Israel, that they looked toward the wilderness, and, behold, the glory of the Lord appeared in the cloud. ¹¹And the Lord spoke unto Moses, saying: ¹²'I have heard the murmurings of the children of Israel. Speak unto them, saying: At dusk ye shall eat flesh, and in the morning ye shall be filled with bread; and ye shall know that I am the Lord your God.'

¹³And it came to pass at even, that the quails came up, and covered

food in the wilderness, one about manna in Exodus, and one about quails in Numbers.

This edition is meant to allow readers to compare doublets by reading across columns, so it moves the J passage about quails that begins at Numbers 11:4 so it follows the J passage about Manna that begins at Exodus 16:1, allowing readers to compare these two J texts with the P text about manna and quails.

**J Text**

There is clearly a change to a different text beginning at Numbers 11:4. In Numbers 11:1-3, God has summarily crushed the complaints of the Israelites, but in Numbers 11:4, the Israelites are just beginning to complain. There are two reasons to assign this second passage to J:

J also uses the phrase "mixed multitude" in Exodus 12:29

In J, these seventy elders also see God in the passage beginning at Exodus 24:1.

**P Text**

Presumably, the following passage is about a relic that the Aaronid priests claimed to have, a jar of manna kept since the exodus:

"ᴱˣ ¹⁶:³³And Moses said unto Aaron: 'Take a jar, and put an omerful of manna therein, and lay it up before the Lord, to be kept throughout your generations.' ³⁴As the Lord commanded Moses, so Aaron laid it up before the Testimony, to be kept. ³⁶Now an omer is the tenth part of an ephah."

| [ used more than once ] | " quoting older text " |
|---|---|

| **E** | **J** |
|---|---|
| | was as the taste of a cake baked with oil. ⁹And when the dew fell upon the camp in the night, the manna fell upon it.— |
| **Establishing Judges** | ¹⁰And Moses heard the people weeping, family by family, every man at the door of his tent; and the anger of the Lord was kindled greatly; and Moses was displeased. |
| EX 18:1Now Jethro, the priest of Midian, Moses' father-in-law, heard of all that God had done for Moses, and for Israel His people, how that the Lord had brought Israel out of Egypt. ²And Jethro, Moses' father-in-law, took Zipporah, Moses' wife, after he had sent her away, ³and her two sons; of whom the name of the one was Gershom; for he said: 'I have been a stranger in a strange land'; ⁴and the name of the other was Eliezer: 'for the God of my father was my help, and delivered me from the sword of Pharaoh.' | ¹¹And Moses said unto the Lord: 'Wherefore hast Thou dealt ill with Thy servant? and wherefore have I not found favour in Thy sight, that Thou layest the burden of all this people upon me? ¹²Have I conceived all this people? have I brought them forth, that Thou shouldest say unto me: Carry them in thy bosom, as a nursing-father carrieth the sucking child, unto the land which Thou didst swear unto their fathers? ¹³Whence should I have flesh to give unto all this people? for they trouble me with their weeping, saying: Give us flesh, that we may eat. |
| ⁵And Jethro, Moses' father-in-law, came with his sons and his wife unto Moses into the wilderness where he was encamped, at the mount of God; ⁶and he said unto Moses: 'I thy father-in-law Jethro am coming unto thee, and thy wife, and her two sons with her.' ⁷And Moses went out to meet his father-in-law, and bowed down and kissed him; and they asked each other of their welfare; and they came into the tent. ⁸And Moses told his father-in-law all that the Lord had done unto Pharaoh and to the Egyptians for Israel's sake, all the travail that had come upon them by the way, and how the Lord delivered them. ⁹And Jethro rejoiced for all the goodness which the Lord had done to Israel, in that He had delivered them out of | ¹⁴I am not able to bear all this people myself alone, because it is too heavy for me. ¹⁵And if Thou deal thus with me, kill me, I pray Thee, out of hand, if I have found favour in Thy sight; and let me not look upon my wretchedness.' |
| | ¹⁶And the Lord said unto Moses: 'Gather unto Me seventy men of the elders of Israel, whom thou knowest to be the elders of the people, and officers over them; and bring them unto the tent of meeting, that they may stand there with thee. ¹⁷And I will come down and speak with thee there; and I will take of the spirit which is upon thee, and will put it |
| ( added by redactor ) | { problematic } |

| P | Notes |
|---|---|

the camp; and in the morning there was a layer of dew round about the camp. [14]And when the layer of dew was gone up, behold upon the face of the wilderness a fine, scale-like thing, fine as the hoar-frost on the ground. [15]And when the children of Israel saw it, they said one to another: 'What is it?'—for they knew not what it was. And Moses said unto them: 'It is the bread which the Lord hath given you to eat. [16]This is the thing which the Lord hath commanded: Gather ye of it omer a head, according to the number of your persons, shall ye take it, every man for them that are in his tent.'

[17]And the children of Israel did so, and gathered some more, some less. [18]And when they did mete it with an omer, he that gathered much had nothing over, and he that gathered little had no lack; they gathered every man according to his eating. [19]And Moses said unto them: 'Let no man leave of it till the morning.' [20]Notwithstanding they hearkened not unto Moses; but some of them left of it until the morning, and it bred worms, and rotted; and Moses was wroth with them.

[21]And they gathered it morning by morning, every man according to his eating; and as the sun waxed hot, it melted. [22]And it came to pass that on the sixth day they gathered twice as much bread, two omers for each one; and all the rulers of the congregation came and told Moses. [23]And he said unto them: 'This is that which the Lord hath spoken: To-morrow is a solemn rest, a holy

Notice that P is a pedantically precise as usual, ending with a definition of what an omer is.

### Establishing Judges

Perhaps E includes this because, as a Mushite priest, he still has traditions about the Israelite government during the time of the judges, before the monarchy moved the religious center away from Shiloh (where the Mushite priests had been in charge) to Jerusalem.

In the original Hebrew, this passage does not use the word "judge" (*shofet*), but it does use a word with the same root *ShFT* when it says that Moses should appoint rulers "and let them judge" (*v'shaftu*) the people.

| [ used more than once ] | " quoting older text " |
|---|---|

| **E** | **J** |
|---|---|
| the hand of the Egyptians. ¹⁰And Jethro said: 'Blessed be the Lord, who hath delivered you out of the hand of the Egyptians, and out of the hand of Pharaoh; who hath delivered the people from under the hand of the Egyptians. ¹¹Now I know that the Lord is greater than all gods; yea, for that they dealt proudly against them.' ¹²And Jethro, Moses' father-in-law, took a burnt-offering and sacrifices for God; and Aaron came, and all the elders of Israel, to eat bread with Moses' father-in-law before God. | upon them; and they shall bear the burden of the people with thee, that thou bear it not thyself alone. |
| | ¹⁸And say thou unto the people: Sanctify yourselves against to-morrow, and ye shall eat flesh; for ye have wept in the ears of the Lord, saying: Would that we were given flesh to eat! for it was well with us in Egypt; therefore the Lord will give you flesh, and ye shall eat. ¹⁹Ye shall not eat one day, nor two days, nor five days, neither ten days, nor twenty days; ²⁰but a whole month, until it come out at your nostrils, and it be loathsome unto you; because that ye have rejected the Lord who is among you, and have troubled Him with weeping, saying: Why, now, came we forth out of Egypt?' |
| ¹³And it came to pass on the morrow, that Moses sat to judge the people; and the people stood about Moses from the morning unto the evening. ¹⁴And when Moses' father-in-law saw all that he did to the people, he said: 'What is this thing that thou doest to the people? why sittest thou thyself alone, and all the people stand about thee from morning unto even?' ¹⁵And Moses said unto his father-in-law: 'Because the people come unto me to inquire of God; ¹⁶when they have a matter, it cometh unto me; and I judge between a man and his neighbour, and I make them know the statutes of God, and His laws.' | ²¹And Moses said: 'The people, among whom I am, are six hundred thousand men on foot; and yet Thou hast said: I will give them flesh, that they may eat a whole month! ²²If flocks and herds be slain for them, will they suffice them? or if all the fish of the sea be gathered together for them, will they suffice them?' ²³And the Lord said unto Moses: 'Is the Lord's hand waxed short? now shalt thou see whether My word shall come to pass unto thee or not.' |
| ¹⁷And Moses' father-in-law said unto him: 'The thing that thou doest is not good. ¹⁸Thou wilt surely wear away, both thou, and this people that is with thee; for the thing is too heavy for thee; thou art not able to perform it thyself alone. ¹⁹Hearken now unto my voice, I will give thee counsel, and God be with thee: be | ²⁴And Moses went out, and told the people the words of the Lord; and he gathered seventy men of the elders of the people, and set them round about the Tent. ²⁵And the Lord came down in the cloud, and spoke unto him, and took of the spirit that was upon him, and put it |
| ( added by redactor ) | { problematic } |

| **P** | **Notes** |
|---|---|
| sabbath unto the Lord. Bake that which ye will bake, and seethe that which ye will seethe; and all that remaineth over lay up for you to be kept until the morning.' ²⁴And they laid it up till the morning, as Moses bade; and it did not rot, neither was there any worm therein. ²⁵And Moses said: 'Eat that to-day; for to-day is a sabbath unto the Lord; to-day ye shall not find it in the field. ²⁶Six days ye shall gather it; but on the seventh day is the sabbath, in it there shall be none.' ²⁷And it came to pass on the seventh day, that there went out some of the people to gather, and they found none.<br><br>²⁸And the Lord said unto Moses: 'How long refuse ye to keep My commandments and My laws? ²⁹See that the Lord hath given you the sabbath; therefore He giveth you on the sixth day the bread of two days; abide ye every man in his place, let no man go out of his place on the seventh clay.' ³⁰So the people rested on the seventh day.<br><br>³¹And the house of Israel called the name thereof Manna; and it was like coriander seed, white; and the taste of it was like wafers made with honey.<br><br>³²And Moses said: 'This is the thing which the Lord hath commanded: Let an omerful of it be kept throughout your generations; that they may see the bread wherewith I fed you in the wilderness, when I brought you forth from the land of Egypt.' ³³And Moses said unto Aaron: 'Take a jar, and put an omerful of manna therein, and lay it up | *[Continued on p. 273]* |
| [ used more than once ] | " quoting older text " |

*[Continued on p. 273]*

| **E** | **J** |
|---|---|
| thou for the people before God, and bring thou the causes unto God. [20]And thou shalt teach them the statutes and the laws, and shalt show them the way wherein they must walk, and the work that they must do. [21]Moreover thou shalt provide out of all the people able men, such as fear God, men of truth, hating unjust gain; and place such over them, to be rulers of thousands, rulers of hundreds, rulers of fifties, and rulers of tens. [22]And let them judge the people at all seasons; and it shall be, that every great matter they shall bring unto thee, but every small matter they shall judge themselves; so shall they make it easier for thee and bear the burden with thee. [23]If thou shalt do this thing, and God command thee so, then thou shalt be able to endure, and all this people also shall go to their place in peace.' | upon the seventy elders; and it came to pass, that, when the spirit rested upon them, they prophesied, but they did so no more. |
| | [26]But there remained two men in the camp, the name of the one was Eldad, and the name of the other Medad; and the spirit rested upon them; and they were of them that were recorded, but had not gone out unto the Tent; and they prophesied in the camp. [27]And there ran a young man, and told Moses, and said: 'Eldad and Medad are prophesying in the camp.' [28]And Joshua the son of Nun, the minister of Moses from his youth up, answered and said: 'My lord Moses, shut them in.' [29]And Moses said unto him: 'Art thou jealous for my sake? would that all the Lord's people were prophets, that the Lord would put His spirit upon them! ' |
| [24]So Moses hearkened to the voice of his father-in-law, and did all that he had said. [25]And Moses chose able men out of all Israel, and made them heads over the people, rulers of thousands, rulers of hundreds, rulers of fifties, and rulers of tens. [26]And they judged the people at all seasons: the hard causes they brought unto Moses, but every small matter they judged themselves. [27]And Moses let his father-in-law depart; and he went his way into his own land. | [30]And Moses withdrew into the camp, he and the elders of Israel. [31]And there went forth a wind from the Lord, and brought across quails from the sea, and let them fall by the camp, about a day's journey on this side, and a day's journey on the other side, round about the camp, and about two cubits above the face of the earth. [32]And the people rose up all that day, and all the night, and all the next day, and gathered the quails; he that gathered least gathered ten heaps; and they spread them all abroad for themselves round about the camp. |
| | [33]While the flesh was yet between their teeth, ere it was chewed, the anger of the Lord was kindled against the people, and the Lord smote the people with a very great plague. [34]And the name of that place was called Kibroth-hattaavah, because there they bur- |
| ( added by redactor ) | { problematic } |

| P | Notes |
|---|---|
| before the Lord, to be kept throughout your generations.' [34]As the Lord commanded Moses, so Aaron laid it up before the Testimony, to be kept. [36]Now an omer is the tenth part of an ephah. | *[Continued on p. 273]* |
| [ used more than once ] | " quoting older text " |

| **E** | **J** |
|---|---|
|  | ied the people that lusted. [35]From Kibroth-hattaavah the people journeyed unto Hazeroth; and they abode at Hazeroth. |

### Approaching the Mountain

**E**

EX 19.2And when they were departed from Rephidim, [and were come to the wilderness of Sinai, and there Israel ... encamped before the mount.] [3]And Moses went up unto God, and the Lord called unto him out of the mountain, saying: 'Thus shalt thou say to the house of Jacob, and tell the children of Israel: [4]Ye have seen what I did unto the Egyptians, and how I bore you on eagles' wings, and brought you unto Myself. [5]Now therefore, if ye will hearken unto My voice indeed, and keep My covenant, then ye shall be Mine own treasure from among all peoples; for all the earth is Mine; [6]and ye shall be unto Me a kingdom of priests, and a holy nation. These are the words which thou shalt speak unto the children of Israel.'

[7]And Moses came and called for the elders of the people, and set before them all these words which the Lord commanded him. [8]And all the people answered together, and said: 'All that the Lord hath spoken we will do.' And Moses reported the words of the people unto the Lord. [9]And the Lord said unto Moses: 'Lo, I come unto thee in a thick cloud, that the people may hear when I speak with thee, and may also believe thee for ever.' And Moses told the words of the people unto the

### Approaching the Mountain

**J**

EX 19.2[... And they were come to the wilderness of Sinai, and there Israel ... encamped before the mount.] [10][And the Lord said unto Moses:] [12]And thou shalt set bounds unto the people round about, saying: Take heed to yourselves, that ye go not up into the mount, or touch the border of it; whosoever toucheth the mount shall be surely put to death; [13a]No hand shall touch him, but he shall surely be stoned, or shot through; whether it be beast or man, it shall not live;

[20]And the Lord came down upon mount Sinai, to the top of the mount; and the Lord called Moses to the top of the mount; and Moses went up. And the Lord said unto Moses: Go down, charge the people, lest they break through unto the Lord to gaze, and many of them perish. [22]And let the priests also, that come near to the Lord, sanctify themselves, lest the Lord break forth upon them.' [23]And Moses said unto the Lord: 'The people cannot come up to mount Sinai; for thou didst charge us, saying: Set bounds about the mount, and sanctify it.' [24]And the Lord said unto him: 'Go, get thee down, and thou shalt come up, thou, (and Aaron with thee); but let not the priests and the people break through to come up unto the

| ( added by redactor ) | { problematic } |
|---|---|

| P | Notes |
|---|---|
| **Approaching the Mountain** | **Approaching the Mountain** |

**Approaching the Mountain**

EX 19:1In the third month after the children of Israel were gone forth out of the land of Egypt, the same day came they into the wilderness of Sinai. 2And ... they encamped in the wilderness; 18Now mount Sinai was altogether on smoke, because the Lord descended upon it in fire; and the smoke thereof ascended as the smoke of a furnace, and the whole mount quaked greatly.

**Approaching the Mountain**

In J and P, the mountain is Mt. Sinai. In E and D, it is Mt. Horeb in the wilderness of Sinai. Deuteronomy, which is by Mushite priests like E, says explicitly that Moses received the Ten Commandments on Mt. Horeb:

DEUT 4:10the day that thou stoodest before the Lord thy God in Horeb ... 12And the Lord spoke unto you out of the midst of the fire; ye heard the voice of words, but ye saw no form; only a voice. 13And He declared unto you His covenant, which He commanded you to perform, even the Ten Commandments; and He wrote them upon two tables of stone.

(In Hebrew, the Ten Commandments are called "*Aseret Hadevarim*." JPS translates this as "Ten Words," because *davar* literally means "word," but this edition follows common English usage by translating it as "Ten Commandments.")

**E Text**

The name Horeb is not mentioned in E at this point, and it was probably removed by RJE to remove the contradiction with J. Earlier in E, Moses saw the burning bush on Mt. Horeb and God said that he would bring the children of Israel to serve God on this mountain (Ex. 3:12).

| [ used more than once ] | " quoting older text " |

| **E** | **J** |
|---|---|
| Lord. | Lord, lest He break forth upon them.' |
| [10][And the Lord said unto Moses:] 'Go unto the people, and sanctify them to-day and to-morrow, and let them wash their garments, [11]and be ready against the third day; for the third day the Lord will come down in the sight of all the people upon mount Sinai. [13b]When the ram's horn soundeth long, they shall come up to the mount.'[14]And Moses went down from the mount unto the people, and sanctified the people; and they washed their garments. [15]And he said unto the people: 'Be ready against the third day; come not near a woman.' | |
| [16]And it came to pass on the third day, when it was morning, that there were thunders and lightnings and a thick cloud upon the mount, and the voice of a horn exceeding loud; and all the people that were in the camp trembled. [17]And Moses brought forth the people out of the camp to meet God; and they stood at the nether part of the mount. [19]And when the voice of the horn waxed louder and louder, Moses spoke, and God answered him by a voice. | |
| [EX20:15]And all the people perceived the thunderings, and the lightnings, and the voice of the horn, and the mountain smoking; and when the people saw it, they trembled, and stood afar off. [16]And they said unto Moses: 'Speak thou with us, and we will hear; but let not God speak with us, lest we die.' [17]And Moses said unto the people: 'Fear not; for God is come to prove you, and that His fear may be before you, that ye sin not.' [18]And the people stood afar off; but Moses drew near unto the thick darkness where God was. | |
| ( added by redactor ) | { problematic } |

| **P** | **Notes** |
|---|---|
| | Later, as they are leaving the mountain, E says: "EX 33:6 And the children of Israel stripped themselves of their ornaments from mount Horeb onward." But including the name Horeb while they are at the mountain, would make the contradiction too blatant. |

In E, the Lord comes down in a cloud, but the people perceive the thunder and lightening and sound of the horn, and they run away because they are afraid to hear God speak (Ex. 20:15-16). Thus, this passage does not violate E's principle that God appears and speaks directly only to Moses.

**J Text**

In this text, Moses is on Mt. Sinai forty days and forty nights, the same amount of time that J said the flood lasted (Gen. 7:12).

A redactor made additions to this text that refer to the first set of tablets that Moses broke, in order to reconcile this story in J with E's story of the golden calf. For more information about the golden calf, see page 27.

*[Continued on p. 279]*

In "EX 19:24 And the Lord said unto him: 'Go, get thee down, and thou shalt come up, thou, (and Aaron with thee)," the mention of Aaron was presumably added by a redactor, since Aaron does not go up with Moses to receive the Ten Commandments in J, though Aaron does go up with seventy elders later in J (Ex. 24).

**P Text**

In P, Aaron goes up to Mt. Sinai with Moses (Ex. 19:24). This is typical of the importance that P gives to Aaron, who he thinks is his ancestor.

Exodus 19:23 was added by R to reconcile this passage in P, where God says Moses should tell the people to stay away from the mountain, with the text in J where God has already told Moses to stay away from the mountain (Ex. 19:12).

**Translation**

J Text: The JPS translation says "EX 19:2... And were come to the wilderness of Sinai." In the J text, this edition translates it as "And they were come to the wilderness of Sinai." Hebrew does not use the pronoun, so this translation is just as accurate.

| [ used more than once ] | " quoting older text " |
|---|---|

| E | J |
|---|---|

**Carving the Tablets**

EX 34:1And the Lord said unto Moses: 'Hew thee two tables of stone (like unto the first; and I will write upon the tables the words that were on the first tables, which thou didst break.) 2And be ready by the morning, and come up in the morning unto mount Sinai, and present thyself there to Me on the top of the mount. 3And no man shall come up with thee, neither let any man be seen throughout all the mount; neither let the flocks nor herds feed before that mount.' 4And he hewed two tables of stone (like unto the first); and Moses rose up early in the morning, and went up unto mount Sinai, as the Lord had commanded him, and took in his hand two tables of stone.

5And the Lord descended in the cloud, and stood with him there, and proclaimed the name of the Lord. 6And the Lord passed by before him, and proclaimed: 'The Lord, the Lord, God, merciful and gracious, long-suffering, and abundant in goodness and truth; 7keeping mercy unto the thousandth generation, forgiving iniquity and transgression and sin; and that will by no means clear the guilty; visiting the iniquity of the fathers upon the children, and upon the children's children, unto the third and unto the fourth generation.'

8And Moses made haste, and bowed his head toward the earth, and worshipped. 9And he said: 'If now I have found grace in Thy sight, O Lord, let the Lord, I pray Thee, go in the midst of us; for it is a stiffnecked people; and pardon our iniquity and our sin, and take us for Thine inheritance.' 10And He said: 'Behold, I make a covenant; before all thy people I will do marvels, such as have not been wrought in all the earth, nor in any nation; and all the people among which thou art shall see the work of the Lord that I am about to do with thee, that it is tremendous. 11Observe thou that which I am commanding thee this day; behold, I am driving out before thee the Amorite, and the Canaanite, and the Hittite, and the Perizzite, and the Hivite, and the Jebusite. 12Take heed to thyself, lest thou make a covenant with the

*[Continued on p. 282]*

| ( added by redactor ) | { problematic } |
|---|---|

| P | Notes |
|---|-------|
| | **Carving the Tablets** |
| | Exodus 34:1,4: Perhaps RJE added mentions of the broken tablets to these two verses in order to reconcile this story in J with E's story of Moses breaking the tablets after seeing the Golden Calf. Or perhaps they were added when the story of the Golden Calf was added to the JE text. For more information about the Golden Calf, see page 27. |
| *[Continued on p. 279]* | |
| [ used more than once ] | " quoting older text " |

*[Continued on p. 279]*

| **E** | **J** |
|---|---|

inhabitants of the land whither thou goest, lest they be for a snare in the midst of thee. [13]But ye shall break down their altars, and dash in pieces their pillars, and ye shall cut down their Asherim. [14]For thou shalt bow down to no other god; for the Lord, whose name is Jealous, is a jealous God; [15]lest thou make a covenant with the inhabitants of the land, and they go astray after their gods, and do sacrifice unto their gods, and they call thee, and thou eat of their sacrifice; [16]and thou take of their daughters unto thy sons, and their daughters go astray after their gods, and make thy sons go astray after their gods.

### The Ten Commandments

EX 34:17Thou shalt make thee no molten gods.

[18]The feast of unleavened bread shalt thou keep. Seven days thou shalt eat unleavened bread, as I commanded thee, at the time appointed in the month Abib, for in the month Abib thou camest out from Egypt.

*[Continued on p. 282]*

[19]All that openeth the womb *[=every first born]* is Mine; and of all thy cattle thou shalt sanctify the males, the firstlings of ox and sheep. [20]And the firstling of an ass thou shalt redeem with a lamb; and if thou wilt not redeem it, then thou shalt break its neck. All the first-born of thy sons thou shalt redeem. And none shall appear before Me empty.

[21]Six days thou shalt work, but on the seventh day thou shalt rest; in plowing time and in harvest thou shalt rest.

[22]And thou shalt observe the feast of weeks, even of the first-fruits of wheat harvest, and the feast of ingathering at the turn of the year.

[23]Three times in the year shall all thy males appear before the Lord God, the God of Israel. [24]For I will cast out nations before thee, and enlarge thy borders; neither shall any man covet thy land, when thou goest up to appear before the Lord thy God three times in the year.

[25]Thou shalt not offer the blood of My sacrifice with leavened bread;

| ( added by redactor ) | { problematic } |
|---|---|

| **P** | **Notes** |
|---|---|

## The Ten Commandments

EX 20:1And God spoke all these words, saying:

"2I am the Lord thy God, who brought thee out of the land of Egypt, out of the house of bondage. 3Thou shalt have no other gods before Me.

4Thou shalt not make unto thee a graven image, nor any manner of likeness, of any thing that is in heaven above, or that is in the earth beneath, or that is in the water under the earth; 5thou shalt not bow down unto them, nor serve them; for I the Lord thy God am a jealous God, visiting the iniquity of the fathers upon the children unto the third and fourth generation of them that hate Me; 6and showing mercy unto the thousandth generation of them that love Me and keep My commandments.

7Thou shalt not take the name of the Lord thy God in vain; for the Lord will not hold him guiltless that taketh His name in vain.

8Remember the sabbath day, to keep it holy. 9Six days shalt thou labour, and do all thy work; 10but the sev-

## The Ten Commandments

**E Text**

E has no text of the Ten Commandments. Instead, it has the much longer Covenant Code in Exodus 20:15-24:15.

**J Text**

In J, Moses carves two tablets and then goes up the mountain to receive the Ten Commandments.

J has an often ignored text of the Ten Commandments in Exodus 34, with ritualist commandments, such as keeping Passover and keeping the sabbath, and without the moral commandments, such as "Thou shalt not kill.

**P Text**

In P, God speaks the Ten Commandments, and then Moses goes up to the mountain for forty days and gets the Ten Commandments on tablets of stone plus the rest of the law.

P has the familiar text of the Ten Commandments in Exodus 20, which is very similar to the Ten Commandments in Deuteronomy

| [ used more than once ] | " quoting older text " |
|---|---|

| **E** | **J** |
|---|---|
| | neither shall the sacrifice of the feast of the passover be left unto the morning. |
| | [26]The choicest first-fruits of thy land thou shalt bring unto the house of the Lord thy God. |
| | Thou shalt not seethe a kid in its mother's milk.' |
| | [27]And the Lord said unto Moses: 'Write thou these words, for after the tenor of these words I have made a covenant with thee and with Israel.' [28]And he was there with the Lord forty days and forty nights; he did neither eat bread, nor drink water. And he wrote upon the tables the words of the covenant, the Ten Commandments. |
| *[Continued on p. 282]* | |
| ( added by redactor ) | { problematic } |

*[Continued on p. 282]*

| P | Notes |
|---|---|

enth day is a sabbath unto the Lord thy God, in it thou shalt not do any manner of work, thou, nor thy son, nor thy daughter, nor thy man-servant, nor thy maid-servant, nor thy cattle, nor thy stranger that is within thy gates; ¹¹for in six days the Lord made heaven and earth, the sea, and all that in them is, and rested on the seventh day; wherefore the Lord blessed the sabbath day, and hallowed it.

¹²Honour thy father and thy mother, that thy days may be long upon the land which the Lord thy God giveth thee.

¹³Thou shalt not murder.

Thou shalt not commit adultery.

Thou shalt not steal.

Thou shalt not bear false witness against thy neighbour.

¹⁴Thou shalt not covet thy neighbour's house; thou shalt not covet thy neighbour's wife, nor his man-servant, nor his maid-servant, nor his ox, nor his ass, nor any thing that is thy neighbour's."

²⁴:¹⁵ᵇAnd the cloud covered the mount. ¹⁶And the glory of the Lord abode upon mount Sinai, and the cloud covered it six days; and the seventh day He called unto Moses out of the midst of the cloud. ¹⁷And the appearance of the glory of the Lord was like devouring fire on the top of the mount in the eyes of the children of Israel. ¹⁸And Moses entered into the midst of the cloud, and went up into the mount; and Moses was in the mount forty days and forty nights.

ᴱˣ ³⁴:²⁹And it came to pass, when Moses came down from mount Sinai with the two tables of the testimony in Mo-

5:6-18. Much of this is quoted from an earlier source by both P and D, but P gives a different reason for keeping the sabbath. In Deuteronomy, the Ten Commandments say:

ᴰᴱᵁᵀ ⁵:¹⁵And thou shalt remember that thou was a servant in the land of Egypt, and the Lord thy God brought thee out thence by a mighty hand and by an outstretched arm; therefore the Lord thy God commanded thee to keep the sabbath day.

In Exodus, the Ten Commandments say:

ᴱˣ ²⁰:¹¹for in six days the Lord made heaven and earth, the sea, and all that in them is, and rested on the seventh day; wherefore the Lord blessed the sabbath day, and hallowed it.

Thus, P's version of the Ten Commandments in Exodus is different from D's version in Deuteronomy because it uses P's story of the creation as the reason for observing the sabbath, which is why this edition assigns it to P, though some scholars say it is a separate text added by a redactor.

One of the commandments may indicate that both the P and D version of the Ten Commandments have a late date:

ᴱˣ ²⁰:⁴Thou shalt not make unto thee a graven image, nor any manner of likeness, of any thing that is in heaven above, or that is in the earth

| [ used more than once ] | " quoting older text " |

| **E** | **J** |
|---|---|
| | |

*[Continued on p. 306]*

### The Law

"EX 20:19And the Lord said unto Moses: Thus thou shalt say unto the children of Israel: Ye yourselves have seen that I have talked with you from heaven. 20Ye shall not make with Me—gods of silver, or gods of gold, ye shall not make unto you. 21An altar of earth thou shalt make unto Me, and shalt sacrifice thereon thy burnt-offerings, and thy peace-offerings, thy sheep, and thine oxen; in every place where I cause My name to be mentioned I will come

| ( added by redactor ) | { problematic } |
|---|---|

| P | Notes |
|---|---|

ses' hand, when he came down from the mount, that Moses knew not that the skin of his face sent forth beams while He talked with him. ³⁰And when Aaron and all the children of Israel saw Moses, behold, the skin of his face sent forth beams; and they were afraid to come nigh him. ³¹And Moses called unto them; and Aaron and all the rulers of the congregation returned unto him; and Moses spoke to them. ³²And afterward all the children of Israel came nigh, and he gave them in commandment all that the Lord had spoken with him in mount Sinai. ³³And when Moses had done speaking with them, he put a veil on his face. ³⁴But when Moses went in before the Lord that He might speak with him, he took the veil off, until he came out; and he came out; and spoke unto the children of Israel that which he was commanded. ³⁵And the children of Israel saw the face of Moses, that the skin of Moses' face sent forth beams; and Moses put the veil back upon his face, until he went in to speak with Him.

beneath, or that is in the water under the earth; ⁵thou shalt not bow down unto them, nor serve them.

This commandment seems to forbid making images as well as worshiping them. There was an early law against worshipping images (as we see in the Covenant Code in Exodus 20:20), but the law against making images seems to date to the religious reform of Hezekiah. See page. 18.

**Translation**

J Text: The JPS translation ends J's version of the ten commandments by saying: "ᴱˣ ³⁴:²⁸ᵇAnd he wrote upon the tables the words of the covenant, the ten words." "Ten words" is a literal translation of the Hebrew *aseret hadevarim*, since *davar* means word, thing, or principle, but this phrase is used in Hebrew to mean the Ten Commandments, so this edition translates it as "Ten Commandments."

### The Law - Abridged
### [The Holy Objects - Ex 35-40]

ᴱˣ ³⁵:⁴And Moses spoke unto all the congregation of the children of Israel, saying: 'This is the thing which the Lord commanded, saying: ¹⁰And let every wise-hearted man among you come, and make all that the Lord hath commanded: ¹¹the tabernacle, its tent, and its covering, its clasps, and its boards, its bars, its pillars, and its sockets; ¹²the ark, and the staves thereof, the ark-cover, and the veil of the screen;

### The Law

Because the goal of this edition is to place parallel passages from the three texts next to each other, it provides abridged versions of some lengthy and repetitive passages from the P text. To read the complete law in the P text, read the passages specified in each subheading in any Bible.

**E Text**

E has no text of the Ten Commandments but has a fairly

| [ used more than once ] | " quoting older text " |
|---|---|

| **E** | **J** |
| --- | --- |

unto thee and bless thee. [22]And if thou make Me an altar of stone, thou shalt not build it of hewn stones; for if thou lift up thy tool upon it, thou hast profaned it. [23]Neither shalt thou go up by steps unto Mine altar, that thy nakedness be not uncovered thereon.

EX 21:1[1]Now these are the ordinances which thou shalt set before them. [2]If thou buy a Hebrew servant, six years he shall serve; and in the seventh he shall go out free for nothing. [3]If he come in by himself, he shall go out by himself; if he be married, then his wife shall go out with him. [4]If his master give him a wife, and she bear him sons or daughters; the wife and her children shall be her master's, and he shall go out by himself. [5]But if the servant shall plainly say: I love my master, my wife, and my children; I will not go out free; [6]then his master shall bring him unto God, and shall bring him to the door, or unto the door-post; and his master shall bore his ear through with an awl; and he shall serve him for ever.

[7]And if a man sell his daughter to be a maid-servant, she shall not go out as the men-servants do. [8]If she please not her master, who hath espoused her to himself, then shall he let her be redeemed; to sell her unto a foreign people he shall have no power, seeing he hath dealt deceitfully with her. [9]And if he espouse her unto his son, he shall deal with her after the manner of daughters. [10]If he take him another wife, her food, her raiment, and her conjugal rights, shall he not diminish. [11]And if he do not these three unto her, then shall she go out for nothing, without money.

*[Continued on p. 306]*

[12]He that smiteth a man, so that he dieth, shall surely be put to death. [13]And if a man lie not in wait, but God cause it to come to hand; then I will appoint thee a place whither he may flee.

[14]And if a man come presumptuously upon his neighbour, to slay him with guile; thou shalt take him from Mine altar, that he may die.

[15]And he that smiteth his father, or his mother, shall be surely put to death.

[16]And he that stealeth a man, and selleth him, or if he be found in his hand, he shall surely be put to death.

[17]And he that curseth his father or his mother, shall

| ( added by redactor ) | { problematic } |
| --- | --- |

| **P** | **Notes** |
|---|---|

<sup>13</sup>the table, and its staves, and all its vessels, and the showbread; <sup>14</sup>the candlestick also for the light, and its vessels, and its lamps, and the oil for the light; <sup>15</sup>and the altar of incense, and its staves, and the anointing oil, and the sweet incense, and the screen for the door, at the door of the tabernacle; <sup>16</sup>the altar of burnt-offering, with its grating of brass, its staves, and all its vessels, the laver and its base; <sup>17</sup>the hangings of the court, the pillars thereof, and their sockets, and the screen for the gate of the court; <sup>18</sup>the pins of the tabernacle, and the pins of the court, and their cords; <sup>19</sup>the plaited garments, for ministering in the holy place, the holy garments for Aaron the priest, and the garments of his sons, to minister in the priest's office.'

EX 36:1And Bezalel and Oholiab shall work, and every wise-hearted man, in whom the Lord hath put wisdom and understanding to know how to work all the work for the service of the sanctuary, according to all that the Lord hath commanded.'

**[Laws of Sacrifices - Lev 1-8]**

LEV 1:1And the Lord called unto Moses, and spoke unto him out of the tent of meeting, saying: <sup>2</sup>Speak unto the children of Israel, and say unto them:

When any man of you bringeth an offering unto the Lord, ye shall bring your offering of the cattle, even of the herd or of the flock. <sup>3</sup>If his offering be a burnt-offering of the herd, he shall offer it a male without blemish; he shall bring it to the door of the tent of meeting, that he may be accepted before the Lord. <sup>10</sup>And if his offering be of the flock, whether of the sheep, or of the goats, for a burnt-offering, he shall offer it a male without blemish. <sup>11</sup>And he shall kill it on the side of the altar northward before the Lord; and Aaron's sons, the priests, shall dash its blood against the altar round about.

lengthy code of law, which is called The Covenant Code. This Code existed in an earlier document, which E quoted, and it is the closest thing we have to the original laws adopted when the Israelites entered Canaan.

It has three main elements.

Many of its laws are a rough legal system to resolve conflicts in a fairly primitive society. An example is:

EX 21:28And if an ox gore a man or a woman, that they die, the ox shall be surely stoned, and its flesh shall not be eaten; but the owner of the ox shall be quit. <sup>29</sup>But if the ox was wont to gore in time past, and warning hath been given to its owner, and he hath not kept it in, but it hath killed a man or a woman; the ox shall be stoned, and its owner also shall be put to death.

Many of tis laws prescribe rituals. An example is:

EX 23:14Three times thou shalt keep a feast unto Me in the year. <sup>15</sup>The feast of unleavened bread shalt thou keep; seven days thou shalt eat unleavened bread,

| [ used more than once ] | " quoting older text " |
|---|---|

| **E** | **J** |
|---|---|
| surely be put to death. | |

*[Continued on p. 306]*

(Column E continues:)

surely be put to death.

¹⁸And if men contend, and one smite the other with a stone, or with his fist, and he die not, but keep his bed; ¹⁹if he rise again, and walk abroad upon his staff, then shall he that smote him be quit; only he shall pay for the loss of his time, and shall cause him to be thoroughly healed.

²⁰And if a man smite his bondman, or his bond-woman, with a rod, and he die under his hand, he shall surely be punished. ²¹Notwithstanding if he continue a day or two, he shall not be punished; for he is his money.

²²And if men strive together, and hurt a woman with child, so that her fruit depart, and yet no harm follow, he shall be surely fined, according as the woman's husband shall lay upon him; and he shall pay as the judges determine. ²³But if any harm follow, then thou shalt give life for life, ²⁴eye for eye, tooth for tooth, hand for hand, foot for foot, ²⁵burning for burning, wound for wound, stripe for stripe.

²⁶And if a man smite the eye of his bondman, or the eye of his bondwoman, and destroy it, he shall let him go free for his eye's sake. ²⁷And if he smite out his bondman's tooth, or his bondwoman's tooth, he shall let him go free for his tooth's sake.

²⁸And if an ox gore a man or a woman, that they die, the ox shall be surely stoned, and its flesh shall not be eaten; but the owner of the ox shall be quit. ²⁹But if the ox was wont to gore in time past, and warning hath been given to its owner, and he hath not kept it in, but it hath killed a man or a woman; the ox shall be stoned, and its owner also shall be put to death. ³⁰If there be laid on him a ransom, then he shall give for the redemption of his life whatsoever is laid upon him. ³¹Whether it have gored a son, or have gored a daughter, according to this judgment shall it be done unto him. ³²If the ox gore a bondman or a bondwoman, he shall give unto their master thirty shekels of silver, and the ox shall be stoned.

³³And if a man shall open a pit, or if a man shall dig a pit and not cover it, and an ox or an ass fall therein, ³⁴the owner of the pit shall make it good;

| ( added by redactor ) | { problematic } |
|---|---|

| P | Notes |
|---|---|
| LEV 4:22When a ruler sinneth, and doeth through error any one of all the things which the Lord his God hath commanded not to be done, and is guilty: 23if his sin, wherein he hath sinned, be known to him, he shall bring for his offering a goat, a male without blemish. 25And the priest shall take of the blood of the sin-offering with his finger, and put it upon the horns of the altar of burnt-offering, and the remaining blood thereof shall he pour out at the base of the altar of burnt-offering. 26And all the fat thereof shall he make smoke upon the altar, as the fat of the sacrifice of peace-offerings; and the priest shall make atonement for him as concerning his sin, and he shall be forgiven. | as I commanded thee, at the time appointed in the month Abib—for in it thou camest out from Egypt; and none shall appear before Me empty; 16and the feast of harvest, the first-fruits of thy labours, which thou sowest in the field; and the feast of ingathering, at the end of the year, when thou gatherest in thy labours out of the field. 17Three times in the year all thy males shall appear before the Lord God. |

**[Performing Sacrifices - Lev 9-10]**

LEV 9:1And it came to pass on the eighth day, that Moses called Aaron and his sons, and the elders of Israel; 2and he said unto Aaron: 'Take thee a bullcalf for a sin-offering, and a ram for a burnt-offering, without blemish, and offer them before the Lord.

LEV 10:1And Nadab and Abihu, the sons of Aaron, took each of them his censer, and put fire therein, and laid incense thereon, and offered strange fire before the Lord, which He had not commanded them. 2And there came forth fire from before the Lord, and devoured them, and they died before the Lord.

**[Kosher Meat - Lev 11]**

LEV 11:1And the Lord spoke unto Moses and to Aaron, saying unto them: 2Speak unto the children of Israel, saying: These are the living things which ye may eat among all the beasts that are on the earth. 3Whatsoever parteth the hoof, and is wholly cloven-footed, and cheweth the cud, among the beasts, that may ye eat. 4Nevertheless these shall ye not eat of them that only chew the cud, or of them that only part the hoof: the camel, because he cheweth the cud but parteth not

Many laws prescribe moral behavior. An example is,

EX 22:20And a stranger shalt thou not wrong, neither shalt thou oppress him; for ye were strangers in the land of Egypt. 21Ye shall not afflict any widow, or fatherless child.

One striking different between E and J is that E's religion has a moral element, while J's does not. See page 25-26.

**J Text**

The J text has no lengthy code of laws. It just has its version of the Ten Commandments, which are ritualistic rather than moral. J, who was a member of

| [ used more than once ] | " quoting older text " |
|---|---|

| **E** | **J** |
|---|---|
| he shall give money unto the owner of them, and the dead beast shall be his. | |

**E**

he shall give money unto the owner of them, and the dead beast shall be his.

[35]And if one man's ox hurt another's, so that it dieth; then they shall sell the live ox, and divide the price of it; and the dead also they shall divide. [36]Or if it be known that the ox was wont to gore in time past, and its owner hath not kept it in; he shall surely pay ox for ox, and the dead beast shall be his own.

[37]If a man steal an ox, or a sheep, and kill it, or sell it, he shall pay five oxen for an ox, and four sheep for a sheep.

EX 22:1If a thief be found breaking in, and be smitten so that he dieth, there shall be no bloodguiltiness for him. [2]If the sun be risen upon him, there shall be bloodguiltiness for him—he shall make restitution; if he have nothing, then he shall be sold for his theft. [3]If the theft be found in his hand alive, whether it be ox, or ass, or sheep, he shall pay double.

[4]If a man cause a field or vineyard to be eaten, and shall let his beast loose, and it feed in another man's field; of the best of his own field, and of the best of his own vineyard, shall he make restitution.

[5]If fire break out, and catch in thorns, so that the shocks of corn, or the standing corn, or the field are consumed; he that kindled the fire shall surely make restitution.

[6]If a man deliver unto his neighbour money or stuff to keep, and it be stolen out of the man's house; if the thief be found, he shall pay double. [7]If the thief be not found, then the master of the house shall come near unto God, to see whether he have not put his hand unto his neighbour's goods. [8]For every matter of trespass, whether it be for ox, for ass, for sheep, for raiment, or for any manner of lost thing, whereof one saith: 'This is it,' the cause of both parties shall come before God; he whom God shall condemn shall pay double unto his neighbour.

[9]If a man deliver unto his neighbour an ass, or an ox, or a sheep, or any beast, to keep, and it die, or be hurt, or driven away, no man seeing it; [10]the oath of the Lord shall be between them both, to see whether he have not put his hand unto his neighbour's goods;

**J**

*[Continued on p. 306]*

( added by redactor )  { problematic }

| **P** | **Notes** |
|---|---|

the hoof, he is unclean unto you.

### [Purity - Lev 12-15]

LEV 12:1And the Lord spoke unto Moses, saying: 2Speak unto the children of Israel, saying: If a woman be delivered, and bear a man-child, then she shall be unclean seven days; as in the days of the impurity of her sickness shall she be unclean. 6And when the days of her purification are fulfilled, for a son, or for a daughter, she shall bring a lamb of the first year for a burnt-offering, and a young pigeon, or a turtle-dove, for a sin-offering, unto the door of the tent of meeting, unto the priest.

LEV 13:1And the Lord spoke unto Moses and unto Aaron, saying: 2When a man shall have in the skin of his flesh a rising, or a scab, or a bright spot, and it become in the skin of his flesh the plague of leprosy, then he shall be brought unto Aaron the priest, or unto one of his sons the priests. 3And the priest shall look upon the plague in the skin of the flesh; and if the hair in the plague be turned white, and the appearance of the plague be deeper than the skin of his flesh, it is the plague of leprosy; and the priest shall look on him, and pronounce him unclean.

### [Laws for Priests - Lev 16]

LEV 16:3Herewith shall Aaron come into the holy place: with a young bullock for a sin-offering, and a ram for a burnt-offering. 4He shall put on the holy linen tunic, and he shall have the linen breeches upon his flesh, and shall be girded with the linen girdle, and with the linen mitre shall he be attired; they are the holy garments; and he shall bathe his flesh in water, and put them on.

### [Beginning of the Holiness Code]
### [Eating Meat - Lev 17]

"LEV 17:1And the Lord spoke unto Moses, saying: 2Speak unto Aaron, and unto his sons, and unto all the children of Israel, and say unto them: This is the thing which the Lord

---

the Judean court, does not care as much about the law as P and E, who were priests.

**P Text**

P has the familiar version of the ten commandments, which is largely moral, followed by a very lengthy code of law. A large portion of P's law (Lev. 17-26) is quoted from an earlier source and is called The Holiness Code.

The laws that P himself wrote are ritualistic, with lengthy descriptions of how to build the ark of the covenant, the tabernacle, and other items used by priests, lengthy descriptions of different sacrifices performed on different occasions, laws about what food can be eaten, laws about sacrifices needed after one becomes impure, and other laws about priests' behavior.

The Holiness Code, which P quotes, has moral laws in addition to ritual laws, such as:

LEV 19:13Thou shalt not oppress thy neighbour, nor rob him; the wages of a hired servant shall not abide with thee all night until the morning. 14Thou shalt not curse the deaf, nor put a stumblingblock

---

| [ used more than once ] | " quoting older text " |

| **E** | **J** |
|---|---|
| and the owner thereof shall accept it, and he shall not make restitution. [11]But if it be stolen from him, he shall make restitution unto the owner thereof. [12]If it be torn in pieces, let him bring it for witness; he shall not make good that which was torn. | |

and the owner thereof shall accept it, and he shall not make restitution. [11]But if it be stolen from him, he shall make restitution unto the owner thereof. [12]If it be torn in pieces, let him bring it for witness; he shall not make good that which was torn.

[13]And if a man borrow aught of his neighbour, and it be hurt, or die, the owner thereof not being with it, he shall surely make restitution. [14]If the owner thereof be with it, he shall not make it good; if it be a hireling, he loseth his hire.

[15]And if a man entice a virgin that is not betrothed, and lie with her, he shall surely pay a dowry for her to be his wife. [16]If her father utterly refuse to give her unto him, he shall pay money according to the dowry of virgins.

[17]Thou shalt not suffer a sorceress to live.

[18]Whosoever lieth with a beast shall surely be put to death.

[19]He that sacrificeth unto the gods, save unto the Lord only, shall be utterly destroyed.

*[Continued on p. 306]*

[20]And a stranger shalt thou not wrong, neither shalt thou oppress him; for ye were strangers in the land of Egypt.

[21]Ye shall not afflict any widow, or fatherless child. [22]If thou afflict them in any wise—for if they cry at all unto Me, I will surely hear their cry— [23]My wrath shall wax hot, and I will kill you with the sword; and your wives shall be widows, and your children fatherless.

[24]If thou lend money to any of My people, even to the poor with thee, thou shalt not be to him as a creditor; neither shall ye lay upon him interest. [25]If thou at all take thy neighbour's garment to pledge, thou shalt restore it unto him by that the sun goeth down; [26]for that is his only covering, it is his garment for his skin; wherein shall he sleep? and it shall come to pass, when he crieth unto Me, that I will hear; for I am gracious.

[27]Thou shalt not revile God, nor curse a ruler of thy people.

[28]Thou shalt not delay to offer of the fulness of thy harvest, and of the outflow of thy presses.

| ( added by redactor ) | { problematic } |

| P | Notes |
|---|---|

hath commanded, saying:

³What man soever there be of the house of Israel, that killeth an ox, or lamb, or goat, in the camp, or that killeth it without the camp, ⁴and hath not brought it unto the door of the tent of meeting, to present it as an offering unto the Lord before the tabernacle of the Lord, blood shall be imputed unto that man; he hath shed blood; and that man shall be cut off from among his people.

**[Sexual Restrictions - Lev 18]**

"LEV 18:1And the Lord spoke unto Moses, saying: ²Speak unto the children of Israel, and say unto them: ⁶None of you shall approach to any that is near of kin to him, to uncover their nakedness. I am the Lord. ⁷The nakedness of thy father, and the nakedness of thy mother, shalt thou not uncover: she is thy mother; thou shalt not uncover her nakedness. ⁸The nakedness of thy father's wife shalt thou not uncover: it is thy father's nakedness.

**[Other Restrictions - Lev 19-21]**

"LEV 19:1And the Lord spoke unto Moses, saying: ²Speak unto all the congregation of the children of Israel, and say unto them: Ye shall be holy; for I the Lord your God am holy. ³Ye shall fear every man his mother, and his father, and ye shall keep My sabbaths: I am the Lord your God. ⁴Turn ye not unto the idols, nor make to yourselves molten gods: I am the Lord your God.

⁹And when ye reap the harvest of your land, thou shalt not wholly reap the corner of thy field, neither shalt thou gather the gleaning of thy harvest. ¹⁰And thou shalt not glean thy vineyard, neither shalt thou gather the fallen fruit of thy vineyard; thou shalt leave them for the poor and for the stranger: I am the Lord your God.

¹¹Ye shall not steal; neither shall ye deal falsely, nor lie one to another. ¹²And ye shall not swear by My name falsely, so that thou

before the blind, but thou shalt fear thy God: I am the Lord. ¹⁵Ye shall do no unrighteousness in judgment; thou shalt not respect the person of the poor, nor favour the person of the mighty; but in righteousness shalt thou judge thy neighbour. ... ¹⁸Thou shalt not take vengeance, nor bear any grudge against the children of thy people, but thou shalt love thy neighbour as thyself: I am the Lord."

As evidence that this holiness code was inserted, P's version of the law has two conclusions. The Holiness Code has this conclusion: "LEV 26:46These are the statutes and ordinances and laws, which the Lord made between Him and the children of Israel in mount Sinai by the hand of Moses." Then P added a chapter about paying priests in silver, apparently a later innovation, and then has this second conclusion for the entire set of commandments: "LEV 27:34These are the commandments, which the Lord commanded Moses for the children of Israel in mount Sinai."

We can speculate about

| [ used more than once ] | " quoting older text " |
|---|---|

| **E** | **J** |
|---|---|

The first-born of thy sons shalt thou give unto Me. [29]Likewise shalt thou do with thine oxen, and with thy sheep; seven days it shall be with its dam; on the eighth day thou shalt give it Me.

[30]And ye shall be holy men unto Me; therefore ye shall not eat any flesh that is torn of beasts in the field; ye shall cast it to the dogs.

EX 23:1Thou shalt not utter a false report; put not thy hand with the wicked to be an unrighteous witness.

[2]Thou shalt not follow a multitude to do evil; neither shalt thou bear witness in a cause to turn aside after a multitude to pervert justice; [3]neither shalt thou favour a poor man in his cause.

[4]If thou meet thine enemy's ox or his ass going astray, thou shalt surely bring it back to him again.

[5]If thou see the ass of him that hateth thee lying under its burden, thou shalt forbear to pass by him; thou shalt surely release it with him.

[6]Thou shalt not wrest the judgment of thy poor in his cause. [7]Keep thee far from a false matter; and the innocent and righteous slay thou not; for I will not justify the wicked. [8]And thou shalt take no gift; for a gift blindeth them that have sight, and perverteth the words of the righteous.

[9]And a stranger shalt thou not oppress; for ye know the heart of a stranger, seeing ye were strangers in the land of Egypt.

[10]And six years thou shalt sow thy land, and gather in the increase thereof; [11]but the seventh year thou shalt let it rest and lie fallow, that the poor of thy people may eat; and what they leave the beast of the field shall eat. In like manner thou shalt deal with thy vineyard, and with thy oliveyard. [12]Six days thou shalt do thy work, but on the seventh day thou shalt rest; that thine ox and thine ass may have rest, and the son of thy handmaid, and the stranger, may be refreshed.

[13]And in all things that I have said unto you take ye heed; and make no mention of the name of other gods, neither let it be heard out of thy mouth.

[14]Three times thou shalt keep a feast unto Me in the year. [15]The feast of unleavened bread shalt thou keep; seven days thou shalt eat unleavened bread, as I

*[Continued on p. 306]*

( added by redactor )                    { problematic }

| **P** | **Notes** |
|---|---|

profane the name of thy God: I am the Lord. ¹³Thou shalt not oppress thy neighbour, nor rob him; the wages of a hired servant shall not abide with thee all night until the morning. ¹⁴Thou shalt not curse the deaf, nor put a stumblingblock before the blind, but thou shalt fear thy God: I am the Lord. ¹⁵Ye shall do no unrighteousness in judgment; thou shalt not respect the person of the poor, nor favour the person of the mighty; but in righteousness shalt thou judge thy neighbour.

¹⁸Thou shalt not take vengeance, nor bear any grudge against the children of thy people, but thou shalt love thy neighbour as thyself: I am the Lord.

¹⁹Ye shall keep My statutes. Thou shalt not let thy cattle gender with a diverse kind; thou shalt not sow thy field with two kinds of seed; neither shall there come upon thee a garment of two kinds of stuff mingled together. ²⁶Ye shall not eat with the blood; neither shall ye practise divination nor soothsaying. ²⁷Ye shall not round the corners of your heads, neither shalt thou mar the corners of thy beard.

³³And if a stranger sojourn with thee in your land, ye shall not do him wrong. ³⁴The stranger that sojourneth with you shall be unto you as the home-born among you, and thou shalt love him as thyself; for ye were strangers in the land of Egypt: I am the Lord your God.

**[Restrictions on Rituals - Lev 22]**

"ᴸᴱⱽ ²²:¹And the Lord spoke unto Moses, saying: ²Speak unto Aaron and to his sons, that they separate themselves from the holy things of the children of Israel, which they hallow unto Me, and that they profane not My holy name: I am the Lord. ³Say unto them: Whosoever he be of all your seed throughout your generations, that approacheth unto the holy things, which the children of Israel hallow unto the Lord, having his uncleanness upon him, that soul shall be cut off from before

why the earlier documents that P quotes, the Ten Commandments and the Holiness Code, have a strong moral element, while the text that P himself wrote focuses on ritual. Perhaps the dogmas of the Aaronid priests changed over time, putting less focus on morality and more on ritual. Or perhaps the P text was written during a religious reform that focused on ritual or at a time when P hoped these rituals would be restored in a rebuilt Temple.

Many of these descriptions of laws are very repetitive and boring to read, but readers who want to read the entire P text can read Exodus 35 through the end of Leviticus in any Bible rather than reading the brief selections included in this edition.

**Holidays**

Notice that the Holiness Code in P mentions five holidays, Passover, Shavuot, Rosh Hashannah, Yom Kippur, and Sukkot (Lev. 23:4-35).

The other texts mention only three holidays, Passover, Shavuot, and Sukkot. (E text: Exodus 23:14; J text: Exodus 34:18-23, and D text: Deuteronomy 16:1-17).

[ used more than once ]　　" quoting older text "

| **E** | **J** |
|---|---|
| commanded thee, at the time appointed in the month Abib—for in it thou camest out from Egypt; and none shall appear before Me empty; [16]and the feast of harvest, the first-fruits of thy labours, which thou sowest in the field; and the feast of ingathering, at the end of the year, when thou gatherest in thy labours out of the field. [17]Three times in the year all thy males shall appear before the Lord God. | |
| [18]Thou shalt not offer the blood of My sacrifice with leavened bread; neither shall the fat of My feast remain all night until the morning. [19]The choicest first-fruits of thy land thou shalt bring into the house of the Lord thy God. Thou shalt not seethe a kid in its mother's milk. | |
| [20]Behold, I send an angel before thee, to keep thee by the way, and to bring thee into the place which I have prepared. [21]Take heed of him, and hearken unto his voice; be not rebellious against him; for he will not pardon your transgression; for My name is in him. [22]But if thou shalt indeed hearken unto his voice, and do all that I speak; then I will be an enemy unto thine enemies, and an adversary unto thine adversaries. [23]For Mine angel shall go before thee, and bring thee in unto the Amorite, and the Hittite, and the Perizzite, and the Canaanite, the Hivite, and the Jebusite; and I will cut them off. [24]Thou shalt not bow down to their gods, nor serve them, nor do after their doings; but thou shalt utterly overthrow them, and break in pieces their pillars. | *[Continued on p. 306]* |
| [25]And ye shall serve the Lord your God, and He will bless thy bread, and thy water; and I will take sickness away from the midst of thee. [26]None shall miscarry, nor be barren, in thy land; the number of thy days I will fulfil. [27]I will send My terror before thee, and will discomfit all the people to whom thou shalt come, and I will make all thine enemies turn their backs unto thee. [28]And I will send the hornet before thee, which shall drive out the Hivite, the Canaanite, and the Hittite, from before thee. [29]I will not drive them out from before thee in one year, lest the land become desolate, and the beasts of the field multiply against thee. [30]By little and little I will drive them out from before thee, until thou be increased, and inherit the land. [31]And I | |
| ( added by redactor ) | { problematic } |

| **P** | **Notes** |
|---|---|
| Me: I am the Lord.<br><br>⁴What man soever of the seed of Aaron is a leper, or hath an issue, he shall not eat of the holy things, until he be clean. And whoso toucheth any one that is unclean by the dead; or from whomsoever the flow of seed goeth out; ⁵or whosoever toucheth any swarming thing, whereby he may be made unclean, or a man of whom he may take uncleanness, whatsoever uncleanness he hath; ⁶the soul that toucheth any such shall be unclean until the even, and shall not eat of the holy things, unless he bathe his flesh in water.<br><br>**[Holy Days - Lev 23]**<br>"ᴸᴱⱽ²³﹕¹And the Lord spoke unto Moses, saying: ²Speak unto the children of Israel, and say unto them: The appointed seasons of the Lord, which ye shall proclaim to be holy convocations, even these are My appointed seasons. ³Six days shall work be done; but on the seventh day is a sabbath of solemn rest, a holy convocation; ye shall do no manner of work; it is a sabbath unto the Lord in all your dwellings.<br><br>⁵In the first month, on the fourteenth day of the month at dusk, is the Lord's passover. ⁶And on the fifteenth day of the same month is the feast of unleavened bread unto the Lord; seven days ye shall eat unleavened bread.<br><br>¹⁵And ye shall count unto you from the morrow after the day of rest, from the day that ye brought the sheaf of the waving; seven weeks shall there be complete; ¹⁶even unto the morrow after the seventh week shall ye number fifty days; and ye shall present a new meal-offering unto the Lord.<br><br>²³And the Lord spoke unto Moses, saying: ²⁴Speak unto the children of Israel, saying: In the seventh month, in the first day of the month, shall be a solemn rest unto you, a memorial proclaimed with the blast of horns, a holy convocation. ²⁵Ye shall do no manner of | *[Continued on p. 297]* |

| [ used more than once ] | " quoting older text " |

| **E** | **J** |
|---|---|

will set thy border from the Red Sea even unto the sea of the Philistines, and from the wilderness unto the River; for I will deliver the inhabitants of the land into your hand; and thou shalt drive them out before thee. [32]Thou shalt make no covenant with them, nor with their gods. [33]They shall not dwell in thy land— lest they make thee sin against Me, for thou wilt serve their gods—for they will be a snare unto thee."

## Israel Accepts the Covenant

[EX 24:3]And Moses came and told the people all the words of the Lord, and all the ordinances; and all the people answered with one voice, and said: 'All the words which the Lord hath spoken will we do.' [4]And Moses wrote all the words of the Lord, and rose up early in the morning, and builded an altar under the mount, and twelve pillars, according to the twelve tribes of Israel. [5]And he sent the young men of the children of Israel, who offered burnt-offerings, and sacrificed peace-offerings of oxen unto the Lord. [6]And Moses took half of the blood, and put it in basins; and half of the blood he dashed against the altar. [7]And he took the book of the covenant, and read in the hearing of the people; and they said: 'All that the Lord hath spoken will we do, and obey.' [8]And Moses took the blood, and sprinkled it on the people, and said: 'Behold the blood of the covenant, which the Lord hath made with you in agreement with all these words.'

*[Continued on p. 306]*

## The Golden Calf

{[EX 24:12]And the Lord said unto Moses: 'Come up to Me into the mount and be there; and I will give thee the tables of stone, and the law and the commandment, which I have written, that thou mayest teach them.' [13]And Moses rose up, and Joshua his minister; and Moses went up into the mount of God. [14]And unto the elders he said: 'Tarry ye here for us, until we come back unto you; and, behold, Aaron and Hur are with you; whosoever hath a cause, let him come near unto them.' [15]And Moses went up into the mount,

[EX 32:1]And when the people saw that Moses delayed

| ( added by redactor ) | { problematic } |
|---|---|

| P | Notes |
|---|---|

servile work; and ye shall bring an offering made by fire unto the Lord.

²⁶And the Lord spoke unto Moses, saying: ²⁷Howbeit on the tenth day of this seventh month is the day of atonement; there shall be a holy convocation unto you, and ye shall afflict your souls; and ye shall bring an offering made by fire unto the Lord. ²⁸And ye shall do no manner of work in that same day; for it is a day of atonement, to make atonement for you before the Lord your God.

³³And the Lord spoke unto Moses, saying: ³⁴Speak unto the children of Israel, saying: On the fifteenth day of this seventh month is the feast of tabernacles for seven days unto the Lord. ³⁵On the first day shall be a holy convocation; ye shall do no manner of servile work. ³⁶Seven days ye shall bring an offering made by fire unto the Lord; on the eighth day shall be a holy convocation unto you; and ye shall bring an offering made by fire unto the Lord; it is a day of solemn assembly; ye shall do no manner of servile work."

**[Various Laws - Lev 24]**

"ᴸᴱⱽ ²⁴:¹And the Lord spoke unto Moses, saying: ²'Command the children of Israel, that they bring unto thee pure olive oil beaten for the light, to cause a lamp to burn continually.

¹⁰And the son of an Israelitish woman, whose father was an Egyptian, went out among the children of Israel; and the son of the Israelitish woman and a man of Israel strove together in the camp. ¹¹And the son of the Israelitish woman blasphemed the Name, and cursed; and they brought him unto Moses. And his mother's name was Shelomith, the daughter of Dibri, of the tribe of Dan. ¹³And the Lord spoke unto Moses, saying: ¹⁴'Bring forth him that hath cursed without the camp; and let all that heard him lay their hands upon his head, and let all the congregation stone him. ¹⁶And he that blasphemeth the name of the Lord, he

**The Golden Calf**

**E Text**

The story of the Golden Calf seems to be out of place in the E text. God calls Moses to receive the Ten Commandments after God has given the Covenant Code and Israel has accepted the covenant (Ex. 24:3), but it does not make

---

[ used more than once ]     " quoting older text "

| **E** | **J** |
|---|---|
| to come down from the mount, the people gathered themselves together unto Aaron, and said unto him: 'Up, make us a god who shall go before us; for as for this Moses, the man that brought us up out of the land of Egypt, we know not what is become of him.' | |

**E**

to come down from the mount, the people gathered themselves together unto Aaron, and said unto him: 'Up, make us a god who shall go before us; for as for this Moses, the man that brought us up out of the land of Egypt, we know not what is become of him.'

²And Aaron said unto them: 'Break off the golden rings, which are in the ears of your wives, of your sons, and of your daughters, and bring them unto me.' ³And all the people broke off the golden rings which were in their ears, and brought them unto Aaron. ⁴And he received it at their hand, and fashioned it with a graving tool, and made it a molten calf; and they said: 'This is thy god, O Israel, which brought thee up out of the land of Egypt.'

⁵And when Aaron saw this, he built an altar before it; and Aaron made proclamation, and said: 'To-morrow shall be a feast to the Lord.' ⁶And they rose up early on the morrow, and offered burnt-offerings, and brought peace-offerings; and the people sat down to eat and to drink, and rose up to make merry.

⁷And the Lord spoke unto Moses: 'Go, get thee down; for thy people, that thou broughtest up out of the land of Egypt, have dealt corruptly; ⁸they have turned aside quickly out of the way which I commanded them; they have made them a molten calf, and have worshipped it, and have sacrificed unto it, and said: This is thy god, O Israel, which brought thee up out of the land of Egypt.' ⁹And the Lord said unto Moses: 'I have seen this people, and, behold, it is a stiffnecked people. ¹⁰Now therefore let Me alone, that My wrath may wax hot against them, and that I may consume them; and I will make of thee a great nation.'

¹¹And Moses besought the Lord his God, and said: 'Lord, why doth Thy wrath wax hot against Thy people, that Thou hast brought forth out of the land of Egypt with great power and with a mighty hand? ¹²Wherefore should the Egyptians speak, saying: For evil did He bring them forth, to slay them in the mountains, and to consume them from the face of the earth? Turn from Thy fierce wrath, and repent of this evil against Thy people. ¹³Remember Abraham, Isaac, and Israel, Thy servants, to whom Thou didst swear by

**J**

*[Continued on p. 306]*

( added by redactor )                    { problematic }

| P | Notes |
|---|---|

shall surely be put to death.

¹⁷And he that smiteth any man mortally shall surely be put to death. ¹⁸And he that smiteth a beast mortally shall make it good: life for life. ¹⁹And if a man maim his neighbour; as he hath done, so shall it be done to him: ²⁰breach for breach, eye for eye, tooth for tooth; as he hath maimed a man, so shall it be rendered unto him.'

**[Laws Helping the Poor - Lev 25]**

"ᴸᴱⱽ ²⁵:¹And the Lord spoke unto Moses in mount Sinai, saying: ²Speak unto the children of Israel, and say unto them: ³Six years thou shalt sow thy field, and six years thou shalt prune thy vineyard, and gather in the produce thereof. ⁴But in the seventh year shall be a sabbath of solemn rest for the land, a sabbath unto the Lord; thou shalt neither sow thy field, nor prune thy vineyard.

⁸And thou shalt number seven sabbaths of years unto thee, seven times seven years; and there shall be unto thee the days of seven sabbaths of years, even forty and nine years. ⁹Then shalt thou make proclamation with the blast of the horn on the tenth day of the seventh month; in the day of atonement shall ye make proclamation with the horn throughout all your land. ¹⁰And ye shall hallow the fiftieth year, and proclaim liberty throughout the land unto all the inhabitants thereof; it shall be a jubilee unto you; and ye shall return every man unto his possession, and ye shall return every man unto his family.

²⁹And if a man sell a dwelling-house in a walled city, then he may redeem it within a whole year after it is sold; for a full year shall he have the right of redemption. ³⁰And if it be not redeemed within the space of a full year, then the house that is in the walled city shall be made sure in perpetuity to him that bought it, throughout his generations; it shall not go out in the jubilee. ³¹But the houses of

sense to give a new set of commandments after Israel has already accepted the covenant. In the story of the Golden Calf, Moses smashes the first version of the Ten Commandments, but in the E text, he does not receive the first version of Ten Commandments and does not receive a second version to replace the smashed first version; and E has no text of the Ten Commandments. The awkward position of this episode within the E text may indicate that it was written later than the rest of the E text.

The Covenant Code is based on an early tradition about the revelation. This text about the Golden Calf is based on a tradition that became important after Jeroboam established religious centers with statues of Golden Calves in Bethel and Dan. This text gets back at Jeroboam for dismantling the religious center at Shiloh and establishing these new religious centers with statues of Golden Calves by showing that the Golden Calf is a shameful symbol. It also gets back at the Aaronid priests by showing that their supposed ancestor Aaron led the worship of the Golden Calf.

| [ used more than once ] | " quoting older text " |
|---|---|

## E                                              J

Thine own self, and saidst unto them: I will multiply your seed as the stars of heaven, and all this land that I have spoken of will I give unto your seed, and they shall inherit it for ever.' [14]And the Lord repented of the evil which He said He would do unto His people.

[15]And Moses turned, and went down from the mount, with the two tables of the testimony in his hand; tables that were written on both their sides; on the one side and on the other were they written. [16]And the tables were the work of God, and the writing was the writing of God, graven upon the tables.

[17]And when Joshua heard the noise of the people as they shouted, he said unto Moses: 'There is a noise of war in the camp.' [18]And he said: 'It is not the voice of them that shout for mastery, neither is it the voice of them that cry for being overcome, but the noise of them that sing do I hear.' [19]And it came to pass, as soon as he came nigh unto the camp, that he saw the calf and the dancing; and Moses' anger waxed hot, and he cast the tables out of his hands, and broke them beneath the mount. [20]And he took the calf which they had made, and burnt it with fire, and ground it to powder, and strewed it upon the water, and made the children of Israel drink of it.

[21]And Moses said unto Aaron: 'What did this people unto thee, that thou hast brought a great sin upon them?' [22]And Aaron said: 'Let not the anger of my lord wax hot; thou knowest the people, that they are set on evil. [23]So they said unto me: Make us a god, which shall go before us; for as for this Moses, the man that brought us up out of the land of Egypt, we know not what is become of him. [24]And I said unto them: Whosoever hath any gold, let them break it off; so they gave it me; and I cast it into the fire, and there came out this calf.'

[25]And when Moses saw that the people were broken loose—for Aaron had let them loose for a derision among their enemies— [26]then Moses stood in the gate of the camp, and said: 'Whoso is on the Lord's side, let him come unto me.' And all the sons of Levi gathered themselves together unto him. [27]And he said unto them: 'Thus saith the Lord, the God of Israel:

*[Continued on p. 306]*

( added by redactor )                    { problematic }

| P | Notes |
|---|---|

the villages which have no wall round about them shall be reckoned with the fields of the country; they may be redeemed, and they shall go out in the jubilee.

### [Blessings and Cursings - Lev 26]

"LEV 26: 3If ye walk in My statutes, and keep My commandments, and do them; 4then I will give your rains in their season, and the land shall yield her produce, and the trees of the field shall yield their fruit. 6And I will give peace in the land, and ye shall lie down, and none shall make you afraid; and I will cause evil beasts to cease out of the land, neither shall the sword go through your land.

14But if ye will not hearken unto Me, and will not do all these commandments; 16I also will do this unto you: I will appoint terror over you, even consumption and fever, that shall make the eyes to fail, and the soul to languish; and ye shall sow your seed in vain, for your enemies shall eat it. 17And I will set My face against you, and ye shall be smitten before your enemies; they that hate you shall rule over you; and ye shall flee when none pursueth you.

27And if ye will not for all this hearken unto Me, but walk contrary unto Me; 28then I will walk contrary unto you in fury; and I also will chastise you seven times for your sins. 29And ye shall eat the flesh of your sons, and the flesh of your daughters shall ye eat. 30And I will destroy your high places, and cut down your sun-pillars, and cast your carcasses upon the carcasses of your idols; and My soul shall abhor you. 31And I will make your cities a waste, and will bring your sanctuaries unto desolation, and I will not smell the savour of your sweet odours. 33And you will I scatter among the nations, and I will draw out the sword after you; and your land shall be a desolation, and your cities shall be a waste.

46These are the statutes and ordinances and laws, which the Lord made between Him and

---

**Notes**

There are so many gaps in the E text, where material has been removed by RJE, that the E text may have originally contained a version of the Ten Commandments and other material that integrated the story of the Golden Calf with the rest of the text, but it is also possible that this story was a later addition, raising questions about how the E text was written.

This story also has an anthropomorphic view of God that is typical of J but not of E. God wants to destroy Israel and make a new nation just from Moses, but Moses convinces Him not to (Ex. 32:10-14). God changes his mind because Moses argues that people will think badly of Him. This atypical behavior also raises questions about how the E text was written

For more information, see page 27-29.

### The Census - Relocated

Both the census in Numbers 1-4 and the census in Numbers 25:19-27:11 are separate documents added by an editor. Both are meant to justify the

---

[ used more than once ]    " quoting older text "

| E | J |
|---|---|
| Put ye every man his sword upon his thigh, and go to and fro from gate to gate throughout the camp, and slay every man his brother, and every man his companion, and every man his neighbour.' [28]And the sons of Levi did according to the word of Moses; and there fell of the people that day about three thousand men. [29]And Moses said: 'Consecrate yourselves to-day to the Lord, for every man hath been against his son and against his brother; that He may also bestow upon you a blessing this day.'<br><br>[30]And it came to pass on the morrow, that Moses said unto the people: 'Ye have sinned a great sin; and now I will go up unto the Lord, peradventure I shall make atonement for your sin.' [31]And Moses returned unto the Lord, and said: 'Oh, this people have sinned a great sin, and have made them a god of gold. [32]Yet now, if Thou wilt forgive their sin—; and if not, blot me, I pray Thee, out of Thy book which Thou hast written.'<br><br>[33]And the Lord said unto Moses: 'Whosoever hath sinned against Me, him will I blot out of My book. [34]And now go, lead the people unto the place of which I have spoken unto thee; behold, Mine angel shall go before thee; nevertheless in the day when I visit, I will visit their sin upon them.' [35]And the Lord smote the people, because they made the calf, which Aaron made.} | *[Continued on p. 306]* |
| ( added by redactor ) | { problematic } |

| P | Notes |
|---|---|
| the children of Israel in mount Sinai by the hand of Moses." | amount of land allocated to each tribe, as is the section of P titled "Inheriting the Land" (beginning at Numbers 33:50), and both have much more detail than this section—but their details contradict each other. The allocation of land fits into the narrative in the section "Inheriting the Land," but the other two censuses interrupt the narrative. Therefore, this edition moves these two censuses to the section of Other Texts. |
| **[End of the Holiness Code]** | |
| **[Valuing for Money - Lev 27]** | |
| LEV 27:1And the Lord spoke unto Moses, saying: ²Speak unto the children of Israel, and say unto them: When a man shall clearly utter a vow of persons unto the Lord, according to thy valuation, ³then thy valuation shall be for the male from twenty years old even unto sixty years old, even thy valuation shall be fifty shekels of silver, after the shekel of the sanctuary. | |
| ¹⁴And when a man shall sanctify his house to be holy unto the Lord, then the priest shall value it, whether it be good or bad; as the priest shall value it, so shall it stand. ¹⁵And if he that sanctified it will redeem his house, then he shall add the fifth part of the money of thy valuation unto it, and it shall be his. | |
| ³⁴These are the commandments, which the Lord commanded Moses for the children of Israel in mount Sinai. | |
| **Purity and Guilt - Abridged** | **Purity and Guilt** |
| NUM 5:1And the Lord spoke unto Moses, saying: ²'Command the children of Israel, that they put out of the camp every leper, and every one that hath an issue, and whosoever is unclean by the dead; | Because the goal of this edition is to place parallel passages from the three texts next to each other, it provides abridged versions of some lengthy and repetitive passages from the P text. For all these commandments about purity and guilt, read Numbers 5. |
| ⁵And the Lord spoke unto Moses, saying: ⁶Speak unto the children of Israel: When a man or woman shall commit any sin that men commit, to commit a trespass against the Lord, and that soul be guilty; ⁷then they shall confess their sin which they have done; and he shall make restitution for his guilt in full, and add unto it the fifth part thereof, and give it unto him in respect of whom he hath been guilty. | |

| [ used more than once ] | " quoting older text " |
|---|---|

| **E** | **J** |
|---|---|
| *[Continued on p. 306]* | *[Continued on p. 306]* |
| ( added by redactor ) | { problematic } |

| **P** | **Notes** |
|---|---|

### Nazarites and Blessing - Abridged

NUM 6:1 And the Lord spoke unto Moses, saying: <sup>2</sup>Speak unto the children of Israel, and say unto them: When either man or woman shall clearly utter a vow, the vow of a Nazirite, to consecrate himself unto the Lord, <sup>3</sup>he shall abstain from wine and strong drink: he shall drink no vinegar of wine, or vinegar of strong drink, neither shall he drink any liquor of grapes, nor eat fresh grapes or dried. <sup>5</sup>All the days of his vow of Naziriteship there shall no razor come upon his head; until the days be fulfilled, in which he consecrateth himself unto the Lord, he shall be holy, he shall let the locks of the hair of his head grow long.

<sup>22</sup>And the Lord spoke unto Moses, saying: <sup>23</sup>'Speak unto Aaron and unto his sons, saying: On this wise ye shall bless the children of Israel; ye shall say unto them: <sup>24</sup>The Lord bless thee, and keep thee; <sup>25</sup>The Lord make His face to shine upon thee, and be gracious unto thee; <sup>26</sup>The Lord lift up His countenance upon thee, and give thee peace.

### The First Sacrifices - Abridged

NUM 7:1 And it came to pass on the day that Moses had made an end of setting up the tabernacle,... <sup>2</sup>that the princes of Israel, the heads of their fathers' houses, offered—these were the princes of the tribes, these are they that were over them that were numbered.

<sup>12</sup>And he that presented his offering the first day was Nahshon the son of Amminadab, of the tribe of Judah; <sup>13</sup>and his offering was one silver dish, the weight thereof was a hundred and thirty shekels, one silver basin of seventy shekels, after the shekel of the sanctuary; both of them full of fine flour mingled with oil for a meal-offering; <sup>14</sup>one golden pan of ten shekels, full of incense; <sup>15</sup>one young bullock, one ram, one he-lamb of the first year, for a burnt-offering; <sup>16</sup>one male of the goats for a sin-offering; <sup>17</sup>and for the sacrifice of peace-offerings, two oxen, five rams, five he-goats, five

### Nazarites and Blessing

Because the goal of this edition is to place parallel passages from the three texts next to each other, it provides abridged versions of some lengthy and repetitive passages from the P text. For all of the commandments about Nazarites, read Numbers 6.

This edition does include the entire priestly blessing.

### The First Sacrifices

Because the goal of this edition is to place parallel passages from the three texts next to each other, it provides abridged versions of some lengthy and repetitive passages from the P text. For the entire account of the first sacrifices, read Numbers 7.

| [ used more than once ] | " quoting older text " |
|---|---|

| **E** | **J** |
|-------|-------|
| | |

### Seeing God

EX 33:12And Moses said unto the Lord: 'See, Thou sayest unto me: Bring up this people; and Thou hast not let me know whom Thou wilt send with me. Yet Thou hast said: I know thee by name, and thou hast also found grace in My sight. 13Now therefore, I pray Thee, if I have found grace in Thy sight, show me now Thy ways, that I may know

### Seeing God

EX 24:1And unto Moses He said: 'Come up unto the Lord, thou, and Aaron, Nadab, and Abihu, and seventy of the elders of Israel; and worship ye afar off; 2and Moses alone shall come near unto the Lord; but they shall not come near; neither shall the people go up with him.'
9Then went up Moses, and Aaron, Nadab, and Abihu, and seventy of

( added by redactor )                    { problematic }

| **P** | **Notes** |
|---|---|

he-lambs of the first year. This was the offering of Nahshon the son of Amminadab.

### Readying the Levites - Abridged

NUM 8:5 And the Lord spoke unto Moses, saying: 6'Take the Levites from among the children of Israel, and cleanse them. 7And thus shalt thou do unto them, to cleanse them: sprinkle the water of purification upon them, and let them cause a razor to pass over all their flesh, and let them wash their clothes, and cleanse themselves. 8Then let them take a young bullock, and its meal-offering, fine flour mingled with oil, and another young bullock shalt thou take for a sin-offering.

### Keeping Passover - Abridged

NUM 9:1 And the Lord spoke unto Moses in the wilderness of Sinai, in the first month of the second year after they were come out of the land of Egypt, saying: 2'Let the children of Israel keep the passover in its appointed season. 3In the fourteenth day of this month, at dusk, ye shall keep it in its appointed season; according to all the statutes of it, and according to all the ordinances thereof, shall ye keep it.'

9And the Lord spoke unto Moses, saying: 10'Speak unto the children of Israel, saying: If any man of you or of your generations shall be unclean by reason of a dead body, or be in a journey afar off, yet he shall keep the passover unto the Lord; 11in the second month on the fourteenth day at dusk they shall keep it; they shall eat it with unleavened bread and bitter herbs; 12they shall leave none of it unto the morning, nor break a bone thereof; according to all the statute of the passover they shall keep it. 13But the man that is clean, and is not on a journey, and forbeareth to keep the passover, that soul shall be cut off from his people.'

### Readying the Levites

Because the goal of this edition is to place parallel passages from the three texts next to each other, it provides abridged versions of some lengthy and repetitive passages from the P text. For the entire account of readying the Levites, read Numbers 8.

### Keeping Passover

Because the goal of this edition is to place parallel passages from the three texts next to each other, it provides abridged versions of some lengthy and repetitive passages from the P text. For the entire account of keeping Passover, read Numbers 9.

### Seeing God
### Separating the Texts

There is an obvious discontinuity in the received text of the Bible. One passage ends by saying, "EX 33:11 And the Lord spoke unto Moses face to face." Immediately afterwards, it has a passage that begins by saying that Moses has

| [ used more than once ] | " quoting older text " |
|---|---|

| **E** | **J** |
|---|---|
| Thee, to the end that I may find grace in Thy sight; and consider that this nation is Thy people.' | the elders of Israel; {¹⁰and they saw the God of Israel; and there was under His feet the like of a paved work of sapphire stone, and the like of |
| ¹⁴And He said: 'My presence shall go with thee, and I will give thee rest.' | the very heaven for clearness. ¹¹And upon the nobles of the children of Israel He laid not His hand; and they |
| ¹⁵And he said unto Him: 'If Thy presence go not with me, carry us not up hence. ¹⁶For wherein now shall it be known that I have found grace in Thy sight, I and Thy people? is it not in that Thou goest with us, so that we are distinguished, I and Thy people, from all the people that are upon the face of the earth?' ¹⁷And the Lord said unto Moses: 'I will do this thing also that thou hast spoken, for thou hast found grace in My sight, and I know thee by name.' | beheld God, and did eat and drink.} |
| | EX 33:7Now Moses used to take the tent and to pitch it without the camp, afar off from the camp; and he called it The tent of meeting. And it came to pass, that every one that sought the Lord went out unto the tent of meeting, which was without the camp. ⁸And it came to pass, when Moses went out unto the Tent, that all the people rose up, and stood, every man at his tent door, and looked after Moses, until he was gone into the Tent. ⁹And it came to pass, when Moses entered into the Tent, the pillar of cloud descended, and stood at the door of the Tent; and [the Lord] spoke with Moses. ¹⁰And when all the people saw the pillar of cloud stand at the door of the Tent, all the people rose up and worshipped, every man at his tent door. ¹¹And the Lord spoke unto Moses face to face, as a man speaketh unto his friend. And he would return into the camp; but his minister Joshua, the son of Nun, a young man, departed not out of the Tent. |
| ¹⁸And he said: 'Show me, I pray Thee, Thy glory.' ¹⁹And He said: 'I will make all My goodness pass before thee, and will proclaim the name of the Lord before thee; and I will be gracious to whom I will be gracious, and will show mercy on whom I will show mercy.' ²⁰And He said: 'Thou canst not see My face, for man shall not see Me and live.' ²¹And the Lord said: 'Behold, there is a place by Me, and thou shalt stand upon the rock. ²²And it shall come to pass, while My glory passeth by, that I will put thee in a cleft of the rock, and will cover thee with My hand until I have passed by. ²³And I will take away My hand, and thou shalt see My back; but My face shall not be seen.' | |
| ( added by redactor ) | { problematic } |

| P | Notes |
|---|---|

### The Tabernacle and Travel

NUM 9:15And on the day that the tabernacle was reared up the cloud covered the tabernacle, even the tent of the testimony; and at even there was upon the tabernacle as it were the appearance of fire, until morning. 16So it was alway: the cloud covered it, and the appearance of fire by night.

17And whenever the cloud was taken up from over the Tent, then after that the children of Israel journeyed; and in the place where the cloud abode, there the children of Israel encamped. 22Whether it were two days, or a month, or a year, that the cloud tarried upon the tabernacle, abiding thereon, the children of Israel remained encamped, and journeyed not; but when it was taken up, they journeyed.

23At the commandment of the Lord they encamped, and at the commandment of the Lord they journeyed; they kept the charge

not seen God's glory and ends by saying that he can see God's back but not His face (Ex. 33:12-23). Clearly, the first passage is from J, where it is easy to see God and many people do it, and the second is from E, where it is much harder to see God and only Moses does it.

**E Text**

In the E text, only Moses can see God, and here we learn that even Moses can see only His back and not His face.

**J Text**

Exodus 24:1-11 is problematic because the narrator uses the word God. As a rule, the narrator in J always says "the Lord" rather than "God."

Exodus 24 overall has J's typical anthropomorphic view of God and her typical view that many people have seen God.

The seventy elders mentioned here are also present later in J when God comes down to speak to Moses:

NUM 11: 24And Moses went out, and told the people the words of the Lord; and he gathered seventy men of the elders of the people, and set them round about the Tent. 25And the Lord came down in the cloud, and spoke unto him, and took of the spirit that was upon him, and put it upon the seventy elders; and it came to pass, that, when the spirit rested upon them, they prophesied, but they did so no more.

The pillar of cloud also appears in J and not in E.

**P Text**

The P text does not talk specifically about seeing God, but it does have the following passage about Moses's appearance after receiving the Ten Commandments, which is much closer to E's than to J's view of seeing God:

EX 34:29And it came to pass, when Moses came down from mount Sinai with the two tables of the testimony in Moses' hand, when he came down from the mount, that Moses knew not that the skin of his face sent forth beams while He talked with him. 30And when Aaron

| [ used more than once ] | " quoting older text " |
|---|---|

| **E** | **J** |
|---|---|
| | |

### Leaving the Mountain

<sup>EX 33:1</sup>And the Lord spoke unto Moses: 'Depart, go up hence, thou and the people that thou hast brought up out of the land of Egypt, unto the land of which I swore unto Abraham, to Isaac, and to Jacob, saying: Unto thy seed will I give it—<sup>2</sup>and I will send an angel before thee; and I will drive out the Canaanite, the Amorite, and the Hittite, and the Perizzite, the Hivite, and the Jebusite—<sup>3</sup>unto a land flowing with milk and honey; for I will not go up in the midst of thee; for thou art a stiffnecked people; lest I consume thee in the way.'

<sup>4</sup>And when the people heard these evil tidings, they mourned; and no

### Leaving the Mountain

<sup>NUM 10:29</sup>And Moses said unto Hobab, the son of Reuel the Midianite, Moses' father-in-law: 'We are journeying unto the place of which the Lord said: I will give it you; come thou with us, and we will do thee good; for the Lord hath spoken good concerning Israel.' <sup>30</sup>And he said unto him: 'I will not go; but I will depart to mine own land, and to my kindred.' <sup>31</sup>And he said: 'Leave us not, I pray thee; forasmuch as thou knowest how we are to encamp in the wilderness, and thou shalt be to us instead of eyes. <sup>32</sup>And it shall be, if thou go with us, yea, it shall be, that what good soever the Lord shall do unto us, the same will we

( added by redactor )        { problematic }

| **P** | **Notes** |
|---|---|
| of the Lord, at the commandment of the Lord by the hand of Moses. | and all the children of Israel saw Moses, behold, the skin of his face sent forth beams; and they were afraid to come nigh him. |

After he saw God, Moses' face was so awesome that the second-hand glory made it hard for other people to look even at Moses.

The Hebrew root *KRN* is used in words connected with both beams and horns. As a result, the Latin Vulgate Bible translated this passage by saying that Moses had "horns" rather than "beams" coming from his face—which is why Michelangelo's Moses and many other works of arts depict him with horns.

### Seeing God/Leaving the Mountain - Relocated

Because this edition is meant to place doublets next to each other so readers can compare them, it reverses the order of the sections Seeing God and Leaving the Mountain in the E text so they are next to the similar sections in the J text.

## Leaving the Mountain

NUM 10:1 And the Lord spoke unto Moses, saying: 2'Make thee two trumpets of silver; of beaten work shalt thou make them; and they shall be unto thee for the calling of the congregation, and for causing the camps to set forward. 3And when they shall blow with them, all the congregation shall gather themselves unto thee at the door

### Leaving the Mountain

**E Text**

E does not mention the name of Mt. Horeb when it tells the story of giving the law. It mentioned Mt. Horeb earlier, when Moses saw the burning bush at Mt. Horeb and that Moses would bring the children of Israel to serve Him there (Ex. 3:1-2b). It mentions Mt. Horeb again here, when they leave the mountain (Ex. 33:6). But it does not mention the name of Mt. Horeb between these two points. In the J and P text, the law is given on Mt. Sinai. Presumably, RJE stripped out other mentions of Horeb in E because the contradiction with the J text would be too blatant, but he kept Mt. Horeb here and in the story of the burning bush because they are far enough from the story of Sinai that the contradiction is not so obvious.

**J Text**

Mentions of the ark of the covenant are prob-

| [ used more than once ] | " quoting older text " |
|---|---|

## E

man did put on him his ornaments. [5]And the Lord said unto Moses: 'Say unto the children of Israel: Ye are a stiffnecked people; if I go up into the midst of thee for one moment, I shall consume thee; therefore now put off thy ornaments from thee, that I may know what to do unto thee.' [6]And the children of Israel stripped themselves of their ornaments from mount Horeb onward.

### The Israelites Complain

NUM 11:1And the people were as murmurers, speaking evil in the ears of the Lord; and when the Lord heard it, His anger was kindled; and the fire of the Lord burnt among them, and devoured in the uttermost part of the camp. [2]And the people cried unto Moses; and Moses prayed unto the Lord, and the fire abated. [3]And the name of that place was called Taberah, because the fire of the Lord burnt among them.

### Miriam and Aaron Complain

{NUM 12:1And Miriam and Aaron spoke against Moses because of the Cushite woman whom he had married; for he had married a Cushite woman. [2]And they said: 'Hath the Lord indeed spoken only with Moses? hath He not spoken also with us?' And the Lord heard it.— [3]Now the man Moses was very meek, above all the men that were upon

## J

do unto thee.'

[33]And they set forward from the mount of the Lord three days' journey; {and the ark of the covenant of the Lord went before them three days' journey, to seek out a resting-place for them.} [34]And the cloud of the Lord was over them by day, when they set forward from the camp.

{[35]And it came to pass, when the ark set forward, that Moses said: 'Rise up, O Lord, and let Thine enemies be scattered; and let them that hate Thee flee before Thee.' [36]And when it rested, he said: 'Return, O Lord, unto the ten thousands of the families of Israel.'}

( added by redactor )          { problematic }

| **P** | **Notes** |
|---|---|

of the tent of meeting. ⁴And if they blow but with one, then the princes, the heads of the thousands of Israel, shall gather themselves unto thee. ⁵And when ye blow an alarm, the camps that lie on the east side shall take their journey. ⁶And when ye blow an alarm the second time, the camps that lie on the south side shall set forward; they shall blow an alarm for their journeys. ⁷But when the assembly is to be gathered together, ye shall blow, but ye shall not sound an alarm.

⁸And the sons of Aaron, the priests, shall blow with the trumpets; and they shall be to you for a statute for ever throughout your generations. ⁹And when ye go to war in your land against the adversary that oppresseth you, then ye shall sound an alarm with the trumpets; and ye shall be remembered before the Lord your God, and ye shall be saved from your enemies. ¹⁰Also in the day of your gladness, and in your appointed seasons, and in your new moons, ye shall blow with the trumpets over your burnt-offerings, and over the sacrifices of your peace-offerings; and they shall be to you for a memorial before your God: I am the Lord your God.'

¹¹And it came to pass in the second year, in the second month, on the twentieth day of the month, that the cloud was taken up from over the tabernacle of the testimony. ¹²And the children of Israel set forward by their stages out of the wilderness of Sinai; and the cloud abode in the wilderness of Paran.— ¹³And they

lematic here, because there is no preparation for it; there is no earlier mention of the ark in J, though it is described at length in P before this point. There is only one other mention of the ark in J (Num. 14:44). The ark of the covenant is not mentioned at all in E. It possible that the ark of the covenant is a tradition introduced by the Aaronid priests who wrote P and inserted it later in these passages in the J text, since P uses stories about the ark of the covenant to justify allowing sacrifices only at the Temple in Jerusalem, where the Aaronid priests presided.

**P Text**

In the P text, written by a Aaronid priest, priests descended from Aaron lead the departure by blowing silver trumpets (Num. 10:8), which is used to explain the priests' practices of blowing trumpets in the time of the Temple.

The P text gives the exact date of the event (Num. 10:11) and says it is in the second year of the exodus, placing it on the timeline in P that goes back to creation. See Appendix 1.

### Miriam and Aaron Complain

The thrust of this passage is typical of E. It states the principle that God spoke directly only to Moses and appears to others in dreams and visions, which we see at work throughout the E text. It establishes Moses' superiority over Miriam and Aaron. These are things that E believes as a Mushite priest, who claimed to be descended from Moses.

| [ used more than once ] | " quoting older text " |
|---|---|

| **E** | **J** |
|---|---|
| the face of the earth.— <sup>4</sup>And the Lord spoke suddenly unto Moses, and unto Aaron, and unto Miriam: 'Come out ye three unto the tent of meeting.' And they three came out.<br><br><sup>5</sup>And the Lord came down in a pillar of cloud, and stood at the door of the Tent, and called Aaron and Miriam; and they both came forth. <sup>6</sup>And He said: 'Hear now My words: if there be a prophet among you, I the Lord do make Myself known unto him in a vision, I do speak with him in a dream. <sup>7</sup>My servant Moses is not so; he is trusted in all My house; <sup>8</sup>with him do I speak mouth to mouth, even manifestly, and not in dark speeches; and the similitude of the Lord doth he behold; wherefore then were ye not afraid to speak against My servant, against Moses?' <sup>9</sup>And the anger of the Lord was kindled against them; and He departed.<br><br><sup>10</sup>And when the cloud was removed from over the Tent, behold, Miriam was leprous, as white as snow; and Aaron looked upon Miriam; and, behold, she was leprous. <sup>11</sup>And Aaron said unto Moses: 'Oh my lord, lay not, I pray thee, sin upon us, for that we have done foolishly, and for that we have sinned. <sup>12</sup>Let her not, I pray, be as one dead, of whom the flesh is half consumed when he cometh out of his mother's womb.' <sup>13</sup>And Moses cried unto the Lord, saying: 'Heal her now, O God, I beseech Thee.'<br><br><sup>14</sup>And the Lord said unto Moses: 'If her father had but spit in her face, should she not hide in shame seven days? let her be shut up with- | *[Continued on p. 316]* |
| ( added by redactor ) | { problematic } |

| P | Notes |
|---|---|

took their first journey, according to the commandment of the Lord by the hand of Moses.

¹⁴And in the first place the standard of the camp of the children of Judah set forward according to their hosts; and over his host was Nahshon the son of Amminadab. ¹⁵And over the host of the tribe of the children of Issachar was Nethanel the son of Zuar. ¹⁶And over the host of the tribe of the children of Zebulun was Eliab the son of Helon. ¹⁷And the tabernacle was taken down; and the sons of Gershon and the sons of Merari, who bore the tabernacle, set forward.

¹⁸And the standard of the camp of Reuben set forward according to their hosts; and over his host was Elizur the son of Shedeur. ¹⁹And over the host of the tribe of the children of Simeon was Shelumiel the son of Zurishaddai. ²⁰And over the host of the tribe of the children of Gad was Eliasaph the son of Deuel.

²¹And the Kohathites the bearers of the sanctuary set forward, that the tabernacle might be set up against their coming.

²²And the standard of the camp of the children of Ephraim set forward according to their hosts; and over his host was Elishama the son of Ammihud. ²³And over the host of the tribe of the children of Manasseh was Gamaliel the son of Pedahzur. ²⁴And over the host of the tribe of the children of Benjamin was Abidan the son of Gideoni. ²⁵And the standard of the camp of the children of Dan, which was the rearward of

Yet in this passage, God comes down in a pillar of cloud to speak to Aaron and Miriam. Apart from this passage, the pillar of cloud appears only in the J text. And it is self-contradictory for God as a pillar of cloud to speak directly to Aaron and Miriam in order to tell them that He speaks directly only to Moses.

One plausible explanation is that this passage is a later addition to the text, added by a Mushite priest who only knew the combined JE text, not the J text. The pillar of cloud is so prominent in the JE text that this later author could have taken it for granted and not seen the contradiction involved.

The mention of Moses' Cushite wife supports the idea that this is a later addition. In the rest of the E and J text, Moses' wife is from Midian, and in later times, Cushan was used as another name for Midian.

For more information about the theory that this is a later addition, see page 27.

P does not mention Moses' going to Midian and marrying a Midianite wife, though both J and E do. P condemns Midian (Num. 25:6-8, Num 31:10), implicitly criticizing the stories that Moses married a Midianite. Here, a Mushite priest responds to the Aaronid priests who condemned Midian by defending Moses' marriage to a Midianite (=Cushite) woman and condemning Aaron.

This dispute in the text between Aaron and Moses reflects a dispute between the Aaronid priests, claiming descent from Aaron, and the

| [ used more than once ] | " quoting older text " |
|---|---|

| **E** | **J** |
|---|---|
| out the camp seven days, and after that she shall be brought in again.' ¹⁵And Miriam was shut up without the camp seven days; and the people journeyed not till Miriam was brought in again.} ¹⁶And afterward the people journeyed from Hazeroth, and pitched in the wilderness of Paran. | |

**The Spies' Report**

*[Gap in J: They arrive in Kadesh and Moses chooses spies]*

NUM 13:17And Moses sent them to spy out the land of Canaan, and said unto them: 'Get you up here into the South, and go up into the mountains; ¹⁸and see the land, what it is; and the people that dwelleth therein, whether they are strong or weak, whether they are few or many; ¹⁹and what the land is that they dwell in, whether it is good or bad; and what cities they are that they dwell in, whether in camps, or in strongholds; ²⁰and what the land is, whether it is fat or lean, whether there is wood therein, or not. And be ye of good courage, and bring of the fruit of the land.'—Now the time was the time of the first-ripe grapes.—

²²And they went up into the South, and came unto Hebron; and Ahiman, Sheshai, and Talmai, the children of Anak, were there.—Now Hebron was built seven years before Zoan in Egypt.— ²³And they came unto the valley of Eshcol, and cut down from thence a branch with one cluster of grapes, and they bore

| ( added by redactor ) | { problematic } |
|---|---|

| P | Notes |
|---|---|

all the camps, set forward according to their hosts; and over his host was Ahiezer the son of Ammishaddai. 26And over the host of the tribe of the children of Asher was Pagiel the son of Ochran. 27And over the host of the tribe of the children of Naphtali was Ahira the son of Enan.

28Thus were the journeyings of the children of Israel according to their hosts.—And they set forward.

### The Spies' Report

NUM 13:1And the Lord spoke unto Moses, saying: 2'Send thou men, that they may spy out the land of Canaan, which I give unto the children of Israel; of every tribe of their fathers shall ye send a man, every one a prince among them.' 3And Moses sent them from the wilderness of Paran according to the commandment of the Lord; all of them men who were heads of the children of Israel.

4And these were their names: of the tribe of Reuben, Shammua the son of Zaccur. 5Of the tribe of Simeon, Shaphat the son of Hori. 6Of the tribe of Judah, Caleb the son of Jephunneh. 7Of the tribe of Issachar, Igal the son of Joseph. 8Of the tribe of Ephraim, Hoshea the son of Nun. 9Of the tribe of Benjamin, Palti the son of Raphu. 10Of the tribe of Zebulun, Gaddiel the son of Sodi. 11Of the tribe of Joseph, namely, of the tribe of Manasseh, Gaddi the son of Susi. 12Of the tribe of Dan, Ammiel the son of Gemalli. 13Of the tribe of Asher, Sethur the son of Michael.

Mushite priests, claiming descent from Moses and therefore also from Moses' Midianite wife.

### The Spies' Report

**Separating the Texts**

The following verse is hard to assign to texts:

NUM 13:26And they went and came to Moses, and to Aaron, and to all the congregation of the children of Israel, unto the wilderness of Paran, to Kadesh; and brought back word unto them, and unto all the congregation, and showed them the fruit of the land.

Notice the repetition of "all the congregation," which presumably shows that this verse is from two texts.

This edition assigns the verse to texts based on the following:

In P, Kadesh is in the Wilderness of Zin (Num. 20:1), so the reference to Kadesh in the Wilderness of Paran must be from J.

The story of bringing back the fruit is in J but not in P.

The mention of Aaron is presumably from P.

Thus, we assign the following text to J:

NUM 13:26[And they went and came to Moses], ...and to all

| [ used more than once ] | " quoting older text " |
|---|---|

| E | J |
|---|---|
| | it upon a pole between two; they took also of the pomegranates, and of the figs.— ²⁴That place was called the valley of Eshcol, because of the cluster which the children of Israel cut down from thence.— |

it upon a pole between two; they took also of the pomegranates, and of the figs.— ²⁴That place was called the valley of Eshcol, because of the cluster which the children of Israel cut down from thence.—

²⁶[And they went and came to Moses], ...and to all the congregation of the children of Israel, unto the wilderness of Paran, to Kadesh; [And they brought back word unto them,] ... and showed them the fruit of the land.

²⁷And they told him, and said: 'We came unto the land whither thou sentest us, and surely it floweth with milk and honey; and this is the fruit of it. ²⁸Howbeit the people that dwell in the land are fierce, and the cities are fortified, and very great; and moreover we saw the children of Anak there. ²⁹Amalek dwelleth in the land of the South; and the Hittite, and the Jebusite, and the Amorite, dwell in the mountains; and the Canaanite dwelleth by the sea, and along by the side of the Jordan.'

*[Continued on p. 326]*

³⁰And Caleb stilled the people toward Moses, and said: 'We should go up at once, and possess it; for we are well able to overcome it.' ³¹But the men that went up with him said: 'We are not able to go up against the people; for they are stronger than we. ³³And there we saw the Nephilim *[giants]*, the sons of Anak, who come of the Nephilim; and we were in our own sight as grasshoppers, and so we were in their sight.

NUM 14:3 And wherefore doth the Lord bring us unto this land, to fall by the sword? Our wives and our little ones will be a prey; were it not better for us to return into Egypt?' ⁴And they said one to another: 'Let us make a captain, and let us return into Egypt.'

¹¹And the Lord said unto Moses: 'How long will this people despise Me? and how long will they not believe in Me, for all the signs which I have wrought among them? ¹²I will smite them with the pestilence, and destroy them,

| ( added by redactor ) | { problematic } |

| P | Notes |
|---|---|

[14]Of the tribe of Naphtali, Nahbi the son of Vophsi. [15]Of the tribe of Gad, Geuel the son of Machi. [16]These are the names of the men that Moses sent to spy out the land. And Moses called Hoshea the son of Nun Joshua.

[21]So they went up, and spied out the land from the wilderness of Zin unto Rehob, at the entrance to Hamath. [25]And they returned from spying out the land at the end of forty days.

[26][And they went and came to Moses], and to Aaron... [And they brought back word unto them,] and unto all the congregation....

[32]And they spread an evil report of the land which they had spied out unto the children of Israel, saying: 'The land, through which we have passed to spy it out, is a land that eateth up the inhabitants thereof; and all the people that we saw in it are men of great stature.

NUM 14:1And all the congregation lifted up their voice, and cried; and the people wept that night. [2]And all the children of Israel murmured against Moses and against Aaron; and the whole congregation said unto them: 'Would that we had died in the land of Egypt! or would we had died in this wilderness!

[5]Then Moses and Aaron fell on their faces before all the assembly of the congregation of the children of Israel. [6]And Joshua the son of Nun and Caleb the son of Jephunneh, who were of them that spied out the land, rent their clothes. [7]And they spoke unto all the congrega-

the congregation of the children of Israel, unto the wilderness of Paran, to Kadesh; [And they brought back word unto them,] ... and showed them the fruit of the land,

and we assign the following text to P:

NUM 13:26[And they went and came to Moses], and to Aaron... [And they brought back word unto them,] and unto all the congregation....

R eliminated many repetitive phrases, so we have to use the phrases in square brackets in both J and P.

**J Text**

There is a gap in the J text: J does not have the Israelites arrive in Kadesh and does not have Moses choose the spies. It begins by saying "NUM 13:17Moses sent them to spy," without giving us any clue about whom the word "them" refers to.

Later in the J text, we can see why R left this gap. In Numbers 32, Gad and Reuben do not want to enter the land of Canaan and Moses says that they are just like their fathers, the spies from Gad and Reuben who went to the valley of Eshcol and did not want to go into the land. Though R usually keeps the entire source text, even when there are contradictions, it is plausible that he thought it would create too blatant a contradiction to include both descriptions of choosing the spies, with J having spies from Gad and Reuben and P having spies from all the tribes, so he choose to keep only the version from the P text. See Appendix 3.

| [ used more than once ] | " quoting older text " |
|---|---|

| **E** | **J** |
|---|---|
| | and will make of thee a nation greater and mightier than they.' [13]And Moses said unto the Lord: 'When the Egyptians shall hear— for Thou broughtest up this people in Thy might from among them—[14]they will say to the inhabitants of this land, who have heard that Thou Lord art in the midst of this people; inasmuch as Thou Lord art seen face to face, and Thy cloud standeth over them, and Thou goest before them, in a pillar of cloud by day, and in a pillar of fire by night; [15]now if Thou shalt kill this people as one man, then the nations which have heard the fame of Thee will speak, saying: [16]Because the Lord was not able to bring this people into the land which He swore unto them, therefore He hath slain them in the wilderness. |
| *[Continued on p. 326]* | [17]And now, I pray Thee, let the power of the Lord be great, according as Thou hast spoken, saying: [18]The Lord is slow to anger, and plenteous in lovingkindness, forgiving iniquity and transgression, and that will by no means clear the guilty; visiting the iniquity of the fathers upon the children, upon the third and upon the fourth generation. [19]Pardon, I pray Thee, the iniquity of this people according unto the greatness of Thy lovingkindness, and according as Thou hast forgiven this people, from Egypt even until now.' |
| | [20]And the Lord said: 'I have pardoned according to thy word'[21]But in very deed, as I live—and all the earth shall be filled with the glory of the Lord— [22]surely all those men that have seen My glory, and My signs, which I wrought in Egypt and in the wilderness, yet have put Me to proof these ten times, and have not hearkened to My voice; [23]surely they shall not see the land which I swore unto their fathers, neither shall any of them that despised Me see it. [24]But My servant Caleb, because he had another spirit with him, and hath followed Me fully, him will I bring into |
| ( added by redactor ) | { problematic } |

| P | Notes |
|---|---|
| tion of the children of Israel, saying: 'The land, which we passed through to spy it out, is an exceeding good land. ⁸If the Lord delight in us, then He will bring us into this land, and give it unto us—a land which floweth with milk and honey. ⁹Only rebel not against the Lord, neither fear ye the people of the land; for they are bread for us; their defence is removed from over them, and the Lord is with us; fear them not.' ¹⁰But all the congregation bade stone them with stones, when the glory of the Lord appeared in the tent of meeting unto all the children of Israel. | J says the Nephilim, a race of giants, were in Canaan (Num. 13:33), but P just says that men of great stature were in Canaan. For more about the Nephilim, see the note to Genesis 6:1-4. |

J's anthropomorphic view of God appears again in this verse:

NUM 14::15 now if Thou shalt kill this people as one man, then the nations which have heard the fame of Thee will speak, saying: ¹⁶Because the Lord was not able to bring this people into the land which He swore unto them, therefore He hath slain them in the wilderness.

Moses gets God to change His mind by appealing to His vanity.

The mention of the ark of the covenant is problematic here, because there is only one earlier mention of the ark in J (Num. 10:33, 35-36), where there is no preparation for it, though it is described at length in P. The text here (Num. 14:44) is the only other mention of the ark in J. The ark of the covenant is not mentioned at all in E. It is possible that the ark of the covenant is a tradition introduced by the Aaronid priests who wrote P, and that R inserted the ark in these passages in J, since P used stories about the ark to claim that sacrifices are allowed only in the Temple in Jerusalem, where the Aaronid priests presided.

²⁶And the Lord spoke unto Moses and unto Aaron, saying: ²⁷'How long shall I bear with this evil congregation, that keep murmuring against Me? I have heard the murmurings of the children of Israel, which they keep murmuring against Me. ²⁸Say unto them: As I live, saith the Lord, surely as ye have spoken in Mine ears, so will I do to you: ²⁹your carcasses shall fall in this wilderness, and all that were numbered of you, according to your whole number, from twenty years old and upward, ye that have murmured against Me; ³⁰surely ye shall not come into the land, concerning which I lifted up My hand that I would make you dwell therein, save Caleb the son of Jephunneh, and Joshua the son of Nun. ³¹But your little ones, that ye said would be a prey, them will I bring in, and they shall know the land which ye have rejected. ³²But as for you, your carcasses shall fall

| [ used more than once ] | " quoting older text " |

| **E** | **J** |
|---|---|
|  | the land whereinto he went; and his seed shall possess it. [25]Now the Amalekite and the Canaanite dwell in the Vale; to-morrow turn ye, and get you into the wilderness by the way to the Red Sea.' |
|  | [39]And Moses told these words unto all the children of Israel; and the people mourned greatly. [40]And they rose up early in the morning, and got them up to the top of the mountain, saying: 'Lo, we are here, and will go up unto the place which the Lord hath promised; for we have sinned.' [41]And Moses said: 'Wherefore now do ye transgress the commandment of the Lord, seeing it shall not prosper? [42]Go not up, for the Lord is not among you; that ye be not smitten down before your enemies. [43]For there the Amalekite and the Canaanite are before you, and ye shall fall by the sword; forasmuch as ye are turned back from following the Lord, and the Lord will not be with you.' [44]But they presumed to go up to the top of the mountain; nevertheless {the ark of the covenant of the Lord, and} Moses, departed not out of the camp. [45]Then the Amalekite and the Canaanite, who dwelt in that hill-country, came down, and smote them and beat them down, even unto Hormah. |
| *[Continued on p. 326]* | |
|  | **Rebellion in the Desert** |
|  | NUM 16:1b And Dathan and Abiram, the sons of Eliab, and On, the son of Peleth, sons of Reuben, took men; [2a]And they rose up in face of Moses. [12]And Moses sent to call Dathan and Abiram, the sons of Eliab; and they said: 'We will not come up; [13]is it a small thing that thou hast brought us up out of a land flowing with milk and honey, to kill us in the wilderness, but thou must needs make thyself also a prince over us? [14]Moreover thou hast not brought us into a land flowing with milk and honey, nor given us inheritance of fields and vineyards; |
| ( added by redactor ) | { problematic } |

[Continued on p. 326]

| **P** | **Notes** |
|---|---|
| in this wilderness. ³³And your children shall be wanderers in the wilderness forty years, and shall bear your strayings, until your carcasses be consumed in the wilderness. ³⁴After the number of the days in which ye spied out the land, even forty days, for every day a year, shall ye bear your iniquities, even forty years, and ye shall know My displeasure. ³⁵I the Lord have spoken, surely this will I do unto all this evil congregation, that are gathered together against Me; in this wilderness they shall be consumed, and there they shall die.' | **Grain Offerings and Other Commandments - Relocated** |

³⁶And the men, whom Moses sent to spy out the land, and who, when they returned, made all the congregation to murmur against him, by bringing up an evil report against the land, ³⁷even those men that did bring up an evil report of the land, died by the plague before the Lord. ³⁸But Joshua the son of Nun, and Caleb the son of Jephunneh, remained alive of those men that went to spy out the land.

Numbers 15 largely duplicates commandment about sacrifices that exist in Leviticus. It also duplicates the commandment about fringes that exists in Deuteronomy 22:12, and it includes the punishment for breaking the commandment to observe the sabbath.

This chapter interrupts the narrative flow in Numbers. Apparently, it is a summary of commandments in an independent text, which was put here by a redactor.

Because the goal of this edition is to put parallel passages from J, E, and P next to each other, this passage is relocated to the section of Other Texts.

### Rebellion in the Desert

NUM 16:1a Now Korah, the son of Izhar, the son of Kohath, the son of Levi, ²ᵇwith certain of the children of Israel, two hundred and fifty men; they were princes of the congregation, the elect men of the assembly, men of renown; ³and they assembled themselves together against Moses and against Aaron, and said unto them: 'Ye take too much upon you, seeing all the congregation are holy, every one of them, and the Lord is among them; wherefore then lift ye

### Rebellion in the Desert

**Separating Texts**

In J, the rebel leaders are Dathan and Abiram. In P, the rebel leaders are Korah and Kohath. In Numbers 16:24 and 16:27, R added the names Dathan and Abiram after the name Korah to combine the two narratives.

**J Text**

In J, there is a rebellion by Reubenites against Moses (not Aaron). We have seen earlier

| [ used more than once ] | " quoting older text " |
|---|---|

| **E** | **J** |
|---|---|
| | wilt thou put out the eyes of these men? we will not come up.'<br><br>²⁵And Moses rose up and went unto Dathan and Abiram; and the elders of Israel followed him. ²⁶And he spoke unto the congregation, saying: 'Depart, I pray you, from the tents of these wicked men, and touch nothing of theirs, lest ye be swept away in all their sins.'<br><br>²⁷ᵇAnd Dathan and Abiram came out, and stood at the door of their tents, with their wives, and their sons, and their little ones. ²⁸And Moses said: 'Hereby ye shall know that the Lord hath sent me to do all these works, and that I have not done them of mine own mind. ²⁹If these men die the common death of all men, and be visited after the visitation of all men, then the Lord hath not sent Me. ³⁰But if the Lord make a new thing, and the ground open her mouth, and swallow them up, with all that appertain unto them, and they go down alive into the pit, then ye shall understand that these men have despised the Lord.'<br><br>³¹And it came to pass, as he made an end of speaking all these words, that the ground did cleave asunder that was under them. ³²ᵃAnd the earth opened her mouth and swallowed them up, and their households, ³³So they, and all that appertained to them, went down alive into the pit; and the earth closed upon them, and they perished from among the assembly. ³⁴And all Israel that were round about them fled at the cry of them; for they said: 'Lest the earth swallow us up.' |
| *[Continued on p. 326]* | |
| ( added by redactor ) | { problematic } |

*[Continued on p. 326]*

| P | Notes |
|---|---|

up yourselves above the assembly of the Lord?'

[4]And when Moses heard it, he fell upon his face. [5]And he spoke unto Korah and unto all his company, saying: 'In the morning the Lord will show who are His, and who is holy, and will cause him to come near unto Him; even him whom He may choose will He cause to come near unto Him. [6]This do: take you censors, Korah, and all his company; [7]and put fire therein, and put incense upon them before the Lord to-morrow; and it shall be that the man whom the Lord doth choose, he shall be holy; ye take too much upon you, ye sons of Levi.'

[8]And Moses said unto Korah: 'Hear now, ye sons of Levi: [9]is it but a small thing unto you, that the God of Israel hath separated you from the congregation of Israel, to bring you near to Himself, to do the service of the tabernacle of the Lord, and to stand before the congregation to minister unto them; [10]and that He hath brought thee near, and all thy brethren the sons of Levi with thee? and will ye seek the priesthood also? [11]Therefore thou and all thy company that are gathered together against the Lord—; and as to Aaron, what is he that ye murmur against him?'

[15]And Moses was very wroth, and said unto the Lord: 'Respect not thou their offering; I have not taken one ass from them, neither have I hurt one of them.' [16]And Moses said unto Korah: 'Be thou and all thy congregation before the Lord, thou,

that Judah was not the first-born son of Jacob, and the dominance of J's tribe of Judah is justified by the misbehavior of his elder brothers Reuben, Simeon and Levi (Gen. 49). Here, we have another case of the misbehavior of the Reubenites, another reason why Judah should be dominant even though Reuben was Jacob's eldest son.

**P Text**

In P, there is a rebellion of Levites against both Moses and Aaron. This is a warning to Levites living in P's time that they should accept the superiority of P's group within the tribe of Levi, the priests who claimed to be descended from Aaron.

The P text makes this warning explicit: "[NUM 17:5]...no common man, that is not of the seed of Aaron, draw near to burn incense before the Lord; that he fare not as Korah, and as his company...."

Numbers 17:6-12 reinforces the warning by showing that you will be punished if you grumble against Moses and Aaron, and the only thing that will be able to save you is Aaron (or a priest who is one of his descendents) performing the proper ritual.

**Translation**

J Text: The JPS translation says "[NUM 16:1]Now Korah, the son of Izhar, the son of Kohath, the son of Levi, with Dathan and Abiram, the sons of Eliab, and On, the son of Peleth, sons of Reuben, took men," combining the two version of the stories.

After separating the stories, this

| [ used more than once ] | " quoting older text " |
|---|---|

| **E** | **J** |
|---|---|
| **Israel Approaches Canaan** | **Israel Approaches Canaan** |
| NUM 20:14And Moses sent messengers from Kadesh unto the king of Edom: 'Thus saith thy brother Israel: Thou knowest all the travail that hath befallen us; 15how our fathers went down into Egypt, and we dwelt in Egypt a long time; and the Egyptians dealt ill with us, and our fathers; 16and when we cried unto the Lord, He heard our voice, and sent an angel, and brought us forth out of Egypt; and, behold, we are in Kadesh, a city in the uttermost of thy border. 17Let us pass, I pray thee, through thy land; we will not pass through field or through vineyard, neither will we drink of the water of the wells; we will go along the king's highway, we will not turn aside to the right hand nor to the left, until we have passed thy border.' 18And Edom said unto him: 'Thou shalt not pass through me, lest I come out with the sword against thee.' 19And the children of Israel said unto him: 'We will go up by the highway; and if we drink of thy water, I and my cattle, then will I give the price thereof; let me only | NUM 21:1And the Canaanite, the king of Arad, who dwelt in the South, heard tell that Israel came by the way of Atharim; and he fought against Israel, and took some of them captive. 2And Israel vowed a vow unto the Lord, and said: 'If Thou wilt indeed deliver this people into my hand, then I will utterly destroy their cities.' 3And the Lord hearkened to the voice of Israel, and delivered up the Canaanites; and they utterly destroyed them and their cities; and the name of the place was called Hormah.<br><br>NUM 21:10And the children of Israel journeyed, and pitched in Oboth. 11And they journeyed from Oboth, and pitched at Ije-abarim, in the wilderness which is in front of Moab, toward the sunrising. 12From thence they journeyed, and pitched in the valley of Zered. 13From thence they journeyed, and pitched on the other side of the Arnon, which is in the wilderness, that cometh out of the border of the Amorites.—For Arnon is the border of Moab, between Moab and the Amorites; 14where- |
| ( added by redactor ) | { problematic } |

| **P** | **Notes** |

and they, and Aaron, to-morrow; [17]and take ye every man his fire-pan, and put incense upon them, and bring ye before the Lord every man his fire-pan, two hundred and fifty fire-pans; thou also, and Aaron, each his fire-pan.' [18]And they took every man his fire-pan, and put fire in them, and laid incense thereon, and stood at the door of the tent of meeting with Moses and Aaron. [19]And Korah assembled all the congregation against them unto the door of the tent of meeting; and the glory of the Lord appeared unto all the congregation.

[20]And the Lord spoke unto Moses and unto Aaron, saying: [21]'Separate yourselves from among this congregation, that I may consume them in a moment.' [22]And they fell upon their faces, and said: 'O God, the God of the spirits of all flesh, shall one man sin, and wilt Thou be wroth with all the congregation?'

[23]And the Lord spoke unto Moses, saying: [24]'Speak unto the congregation, saying: Get you up from about the dwelling of Korah, (Dathan, and Abiram).' [27a]So they got them up from the dwelling of Korah, (Dathan, and Abiram,) on every side; [32b]and all the men that appertained unto Korah, and all their goods. [35]And fire came forth from the Lord, and devoured the two hundred and fifty men that offered the incense.

NUM 17:1And the Lord spoke unto Moses, saying: [2]'Speak unto Eleazar the son of Aaron the priest, that he take up the fire-pans out of the burning, and scatter thou the fire yonder; for they are become holy; [3]even the fire-pans of these men who have sinned at the cost of their lives, and let them be made

translation begins J's version by saying "And Dathan and Abiram" rather than "with Dathan and Abiram." The original Hebrew says "*v'datan*" which literally means "and Dathan," so this translation is more literal than the JPS translation. Many other translations also say "and Dathan and Abiram."

### Israel Approaches Canaan
### E Text

The previous passage in E said NUM 12:16And afterward the people journeyed from Hazeroth, and pitched in the wilderness of Paran.

Now, it says they are in Kadesh, but this is not a significant gap in the text, since Kadesh is in the wilderness of Paran, as we learn in the J text (Num. 13:26).

In the P text, by contrast, Kadesh is in the wilderness of Zin:

NUM 20:1And the children of Israel, even the whole congregation, came into the wilderness of Zin in the first month; and the people abode in Kadesh.

In the E text, an angel leads the Israelites out of Egypt (Ex. 13:19a) but not in J or P, which is why this verse must be from E:

NUM 20:16and when we cried unto the Lord, He heard our voice, and sent an angel,

| [ used more than once ] | " quoting older text " |

| **E** | **J** |
|---|---|
| pass through on my feet; there is no hurt.' [20]And he said: 'Thou shalt not pass through.' And Edom came out against him with much people, and with a strong hand. [21]Thus Edom refused to give Israel passage through his border; wherefore Israel turned away from him. | fore it is said in the book of the Wars of the Lord: |

pass through on my feet; there is no hurt.' [20]And he said: 'Thou shalt not pass through.' And Edom came out against him with much people, and with a strong hand. [21]Thus Edom refused to give Israel passage through his border; wherefore Israel turned away from him.

NUM [21:4]And they journeyed from mount Hor by the way to the Red Sea, to compass the land of Edom; and the soul of the people became impatient because of the way. [5]And the people spoke against God, and against Moses: 'Wherefore have ye brought us up out of Egypt to die in the wilderness? for there is no bread, and there is no water; and our soul loatheth this light bread.'

[6]And the Lord sent fiery serpents among the people, and they bit the people; and much people of Israel died. [7]And the people came to Moses, and said: 'We have sinned, because we have spoken against the Lord, and against thee; pray unto the Lord, that He take away the serpents from us.' And Moses prayed for the people. [8]And the Lord said unto Moses: 'Make thee a fiery serpent, and set it upon a pole; and it shall come to pass, that every one that is bitten, when he seeth it, shall live.' [9]And Moses made a serpent of brass, and set it upon the pole; and it came to pass, that if a serpent had bitten any man, when he looked unto the serpent of brass, he lived.

[21]And Israel sent messengers unto Sihon king of the Amorites, saying: [22]'Let me pass through thy land; we will not turn aside into

fore it is said in the book of the Wars of the Lord:

"Vaheb in Suphah,
And the valleys of Arnon,
[15]And the slope of the valleys
That inclineth toward the seat of Ar,
And leaneth upon the border of Moab."

— [16]And from thence to Beer; that is the well whereof the Lord said unto Moses: 'Gather the people together, and I will give them water.' [17]Then sang Israel this song:

"Spring up, O well—sing ye unto it—
[18]The well, which the princes digged,
Which the nobles of the people delved,
With the sceptre, and with their staves."

And from the wilderness to Mattanah; [19]and from Mattanah to Nahaliel; and from Nahaliel to Bamoth; [20]and from Bamoth to the valley that is in the field of Moab, by the top of Pisgah, which looketh down upon the desert. [24b]even unto the children of Ammon; for the border of the children of Ammon was strong.

[25]And Israel took all these cities; and Israel dwelt in all the cities of the Amorites, in Heshbon, and in all the towns thereof. [26]For Heshbon was the city of Sihon the king of the Amorites, who had fought against the former king of Moab, and taken all his land out of his hand, even unto the Arnon. [27]Wherefore they that speak in parables say:

"Come ye to Heshbon!

| ( added by redactor ) | { problematic } |

| P | Notes |
|---|---|

beaten plates for a covering of the altar—for they are become holy, because they were offered before the Lord—that they may be a sign unto the children of Israel.' ⁴And Eleazar the priest took the brazen fire-pans, which they that were burnt had offered; and they beat them out for a covering of the altar, ⁵to be a memorial unto the children of Israel, to the end that no common man, that is not of the seed of Aaron, draw near to burn incense before the Lord; that he fare not as Korah, and as his company; as the Lord spoke unto him by the hand of Moses.

⁶But on the morrow all the congregation of the children of Israel murmured against Moses and against Aaron, saying: 'Ye have killed the people of the Lord.' ⁷And it came to pass, when the congregation was assembled against Moses and against Aaron, that they looked toward the tent of meeting; and, behold, the cloud covered it, and the glory of the Lord appeared. ⁸And Moses and Aaron came to the front of the tent of meeting.

⁹And the Lord spoke unto Moses, saying: ¹⁰'Get you up from among this congregation, that I may consume them in a moment.' And they fell upon their faces. ¹¹And Moses said unto Aaron: 'Take thy fire-pan, and put fire therein from off the altar, and lay incense thereon, and carry it quickly unto the congregation, and make atonement for them; for there is wrath gone out from the Lord: the plague is begun.' ¹²And Aaron took as Moses spoke, and ran into the midst of the assembly; and, behold, the plague was begun among the people; and he put on the incense, and made atonement

## Notes

and brought us forth out of Egypt.

### Sacrifices and Purity - Relocated

It is difficult to tell whether Numbers 18-19 is by P or is another text added by R. In general, the commandments in R are given at Mt. Sinai, so this set of commandments given after leaving the mountain are out of place. These commandments also interrupt the narrative flow.

Because this edition assumes that the J, E, and P texts are cohesive as an experiment to test the documentary hypothesis, it puts this out-of-place text in the section of Other Texts.

### Food and Water - Relocated

This edition is meant to allow readers to compare doublets by reading across columns, so it has moved two passages from Numbers so they are next to parallel passages in Exodus:

Numbers 11:4-35 (J): The people complain about lack of meat and God sends them quails to eat. This passage is moved so it is next to Exodus 16:2-26 (P): the people complain about lack of food, and God sends them Manna and quails to eat.

Numbers 21:1-21 (P) the people complain about lack of water and Moses provides

| [ used more than once ] | " quoting older text " |
|---|---|

| E | J |
|---|---|
| field, or into vineyard; we will not drink of the water of the wells; we will go by the king's highway, until we have passed thy border.' ²³And Sihon would not suffer Israel to pass through his border; but Sihon gathered all his people together, and went out against Israel into the wilderness, and came to Jahaz; and he fought against Israel. ²⁴ᵃAnd Israel smote him with the edge of the sword, and possessed his land from the Arnon unto the Jabbok,<br><br>ᴺᵁᴹ ²²:¹And the children of Israel journeyed, and pitched in the plains of Moab beyond the Jordan at Jericho. | Let the city of Sihon be built and established!<br>²⁸For a fire is gone out of Heshbon,<br>A flame from the city of Sihon;<br>It hath devoured Ar of Moab,<br>The lords of the high places of Arnon.<br>²⁹Woe to thee, Moab!<br>Thou art undone, O people of Chemosh;<br>He hath given his sons as fugitives,<br>And his daughters into captivity,<br>Unto Sihon king of the Amorites.<br>³⁰We have shot at them—Heshbon is perished—even unto Dibon,<br>And we have laid waste even unto Nophah,<br>Which reacheth unto Medeba."<br>³¹Thus Israel dwelt in the land of the Amorites. ³²And Moses sent to spy out Jazer, and they took the towns thereof, and drove out the Amorites that were there. ³³And they turned and went up by the way of Bashan; and Og the king of Bashan went out against them, he and all his people, to battle at Edrei. ³⁴And the Lord said unto Moses: 'Fear him not; for I have delivered him into thy hand, and all his people, and his land; and thou shalt do to him as thou didst unto Sihon king of the Amorites, who dwelt at Heshbon.' ³⁵So they smote him, and his sons, and all his people, until there was none left him remaining; and they possessed his land. |
| ( added by redactor ) | { problematic } |

| P | Notes |
|---|---|

for the people. ¹³And he stood between the dead and the living; and the plague was stayed.

¹⁴Now they that died by the plague were fourteen thousand and seven hundred, besides them that died about the matter of Korah. ¹⁵And Aaron returned unto Moses unto the door of the tent of meeting, and the plague was stayed.

### God Chooses Aaron and the Levites

NUM 17:16And the Lord spoke unto Moses, saying: ¹⁷'Speak unto the children of Israel, and take of them rods, one for each fathers' house, of all their princes according to their fathers' houses, twelve rods; thou shalt write every man's name upon his rod. ¹⁸And thou shalt write Aaron's name upon the rod of Levi, for there shall be one rod for the head of their fathers' houses. ¹⁹And thou shalt lay them up in the tent of meeting before the testimony, where I meet with you. ²⁰And it shall come to pass, that the man whom I shall choose, his rod shall bud; and I will make to cease from Me the murmurings of the children of Israel, which they murmur against you.'

²¹And Moses spoke unto the children of Israel; and all their princes gave him rods, for each prince one, according to their fathers' houses, even twelve rods; and the rod of Aaron was among their rods. ²²And Moses laid up the rods before the Lord in the tent of the testimony. ²³And it came to pass on the morrow, that Moses went into the tent of the testimony; and, behold, the rod of Aaron for the house of Levi was budded, and put forth buds, and bloomed blossoms, and bore ripe almonds. ²⁴And Moses brought out all the rods from before the Lord unto all the children of Israel; and they looked, and took every man his rod.

²⁵And the Lord said unto Moses: 'Put back the rod of Aaron before the testimony, to be kept there, for a token against the rebellious children;

---

**Notes**

water by striking a rock. This passage is moved so it is next to Exodus 17:1-7 (E), where the people complain about lack of water and Moses provides water by striking a rock.

### God Chooses Aaron and the Levites

It goes without saying that this passage was written by P, one of the Aaronid priests. This passage says that rituals can only be performed by the Levites descended from Aaron, the Aaronid priests called *kohanim*, while the other Levites are just their assistants. In the other texts, all Levites can perform religious rituals. In the P text, only the Levites descended from Aaron can.

---

| [ used more than once ] | " quoting older text " |
|---|---|

| E | J |
|---|---|
| *[Continued on p. 334]* | *[Continued on p. 334]* |
| ( added by redactor ) | { problematic } |

| **P** | **Notes** |
|---|---|

that there may be made an end of their murmurings against Me, that they die not.' ²⁶Thus did Moses; as the Lord commanded him, so did he.

²⁷And the children of Israel spoke unto Moses, saying: 'Behold, we perish, we are undone, we are all undone. ²⁸Every one that cometh near, that cometh near unto the tabernacle of the Lord, is to die; shall we wholly perish?'

ᴺᵁᴹ ¹⁸·¹And the Lord said unto Aaron: 'Thou and thy sons and thy fathers' house with thee shall bear the iniquity of the sanctuary; and thou and thy sons with thee shall bear the iniquity of your priesthood. ²And thy brethren also, the tribe of Levi, the tribe of thy father, bring thou near with thee, that they may be joined unto thee, and minister unto thee, thou and thy sons with thee being before the tent of the testimony. ³And they shall keep thy charge, and the charge of all the Tent; only they shall not come nigh unto the holy furniture and unto the altar, that they die not, neither they, nor ye. ⁴And they shall be joined unto thee, and keep the charge of the tent of meeting, whatsoever the service of the Tent may be; but a common man shall not draw nigh unto you. ⁵And ye shall keep the charge of the holy things, and the charge of the altar, that there be wrath no more upon the children of Israel.

⁶And I, behold, I have taken your brethren the Levites from among the children of Israel; for you they are given as a gift unto the Lord, to do the service of the tent of meeting. ⁷And thou and thy sons with thee shall keep your priesthood in everything that pertaineth to the altar, and to that within the veil; and ye shall serve; I give you the priesthood as a service of gift; and the common man that draweth nigh shall be put to death.'

### Death of Aaron

ᴺᵁᴹ ²⁰·²²And they journeyed from Kadesh; and the children of Israel, even the whole congregation, came unto mount Hor. ²³And the Lord spoke

### Death of Aaron

Originally, the P passage about the waters of Meribah, in Num-

| [ used more than once ] | " quoting older text " |
|---|---|

| **E** | **J** |
|---|---|
| **Balaam** | **Balaam** |
| NUM 22:3 And Moab was sore afraid of the people, because they were many; and Moab was overcome with dread because of the children of Israel. ⁴And Moab said unto the elders of Midian: 'Now will this multitude lick up all that is round about us, as the ox licketh up the grass of the field.' | NUM 22:2 And Balak the son of Zippor saw all that Israel had done to the Amorites. |
| —And Balak the son of Zippor was king of Moab at that time.—⁵And he sent messengers unto Balaam the son of Beor, to Pethor, which is by the River, to the land of the children of his people, to call him, saying: | (¹³And Balaam rose up in the morning, and said unto the princes of Balak: 'Get you into your land; for the Lord refuseth to give me leave to go with you.' ¹⁴And the princes of Moab rose up, and they went unto Balak, and said: 'Balaam refuseth to come with us.') |
| | ¹⁵And Balak sent (yet again) princes, (more, and more honourable than they.) ¹⁶And they came to Balaam, and said to him: 'Thus saith Balak the son of Zippor: (Let nothing, I pray thee, hinder thee from coming unto me; ¹⁷for) I will promote thee unto very great honour, and whatsoever thou sayest unto me I will do; come therefore, I pray thee, curse me this people.' |
| | NUM 22:18 And Balaam answered and said unto the servants of Balak: 'If Balak would give me his house full of silver and gold, I cannot go beyond the word of the Lord my God, to do any thing, small or great. ¹⁹Now therefore, I pray you, tarry ye also here (this night), that I may know what the Lord will speak unto me (more).' ²⁰And {God} came unto Balaam (at night), and said unto him: 'If the men are come to call thee, rise up, go with them; but only the word which I speak unto thee, that shalt thou do.' (³⁵And the angel of the Lord said unto Balaam: 'Go with the men; but only the word that I shall speak unto |
| ( added by redactor ) | { problematic } |

| P | Notes |
|---|---|

unto Moses and Aaron in mount Hor, by the border of the land of Edom, saying: ²⁴'Aaron shall be gathered unto his people; for he shall not enter into the land which I have given unto the children of Israel, because ye rebelled against My word at the waters of Meribah. ²⁵Take Aaron and Eleazar his son, and bring them up unto mount Hor. ²⁶And strip Aaron of his garments, and put them upon Eleazar his son; and Aaron shall be gathered unto his people, and shall die there.' ²⁷And Moses did as the Lord commanded; and they went up into mount Hor in the sight of all the congregation. ²⁸And Moses stripped Aaron of his garments, and put them upon Eleazar his son; and Aaron died there in the top of the mount; and Moses and Eleazar came down from the mount. ²⁹And when all the congregation saw that Aaron was dead, they wept for Aaron thirty days, even all the house of Israel.

bers 20:1-21, where Moses strikes the rock to get water and Moses and Aaron are both punished for it, was immediately before this passage about the death of Aaron. As explained above, this passage about the waters of Meribah has been relocated next to Exodus 17:1-7, so readers can compare it with the E passage about Moses striking the rock to get water.

### Balaam

#### Separating the Texts

The story of Balaam is difficult to assign to texts because RJE added a significant amount of text to reconcile the stories from J and E.

The following verses show that the story of Balaam was patched together from two texts:

NUM 22:20And God came unto Balaam at night, and said unto him: 'If the men are come to call thee, rise up, go with them; but only the word which I speak unto thee, that shalt thou do.' ²¹And Balaam rose up in the morning, and saddled his ass, and went with the princes of Moab. ²²And God's anger was kindled because he went; and the angel of the Lord placed himself in the way for an adversary against him.

Notice the self-contradiction: God tells Balaam to go with the men and speak His word to them, but when Balaam obeys him by going, God gets angry and sends an angel to block his way.

The most plausible explanation is

| [ used more than once ] | " quoting older text " |
|---|---|

| **E** | **J** |
|---|---|
| 'Behold, there is a people come out from Egypt; behold, they cover the face of the earth, and they abide over against me. ⁶Come now therefore, I pray thee, curse me this people; for they are too mighty for me; peradventure I shall prevail, that we may smite them, and that I may drive them out of the land; for I know that he whom thou blessest is blessed, and he whom thou cursest is cursed.' | thee, that thou shalt speak.') So Balaam went with the princes of Balak. |

thee, that thou shalt speak.') So Balaam went with the princes of Balak.

³⁶And when Balak heard that Balaam was come, he went out to meet him unto Ir-moab, which is on the border of Arnon, which is in the utmost part of the border. (³⁷And Balak said unto Balaam: 'Did I not earnestly send unto thee to call thee? wherefore camest thou not unto me? am I not able indeed to promote thee to honour?)' ³⁸And Balaam said unto Balak: 'Lo, I am come unto thee; have I now any power at all to speak any thing? the word that God putteth in my mouth, that shall I speak.'

³⁹And Balaam went with Balak, and they came unto Kiriath-huzoth. ⁴⁰And Balak sacrificed oxen and sheep, and sent to Balaam, and to the princes that were with him. ⁴¹And it came to pass in the morning that Balak took Balaam, and brought him up into Bamoth-baal, and he saw from thence the utmost part of the people.

NUM 23:1And Balaam said unto Balak: 'Build me here seven altars, and prepare me here seven bullocks and seven rams.' ²And Balak did as Balaam had spoken; and Balak and Balaam offered on every altar a bullock and a ram. ³And Balaam said unto Balak: 'Stand by thy burnt-offering, and I will go; peradventure the Lord will come to meet me; and whatsoever He showeth me I will tell thee.' And he went to a bare height. ⁴And {God} met Balaam; and he said unto Him: 'I have prepared the seven altars, and I have offered up a bullock and a ram on every altar.' ⁵And the Lord put a word in Balaam's mouth, and said: 'Return unto Balak, and thus thou shalt speak.' ⁶And he returned unto him, and, lo, he stood by his burnt-offering, he, and all the princes of Moab. ⁷And he took up his parable, and said:

"From Aram Balak bringeth me,
The king of Moab from the mountains of the East:
'Come, curse me Jacob,
And come, execrate Israel.'
⁸How shall I curse, whom God hath not cursed?
And how shall I execrate, whom the Lord hath

⁷And the elders of Moab and the elders of Midian departed with the rewards of divination in their hand; and they came unto Balaam, and spoke unto him the words of Balak. ⁸And he said unto them: 'Lodge here this night, and I will bring you back word, as the Lord may speak unto me'; and the princes of Moab abode with Balaam.

⁹And God came

( added by redactor )                    { problematic }

| P | Notes |
|---|---|
| | that the story of Balaam is made up of two texts:<br><br>1. Balaam disobeys God by going to curse Israel, and God sends an angel to block his way.<br><br>2. Balaam obeys God by going and saying only the words that God speaks to Balaam, so Balaam blesses Israel rather than cursing them.<br><br>Story 1 is from the E text. Notice that here, God speaks to Balaam at night, presumably in a dream, and sends an angel to block his way. In E, God speaks directly only to Moses and speaks to others through dreams or through angels.<br><br>Story 2 is from the J text. God repeatedly speaks to Balaam directly, as He typically does in the J text. The story includes the use of repetition to intensify drama that is typical of J, with the three calls for Balaam to curse Israel. The story continues the quotations from earlier poetry that are in the J text in Numbers 21.<br><br>To reconcile these two stories, RJE had to add several sentences, making Balaam ask God twice whether he should go, and these additions are in parentheses in this edition.<br><br>RJE also seems to have added to the J text in Numbers 22:19-20 (where Balaam asks the princes to stay the night and God comes to him at night) in order to make this J text more consistent with E (where Balaam asks the messengers to stay the night so he could ask God what to do in Numbers 22:8 because in E, God only appears in dreams or visions to anyone except Moses). This edition puts the minimum necessary |
| *[Continued on p. 345]* | |
| [ used more than once ] | " quoting older text " |

*[Continued on p. 345]*

| **E** | **J** |
|---|---|
| unto Balaam, and said: 'What men are these with thee?' ¹⁰And Balaam said unto God: 'Balak the son of Zippor, king of Moab, hath sent unto me [saying]: ¹¹Behold the people that is come out of Egypt, it covereth the face of the earth; now, come curse me them; peradventure I shall be able to fight against them, and shall drive them out.' ¹²And God said unto Balaam: 'Thou shalt not go with them; thou shalt not curse the people; for they are blessed.'<br><br>²¹And Balaam rose up in the morning, and saddled his ass, and went with the princes of Moab. ²²And God's anger was kindled because he went; and the angel of the Lord placed himself in the way for an adversary against him.— Now he was riding upon his ass, and his two servants | not execrated?<br>⁹For from the top of the rocks I see him,<br>And from the hills I behold him:<br>Lo, it is a people that shall dwell alone,<br>And shall not be reckoned among the nations.<br>¹⁰Who hath counted the dust of Jacob,<br>Or numbered the stock of Israel?<br>Let me die the death of the righteous,<br>And let mine end be like his!"<br>¹¹And Balak said unto Balaam: 'What hast thou done unto me? I took thee to curse mine enemies, and, behold, thou hast blessed them altogether.' ¹²And he answered and said: 'Must I not take heed to speak that which the Lord putteth in my mouth?'<br>¹³And Balak said unto him: 'Come, I pray thee, with me unto another place, from whence thou mayest see them; thou shalt see but the utmost part of them, and shalt not see them all; and curse me them from thence.' ¹⁴And he took him into the field of Zophim, to the top of Pisgah, and built seven altars, and offered up a bullock and a ram on every altar. ¹⁵And he said unto Balak: 'Stand here by thy burnt-offering, while I go toward a meeting yonder.' ¹⁶And the Lord met Balaam, and put a word in his mouth, and said: 'Return unto Balak, and thus shalt thou speak.' ¹⁷And he came to him, and, lo, he stood by his burnt-offering, and the princes of Moab with him. And Balak said unto him: 'What hath the Lord spoken?' ¹⁸And he took up his parable, and said:<br>"Arise, Balak, and hear;<br>Give ear unto me, thou son of Zippor:<br>¹⁹God is not a man, that He should lie;<br>Neither the son of man, that He should repent:<br>When He hath said, will He not do it?<br>Or when He hath spoken, will He not make it good?<br>²⁰Behold, I am bidden to bless;<br>And when He hath blessed, I cannot call it back.<br>²¹None hath beheld iniquity in Jacob,<br>Neither hath one seen perverseness in Israel;<br>The Lord his God is with him,<br>And the shouting for the King is among them. |
| ( added by redactor ) | { problematic } |

| P | Notes |
|---|---|
| | amount of this text in parentheses to indicate that it was added by RJE, but RJE might have worked over the text more extensively. |

The problem with this division is that the narrator in the J text uses the word "God" three times. As a rule, the narrator in J always says "the Lord" rather than "God," so these three uses of "God" are in curly brackets to indicate that they are problematic. It may also be problematic that in E, Balaam himself uses the name "the Lord" (Num. 22:8), because E believed that this name was only revealed to Moses and the Israelites. The most likely explanation is that RJE made extensive changes to the text to reconcile the two stories, and in the process, he also modified "God" and "the Lord" in a few places.

**J Text**

Note that in J, Balaam says:

NUM 22:18 …'If Balak would give me
his house full of silver and gold,
I cannot go beyond the word of
the Lord my God.

This is typical of J's syncretism: the other texts say that Abraham was the first to worship the Lord and Moses was the first to know His name, but J says that people began to call on the name of the Lord before the flood (Gen. 4:26). Thus, it is not surprising that, in J, a non-Israelite says that the Lord is his God.

**P Text**

The P text has no parallel to this story, but it does have a very different attitude to Balaam elsewhere: In the section titled "Revenge on the

*[Continued on p. 345]*

| [ used more than once ] | " quoting older text " |

| **E** | **J** |
|---|---|
| were with him.—²³And the ass saw the angel of the Lord standing in the way, with his sword drawn in his hand; and the ass turned aside out of the way, and went into the field; and Balaam smote the ass, to turn her into the way. ²⁴Then the angel of the Lord stood in a hollow way between the vineyards, a fence being on this side, and a fence on that side. ²⁵And the ass saw the angel of the Lord, and she thrust herself unto the wall, and crushed Balaam's foot against the wall; and he smote her again. ²⁶And the angel of the Lord went further, and stood in a narrow place, where was no way to turn either to the right hand or to the left. ²⁷And the ass saw the angel of the Lord, and she lay down under Balaam; and Balaam's anger | ²²God who brought them forth out of Egypt Is for them like the lofty horns of the wild-ox. ²³For there is no enchantment with Jacob, Neither is there any divination with Israel; Now is it said of Jacob and of Israel: 'What hath God wrought! ' ²⁴Behold a people that riseth up as a lioness, And as a lion doth he lift himself up; He shall not lie down until he eat of the prey, And drink the blood of the slain." ²⁵And Balak said unto Balaam: 'Neither curse them at all, nor bless them at all.' ²⁶But Balaam answered and said unto Balak: 'Told not I thee, saying: All that the Lord speaketh, that I must do?' ²⁷And Balak said unto Balaam: 'Come now, I will take thee unto another place; peradventure it will please God that thou mayest curse me them from thence.' ²⁸And Balak took Balaam unto the top of Peor, that looketh down upon the desert. ²⁹And Balaam said unto Balak: 'Build me here seven altars, and prepare me here seven bullocks and seven rams.' ³⁰And Balak did as Balaam had said, and offered up a bullock and a ram on every altar. ᴺᵁᴹ ²⁴:¹And when Balaam saw that it pleased the Lord to bless Israel, he went not, as at the other times, to meet with enchantments, but he set his face toward the wilderness. ²And Balaam lifted up his eyes, and he saw Israel dwelling tribe by tribe; and the spirit of {God} came upon him. ³And he took up his parable, and said: "The saying of Balaam the son of Beor, And the saying of the man whose eye is opened; ⁴The saying of him who heareth the words of God, Who seeth the vision of the Almighty, Fallen down, yet with opened eyes: ⁵How goodly are thy tents, O Jacob, Thy dwellings, O Israel! ⁶As valleys stretched out, As gardens by the river-side; As aloes planted of the Lord, As cedars beside the waters; |

( added by redactor )                              { problematic }

| P | Notes |
|---|---|
| | Midianites," it says:<br><br>NUM 31:8And they slew the kings of Midian with the rest of their slain: Evi, and Rekem, and Zur, and Hur, and Reba, the five kings of Midian; Balaam also the son of Beor they slew with the sword"<br><br>and it says<br><br>NUM 31:15And Moses said unto them: 'Have ye saved all the women alive? 16Behold, these caused the children of Israel, through the counsel of Balaam, to revolt so as to break faith with the Lord in the matter of Peor.<br><br>In P, Balaam is a villain who promoted pagan worship. In J, Balaam is a hero who obeyed the Lord. In E, Balaam begins as a villain but finally repents and obeys the Lord. |
| *[Continued on p. 345]* | |
| [ used more than once ] | " quoting older text " |

| E | J |
|---|---|

**E**

was kindled, and he smote the ass with his staff.

²⁸And the Lord opened the mouth of the ass, and she said unto Balaam: 'What have I done unto thee, that thou hast smitten me these three times?' ²⁹And Balaam said unto the ass: 'Because thou hast mocked me; I would there were a sword in my hand, for now I had killed thee.' ³⁰And the ass said unto Balaam: 'Am not I thine ass, upon which thou hast ridden all thy life long unto this day? was I ever wont to do so unto thee?' And he said: 'Nay.'

³¹Then the Lord opened the eyes of Balaam, and he saw the angel of the Lord standing in the way, with his sword drawn in his hand; and he bowed his head, and fell on his face. ³²And the angel of the Lord said unto him: 'Wherefore hast thou smitten

**J**

⁷Water shall flow from his branches,
And his seed shall be in many waters;
And his king shall be higher than Agag,
And his kingdom shall be exalted.
⁸God who brought him forth out of Egypt
Is for him like the lofty horns of the wild-ox;
He shall eat up the nations that are his adversaries,
And shall break their bones in pieces,
And pierce them through with his arrows.
⁹He couched, he lay down as a lion,
And as a lioness; who shall rouse him up?
Blessed be every one that blesseth thee,
And cursed be every one that curseth thee."

¹⁰And Balak's anger was kindled against Balaam, and he smote his hands together; and Balak said unto Balaam: 'I called thee to curse mine enemies, and, behold, thou hast altogether blessed them these three times. ¹¹Therefore now flee thou to thy place; I thought to promote thee unto great honour; but, lo, the Lord hath kept thee back from honour.'

¹²And Balaam said unto Balak: 'Spoke I not also to thy messengers that thou didst send unto me, saying: ¹³If Balak would give me his house full of silver and gold, I cannot go beyond the word of the Lord, to do either good or bad of mine own mind; what the Lord speaketh, that will I speak. ¹⁴And now, behold, I go unto my people; come, and I will announce to thee what this people shall do to thy people in the end of days.' ¹⁵And he took up his parable, and said:
"The saying of Balaam the son of Beor,
And the saying of the man whose eye is opened;
¹⁶The saying of him who heareth the words of God,
And knoweth the knowledge of the Most High,
Who seeth the vision of the Almighty,
Fallen down, yet with opened eyes:
¹⁷I see him, but not now;
I behold him, but not nigh;
There shall step forth a star out of Jacob,
And a scepter shall rise out of Israel,
And shall smite through the corners of Moab,

( added by redactor )        { problematic }

| P | Notes |
|---|---|
| *[Continued on p. 345]* | *[Continued on p. 345]* |
| [ used more than once ] | " quoting older text " |

| **E** | **J** |
|---|---|
| thine ass these three times? behold, I am come forth for an adversary, because thy way is contrary unto me; ³³and the ass saw me, and turned aside before me these three times; unless she had turned aside from me, surely now I had even slain thee, and saved her alive.' ³⁴And Balaam said unto the angel of the Lord: 'I have sinned; for I knew not that thou stoodest in the way against me; now therefore, if it displease thee, I will get me back.' | And break down all the sons of Seth. ¹⁸And Edom shall be a possession, Seir also, even his enemies, shall be a possession; While Israel doeth valiantly. ¹⁹And out of Jacob shall one have dominion, And shall destroy the remnant from the city." ²⁰And he looked on Amalek, and took up his parable, and said: "Amalek was the first of the nations; But his end shall come to destruction." ²¹And he looked on the Kenite, and took up his parable, and said: "Though firm be thy dwelling-place, And though thy nest be set in the rock; ²²Nevertheless Kain shall be wasted; How long? Asshur shall carry thee away captive." ²³And he took up his parable, and said: "Alas, who shall live after God hath appointed him? ²⁴But ships shall come from the coast of Kittim, And they shall afflict Asshur, and shall afflict Eber, And he also shall come to destruction." ²⁵And Balaam rose up, and went and returned to his place; and Balak also went his way. |

### Baal of Peor

NUM 25:1And Israel abode in Shittim, and the people began to commit harlotry with the daughters of Moab. ²And they called the people unto the sacrifices of their gods; and the people did eat, and bowed down to their gods. ³And Israel joined himself unto the Baal of Peor; and the anger of the Lord was kindled against Israel. ⁴And the Lord said unto Moses: 'Take all the chiefs of the people, and hang them up unto the Lord in face of the sun, that the fierce anger of the Lord may turn away from Israel.' ⁵And Moses said unto the judges of Israel: 'Slay ye every one his men that have joined themselves unto the Baal of Peor.'

( added by redactor )                    { problematic }

| P | Notes |
|---|---|
| **The Matter of Peor**<br><br>***[Gap in P: Worshiping Midianite God Causes a Plague]***<br><br>NUM 25:6 And, behold, one of the children of Israel came and brought unto his brethren a Midianitish woman in the sight of Moses, and in the sight of all the congrega- | **Baal/ Matter of Peor**<br>**J Text**<br>At the beginning of Numbers 25, J blames the worship of Baal Peor on the Moabites. We have seen J's hostility to the Moabites earlier, where she says that Moab and Amon descend from incest between Lot and his daughters (Gen. 19:36-38). In J, Moses punishes those who worshipped Baal Peor by telling the judges to slay them.<br>**P Text**<br>Later in Numbers 25, P blames the matter |
| [ used more than once ] | " quoting older text " |

| E | J |
|---|---|
| *[Continued on p. 364]* | *[Continued on p. 354]* |
| ( added by redactor ) | { problematic } |

| P | Notes |
|---|---|

tion of the children of Israel, while they were weeping at the door of the tent of meeting. [7]And when Phinehas, the son of Eleazar, the son of Aaron the priest, saw it, he rose up from the midst of the congregation, and took a spear in his hand. [8]And he went after the man of Israel into the chamber, and thrust both of them through, the man of Israel, and the woman through her belly. So the plague was stayed from the children of Israel. [9]And those that died by the plague were twenty and four thousand.

[10]And the Lord spoke unto Moses, saying: [11]'Phinehas, the son of Eleazar, the son of Aaron the priest, hath turned My wrath away from the children of Israel, in that he was very jealous for My sake among them, so that I consumed not the children of Israel in My jealousy. [12]Wherefore say: Behold, I give unto him My covenant of peace; [13]and it shall be unto him, and to his seed after him, the covenant of an everlasting priesthood; because he was jealous for his God, and made atonement for the children of Israel.'

[14]Now the name of the man of Israel that was slain, who was slain with the Midianitish woman, was Zimri, the son of Salu, a prince of a fa-

of Peor on the Midianites rather than the Moabites (Num. 25:17-18). P's hostility to the Midianites will culminate soon in the section titled "Revenge on the Midianites" (Num. 31). P was an Aaronid priest, and the rival Mushite priests claimed descent from Moses and therefore from Moses' Midianite wife.

In P, a plague punishes those who worshipped Baal Peor. Aaron's grandson Phinehas ends the plague, after it kills twenty four thousand people, by murdering the Midianite woman, Cozbi, and the Israelite man who brought her, Zimri.

There is clearly a gap in the P text here. Phinehas ends the plague, but there is no earlier mention of this plague in the received text of the Bible. The most recent plague in the Bible before this one, also in the P text, was punishment for the Israelites' complaining after Korah's rebellion and was stopped after killing fourteen thousand and seven hundred people when Aaron burned incense. (Num. 17:9-14). The plague we have here is clearly a separate one, a punishment for the Israelites' worshiping Baal Peor after consorting with Midianite women, which kills twenty-four thousand people.

The gap in the P text probably says that Midianite women led the Israelites to worship Baal Peor and God punished them by sending a plague. R must have removed this from the P text because it contradicted the J text.

"[NUM 26:6]...while they were weeping at the door of the tent of meeting" seems to be a reference to what just happened previously in the P text, when Aaron died and Israel mourned him for thirty days. But there is no prior reference in the P text to this plague or to Peor.

| [ used more than once ] | " quoting older text " |
|---|---|

| **E** | **J** |
|---|---|
| *[Continued on p. 364]* | *[Continued on p. 354]* |
| ( added by redactor ) | { problematic } |

*[Continued on p. 364]*

*[Continued on p. 354]*

| P | Notes |
|---|---|

thers' house among the Simeonites. ¹⁵And the name of the Midianitish woman that was slain was Cozbi, the daughter of Zur; he was head of the people of a fathers' house in Midian.

¹⁶And the Lord spoke unto Moses, saying: ¹⁷'Harass the Midianites, and smite them; ¹⁸for they harass you, by their wiles wherewith they have beguiled you in the matter of Peor, and in the matter of Cozbi, the daughter of the prince of Midian, their sister, who was slain on the day of the plague in the matter of Peor.'

### The Census - Relocated

Both this census in Numbers 1-4 and the census in Numbers 25:19-27:11 are separate documents added by an editor. Both are meant to justify the amount of land allocated to each tribe, as is the section of P titled "Inheriting the Land" (beginning at Numbers 33:50), and both add much more detail—but their details contradict each other. The allocation of land fits into the narrative in the section "Inheriting the Land," but the other two censuses interrupt the narrative. Therefore, this edition moves these two censuses to the section of Other Texts.

### Joshua Succeeds Moses

NUM 27:12And the Lord said unto Moses: 'Get thee up into this mountain of Abarim, and behold the land which I have given unto the children of Israel. ¹³And when thou hast seen it, thou also shalt be gathered unto thy people, as Aaron thy brother was gathered; ¹⁴because ye rebelled against My commandment in the wilderness of Zin, in the strife of the congregation, to sanctify Me at the waters before their eyes.'— These are the waters of Meribath-kadesh in the wilderness of Zin.—

¹⁵And Moses spoke unto the Lord, saying: ¹⁶'Let the Lord, the God of the spirits of all flesh, set a man over the con-

### Joshua Succeeds Moses

Here in P, Moses goes to a mountain of Abiram to see the promised land (Num. 27:12). D gives the name of the mountain:

DEUT 32:49'Get thee up into this mountain of Abarim, unto mount Nebo, which is in the land of Moab, that is over against Jericho; and behold the land of Canaan, which I give unto the children of Israel for a possession.'

This story seems to be out of place, since it comes between the P text telling Moses to harass the Midianites (Num. 25:17) and the actual revenge on the Midianites (Num. 31). In addition, it makes sense for Moses to go up to see the promised land just before his death, not at this earlier time.

R inserted many other texts at this point (Num. 26:1 to 27:11 and Numbers 28-30), and this story might have been relocated in the process.

| [ used more than once ] | " quoting older text " |
|---|---|

| E | J |
|---|---|
| | |
| *[Continued on p. 364]* | *[Continued on p. 354]* |
| ( added by redactor ) | { problematic } |

| **P** | **Notes** |
|---|---|

gregation, <sup>17</sup>who may go out before them, and who may come in before them, and who may lead them out, and who may bring them in; that the congregation of the Lord be not as sheep which have no shepherd.'

<sup>18</sup>And the Lord said unto Moses: 'Take thee Joshua the son of Nun, a man in whom is spirit, and lay thy hand upon him; <sup>19</sup>and set him before Eleazar the priest, and before all the congregation; and give him a charge in their sight. <sup>20</sup>And thou shalt put of thy honour upon him, that all the congregation of the children of Israel may hearken. <sup>21</sup>And he shall stand before Eleazar the priest, who shall inquire for him by the judgment of the Urim before the Lord; at his word shall they go out, and at his word they shall come in, both he, and all the children of Israel with him, even all the congregation.'

<sup>22</sup>And Moses did as the Lord commanded him; and he took Joshua, and set him before Eleazar the priest, and before all the congregation. <sup>23</sup>And he laid his hands upon him, and gave him a charge, as the Lord spoke by the hand of Moses.

### Meat Offerings and Sacrifices
### Numbers 28-29 - Relocated

These chapters elaborate on the laws for meat offerings and for holidays that are also in Leviticus. They is probably an independent document added by R, so this edition puts them in the section of Other Documents.

### Miscellaneous Commandments
### Numbers 30 - Relocated

It is difficult to tell whether this text is by P or is another text added by R. In general, the commandments in P are given at Mt. Sinai, so this set of commandments given after leaving the mountain are out of place. These commandments also interrupt the narrative flow.

Because this edition assumes that the J, E, and P texts are continuous as an experiment to test the documentary hypothesis, it puts this out-of-place text in the section of Other Texts.

### Revenge on the Midianites - Abridged

NUM 31:1And the Lord spoke unto Moses, saying: <sup>2</sup>'Avenge the children of Israel of the Midianites; afterward shalt thou be gathered unto thy people.' <sup>3</sup>And Moses spoke unto the people, saying: 'Arm ye men from among you for the war, that they may go against Midian, to

### Revenge on the Midianites

Because the goal of this edition is to place parallel passages from the three texts next to each other, it provides abridged versions of some lengthy and repetitive passages from the P text. To read the complete passage in the P text, read Numbers 31.

**P Text**

This section continues P's story

| [ used more than once ] | " quoting older text " |
|---|---|

| E | J |
|---|---|
| *[Continued on p. 364]* | *[Continued on p. 354]* |
| ( added by redactor ) | { problematic } |

[Continued on p. 364]

[Continued on p. 354]

| P | Notes |
|---|---|

execute the Lord's vengeance on Midian. ⁴Of every tribe a thousand, throughout all the tribes of Israel, shall ye send to the war.' ⁵So there were delivered, out of the thousands of Israel, a thousand of every tribe, twelve thousand armed for war. ⁶And Moses sent them, a thousand of every tribe, to the war, them and Phinehas the son of Eleazar the priest, to the war, with the holy vessels and the trumpets for the alarm in his hand. ⁷And they warred against Midian, as the Lord commanded Moses; and they slew every male. ⁸And they slew the kings of Midian with the rest of their slain: Evi, and Rekem, and Zur, and Hur, and Reba, the five kings of Midian; Balaam also the son of Beor they slew with the sword. ⁹And the children of Israel took captive the women of Midian and their little ones; and all their cattle, and all their flocks, and all their goods, they took for a prey. ¹⁰And all their cities in the places wherein they dwelt, and all their encampments, they burnt with fire. ¹¹And they took all the spoil, and all the prey, both of man and of beast. ¹²And they brought the captives, and the prey, and the spoil, unto Moses, and unto Eleazar the priest, and unto the congregation of the children of Israel, unto the camp, unto the plains of Moab, which are by the Jordan at Jericho.

¹³And Moses, and Eleazar the priest, and all the princes of the congregation, went forth to meet them without the camp. ¹⁴And Moses was wroth with the officers of the host, the captains of thousands and the captains of hundreds, who came from the service of the war. ¹⁵And Moses said unto them: 'Have ye saved all the women alive? ¹⁶Behold, these caused the children of Israel, through the counsel of Balaam, to revolt so as to break faith with the Lord in the matter of Peor, and so the plague was among the congregation of the Lord. ¹⁷Now therefore kill every male among the little ones, and kill every woman that hath known man by lying with him. ¹⁸But all the women children, that have not known man by lying with him, keep alive for yourselves. ¹⁹And encamp ye without the camp seven days; whosoever hath killed any person, and whosoever hath touched any slain, purify your-

of the Matter of Peor, which ended by saying: NUM 25:16And the Lord spoke unto Moses, saying: ¹⁷'Harass the Midianites, and smite them; ¹⁸for they harass you, by their wiles wherewith they have beguiled you in the matter of Peor, and in the matter of Cozbi, the daughter of the prince of Midian, their sister, who was slain on the day of the plague in the matter of Peor.'

P's continuous story of the matter of Peor and revenge on the Midianites is interrupted by many inserted chapters of commandments, which this edition relocates to the section of Other Texts. It is also interrupted by the section in P titled "Joshua Succeeds Moses,"

| [ used more than once ] | " quoting older text " |
|---|---|

| E | J |
|---|---|
| | |

*[Continued on p. 364]*

*[Continued on p. 364]*

### Gad and Reuben Remain

NUM 32:1Now the children of Reuben and the children of Gad had a very great multitude of cattle; and when they saw the land of Jazer, and the land of Gilead, that, behold, the place was a place for cattle. 5aAnd

( added by redactor )        { problematic }

| **P** | **Notes** |
|---|---|
| selves on the third day and on the seventh day, ye and your captives. [20]And as to every garment, and all that is made of skin, and all work of goats' hair, and all things made of wood, ye shall purify.' | which seems to be out of place. |
| [21]And Eleazar the priest said unto the men of war that went to the battle: 'This is the statute of the law which the Lord hath commanded Moses: [22]Howbeit the gold, and the silver, the brass, the iron, the tin, and the lead, [23]every thing that may abide the fire, ye shall make to go through the fire, and it shall be clean; nevertheless it shall be purified with the water of sprinkling; and all that abideth not the fire ye shall make to go through the water. [24]And ye shall wash your clothes on the seventh day, and ye shall be clean, and afterward ye may come into the camp.' | The P text was written by an Aaronid priest, so it is not surprising that Moses commands that half of the booty of war should be given to the Aaronid priests. |
| [25]And the Lord spoke unto Moses, saying: [26]'Take the sum of the prey that was taken, both of man and of beast, thou, and Eleazar the priest, and the heads of the fathers' houses of the congregation; [27]and divide the prey into two parts: between the men skilled in war, that went out to battle, and all the congregation; [28]and levy a tribute unto the Lord of the men of war that went out to battle: one soul of five hundred, both of the persons, and of the beeves, and of the asses, and of the flocks; [29]take it of their half, and give it unto Eleazar the priest, as a portion set apart for the Lord. [30]And of the children of Israel's half, thou shalt take one drawn out of every fifty, of the persons, of the beeves, of the asses, and of the flocks, even of all the cattle, and give them unto the Levites, that keep the charge of the tabernacle of the Lord.' [31]And Moses and Eleazar the priest did as the Lord commanded Moses. | |
| ### Gad and Reuben Remain | ### Gad and Reuben Remain |
| NUM 32:2The children of Gad and the children of Reuben came and spoke unto Moses, and to Eleazar the priest, and unto the princes of the congregation, saying: [3]Ataroth, and Dibon, and Jazer, and Nimrah, and Heshbon, and Elealeh, and Sebam, and Nebo, and Beon, [4]the land which the Lord smote before | **J Text** One of the redactors added "and Joshua the son of Nun" to the fol- |
| [ used more than once ] | " quoting older text " |

| **E** | **J** |
|---|---|
| | they said: 'If we have found favour in thy sight, ⁵ᶜbring us not over the Jordan.'<br><br>⁷[And Moses said] And wherefore will ye turn away the heart of the children of Israel from going over into the land which the Lord hath given them? ⁸Thus did your fathers, when I sent them from Kadesh-barnea to see the land. ⁹For when they went up unto the valley of Eshcol, and saw the land, they turned away the heart of the children of Israel, that they should not go into the land which the Lord had given them. ¹⁰And the Lord's anger was kindled in that day, and He swore, saying: NUM 32:11Surely none of the men that came up out of Egypt, from twenty years old and upward, shall see the land which I swore unto Abraham, unto Isaac, and unto Jacob; because they have not wholly followed Me; ¹²save Caleb the son of Jephunneh the Kenizzite, (and Joshua the son of Nun;) because they have wholly followed the Lord.<br><br>²⁵And the children of Gad and the children of Reuben spoke unto Moses, saying: 'Thy servants will do as my lord commandeth. ²⁶Our little ones, our wives, our flocks, and all our cattle, shall be there in the cities of Gilead; ²⁷but thy servants will pass over, every man that is armed for war, before the Lord to battle, as my lord saith.'<br><br>³³And Moses gave unto them, even to the children of Gad, and to the children of Reuben, and unto the half-tribe of Manasseh the son of Joseph, the kingdom of Sihon king |

*[Continued on p. 364]*

| ( added by redactor ) | { problematic } |
|---|---|

| P | Notes |
|---|---|

the congregation of Israel, is a land for cattle, and thy servants have cattle.'

⁵ᵇLet this land be given unto thy servants for a possession,

[⁶And Moses said] unto the children of Gad and to the children of Reuben: 'Shall your brethren go to the war, and shall ye sit here?

(¹³And the Lord's anger was kindled against Israel, and He made them wander to and fro in the wilderness forty years, until all the generation, that had done evil in the sight of the Lord, was consumed.)

¹⁴And, behold, ye are risen up in your fathers' stead, a brood of sinful men, to augment yet the fierce anger of the Lord toward Israel. ¹⁵For if ye turn away from after Him, He will yet again leave them in the wilderness; and so ye will destroy all this people.'

¹⁶And they came near unto him, and said: 'We will build sheepfolds here for our cattle, and cities for our little ones; ¹⁷but we ourselves will be ready armed to go before the children of Israel, until we have brought them unto their place; and our little ones shall dwell in the fortified cities because of the inhabitants of the land. ¹⁸We will not return unto our houses, until the children of Israel have inherited every man his inheritance. ¹⁹For we will not inherit with them on

lowing in order to make it consistent with the other texts:

ᴺᵁᴹ ³²:¹¹Surely none of the men that came up out of Egypt, from twenty years old and upward, shall see the land which I swore unto Abraham, unto Isaac, and unto Jacob; because they have not wholly followed Me; ¹²save Caleb the son of Jephunneh the Kenizzite, (and Joshua the son of Nun;) because they have wholly followed the Lord.

Earlier in J, Caleb is the only one who wants to invade Canaan after the spies come back and say its inhabitants are too dangerous (Num. 13:30), and as a result that Lord says of the other Israelites:

ᴺᵁᴹ ¹⁴:²³surely they shall not see the land which I swore unto their fathers, neither shall any of them that despised Me see it. ²⁴But My servant Caleb, because he had another spirit with him, and hath followed Me fully, him will I bring into the land whereinto he went; and his seed shall possess it.

In the J text, Joshua is appointed to lead the Israelites into Canaan (Deut. 31:14). Apparently, J thought that Joshua would be allowed to enter Canaan because he was less than twenty years old when they left Egypt. J emphasizes Joshua's youth elsewhere: "ᴱˣ ³³:¹¹Joshua, the son of Nun, a young man" and "ᴺᵁᴹ ¹¹:²⁸And Joshua the son of Nun, the minister of Moses from his youth up."

**P Text**

The following verse is clearly out of place: "ᴺᵁᴹ ³²:¹³He made them wander to and fro in the wilderness forty years." It does not make sense for God to become angry and condemn the Israelites to wander in the wilderness at this point, when

| [ used more than once ] | " quoting older text " |
|---|---|

| E | J |
|---|---|
| | of the Amorites, and the kingdom of Og king of Bashan, the land, according to the cities thereof with their borders, even the cities of the land round about.<br><br>[34]And the children of Gad built Dibon, and Ataroth, and Aroer; [35]and Atrothshophan, and Jazer, and Jogbehah; [36]and Beth-nimrah, and Beth-haran; fortified cities, and folds for sheep. [37]And the children of Reuben built Heshbon, and El-ealeh, and Kiriathaim; [38]and Nebo, and Baal-meon—their names being changed—and Sibmah; and gave their names unto the cities which they builded. [39]And the children of Machir the son of Manasseh went to Gilead, and took it, and dispossessed the Amorites that were therein. [40]And Moses gave Gilead unto Machir the son of Manasseh; and he dwelt therein. [41]And Jair the son of Manasseh went and took the villages thereof, and called them Havvoth-jair. [42]And Nobah went and took Kenath, and the villages thereof, and called it Nobah, after his own name. |

*[Continued on p. 364]*

| ( added by redactor ) | { problematic } |

| P | Notes |
|---|---|
| the other side of the Jordan, and forward, because our inheritance is fallen to us on this side of the Jordan eastward.' | they have already wandered through the wilderness and gotten to Moab and are about to enter Canaan. R must have added this here to accommodate the itinerary in Numbers 33, which R inserted a |

the other side of the Jordan, and forward, because our inheritance is fallen to us on this side of the Jordan eastward.'

<sup></sup>20And Moses said unto them: 'If ye will do this thing: if ye will arm yourselves to go before the Lord to the war, 21and every armed man of you will pass over the Jordan before the Lord, until He hath driven out His enemies from before Him, 22and the land be subdued before the Lord, and ye return afterward; then ye shall be clear before the Lord, and before Israel, and this land shall be unto you for a possession before the Lord. 23But if ye will not do so, behold, ye have sinned against the Lord; and know ye your sin which will find you. 24Build you cities for your little ones, and folds for your sheep; and do that which hath proceeded out of your mouth.'

28So Moses gave charge concerning them to Eleazar the priest, and to Joshua the son of Nun, and to the heads of the fathers' houses of the tribes of the children of Israel. 29And Moses said unto them: 'If the children of Gad and the children of Reuben will pass with you over the Jordan, every man that is armed to battle, before the Lord, and the land shall be subdued before you, then ye shall give them the land of Gilead for a possession; 30but if they will not pass over with you

---

they have already wandered through the wilderness and gotten to Moab and are about to enter Canaan. R must have added this here to accommodate the itinerary in Numbers 33, which R inserted a bit later in the text. The itinerary repeats many locations where the Israelites have already wandered, so it must be an independent document that R inserted here, and R also added Numbers 32:13 as the reason for inserting all this wandering at this late point.

R might have added the forty years of wandering to P in response to this passage from J:

NUM 32:8Thus did your fathers, when I sent them from Kadesh-barnea to see the land. 9For when they went up unto the valley of Eshcol, and saw the land, they turned away the heart of the children of Israel, that they should not go into the land which the Lord had given them. 10And the Lord's anger was kindled in that day, and He swore, saying: 11Surely none of the men that came up out of Egypt, from twenty years old and upward, shall see the land which I swore unto Abraham, unto Isaac, and unto Jacob; because they have not wholly followed Me.

But this passage says that the Lord became angry and condemned Israel to forty years of wandering "on that day"— that is, on the day when Israel sent spies from Kadesh-barnea.

The P text also contains a passage condemning Israel to wandering in the wilderness for 40 years at that earlier time, when the spies first went to see Canaan (Num. 14:33), so the 40 years of wandering are not appropriate at this later location.

| [ used more than once ] | " quoting older text " |
|---|---|

| **E** | **J** |
|---|---|
| *[Continued on p. 364]* | *[Continued on p. 364]* |
| ( added by redactor ) | { problematic } |

[Continued on p. 364]

| P | Notes |
|---|---|

armed, they shall have possessions among you in the land of Canaan.' ³¹And the children of Gad and the children of Reuben answered, saying: 'As the Lord hath said unto thy servants, so will we do. ³²We will pass over armed before the Lord into the land of Canaan, and the possession of our inheritance shall remain with us beyond the Jordan.'

### Stages of the Exodus - Relocated

Numbers 33, which summarizes Israel's journey through the wilderness, is an independent document added by R. See Appendix 2. Because the goal of this edition is to present the J, E, and P texts in columnar form, this passage is moved to the section of Other Texts.

### Inheriting the Land - Abridged

NUM 33:50And the Lord spoke unto Moses in the plains of Moab by the Jordan at Jericho, saying: ⁵¹'Speak unto the children of Israel, and say unto them: When ye pass over the Jordan into the land of Canaan, ⁵²then ye shall drive out all the inhabitants of the land from before you, and destroy all their figured stones, and destroy all their molten images, and demolish all their high places. ⁵³And ye shall drive out the inhabitants of the land, and dwell therein; for unto you have I given the land to possess it. ⁵⁴And ye shall inherit the land by lot according to your families—to the more ye shall give the more inheritance, and to the fewer thou shalt give the less inheritance; wheresoever the lot falleth to any man, that shall be his; according to the tribes of your fathers shall ye inherit.

⁵⁵But if ye will not drive out the inhabitants of the land from before you, then shall those that ye let remain of them be as thorns in your eyes, and as pricks in your sides, and they shall harass you in the land

### Inheriting the Land

Because the goal of this edition is to place parallel passages from the three texts next to each other, it provides abridged versions of some lengthy and repetitive passages from the P text. For the entire section about inheriting the land, read Numbers 33:50 to 36:13.

**P Text**

This section repeats some of what earlier sections about censuses (Num. 1-4 and Numbers 25:19-27:11) say about dividing the land among tribes, but it fits into the narrative while the earlier sections do not, indicating that it is the original text about dividing the land while the earlier sections are independent documents that were added by a redactor. These earlier sections are included in the section of this book named Other Texts.

| [ used more than once ] | " quoting older text " |
|---|---|

| E | J |
|---|---|
| | |

*[Continued on p. 364]*

*[Continued on p. 364]*

| ( added by redactor ) | { problematic } |

| **P** | **Notes** |
|---|---|

wherein ye dwell. ⁵⁶And it shall come to pass, that as I thought to do unto them, so will I do unto you.

NUM 34:1And the Lord spoke unto Moses, saying: 2'Command the children of Israel, and say unto them: When ye come into the land of Canaan, this shall be the land that shall fall unto you for an inheritance, even the land of Canaan according to the borders thereof.

¹³And Moses commanded the children of Israel, saying: 'This is the land wherein ye shall receive inheritance by lot, which the Lord hath commanded to give unto the nine tribes, and to the half-tribe; ¹⁴for the tribe of the children of Reuben according to their fathers' houses, and the tribe of the children of Gad according to their fathers' houses, have received, and the half-tribe of Manasseh have received, their inheritance; ¹⁵the two tribes and the half-tribe have received their inheritance beyond the Jordan at Jericho eastward, toward the sunrising.'

³⁵:1And the Lord spoke unto Moses in the plains of Moab by the Jordan at Jericho, saying: 2'Command the children of Israel, that they give unto the Levites of the inheritance of their possession cities to dwell in; and open land round about the cities shall ye give unto the Levites. ³And the cities shall they have to dwell in; and their open land shall be for their cattle, and for their substance, and for all their beasts.

⁶And the cities which ye shall give unto the Levites, they shall be the six cities of refuge, which ye shall give for the manslayer to flee thither; and beside them ye shall give forty and two cities. ⁷All the cities which ye shall give to the Levites shall be forty and eight cities: them shall ye give with the open land about them.

⁹And the Lord spoke unto Moses, saying: 10'Speak unto the children of Israel, and say unto them: When ye pass over the Jordan into the land of Canaan, ¹¹then ye shall appoint you cities to be cities of refuge for you, that the manslayer that killeth any person through error may flee thither. ¹²And the cities shall be unto you for refuge from the avenger, that the manslayer die not, until he stand before the congregation for judgment.

*[Continued on p. 365]*

| [ used more than once ] | " quoting older text " |
|---|---|

| **E** | **J** |
|---|---|
| | |
| **Death of Moses** | **Death of Moses** |
| DEUT 34:5[So Moses] the servant of the Lord [died there in the land of Moab], according to the word of the Lord. 6And he was buried in the valley in the land of Moab over against Beth-peor; and no man knoweth of his sepulchre unto this day. | DEUT 31:14And the Lord said unto Moses: 'Behold, thy days approach that thou must die; call Joshua, and present yourselves in the tent of meeting, that I may give him a charge.' And Moses and Joshua went, and presented themselves in the tent of meeting. 15And the Lord appeared in the Tent in a pillar of cloud; and the pillar of cloud stood over the door of the Tent. 23And He gave Joshua the son of Nun a |
| ( added by redactor ) | { problematic } |

| P | Notes |
|---|---|

**P**

²⁹And these things shall be for a statute of judgment unto you throughout your generations in all your dwellings. ³⁰Whoso killeth any person, the murderer shall be slain at the mouth of witnesses; but one witness shall not testify against any person that he die. ³¹Moreover ye shall take no ransom for the life of a murderer, that is guilty of death; but he shall surely be put to death. ³²And ye shall take no ransom for him that is fled to his city of refuge, that he should come again to dwell in the land, until the death of the priest. ³³So ye shall not pollute the land wherein ye are; for blood, it polluteth the land; and no expiation can be made for the land for the blood that is shed therein, but by the blood of him that shed it. ³⁴And thou shalt not defile the land which ye inhabit, in the midst of which I dwell; for I the Lord dwell in the midst of the children of Israel.'

³⁶:¹³These are the commandments and the ordinances, which the Lord commanded by the hand of Moses unto the children of Israel in the plains of Moab by the Jordan at Jericho.

### Death of Moses

DEUT 34:5[So Moses died there in the land of Moab], ⁸And the children of Israel wept for Moses in the plains of Moab thirty days; so the days of weeping in the mourning for Moses were ended. ⁹And Joshua the son of Nun was full of the spirit of wisdom; for Moses had laid his hands upon him; and the children of Israel hearkened unto him, and did as the Lord commanded Moses.

**Notes**

### Death of Moses

**E Text**

"Unto this day" implies that this text was written long after the death of Moses, one of many phrases discrediting the traditional view that the Torah is a single text that originated with Moses.

**J Text**

In J, Moses lives to be 120 years old, the maximum life span according to J in Genesis 6:3.

| [ used more than once ] | " quoting older text " |
|---|---|

| **E** | **J** |
|---|---|
| | charge, and said: 'Be strong and of good courage; for thou shalt bring the children of Israel into the land which I swore unto them; and I will be with thee.'<br><br>DEUT 34:7And Moses was a hundred and twenty years old when he died: his eye was not dim, nor his natural force abated. |
| ( added by redactor ) | { problematic } |

| P | Notes |
|---|---|
| | In J, but not in the other texts, it is common for God to appear as a pillar of cloud. Both Moses and Joshua are with the pillar of cloud in the tent of meeting earlier in the J text (Ex. 33:7-11). |
| | **P Text** |
| | The Israelites have the same 30 days of mourning for Moses that they had for Aaron (Num. 20:29), another example of P trying to make his ancestor, Aaron, as important as Moses. |
| | **Translation** |
| | The JPS translation uses "he" with a small "h" in "ᴰᴱᵁᵀ ³¹:²³ And he gave Joshua the son of Nun a charge," because in the combined text, it seems that Moses is giving Joshua this charge. This edition uses "He" with a capital "H," because in the separated text, God gives Joshua this charge. Both are equally adequate translations of the original Hebrew, which does not use pronouns or capitalization. |
| [ used more than once ] | " quoting older text " |

# Part III:
# Other Texts

*This section includes texts from the first four books
of the Bible that are not part of the E, J or P text.*

# A Chronicle of Abraham
## Genesis 14

## Notes

Most of this chapter is not in the style of J, P, or E. It is clearly more historical and less mythological than many of the surrounding texts: in this text, Sodom is defeated militarily, the king of Sodom and Lot are captured, and Abram leads his fighting men to free them. By contrast, in J's much more mythological account, Abram defends Sodom by bargaining with God to spare it if it has ten righteous men,[119] and Lot escapes the destruction of Sodom after being warned by two angels.[120]

Scholars have come up with varied theories about the origin of this chapter. Some have suggested that it may be a Canaanite chronicle incorporated in the Bible, which may give us some idea of the actual history behind the myths. Others have said that writing about mythical material in the style of a historical chronicle is typical of the late Persian and Hellenistic period, which implies that this passage is the last addition to the Torah.[121]

The final portion of this passage is problematic. Parts sound like they might have been written by J or P, but it does not seem possible to untangle them from the rest of this passage and include them in the J or P text.

Genesis 14:18-20, about Melchizedek king of Salem, sounds like it might be by J. It fails to distinguish between the religion of Abraham and pagan religions, which is typical of J. The story of Melchizedek is also something we would expect from a courtly source, because it was used to support the king's authority over the Israelite religion: Melchizedek was both the king and priest in Salem (which is identified with Jerusalem), implying that kings in Jerusalem should control the religion; Psalm 110 also mentions Melchizedek to defend the king's authority over religion.

Genesis 14:21-24, about Abram refusing to accept gifts from the king of Sodom, sounds like it might be by P. Just as P records the purchase of the tomb of the patriarchs in Hebron[122] to show that Abraham gave fair value for it and it legitimately belongs to the Israelites, this passage ends by saying "GEN 14:23 ... I will not take a thread nor a shoe-latchet nor aught that is thine, lest thou shouldest say: I have made Abram rich; 24save only that which the young men have eaten, and the portion of the men which went with me, Aner, Eshcol, and Mamre, let them take their portion," which shows that Abram did not take any Canaanite wealth illegitimately.

But these passages are so brief that it is impossible to incorporate them in the J or P text. Genesis 14:18-20 is clearly a separate text that interrupts the overall story of Genesis 14, while Genesis 14:21-24 may be part of the overall story.

# Text

GEN 14:1And it came to pass in the days of Amraphel king of Shinar, Arioch king of Ellasar, Chedorlaomer king of Elam, and Tidal king of Goiim, 2that they made war with Bera king of Sodom, and with Birsha king of Gomorrah, Shinab king of Admah, and Shemeber king of Zeboiim, and the king of Bela—the same is Zoar. 3All these came as allies unto the vale of Siddim— the same is the Salt Sea. 4Twelve years they served Chedorlaomer, and in the thirteenth year they rebelled. 5And in the fourteenth year came Chedorlaomer and the kings that were with him, and smote the Rephaim in Ashteroth-karnaim, and the Zuzim in Ham, and the Emim in Shavehkiriathaim, 6and the Horites in their mount Seir, unto El-paran, which is by the wilderness. 7And they turned back, and came to En-mishpat—the same is Kadesh—and smote all the country of the Amalekites, and also the Amorites, that dwelt in Hazazon-tamar. 8And there went out the king of Sodom, and the king of Gomorrah, and the king of Admah, and the king of Zeboiim, and the king of Bela—the same is Zoar; and they set the battle in array against them in the vale of Siddim; 9against Chedorlaomer king of Elam, and Tidal king of Goiim, and Amraphel king of Shinar, and Arioch king of Ellasar; four kings against the five. 10Now the vale of Siddim was full of slime pits; and the kings of Sodom and Gomorrah fled, and they fell there, and they that remained fled to the mountain. 11And they took all the goods of Sodom and Gomorrah, and all their victuals, and went their way. 12And they took Lot, Abram's brother's son, who dwelt in Sodom, and his goods, and departed. 13And there came one that had escaped, and told Abram the Hebrew—now he dwelt by the terebinths of Mamre the Amorite, brother of Eshcol, and brother of Aner; and these were confederate with Abram. 14And when Abram heard that his brother was taken captive, he led forth his trained men, born in his house, three hundred and eighteen, and pursued as far as Dan. 15And he divided himself against them by night, he and his servants, and smote them, and pursued them unto Hobah, which is on the left hand of Damascus. 16And he brought back all the goods, and also brought back his brother Lot, and his goods, and the women also, and the people. 17And the king of Sodom went out to meet him, after his return from the slaughter of Chedorlaomer and the kings that were with him, at the vale of Shaveh—the same is the King's Vale. {18And Melchizedek king of Salem brought forth bread and wine; and he was priest of God the Most High *[=El Elyon]*. 19And he blessed him, and said: 'Blessed be Abram of God Most High, Maker of heaven and earth; 20and blessed be God the Most High, who hath delivered thine enemies into thy hand.' And he gave him a tenth of all. 21And the king of Sodom said unto Abram: 'Give me the persons, and take the goods to thyself.' [22]And Abram said to the king of Sodom: 'I have lifted up my hand unto (the Lord,) God Most High, Maker of heaven and earth, [23]that I will not take a thread nor a shoe-latchet nor aught that is thine, lest thou shouldest say: I have made Abram rich; [24]save only that which the young men have eaten, and the portion of the men which went with me, Aner, Eshcol, and Mamre, let them take their portion.'}

# Chiefs of Edom
## Genesis 36:15-42

## Notes

These lists of chiefs and kings of Edom follow the list of the sons and grandsons of Esau in Genesis 36:1-14. These lists are made up of several separate texts.

Genesis 36 overall is clearly patched together.

The first section of this chapter, Genesis 36:1-14, is a conventional genealogy of Esau's descendents. Many scholars attribute it to P but this edition attributes it to J for several reasons.

- P focuses on the mainline genealogy leading from Adam to the Israelites, while J often includes genealogies of other nations. This difference begins with the pre-flood and post-flood genealogies of the two texts.
- P has already had a story about the children of Esau, which contradicts this story. For example, the earlier P story said: "[GEN 26:34]And when Esau was forty years old, he took to wife Judith the daughter of Beeri the Hittite, and Basemath the daughter of Elon the Hittite." This genealogy gives different names for these Canaanite wives: [GEN 36:2]"Esau took his wives of the daughters of Canaan; Adah the daughter of Elon the Hittite, and Oholibamah the daughter of Anah, the daughter of Zibeon the Hivite."
- J is likely to includes the generations of Esau because she is clearly sympathetic to Esau: in her story of Jacob stealing Esau's blessing, Esau is an innocent victim, and in her story of Esau meeting Jacob when he returns from Haran, Esau magnanimously forgives the brother who stole his blessing. In other traditions, Esau is not so sympathetic: in E, Esau disappoints Isaac and Rebekah by marrying Canaanites. Judea was near Edom, and J's sympathetic portrayal of

Esau (the ancestor of Edom) raises the possibility that perhaps she had some Edomite ancestry.

The second section of this chapter, Genesis 36:15-19, lists the ancestry of chiefs of Edomite clans, legitimizing Edom's chiefdoms by saying the chiefs are descended from Esau or from his sons. This section does not follow consecutively from Genesis 36:1-14, since Genesis 36:1-14 includes Esau's grandsons, but then Genesis 36:15-19 goes back to Esau and his sons to establish the ancestry of the chiefs. In addition, this list includes a self-contradiction, since it says in verse 15 that the chief of Korah was descended from Eliphaz, the first son of Esau and then says in verse 18 that the chief of Korah was descended from Esau and his wife Oholibamah, which could explained as a corruption in an earlier document. This is very early history, since it dates back to the days when Edom had chiefs, before it had kings, and the passage goes on to tell us that there were kings in Edom before there were kings in Israel, so there was plenty of time for the document to become corrupt. It seems that this list is an earlier document that was inserted at this point because it does not follow consecutively and because it contradicts the final section, as described below

The next section, Genesis 36:20-30, gives the ancestry of Horite clans, which is not connected with the genealogy that came earlier, making it seem like a separate document that was inserted here.

The next section, Genesis 36:31-39, gives a list of Edomite kings, which also is not connected with the genealogy that came earlier, making it seem like a separate document inserted here.

The final section, Genesis 36:40-42, lists "chiefs who came of Esau," indicating that it is supposedly connected with the earlier genealogy of Esau. In fact, it does duplicate the names of a couple of the clans in the earlier list in Genesis 36:15-19, Teman and Kenaz. Oddly, it also says that there was a clan named Oholibamah, which the earlier list says was the name of Esau's wife, not of one of his sons. But most of the clans in the earlier list are not mentioned in this list, and most of the clans in this list are not mentioned in the earlier list. Thus, it seems that these two lists are two earlier documents that were both inserted here.

## Text

GEN 36:15These are the chiefs of the sons of Esau: the sons of Eliphaz the first-born of Esau: the chief of Teman, the chief of Omar, the chief of Zepho, the chief of Kenaz, 16the chief of Korah, the chief of Gatam, the chief of Amalek. These are the chiefs that came of Eliphaz in the land of Edom. These are the sons of Adah. 17And these are the sons of Reuel Esau's son: the chief of Nahath, the chief of Zerah, the chief of Shammah, the chief of Mizzah. These are the chiefs that came of Reuel in the land of Edom.

These are the sons of Basemath Esau's wife. ¹⁸And these are the sons of Oholibamah Esau's wife: the chief of Jeush, the chief of Jalam, the chief of Korah. These are the chiefs that came of Oholibamah the daughter of Anah, Esau's wife. ¹⁹These are the sons of Esau, and these are their chiefs; the same is Edom.

²⁰These are the sons of Seir the Horite, the inhabitants of the land: Lotan and Shobal and Zibeon and Anah, ²¹and Dishon and Ezer and Dishan. These are the chiefs that came of the Horites, the children of Seir in the land of Edom. ²²And the children of Lotan were Hori and Hemam; and Lotan's sister was Timna. ²³And these are the children of Shobal: Alvan and Manahath and Ebal, Shepho and Onam. ²⁴And these are the children of Zibeon: Aiah and Anah—this is Anah who found the hot springs in the wilderness, as he fed the asses of Zibeon his father. ²⁵And these are the children of Anah: Dishon and Oholibamah the daughter of Anah. ²⁶And these are the children of Dishon: Hemdan and Eshban and Ithran and Cheran. ²⁷These are the children of Ezer: Bilhan and Zaavan and Akan. ²⁸These are the children of Dishan: Uz and Aran. ²⁹These are the chiefs that came of the Horites: the chief of Lotan, the chief of Shobal, the chief of Zibeon, the chief of Anah, ³⁰the chief of Dishon, the chief of Ezer, the chief of Dishan. These are the chiefs that came of the Horites, according to their chiefs in the land of Seir.

³¹And these are the kings that reigned in the land of Edom, before there reigned any king over the children of Israel. ³²And Bela the son of Beor reigned in Edom; and the name of his city was Dinhabah. ³³And Bela died, and Jobab the son of Zerah of Bozrah reigned in his stead. ³⁴And Jobab died, and Husham of the land of the Temanites reigned in his stead. ³⁵And Husham died, and Hadad the son of Bedad, who smote Midian in the field of Moab, reigned in his stead; and the name of his city was Avith. ³⁶And Hadad died, and Samlah of Masrekah reigned in his stead. ³⁷And Samlah died, and Shaul of Rehoboth by the River reigned in his stead. ³⁸And Shaul died, and Baal-hanan the son of Achbor reigned in his stead. ³⁹And Baal-hanan the son of Achbor died, and Hadar reigned in his stead; and the name of the city was Pau; and his wife's name was Mehetabel, the daughter of Matred, the daughter of Me-zahab. ⁴⁰And these are the names of the chiefs that came of Esau, according to their families, after their places, by their names: the chief of Timna, the chief of Alvah, the chief of Jetheth; ⁴¹the chief of Oholibamah, the chief of Elah, the chief of Pinon; ⁴²the chief of Kenaz, the chief of Teman, the chief of Mibzar; ⁴³the chief of Magdiel, the chief of Iram. These are the chiefs of Edom, according to their habitations in the land of their possession. This is Esau the father of the Edomites.

# Heads of Tribes
## Exodus 6:13-30

## Notes

The catalog of heads of tribes in Exodus 6:13-30 seems to have been inserted by a redactor.

This passage interrupts a passage from P. It is framed by passages that repeat each other. The statement at the end of the passage, "[EX 6:30]And Moses said before the Lord: 'Behold, I am of uncircumcised lips, and how shall Pharaoh hearken unto me?'" says the same thing as the statement that comes immediately before the passage, "[EX 6:12]And Moses spoke before the Lord, saying: 'Behold, the children of Israel have not hearkened unto me; how then shall Pharaoh hear me, who am of uncircumcised lips?'" Redactors often use this sort of repetition to frame an insertion, since the repetition takes up the thread of the narrative again after it is interrupted by the insertion.

The odd thing about this passage is that begins by saying it will list the heads of all the tribes: "[EX 6:14]These are the heads of their fathers' houses:" Then it gives brief lists of the heads of Reuben and Simeon, Jacob's first two sons. Then it gives a more elaborate genealogy of the sons of Levi, Jacob's third son. But it never gets around to giving the heads of the other tribes.

R was a priest, so it makes sense that he would give a longer genealogy of the descendents of Levi, his own tribe. But why did he forget about the other tribes? It seems that, after a redactor added the list of the sons of Levi, which includes Moses and Aaron, he lost the thread of this insertion and went back to the main narrative about Moses and Aaron, with this transition: "[EX 6:26]These are that Aaron and Moses, to whom the Lord said: 'Bring out the children of Israel from the land of Egypt according to their hosts.'"

## Text

"[EX 6:13]And the Lord spoke unto Moses and unto Aaron, and gave them a charge unto the children of Israel, and unto Pharaoh king of Egypt, to bring the children of Israel out of the land of Egypt.

[14]These are the heads of their fathers' houses: the sons of Reuben the first-born of Israel: Hanoch, and Pallu, Hezron, and Carmi. These are the families of Reuben.

[15]And the sons of Simeon: Jemuel, and Jamin, and Ohad, and Jachin, and Zohar, and Shaul the son of a Canaanitish woman. These are the families of Simeon.

[16]And these are the names of the sons of Levi according to their generations: Gershon and Kohath, and Merari. And the years of the life of Levi were a hundred thirty and seven years. [17]The sons of Gershon: Libni and Shimei, according to their families. [18]And the sons of Kohath: Amram,

and Izhar, and Hebron, and Uzziel. And the years of the life of Kohath were a hundred thirty and three years. ¹⁹And the sons of Merari: Mahli and Mushi. These are the families of the Levites according to their generations. ²⁰And Amram took him Jochebed his father's sister to wife; and she bore him Aaron and Moses. And the years of the life of Amram were a hundred and thirty and seven years. ²¹And the sons of Izhar: Korah, and Nepheg, and Zichri. ²²And the sons of Uzziel: Mishael, and Elzaphan, and Sithri. ²³And Aaron took him Elisheba, the daughter of Amminadab, the sister of Nahshon, to wife; and she bore him Nadab and Abihu, Eleazar and Ithamar. ²⁴And the sons of Korah: Assir, and Elkanah, and Abiasaph; these are the families of the Korahites. ²⁵And Eleazar Aaron's son took him one of the daughters of Putiel to wife; and she bore him Phinehas. These are the heads of the fathers' houses of the Levites according to their families. (²⁶These are that Aaron and Moses, to whom the Lord said: 'Bring out the children of Israel from the land of Egypt according to their hosts.' ²⁷These are they that spoke to Pharaoh king of Egypt, to bring out the children of Israel from Egypt. These are that Moses and Aaron. ²⁸And it came to pass on the day when the Lord spoke unto Moses in the land of Egypt, ²⁹that the Lord spoke unto Moses, saying: 'I am the Lord; speak thou unto Pharaoh king of Egypt all that I speak unto thee.' ³⁰And Moses said before the Lord: 'Behold, I am of uncircumcised lips, and how shall Pharaoh hearken unto me?')

# The First Census
## Numbers 1-4

## Notes

The census in Numbers 1-4 seems to be a separate document added by a later redactor.

It repeats a point made later, in the section of P that this edition titles "Inheriting the Land":

> NUM 33:54And ye shall inherit the land by lot according to your families—to the more ye shall give the more inheritance, and to the fewer thou shalt give the less inheritance; wheresoever the lot falleth to any man, that shall be his; according to the tribes of your fathers shall ye inherit."

It adds much more detail, giving the actual populations that justify the division of the land into the territories of tribes, so it looks like this Census is a later document added to flesh out the point made in "Inheriting the Land."

This section about "Inheriting the Land" fits into the narrative, while the first census in Numbers 1-4 interrupts the narrative. The first census also contradicts the second census, described below. Therefore, both the first and second census seem to be texts that were added later.

## Text

NUM 1:1And the Lord spoke unto Moses in the wilderness of Sinai, in the tent of meeting, on the first day of the second month, in the second year after the were come out of the land of Egypt, saying: 2'Take ye the sum of all the congregation of the children of Israel, by their families, by their fathers' houses, according to the number of names, every male, by their polls; 3from twenty years old and upward, all that are able to go forth to war in Israel: ye shall number them by their hosts, even thou and Aaron. 4And with you there shall be a man of every tribe, every one head of his fathers' house. 5And these are the names of the men that shall stand with you: of Reuben, Elizur the son of Shedeur. 6Of Simeon, Shelumiel the son of Zurishaddai. 7Of Judah, Nahshon the son of Amminadab. 8Of Issachar, Nethanel the son of Zuar. 9Of Zebulun, Eliab the son of Helon. 10Of the children of Joseph: of Ephraim, Elishama the son of Ammihud; of Manasseh, Gamaliel the son of Pedahzur. 11Of Benjamin, Abidan the son of Gideoni. 12Of Dan, Ahiezer the son of Ammishaddai. 13Of Asher, Pagiel the son of Ochran. 14Of Gad, Eliasaph the son of Deuel. 15Of Naphtali, Ahira the son of Enan.' 16These were the elect of the congregation, the princes of the tribes of their fathers; they were the heads of the thousands of Israel. 17And Moses and Aaron took these men that are pointed out by name. 18And they assembled all the congregation together on the first day of the second month, and they declared their pedigrees after their families, by their fathers' houses, according to the number of names, from twenty years old and upward, by their polls. 19As the Lord commanded Moses, so did he number them in the wilderness of Sinai.

20And the children of Reuben, Israel's first-born, their generations, by their families, by their fathers' houses, according to the number of names, by their polls, every male from twenty years old and upward, all that were able to go forth to war; 21those that were numbered of them, of the tribe of Reuben, were forty and six thousand and five hundred.

22Of the children of Simeon, their generations, by their families, by their fathers' houses, those that were numbered thereof, according to the number of names, by their polls, every male from twenty years old and upward, all that were able to go forth to war; 23those that were numbered of them, of the tribe of Simeon, were fifty and nine thousand and three hundred.

24Of the children of Gad, their generations, by their families, by their fathers' houses, according to the number of names, from twenty years old and upward, all that were able to go forth to war; 25those that were numbered of them, of the tribe of Gad, were forty and five thousand six hundred and fifty.

26Of the children of Judah, their generations, by their families, by their fathers' houses, according to the number of names, from twenty years old and upward, all that were able to go forth to war; ²⁷those that were numbered of them, of the tribe of Judah, were threescore and fourteen thousand and six hundred.

²⁸Of the children of Issachar, their generations, by their families, by their fathers' houses, according to the number of names, from twenty years old and upward, all that were able to go forth to war; ²⁹those that were numbered of them, of the tribe of Issachar, were fifty and four thousand and four hundred.

³⁰Of the children of Zebulun, their generations, by their families, by their fathers' houses, according to the number of names, from twenty years old and upward, all that were able to go forth to war; ³¹those that were numbered of them, of the tribe of Zebulun, were fifty and seven thousand and four hundred.

³²Of the children of Joseph, namely, of the children of Ephraim, their generations, by their families, by their fathers' houses, according to the number of names, from twenty years old and upward, all that were able to go forth to war; ³³those that were numbered of them, of the tribe of Ephraim, were forty thousand and five hundred.

³⁴Of the children of Manasseh, their generations, by their families, by their fathers' houses, according to the number of names, from twenty years old and upward, all that were able to go forth to war; ³⁵those that were numbered of them, of the tribe of Manasseh, were thirty and two thousand and two hundred.

³⁶Of the children of Benjamin, their generations, by their families, by their fathers' houses, according to the number of names, from twenty years old and upward, all that were able to go forth to war; ³⁷those that were numbered of them, of the tribe of Benjamin, were thirty and five thousand and four hundred.

³⁸Of the children of Dan, their generations, by their families, by their fathers' houses, according to the number of names, from twenty years old and upward, all that were able to go forth to war; ³⁹those that were numbered of them, of the tribe of Dan, were threescore and two thousand and seven hundred.

⁴⁰Of the children of Asher, their generations, by their families, by their fathers' houses, according to the number of names, from twenty years old and upward, all that were able to go forth to war; ⁴¹those that were numbered of them, of the tribe of Asher, were forty and one thousand and five hundred.

⁴²Of the children of Naphtali, their generations, by their families, by their fathers' houses, according to the number of names, from twenty years old and upward, all that were able to go forth to war; ⁴³those that were numbered of them, of the tribe of Naphtali, were fifty and three thousand and four hundred.

⁴⁴These are those that were numbered, which Moses and Aaron numbered, and the princes of Israel, being twelve men; they were each one for his fathers' house. ⁴⁵And all those that were numbered of the children of

Israel by their fathers' houses, from twenty years old and upward, all that were able to go forth to war in Israel; 46even all those that were numbered were six hundred thousand and three thousand and five hundred and fifty. 47But the Levites after the tribe of their fathers were not numbered among them.

48And the Lord spoke unto Moses, saying: 49'Howbeit the tribe of Levi thou shalt not number, neither shalt thou take the sum of them among the children of Israel; 50but appoint thou the Levites over the tabernacle of the testimony, and over all the furniture thereof, and over all that belongeth to it; they shall bear the tabernacle, and all the furniture thereof; and they shall minister unto it, and shall encamp round about the tabernacle. 51And when the tabernacle setteth forward, the Levites shall take it down; and when the tabernacle is to be pitched, the Levites shall set it up; and the common man that draweth nigh shall be put to death. 52And the children of Israel shall pitch their tents, every man with his own camp, and every man with his own standard, according to their hosts. 53But the Levites shall pitch round about the tabernacle of the testimony, that there be no wrath upon the congregation of the children of Israel; and the Levites shall keep the charge of the tabernacle of the testimony.' 54Thus did the children of Israel; according to all that the Lord commanded Moses, so did they.

NUM 2:1And the Lord spoke unto Moses and unto Aaron, saying: 2'The children of Israel shall pitch by their fathers' houses; every man with his own standard, according to the ensigns; a good way off shall they pitch round about the tent of meeting. 3Now those that pitch on the east side toward the sunrising shall be they of the standard of the camp of Judah, according to their hosts; the prince of the children of Judah being Nahshon the son of Amminadab, 4and his host, and those that were numbered of them, threescore and fourteen thousand and six hundred; 5and those that pitch next unto him shall be the tribe of Issachar; the prince of the children of Issachar being Nethanel the son of Zuar, 6and his host, even those that were numbered thereof, fifty and four thousand and four hundred; 7and the tribe of Zebulun; the prince of the children of Zebulun being Eliab the son of Helon, 8and his host, and those that were numbered thereof, fifty and seven thousand and four hundred; 9all that were numbered of the camp of Judah being a hundred thousand and fourscore thousand and six thousand and four hundred, according to their hosts; they shall set forth first.

10On the south side shall be the standard of the camp of Reuben according to their hosts; the prince of the children of Reuben being Elizur the son of Shedeur, 11and his host, and those that were numbered thereof, forty and six thousand and five hundred; 12and those that pitch next unto him shall be the tribe of Simeon; the prince of the children of Simeon being Shelumiel the son of Zurishaddai, 13and his host, and those that were numbered of them, fifty and nine thousand and three hundred; 14and the tribe of Gad; the prince of the children of Gad being Eliasaph the son of Reuel, 15and his host, even those that were numbered of them, forty and five thousand and six hundred and fifty; [16]all that were numbered of the camp of Reuben being a hundred thousand and fifty and one thousand and four hundred and fifty, according to their hosts; and they shall set forth second.

[17]Then the tent of meeting, with the camp of the Levites, shall set forward in the midst of the camps; as they encamp, so shall they set forward, every man in his place, by their standards.

[18]On the west side shall be the standard of the camp of Ephraim according to their hosts; the prince of the children of Ephraim being Elishama the son of Ammihud, [19]and his host, and those that were numbered of them, forty thousand and five hundred; [20]and next unto him shall be the tribe of Manasseh; the prince of the children of Manasseh being Gamaliel the son of Pedahzur, [21]and his host, and those that were numbered of them, thirty and two thousand and two hundred; [22]and the tribe of Benjamin; the prince of the children of Benjamin being Abidan the son of Gideoni, [23]and his host, and those that were numbered of them, thirty and five thousand and four hundred; [24]all that were numbered of the camp of Ephraim being a hundred thousand and eight thousand and a hundred, according to their hosts; and they shall set forth third.

[25]On the north side shall be the standard of the camp of Dan according to their hosts; the prince of the children of Dan being Ahiezer the son of Ammishaddai, [26]and his host, and those that were numbered of them, threescore and two thousand and seven hundred; [27]and those that pitch next unto him shall be the tribe of Asher; the prince of the children of Asher being Pagiel the son of Ochran, [28]and his host, and those that were numbered of them, forty and one thousand and five hundred; [29]and the tribe of Naphtali; the prince of the children of Naphtali being Ahira the son of Enan, [30]and his host, and those that were numbered of them, fifty and three thousand and four hundred; [31]all that were numbered of the camp of Dan being a hundred thousand and fifty and seven thousand and six hundred; they shall set forth hindmost by their standards.'

[32]These are they that were numbered of the children of Israel by their fathers' houses; all that were numbered of the camps according to their hosts were six hundred thousand and three thousand and five hundred and fifty. [33]But the Levites were not numbered among the children of Israel; as the Lord commanded Moses. [34]Thus did the children of Israel: according to all that the Lord commanded Moses, so they pitched by their standards, and so they set forward, each one according to its families, and according to its fathers' houses.

NUM 3:1Now these are the generations of Aaron and Moses in the day that the Lord spoke with Moses in mount Sinai. [2]And these are the names of the sons of Aaron: Nadab the first-born, and Abihu, Eleazar, and Ithamar. [3]These are the names of the sons of Aaron, the priests that were anointed, whom he consecrated to minister in the priest's office. [4]And Nadab and

Abihu died before the Lord, when they offered strange fire before the Lord, in the wilderness of Sinai, and they had no children; and Eleazar and Ithamar ministered in the priest's office in the presence of Aaron their father.

[5]And the Lord spoke unto Moses, saying: [6]'Bring the tribe of Levi near, and set them before Aaron the priest, that they may minister unto him. [7]And they shall keep his charge, and the charge of the whole congregation before the tent of meeting, to do the service of the tabernacle. [8]And they shall keep all the furniture of the tent of meeting, and the charge of the children of Israel, to do the service of the tabernacle. [9]And thou shalt give the Levites unto Aaron and to his sons; they are wholly given unto him from the children of Israel. [10]And thou shalt appoint Aaron and his sons, that they may keep their priesthood; and the common man that draweth nigh shall be put to death.'

[11]And the Lord spoke unto Moses, saying: [12]'And I, behold, I have taken the Levites from among the children of Israel instead of every first-born that openeth the womb among the children of Israel; and the Levites shall be Mine; [13]for all the first-born are Mine: on the day that I smote all the first-born in the land of Egypt I hallowed unto Me all the first-born in Israel, both man and beast, Mine they shall be: I am the Lord.' [14]And the Lord spoke unto Moses in the wilderness of Sinai, saying: [15]'Number the children of Levi by their fathers' houses, by their families; every male from a month old and upward shalt thou number them.' [16]And Moses numbered them according to the word of the Lord, as he was commanded. [17]And these were the sons of Levi by their names: Gershon, and Kohath, and Merari. [18]And these are the names of the sons of Gershon by their families: Libni and Shimei. [19]And the sons of Kohath by their families: Amram and Izhar, Hebron and Uzziel. [20]And the sons of Merari by their families: Mahli and Mushi. These are the families of the Levites according to their fathers' houses.

[21]Of Gershon was the family of the Libnites, and the family of the Shimeites; these are the families of the Gershonites. [22]Those that were numbered of them, according to the number of all the males, from a month old and upward, even those that were numbered of them were seven thousand and five hundred. [23]The families of the Gershonites were to pitch behind the tabernacle westward; [24]the prince of the fathers' house of the Gershonites being Eliasaph the son of Lael, [25]and the charge of the sons of Gershon in the tent of meeting the tabernacle, and the Tent, the covering thereof, and the screen for the door of the tent of meeting, [26]and the hangings of the court, and the screen for the door of the court—which is by the tabernacle, and by the altar, round about—and the cords of it, even whatsoever pertaineth to the service thereof.

[27]And of Kohath was the family of the Amramites, and the family of the Izharites, and the family of the Hebronites, and the family of the Uzzielites; these are the families of the Kohathites: [28]according to the number of all the males, from a month old and upward, eight thousand and six hundred,

keepers of the charge of the sanctuary. ²⁹The families of the sons of Kohath were to pitch on the side of the tabernacle southward; ³⁰the prince of the fathers' house of the families of the Kohathites being Elizaphan the son of Uzziel, ³¹and their charge the ark, and the table, and the candlestick, and the altars, and the vessels of the sanctuary wherewith the priests minister, and the screen, and all that pertaineth to the service thereof; ³²Eleazar the son of Aaron the priest being prince of the princes of the Levites, and having the oversight of them that keep the charge of the sanctuary.

³³Of Merari was the family of the Mahlites, and the family of the Mushites; these are the families of Merari. ³⁴And those that were numbered of them, according to the number of all the males, from a month old and upward, were six thousand and two hundred; ³⁵the prince of the fathers' house of the families of Merari being Zuriel the son of Abihail; they were to pitch on the side of the tabernacle northward; ³⁶the appointed charge of the sons of Merari being the boards of the tabernacle, and the bars thereof, and the pillars thereof, and the sockets thereof, and all the instruments thereof, and all that pertaineth to the service thereof; ³⁷and the pillars of the court round about, and their sockets, and their pins, and their cords. ³⁸And those that were to pitch before the tabernacle eastward, before the tent of meeting toward the sunrising, were Moses, and Aaron and his sons, keeping the charge of the sanctuary, even the charge for the children of Israel; and the common man that drew nigh was to be put to death. ³⁹All that were numbered of the Levites, whom Moses and Aaron numbered at the commandment of the Lord, by their families, all the males from a month old and upward, were twenty and two thousand.

⁴⁰And the Lord said unto Moses: 'Number all the first-born males of the children of Israel from a month old and upward, and take the number of their names. ⁴¹And thou shalt take the Levites for Me, even the Lord, instead of all the first-born among the children of Israel; and the cattle of the Levites instead of all the firstlings among the cattle of the children of Israel.' ⁴²And Moses numbered, as the Lord commanded him, all the first-born among the children of Israel. ⁴³And all the first-born males according to the number of names, from a month old and upward, of those that were numbered of them, were twenty and two thousand two hundred and threescore and thirteen.

⁴⁴And the Lord spoke unto Moses, saying: ⁴⁵'Take the Levites instead of all the first-born among the children of Israel, and the cattle of the Levites instead of their cattle; and the Levites shall be Mine, even the Lord's. ⁴⁶And as for the redemption of the two hundred and threescore and thirteen of the first-born of the children of Israel, that are over and above the number of the Levites, ⁴⁷thou shalt take five shekels apiece by the poll; after the shekel of the sanctuary shalt thou take them—the shekel is twenty gerahs. ⁴⁸And thou shalt give the money wherewith they that remain over of them are redeemed unto Aaron and to his sons.' ⁴⁹And Moses took the redemption-money from them that were over and above them that were redeemed by the

Levites; [50]from the first-born of the children of Israel took he the money: a thousand three hundred and threescore and five shekels, after the shekel of the sanctuary. [51]And Moses gave the redemption-money unto Aaron and to his sons, according to the word of the Lord, as the Lord commanded Moses.

NUM 4:1 And the Lord spoke unto Moses and unto Aaron, saying: [2]'Take the sum of the sons of Kohath from among the sons of Levi, by their families, by their fathers' houses, [3]from thirty years old and upward even until fifty years old, all that enter upon the service, to do work in the tent of meeting. [4]This is the service of the sons of Kohath in the tent of meeting, about the most holy things: [5]when the camp setteth forward, Aaron shall go in, and his sons, and they shall take down the veil of the screen, and cover the ark of the testimony with it; [6]and shall put thereon a covering of sealskin, and shall spread over it a cloth all of blue, and shall set the staves thereof. [7]And upon the table of showbread they shall spread a cloth of blue, and put thereon the dishes, and the pans, and the bowls, and the jars wherewith to pour out; and the continual bread shall remain thereon. [8]And they shall spread upon them a cloth of scarlet, and cover the same with a covering of sealskin, and shall set the staves thereof. [9]And they shall take a cloth of blue, and cover the candlestick of the light, and its lamps, and its tongs, and its snuffdishes, and all the oil vessels thereof, wherewith they minister unto it. [10]And they shall put it and all the vessels thereof within a covering of sealskin, and shall put it upon a bar. [11]And upon the golden altar they shall spread a cloth of blue, and cover it with a covering of sealskin, and shall set the staves thereof. [12]And they shall take all the vessels of ministry, wherewith they minister in the sanctuary, and put them in a cloth of blue, and cover them with a covering of sealskin, and shall put them on a bar. [13]And they shall take away the ashes from the altar, and spread a purple cloth thereon. [14]And they shall put upon it all the vessels thereof, wherewith they minister about it, the fire-pans, the flesh-hooks, and the shovels, and the basins, all the vessels of the altar; and they shall spread upon it a covering of sealskin, and set the staves thereof. [15]And when Aaron and his sons have made an end of covering the holy furniture, and all the holy vessels, as the camp is to set forward—after that, the sons of Kohath shall come to bear them; but they shall not touch the holy things, lest they die. These things are the burden of the sons of Kohath in the tent of meeting. [16]And the charge of Eleazar the son of Aaron the priest shall be the oil for the light, and the sweet incense, and the continual meal-offering, and the anointing oil: he shall have the charge of all the tabernacle, and of all that therein is, whether it be the sanctuary, or the furniture thereof.'

[17]And the Lord spoke unto Moses and unto Aaron, saying: [18]'Cut ye not off the tribe of the families of the Kohathites from among the Levites; [19]but thus do unto them, that they may live, and not die, when they approach unto the most holy things: Aaron and his sons shall go in, and appoint them every one to his service and to his burden; [20]but they shall not go in to see the holy things as they are being covered, lest they die.'

²¹And the Lord spoke unto Moses saying: ²²'Take the sum of the sons of Gershon also, by their fathers' houses, by their families; ²³from thirty years old and upward until fifty years old shalt thou number them: all that enter in to wait upon the service, to do service in the tent of meeting. ²⁴This is the service of the families of the Gershonites, in serving and in bearing burdens: ²⁵they shall bear the curtains of the tabernacle, and the tent of meeting, its covering, and the covering of sealskin that is above upon it, and the screen for the door of the tent of meeting; ²⁶and the hangings of the court, and the screen for the door of the gate of the court, which is by the tabernacle and by the altar round about, and their cords, and all the instruments of their service, and whatsoever there may be to do with them, therein shall they serve. ²⁷At the commandment of Aaron and his sons shall be all the service of the sons of the Gershonites, in all their burden, and in all their service; and ye shall appoint unto them in charge all their burden. ²⁸This is the service of the families of the sons of the Gershonites in the tent of meeting; and their charge shall be under the hand of Ithamar the son of Aaron the priest.

²⁹As for the sons of Merari, thou shalt number them by their families, by their fathers' houses; ³⁰from thirty years old and upward even unto fifty years old shalt thou number them, every one that entereth upon the service, to do the work of the tent of meeting. ³¹And this is the charge of their burden, according to all their service in the tent of meeting: the boards of the tabernacle, and the bars thereof, and the pillars thereof, and the sockets thereof; ³²and the pillars of the court round about, and their sockets, and their pins, and their cords, even all their appurtenance, and all that pertaineth to their service; and by name ye shall appoint the instruments of the charge of their burden. ³³This is the service of the families of the sons of Merari, according to all their service, in the tent of meeting, under the hand of Ithamar the son of Aaron the priest.'

³⁴And Moses and Aaron and the princes of the congregation numbered the sons of the Kohathites by their families, and by their fathers' houses, ³⁵from thirty years old and upward even unto fifty years old, every one that entered upon the service, for service in the tent of meeting. ³⁶And those that were numbered of them by their families were two thousand seven hundred and fifty. ³⁷These are they that were numbered of the families of the Kohathites, of all that did serve in the tent of meeting, whom Moses and Aaron numbered according to the commandment of the Lord by the hand of Moses.

³⁸And those that were numbered of the sons of Gershon, by their families, and by their fathers' houses, ³⁹from thirty years old and upward even unto fifty years old, every one that entered upon the service, for service in the tent of meeting, ⁴⁰even those that were numbered of them, by their families, by their fathers' houses, were two thousand and six hundred and thirty. ⁴¹These are they that were numbered of the families of the sons of Gershon, of all

that did serve in the tent of meeting, whom Moses and Aaron numbered according to the commandment of the Lord.

⁴²And those that were numbered of the families of the sons of Merari, by their families, by their fathers' houses, ⁴³from thirty years old and upward even unto fifty years old, every one that entered upon the service, for service in the tent of meeting, ⁴⁴even those that were numbered of them by their families, were three thousand and two hundred. ⁴⁵These are they that were numbered of the families of the sons of Merari, whom Moses and Aaron numbered according to the commandment of the Lord by the hand of Moses.

⁴⁶All those that were numbered of the Levites, whom Moses and Aaron and the princes of Israel numbered, by their families, and by their fathers' houses, ⁴⁷from thirty years old and upward even unto fifty years old, every one that entered in to do the work of service, and the work of bearing burdens in the tent of meeting, ⁴⁸even those that were numbered of them, were eight thousand and five hundred and fourscore. ⁴⁹According to the commandment of the Lord they were appointed by the hand of Moses, every one to his service, and to his burden; they were also numbered, as the Lord commanded Moses.

# Commandments About Sacrifices
## Numbers 15

### Notes

Numbers 15 largely duplicates commandments about sacrifices in Leviticus. It also duplicates the commandment about fringes in Deuteronomy 22:12, and it includes a bit of narrative illustrating the punishment for breaking the commandment about the Sabbath: death by stoning.

This chapter interrupts the narrative flow in Numbers. Apparently, it is a summary of commandments from an independent text, which was put here by a later redactor.

Richard Elliot Friedman points out that the commandments about sacrifices in Leviticus require the tabernacle, but the commandments here do not.[123] Friedman believes that the Tabernacle was built into the first Temple, allowing sacrifices to be performed there while obeying the commandments in Leviticus to sacrifice in the Tabernacle, and that Numbers 15 was written at the time of the second Temple, when the Tabernacle no longer existed, requiring this new set of commandments that allow sacrifices without the Tabernacle.

# Text

NUM 15:1And the Lord spoke unto Moses, saying: 2Speak unto the children of Israel, and say unto them:

When ye are come into the land of your habitations, which I give unto you, 3and will make an offering by fire unto the Lord, a burnt-offering, or a sacrifice, in fulfilment of a vow clearly uttered, or as a freewill-offering, or in your appointed seasons, to make a sweet savour unto the Lord, of the herd, or of the flock; 4then shall he that bringeth his offering present unto the Lord a meal-offering of a tenth part of an ephah of fine flour mingled with the fourth part of a hin of oil; 5and wine for the drink-offering, the fourth part of a hin, shalt thou prepare with the burnt-offering or for the sacrifice, for each lamb. 6Or for a ram, thou shalt prepare for a meal-offering two tenth parts of an ephah of fine flour mingled with the third part of a hin of oil; 7and for the drink-offering thou shalt present the third part of a hin of wine, of a sweet savour unto the Lord. 8And when thou preparest a bullock for a burnt-offering, or for a sacrifice, in fulfilment of a vow clearly uttered, or for peace-offerings unto the Lord; 9then shall there be presented with the bullock a meal-offering of three tenth parts of an ephah of fine flour mingled with half a hin of oil. 10And thou shalt present for the drink-offering half a hin of wine, for an offering made by fire, of a sweet savour unto the Lord. 11Thus shall it be done for each bullock, or for each ram, or for each of the he-lambs, or of the kids. 12According to the number that ye may prepare, so shall ye do for every one according to their number. 13All that are home-born shall do these things after this manner, in presenting an offering made by fire, of a sweet savour unto the Lord. 14And if a stranger sojourn with you, or whosoever may be among you, throughout your generations, and will offer an offering made by fire, of a sweet savour unto the Lord; as ye do, so he shall do. 15As for the congregation, there shall be one statute both for you, and for the stranger that sojourneth with you, a statute for ever throughout your generations; as ye are, so shall the stranger be before the Lord. 16One law and one ordinance shall be both for you, and for the stranger that sojourneth with you.

17And the Lord spoke unto Moses, saying: 18Speak unto the children of Israel, and say unto them:

When ye come into the land whither I bring you, 19then it shall be, that, when ye eat of the bread of the land, ye shall set apart a portion for a gift unto the Lord. 20Of the first of your dough ye shall set apart a cake for a gift; as that which is set apart of the threshing-floor, so shall ye set it apart. 21Of the first of your dough ye shall give unto the Lord a portion for a gift throughout your generations.

22And when ye shall err, and not observe all these commandments, which the Lord hath spoken unto Moses, 23even all that the Lord hath commanded you by the hand of Moses, from the day that the Lord gave commandment, and onward throughout your generations; [24]then it shall be, if it be done in error by the congregation, it being hid from their eyes, that all the congregation shall offer one young bullock for a burnt-offering, for a sweet savour unto the Lord—with the meal-offering thereof, and the drink-offering thereof, according to the ordinance—and one he-goat for a sin-offering. [25]And the priest shall make atonement for all the congregation of the children of Israel, and they shall be forgiven; for it was an error, and they have brought their offering, an offering made by fire unto the Lord, and their sin-offering before the Lord, for their error. [26]And all the congregation of the children of Israel shall be forgiven, and the stranger that sojourneth among them; for in respect of all the people it was done in error.

[27]And if one person sin through error, then he shall offer a she-goat of the first year for a sin-offering. [28]And the priest shall make atonement for the soul that erreth, when he sinneth through error, before the Lord, to make atonement for him; and he shall be forgiven, [29]both he that is home-born among the children of Israel, and the stranger that sojourneth among them: ye shall have one law for him that doeth aught in error. [30]But the soul that doeth aught with a high hand, whether he be home-born or a stranger, the same blasphemeth the Lord; and that soul shall be cut off from among his people. [31]Because he hath despised the word of the Lord, and hath broken His commandment; that soul shall utterly be cut off, his iniquity shall be upon him.

[32]And while the children of Israel were in the wilderness, they found a man gathering sticks upon the sabbath day. [33]And they that found him gathering sticks brought him unto Moses and Aaron, and unto all the congregation. [34]And they put him in ward, because it had not been declared what should be done to him. [35]And the Lord said unto Moses: 'The man shall surely be put to death; all the congregation shall stone him with stones without the camp.' [36]And all the congregation brought him without the camp, and stoned him with stones, and he died, as the Lord commanded Moses.

[37]And the Lord spoke unto Moses, saying: [38]'Speak unto the children of Israel, and bid them that they make them throughout their generations fringes in the corners of their garments, and that they put with the fringe of each corner a thread of blue. [39]And it shall be unto you for a fringe, that ye may look upon it, and remember all the commandments of the Lord, and do them; and that ye go not about after your own heart and your own eyes, after which ye use to go astray; [40]that ye may remember and do all My commandments, and be holy unto your God. [41]I am the Lord your God, who brought you out of the land of Egypt, to be your God: I am the Lord your God.'

# Sacrifices and Purity
## Numbers 18-19

## Notes

It is difficult to tell whether Numbers 18-19 is by P or is a text added by R. In general, the commandments in P are given at Mt. Sinai, so this set of commandments given after leaving the mountain are out of place. These commandments also interrupt the narrative flow.

Because this edition assumes that the J, E, and P texts are continuous as an experiment to test the documentary hypothesis, it puts this out-of-place text in this section of Other Texts.

## Text

NUM 18:1And the Lord said unto Aaron: 'Thou and thy sons and thy fathers' house with thee shall bear the iniquity of the sanctuary; and thou and thy sons with thee shall bear the iniquity of your priesthood. 2And thy brethren also, the tribe of Levi, the tribe of thy father, bring thou near with thee, that they may be joined unto thee, and minister unto thee, thou and thy sons with thee being before the tent of the testimony. 3And they shall keep thy charge, and the charge of all the Tent; only they shall not come nigh unto the holy furniture and unto the altar, that they die not, neither they, nor ye. 4And they shall be joined unto thee, and keep the charge of the tent of meeting, whatsoever the service of the Tent may be; but a common man shall not draw nigh unto you. 5And ye shall keep the charge of the holy things, and the charge of the altar, that there be wrath no more upon the children of Israel. 6And I, behold, I have taken your brethren the Levites from among the children of Israel; for you they are given as a gift unto the Lord, to do the service of the tent of meeting. 7And thou and thy sons with thee shall keep your priesthood in everything that pertaineth to the altar, and to that within the veil; and ye shall serve; I give you the priesthood as a service of gift; and the common man that draweth nigh shall be put to death.'

8And the Lord spoke unto Aaron: 'And I, behold, I have given thee the charge of My heave-offerings; even of all the hallowed things of the children of Israel unto thee have I given them for a consecrated portion, and to thy sons, as a due for ever. 9This shall be thine of the most holy things, reserved from the fire: every offering of theirs, even every meal-offering of theirs, and every sin-offering of theirs, and every guilt-offering of theirs, which they may render unto Me, shall be most holy for thee and for thy sons. 10In a most holy place shalt thou eat thereof; every male may eat thereof; it shall be holy unto thee. 11And this is thine: the heave-offering of their gift, even all the wave-offerings of the children of Israel; I have given them unto thee, and to thy sons and to thy daughters with thee, as a due for ever; every one that is clean in thy house may eat thereof. [12]All the best of the oil, and all the best of the wine, and of the corn, the first part of them which they give unto the Lord, to thee have I given them. [13]The first-ripe fruits of all that is in their land, which they bring unto the Lord, shall be thine; every one that is clean in thy house may eat thereof. [14]Every thing devoted in Israel shall be thine. [15]Every thing that openeth the womb, of all flesh which they offer unto the Lord, both of man and beast, shall be thine; howbeit the first-born of man shalt thou surely redeem, and the firstling of unclean beasts shalt thou redeem. [16]And their redemption-money—from a month old shalt thou redeem them—shall be, according to thy valuation, five shekels of silver, after the shekel of the sanctuary—the same is twenty gerahs. [17]But the firstling of an ox, or the firstling of a sheep, or the firstling of a goat, thou shalt not redeem; they are holy: thou shalt dash their blood against the altar, and shalt make their fat smoke for an offering made by fire, for a sweet savour unto the Lord. [18]And the flesh of them shall be thine, as the wave-breast and as the right thigh, it shall be thine. [19]All the heave-offerings of the holy things, which the children of Israel offer unto the Lord, have I given thee, and thy sons and thy daughters with thee, as a due for ever; it is an everlasting covenant of salt before the Lord unto thee and to thy seed with thee.'

[20]And the Lord said unto Aaron: 'Thou shalt have no inheritance in their land, neither shalt thou have any portion among them; I am thy portion and thine inheritance among the children of Israel. [21]And unto the children of Levi, behold, I have given all the tithe in Israel for an inheritance, in return for their service which they serve, even the service of the tent of meeting. [22]And henceforth the children of Israel shall not come nigh the tent of meeting, lest they bear sin, and die. [23]But the Levites alone shall do the service of the tent of meeting, and they shall bear their iniquity; it shall be a statute for ever throughout your generations, and among the children of Israel they shall have no inheritance. [24]For the tithe of the children of Israel, which they set apart as a gift unto the Lord, I have given to the Levites for an inheritance; therefore I have said unto them: Among the children of Israel they shall have no inheritance.'

[25]And the Lord spoke unto Moses, saying: [26]'Moreover thou shalt speak unto the Levites, and say unto them: When ye take of the children of Israel the tithe which I have given you from them for your inheritance, then ye shall set apart of it a gift for the Lord, even a tithe of the tithe. [27]And the gift which ye set apart shall be reckoned unto you, as though it were the corn of the threshing-floor, and as the fulness of the winepress. [28]Thus ye also shall set apart a gift unto the Lord of all your tithes, which ye receive of the children of Israel; and thereof ye shall give the gift which is set apart unto the Lord to Aaron the priest. [29]Out of all that is given you ye shall set apart all of that which is due unto the Lord, of all the best thereof, even the hallowed part thereof out of it. [30]Therefore thou shalt say unto them: When

ye set apart the best thereof from it, then it shall be counted unto the Levites as the increase of the threshing-floor, and as the increase of the winepress. [31]And ye may eat it in every place, ye and your households; for it is your reward in return for your service in the tent of meeting. [32]And ye shall bear no sin by reason of it, seeing that ye have set apart from it the best thereof; and ye shall not profane the holy things of the children of Israel, that ye die not.'

[19:1]And the Lord spoke unto Moses and unto Aaron, saying: [2]This is the statute of the law which the Lord hath commanded, saying: Speak unto the children of Israel, that they bring thee a red heifer, faultless, wherein is no blemish, and upon which never came yoke. [3]And ye shall give her unto Eleazar the priest, and she shall be brought forth without the camp, and she shall be slain before his face. [4]And Eleazar the priest shall take of her blood with his finger, and sprinkle of her blood toward the front of the tent of meeting seven times. [5]And the heifer shall be burnt in his sight; her skin, and her flesh, and her blood, with her dung, shall be burnt. [6]And the priest shall take cedar-wood, and hyssop, and scarlet, and cast it into the midst of the burning of the heifer. [7]Then the priest shall wash his clothes, and he shall bathe his flesh in water, and afterward he may come into the camp, and the priest shall be unclean until the even. [8]And he that burneth her shall wash his clothes in water, and bathe his flesh in water, and shall be unclean until the even. [9]And a man that is clean shall gather up the ashes of the heifer, and lay them up without the camp in a clean place, and it shall be kept for the congregation of the children of Israel for a water of sprinkling; it is a purification from sin. [10]And he that gathereth the ashes of the heifer shall wash his clothes, and be unclean until the even; and it shall be unto the children of Israel, and unto the stranger that sojourneth among them, for a statute for ever. [11]He that toucheth the dead, even any man's dead body, shall be unclean seven days; [12]the same shall purify himself therewith on the third day and on the seventh day, and he shall be clean; but if he purify not himself the third day and the seventh day, he shall not be clean. [13]Whosoever toucheth the dead, even the body of any man that is dead, and purifieth not himself—he hath defiled the tabernacle of the Lord—that soul shall be cut off from Israel; because the water of sprinkling was not dashed against him, he shall be unclean; his uncleanness is yet upon him. [14]This is the law: when a man dieth in a tent, every one that cometh into the tent, and every thing that is in the tent, shall be unclean seven days. [15]And every open vessel, which hath no covering close-bound upon it, is unclean. [16]And whosoever in the open field toucheth one that is slain with a sword, or one that dieth of himself, or a bone of a man, or a grave, shall be unclean seven days. [17]And for the unclean they shall take of the ashes of the burning of the purification from sin, and running water shall be put thereto in a vessel. [18]And a clean person shall take hyssop, and dip it in the water, and sprinkle it upon the tent, and upon all the vessels, and upon the persons that were there, and upon him that touched the bone, or the slain, or the dead, or the grave. [19]And the clean person shall sprinkle upon the unclean on the third day, and on the seventh day; and on the seventh day he shall purify him; and he shall wash his clothes, and bathe himself in water, and shall be clean at even. [20]But the man that shall be unclean, and shall not purify himself, that soul shall be cut off from the midst of the assembly, because he hath defiled the sanctuary of the Lord; the water of sprinkling hath not been dashed against him: he is unclean. [21]And it shall be a perpetual statute unto them; and he that sprinkleth the water of sprinkling shall wash his clothes; and he that toucheth the water of sprinkling shall be unclean until even. [22]And whatsoever the unclean person toucheth shall be unclean; and the soul that toucheth him shall be unclean until even.

# The Second Census
## Numbers 25:19-27:11

## Notes

Like the census in Numbers 1-4, the census in Numbers 25:19-27:11 is meant to justify the division of the territory of Canaan among the tribes, with larger territories going to tribes that have larger populations.

These two censuses both begin with a similar statement:

- [NUM 1:2]'Take ye the sum of all the congregation of the children of Israel, by their families, by their fathers' houses, according to the number of names, every male, by their polls; [3]from twenty years old and upward, all that are able to go forth to war in Israel: ye shall number them by their hosts, even thou and Aaron.

- [NUM 26:2]'Take the sum of all the congregation of the children of Israel, from twenty years old and upward, by their fathers' houses, all that are able to go forth to war in Israel.'

But the numbers given by the two texts contradict each other. For example:

- From the first census: "[NUM 1:23]those that were numbered of them, of the tribe of Simeon, were fifty and nine thousand and three hundred."

- From the second census: "[NUM 26:14]These are the families of the Simeonites, twenty and two thousand and two hundred."

Thus, it seems that both the census in Numbers 1-4 and the census in Numbers 25:19-27:11 are separate documents added to the Bible to give more detailed information about the division of the land than is found in the older section titled "Inheriting the Land." The section "Inheriting the Land" fits into the narrative, but these two sections interrupt the narrative, so this edition classifies them as separate texts that were added later.

# Text

(<sup>NUM 25:19</sup>And it came to pass after the plague <sup>NUM 26:1</sup>that) the Lord spoke unto Moses and unto Eleazar the son of Aaron the priest, saying: <sup>2</sup>'Take the sum of all the congregation of the children of Israel, from twenty years old and upward, by their fathers' houses, all that are able to go forth to war in Israel.' <sup>3</sup>And Moses and Eleazar the priest spoke with them in the plains of Moab by the Jordan at Jericho, saying: <sup>4</sup>'[Take the sum of the people,] from twenty years old and upward, as the Lord commanded Moses and the children of Israel, that came forth out of the land of Egypt.'

<sup>5</sup>Reuben, the first-born of Israel: the sons of Reuben: of Hanoch, the family of the Hanochites; of Pallu, the family of the Palluites; <sup>6</sup>of Hezron, the family of the Hezronites; of Carmi, the family of the Carmites. <sup>7</sup>These are the families of the Reubenites; and they that were numbered of them were forty and three thousand and seven hundred and thirty. <sup>8</sup>And the sons of Pallu: Eliab. <sup>9</sup>And the sons of Eliab: Nemuel, and Dathan, and Abiram. These are that Dathan and Abiram, the elect of the congregation, who strove against Moses and against Aaron in the company of Korah, when they strove against the Lord; <sup>10</sup>and the earth opened her mouth, and swallowed them up together with Korah, when that company died; what time the fire devoured two hundred and fifty men, and they became a sign. <sup>11</sup>Notwithstanding the sons of Korah died not.

<sup>12</sup>The sons of Simeon after their families: of Nemuel, the family of the Nemuelites; of Jamin, the family of the Jaminites; of Jachin, the family of the Jachinites; <sup>13</sup>of Zerah, the family of the Zerahites; of Shaul, the family of the Shaulites. <sup>14</sup>These are the families of the Simeonites, twenty and two thousand and two hundred.

<sup>15</sup>The sons of Gad after their families: of Zephon, the family of the Zephonites; of Haggi, the family of the Haggites; of Shuni, the family of the Shunites; <sup>16</sup>of Ozni, the family of the Oznites; of Eri, the family of the Erites; <sup>17</sup>of Arod, the family of the Arodites; of Areli, the family of the Arelites. <sup>18</sup>These are the families of the sons of Gad according to those that were numbered of them, forty thousand and five hundred.

<sup>19</sup>The sons of Judah: Er and Onan; and Er and Onan died in the land of Canaan. <sup>20</sup>And the sons of Judah after their families were: of Shelah, the family of the Shelanites; of Perez, the family of the Perezites; of Zerah, the family of the Zerahites. <sup>21</sup>And the sons of Perez were: of Hezron, the family of the Hezronites; of Hamul, the family of the Hamulites. <sup>22</sup>These are the families of Judah according to those that were numbered of them, threescore and sixteen thousand and five hundred.

<sup>23</sup>The sons of Issachar after their families: of Tola, the family of the Tolaites; of Puvah, the family of the Punites; <sup>24</sup>of Jashub, the family of the Jashubites; of Shimron, the family of the Shimronites. <sup>25</sup>These are the families of Issachar according to those that were numbered of them,

threescore and four thousand and three hundred.

²⁶The sons of Zebulun after their families: of Sered, the family of the Seredites; of Elon, the family of the Elonites; of Jahleel, the family of the Jahleelites. ²⁷These are the families of the Zebulunites according to those that were numbered of them, threescore thousand and five hundred.

²⁸The sons of Joseph after their families: Manasseh and Ephraim. ²⁹The sons of Manasseh: of Machir, the family of the Machirites—and Machir begot Gilead; of Gilead, the family of the Gileadites. ³⁰These are the sons of Gilead: of Iezer, the family of the Iezerites; of Helek, the family of the Helekites; ³¹and of Asriel, the family of the Asrielites; and of Shechem, the family of the Shechemites; ³²and of Shemida, the family of the Shemidaites; and of Hepher, the family of the Hepherites. ³³And Zelophehad the son of Hepher had no sons, but daughters; and the names of the daughters of Zelophehad were Mahlah, and Noah, Hoglah, Milcah, and Tirzah. ³⁴These are the families of Manasseh; and they that were numbered of them were fifty and two thousand and seven hundred.'

³⁵These are the sons of Ephraim after their families: of Shuthelah, the family of the Shuthelahites; of Becher, the family of the Becherites; of Tahan, the family of the Tahanites. ³⁶And these are the sons of Shuthelah: of Eran, the family of the Eranites. ³⁷These are the families of the sons of Ephraim according to those that were numbered of them, thirty and two thousand and five hundred. These are the sons of Joseph after their families.

³⁸The sons of Benjamin after their families: of Bela, the family of the Belaites; of Ashbel, the family of the Ashbelites; of Ahiram, the family of the Ahiramites; ³⁹of Shephupham, the family of the Shuphamites; of Hupham, the family of the Huphamites. ⁴⁰And the sons of Bela were Ard and Naaman; [of Ard,] the family of the Ardites; of Naaman, the family of the Naamites. ⁴¹These are the sons of Benjamin after their families; and they that were numbered of them were forty and five thousand and six hundred.

⁴²These are the sons of Dan after their families: of Shuham, the family of the Shuhamites. These are the families of Dan after their families. ⁴³All the families of the Shuhamites, according to those that were numbered of them, were threescore and four thousand and four hundred.

⁴⁴The sons of Asher after their families: of Imnah, the family of the Imnites; of Ishvi, the family of the Ishvites; of Beriah, the family of the Beriites. ⁴⁵Of the sons of Beriah: of Heber, the family of the Heberites; of Malchiel, the family of the Malchielites. ⁴⁶And the name of the daughter of Asher was Serah. ⁴⁷These are the families of the sons of Asher according to those that were numbered of them, fifty and three thousand and four hundred.

⁴⁸The sons of Naphtali after their families: of Jahzeel, the family of the Jahzeelites; of Guni, the family of the Gunites; ⁴⁹of Jezer, the family of the Jezerites; of Shillem, the family of the Shillemites. ⁵⁰These are the families of Naphtali according to their families; and they that were numbered of

them were forty and five thousand and four hundred.

⁵¹These are they that were numbered of the children of Israel, six hundred thousand and a thousand and seven hundred and thirty.

⁵²And the Lord spoke unto Moses, saying: ⁵³'Unto these the land shall be divided for an inheritance according to the number of names. ⁵⁴To the more thou shalt give the more inheritance, and to the fewer thou shalt give the less inheritance; to each one according to those that were numbered of it shall its inheritance be given. ⁵⁵Notwithstanding the land shall be divided by lot; according to the names of the tribes of their fathers they shall inherit. ⁵⁶According to the lot shall their inheritance be divided between the more and the fewer.'

⁵⁷And these are they that were numbered of the Levites after their families: of Gershon, the family of the Gershonites; of Kohath, the family of the Kohathites; of Merari, the family of the Merarites. ⁵⁸These are the families of Levi: the family of the Libnites, the family of the Hebronites, the family of the Mahlites, the family of the Mushites, the family of the Korahites. And Kohath begot Amram. ⁵⁹And the name of Amram's wife was Jochebed, the daughter of Levi, who was born to Levi in Egypt; and she bore unto Amram Aaron and Moses, and Miriam their sister. ⁶⁰And unto Aaron were born Nadab and Abihu, Eleazar and Ithamar. ⁶¹And Nadab and Abihu died, when they offered strange fire before the Lord. ⁶²And they that were numbered of them were twenty and three thousand, every male from a month old and upward; for they were not numbered among the children of Israel, because there was no inheritance given them among the children of Israel.

⁶³These are they that were numbered by Moses and Eleazar the priest, who numbered the children of Israel in the plains of Moab by the Jordan at Jericho. ⁶⁴But among these there was not a man of them that were numbered by Moses and Aaron the priest, who numbered the children of Israel in the wilderness of Sinai. ⁶⁵For the Lord had said of them: 'They shall surely die in the wilderness.' And there was not left a man of them, save Caleb the son of Jephunneh, and Joshua the son of Nun.

NUM 27:1Then drew near the daughters of Zelophehad, the son of Hepher, the son of Gilead, the son of Machir, the son of Manasseh, of the families of Manasseh the son of Joseph; and these are the names of his daughters: Mahlah, Noah, and Hoglah, and Milcah, and Tirzah. ²And they stood before Moses, and before Eleazar the priest, and before the princes and all the congregation, at the door of the tent of meeting, saying: ³'Our father died in the wilderness, and he was not among the company of them that gathered themselves together against the Lord in the company of Korah, but he died in his own sin; and he had no sons. ⁴Why should the name of our father be done away from among his family, because he had no son? Give unto us a possession among the brethren of our father.' ⁵And Moses brought their cause before the Lord. ⁶And the Lord spoke unto Moses, saying: ⁷'The daughters of Zelophehad speak right: thou shalt surely give them a possession of an inheritance among their father's brethren; and thou shalt cause the inheritance of their father to pass unto them. [8]And thou shalt speak unto the children of Israel, saying: If a man die, and have no son, then ye shall cause his inheritance to pass unto his daughter. [9]And if he have no daughter, then ye shall give his inheritance unto his brethren. [10]And if he have no brethren, then ye shall give his inheritance unto his father's brethren. [11]And if his father have no brethren, then ye shall give his inheritance unto his kinsman that is next to him of his family, and he shall possess it. And it shall be unto the children of Israel a statute of judgment, as the Lord commanded Moses.'

# Meat Offerings and Holidays
## Numbers 28-29

## Notes

These chapters about the laws for meat offerings and for holidays give more details about laws that are also in Leviticus. Thus, they are probably an independent document added by the redactor.

## Text

[28:1]And the Lord spoke unto Moses, saying: [2]Command the children of Israel, and say unto them:

My food which is presented unto Me for offerings made by fire, of a sweet savour unto Me, shall ye observe to offer unto Me in its due season. [3]And thou shalt say unto them: This is the offering made by fire which ye shall bring unto the Lord: he-lambs of the first year without blemish, two day by day, for a continual burnt-offering. [4]The one lamb shalt thou offer in the morning, and the other lamb shalt thou offer at dusk; [5]and the tenth part of an ephah of fine flour for a meal-offering, mingled with the fourth part of a hin of beaten oil. [6]It is a continual burnt-offering, which was offered in mount Sinai, for a sweet savour, an offering made by fire unto the Lord. [7]And the drink-offering thereof shall be the fourth part of a hin for the one lamb; in the holy place shalt thou pour out a drink-offering of strong drink unto the Lord. [8]And the other lamb shalt thou present at dusk; as the meal-offering of the morning, and as the drink-offering thereof, thou shalt present it, an offering made by fire, of a sweet savour unto the Lord.

[9]And on the sabbath day two he-lambs of the first year without blemish, and two tenth parts of an ephah of fine flour for a meal-offering, mingled with oil, and the drink-offering thereof. [10]This is the burnt-offering of every sabbath, beside the continual burnt-offering, and the drink-offering thereof.

[11]And in your new moons ye shall present a burnt-offering unto the Lord: two young bullocks, and one ram, seven he-lambs of the first year without blemish; [12]and three tenth parts of an ephah of fine flour for a meal-offering, mingled with oil, for each bullock; and two tenth parts of fine flour for a meal-offering, mingled with oil, for the one ram; [13]and a several tenth part of fine flour mingled with oil for a meal-offering unto every lamb; for a burnt-offering of a sweet savour, an offering made by fire unto the Lord. [14]And their drink-offerings shall be half a hin of wine for a bullock, and the third part of a hin for the ram, and the fourth part of a hin for a lamb. This is the burnt-offering of every new moon throughout the months of the year. [15]And one he-goat for a sin-offering unto the Lord; it shall be offered beside the continual burnt-offering, and the drink-offering thereof.

[16]And in the first month, on the fourteenth day of the month, is the Lord's passover. [17]And on the fifteenth day of this month shall be a feast; seven days shall unleavened bread be eaten. [18]In the first day shall be a holy convocation; ye shall do no manner of servile work; [19]but ye shall present an offering made by fire, a burnt-offering unto the Lord: two young bullocks, and one ram, and seven he-lambs of the first year; they shall be unto you without blemish; [20]and their meal-offering, fine flour mingled with oil; three tenth parts shall ye offer for a bullock, and two tenth parts for the ram; [21]a several tenth part shalt thou offer for every lamb of the seven lambs; [22]and one he-goat for a sin-offering, to make atonement for you. [23]Ye shall offer these beside the burnt-offering of the morning, which is for a continual burnt-offering. [24]After this manner ye shall offer daily, for seven days, the food of the offering made by fire, of a sweet savour unto the Lord; it shall be offered beside the continual burnt-offering, and the drink-offering thereof. [25]And on the seventh day ye shall have a holy convocation; ye shall do no manner of servile work.

[26]Also in the day of the first-fruits, when ye bring a new meal-offering unto the Lord in your feast of weeks, ye shall have a holy convocation: ye shall do no manner of servile work; [27]but ye shall present a burnt-offering for a sweet savour unto the Lord: two young bullocks, one ram, seven he-lambs of the first year; [28]and their meal-offering, fine flour mingled with oil, three tenth parts for each bullock, two tenth parts for the one ram, [29]a several tenth part for every lamb of the seven lambs; [30]one he-goat, to make atonement for you. [31]Beside the continual burnt-offering, and the meal-offering thereof, ye shall offer them—they shall be unto you without blemish—and their drink-offerings.

[29:1]And in the seventh month, on the first day of the month, ye shall have a holy convocation: ye shall do no manner of servile work; it is a day of blowing the horn unto you. [2]And ye shall prepare a burnt-offering for a sweet savour unto the Lord: one young bullock, one ram, seven he-lambs of the first year without blemish; [3]and their meal-offering, fine flour mingled with oil, three tenth parts for the bullock, two tenth part for the ram, [4]and one tenth part for every lamb of the seven lambs; [5]and one he-goat for a sin-offering, to make atonement for you; [6]beside the burnt-offering of the new moon, and the meal-offering thereof, and the continual burnt-offering and the meal-offering thereof, and their drink-offerings, according unto their ordinance, for a sweet savour, an offering made by fire unto the Lord.

[7]And on the tenth day of this seventh month ye shall have a holy convocation; and ye shall afflict your souls; ye shall do no manner of work; [8]but ye shall present a burnt-offering unto the Lord for a sweet savour: one young bullock, one ram, seven he-lambs of the first year; they shall be unto you without blemish; [9]and their meal-offering, fine flour mingled with oil, three tenth parts for the bullock, two tenth parts for the one ram, [10]a several tenth part for every lamb of the seven lambs; [11]one he-goat for a sin-offering; beside the sin-offering of atonement, and the continual burnt-offering, and the meal-offering thereof, and their drink-offerings.

[12]And on the fifteenth day of the seventh month ye shall have a holy convocation: ye shall do no manner of servile work, and ye shall keep a feast unto the Lord seven days; [13]and ye shall present a burnt-offering, an offering made by fire, of a sweet savour unto the Lord: thirteen young bullocks, two rams, fourteen he-lambs of the first year; they shall be without blemish; [14]and their meal-offering, fine flour mingled with oil, three tenth parts for every bullock of the thirteen bullocks, two tenth parts for each ram of the two rams, [15]and a several tenth part for every lamb of the fourteen lambs; [16]and one he-goat for a sin-offering; beside the continual burnt-offering, the meal-offering thereof, and the drink-offering thereof.

[17]And on the second day ye shall present twelve young bullocks, two rams, fourteen he-lambs of the first year without blemish; [18]and their meal-offering and their drink-offerings for the bullocks, for the rams, and for the lambs, according to their number, after the ordinance; [19]and one he-goat for a sin-offering; beside the continual burnt-offering, and the meal-offering thereof, and their drink-offerings.

[20]And on the third day eleven bullocks, two rams, fourteen he-lambs of the first year without blemish; [21]and their meal-offering and their drink-offerings for the bullocks, for the rams, and for the lambs, according to their number, after the ordinance; [22]and one he-goat for a sin-offering; beside the continual burnt-offering, and the meal-offering thereof, and the drink-offering thereof.

[23]And on the fourth day ten bullocks, two rams, fourteen he-lambs of the first year without blemish; [24]their meal-offering and their drink-offerings for the bullocks, for the rams, and for the lambs, according to their number, after the ordinance; [25]and one he-goat for a sin-offering; beside the continual burnt-offering, the meal-offering thereof, and the drink-offering thereof.

[26]And on the fifth day nine bullocks, two rams, fourteen he-lambs of the first year without blemish; [27]and their meal-offering and their drink-offerings for the bullocks, for the rams, and for the lambs, according to their

number, after the ordinance; <sup>28</sup>and one he-goat for a sin-offering; beside the continual burnt-offering, and the meal-offering thereof, and the drink-offering thereof.

<sup>29</sup>And on the sixth day eight bullocks, two rams, fourteen he-lambs of the first year without blemish; <sup>30</sup>and their meal-offering and their drink-offerings for the bullocks, for the rams, and for the lambs, according to their number, after the ordinance; <sup>31</sup>and one he-goat for a sin-offering; beside the continual burnt-offering, the meal-offering thereof, and the drink-offerings thereof.

<sup>32</sup>And on the seventh day seven bullocks, two rams, fourteen he-lambs of the first year without blemish; <sup>33</sup>and their meal-offering and their drink-offerings for the bullocks, for the rams, and for the lambs, according to their number, after the ordinance; <sup>34</sup>and one he-goat for a sin-offering; beside the continual burnt-offering, the meal-offering thereof, and the drink-offering thereof.

<sup>35</sup>On the eighth day ye shall have a solemn assembly: ye shall do no manner of servile work; <sup>36</sup>but ye shall present a burnt-offering, an offering made by fire, of a sweet savour unto the Lord: one bullock, one ram, seven he-lambs of the first year without blemish; <sup>37</sup>their meal-offering and their drink-offerings for the bullock, for the ram, and for the lambs, shall be according to their number, after the ordinance; <sup>38</sup>and one he-goat for a sin-offering; beside the continual burnt-offering, and the meal-offering thereof, and the drink-offering thereof.

<sup>39</sup>These ye shall offer unto the Lord in your appointed seasons, beside your vows, and your freewill-offerings, whether they be your burnt-offerings, or your meal-offerings, or your drink-offerings, or your peace-offerings.

# Miscellaneous Commandments
# Numbers 30

## Notes

It is difficult to tell whether this text is by P or is a separate text added by R. In general, the commandments in P are given at Mt. Sinai, so this set of commandments given after leaving the mountain are out of place. These commandments also interrupt the narrative flow.

Because this edition assumes that the J, E, and P texts are continuous as an experiment to test the documentary hypothesis, it puts this out-of-place text in this section of Other Texts.

# Text

NUM 30:1And Moses told the children of Israel according to all that the Lord commanded Moses.

²And Moses spoke unto the heads of the tribes of the children of Israel, saying:

This is the thing which the Lord hath commanded. ³When a man voweth a vow unto the Lord, or sweareth an oath to bind his soul with a bond, he shall not break his word; he shall do according to all that proceedeth out of his mouth. ⁴Also when a woman voweth a vow unto the Lord, and bindeth herself by a bond, being in her father's house, in her youth, ⁵and her father heareth her vow, or her bond wherewith she hath bound her soul, and her father holdeth his peace at her, then all her vows shall stand, and every bond wherewith she hath bound her soul shall stand. ⁶But if her father disallow her in the day that he heareth, none of her vows, or of her bonds wherewith she hath bound her soul, shall stand; and the Lord will forgive her, because her father disallowed her. ⁷And if she be married to a husband, while her vows are upon her, or the clear utterance of her lips, wherewith she hath bound her soul; ⁸and her husband hear it, whatsoever day it be that he heareth it, and hold his peace at her; then her vows shall stand, and her bonds wherewith she hath bound her soul shall stand. ⁹But if her husband disallow her in the day that he heareth it, then he shall make void her vow which is upon her, and the clear utterance of her lips, wherewith she hath bound her soul; and the Lord will forgive her. ¹⁰But the vow of a widow, or of her that is divorced, even every thing wherewith she hath bound her soul, shall stand against her. ¹¹And if a woman vowed in her husband's house, or bound her soul by a bond with an oath, ¹²and her husband heard it, and held his peace at her, and disallowed her not, then all her vows shall stand, and every bond wherewith she bound her soul shall stand. ¹³But if her husband make them null and void in the day that he heareth them, then whatsoever proceeded out of her lips, whether it were her vows, or the bond of her soul, shall not stand: her husband hath made them void; and the Lord will forgive her. ¹⁴Every vow, and every binding oath to afflict the soul, her husband may let it stand, or her husband may make it void. ¹⁵But if her husband altogether hold his peace at her from day to day, then he causeth all her vows to stand, or all her bonds, which are upon her; he hath let them stand, because he held his peace at her in the day that he heard them. ¹⁶But if he shall make them null and void after that he hath heard them, then he shall bear her iniquity. ¹⁷These are the statutes, which the Lord commanded Moses, between a man and his wife, between a father and his daughter, being in her youth, in her father's house.

# The Stages of the Exodus
## Numbers 33

## Notes

Numbers 33, which summarizes all the stages of Israel's journey through the wilderness, is an independent document added by R.

Some scholars believe that R took information from Numbers 33 and added it to the narratives in the other texts to give the narratives more continuity. For reasons that are discussed in Appendix 2, this edition considers the stages of Israel's journey that are contained in the narratives to be independent of this summary of the stages of the exodus in Numbers 33.

## Text

NUM 33:1These are the stages of the children of Israel, by which they went forth out of the land of Egypt by their hosts under the hand of Moses and Aaron. 2And Moses wrote their goings forth, stage by stage, by the commandment of the Lord; and these are their stages at their goings forth. 3And they journeyed from Rameses in the first month, on the fifteenth day of the first month; on the morrow after the passover the children of Israel went out with a high hand in the sight of all the Egyptians, 4while the Egyptians were burying them that the Lord had smitten among them, even all their first-born; upon their gods also the Lord executed judgments. 5And the children of Israel journeyed from Rameses, and pitched in Succoth. 6And they journeyed from Succoth, and pitched in Etham, which is in the edge of the wilderness. 7And they journeyed from Etham, and turned back unto Pi-hahiroth, which is before Baal-zephon; and they pitched before Migdol. 8And they journeyed from Penehahiroth, and passed through the midst of the sea into the wilderness; and they went three days' journey in the wilderness of Etham, and pitched in Marah. 9And they journeyed from Marah, and came unto Elim; and in Elim were twelve springs of water, and threescore and ten palm-trees; and they pitched there. 10And they journeyed from Elim, and pitched by the Red Sea. 11And they journeyed from the Red Sea, and pitched in the wilderness of Sin. 12And they journeyed from the wilderness of Sin, and pitched in Dophkah. 13And they journeyed from Dophkah, and pitched in Alush. 14And they journeyed from Alush, and pitched in Rephidim, where was no water for the people to drink. 15And they journeyed from Rephidim, and pitched in the wilderness of Sinai. 16And they journeyed from the wilderness of Sinai, and pitched in Kibroth-hattaavah. 17And they journeyed from Kibroth-hattaavah, and pitched in Hazeroth. 18And they journeyed from Hazeroth, and pitched in Rithmah. 19And they journeyed from Rithmah, and pitched in Rimmon-perez. 20And they journeyed from Rimmon-perez, and pitched in Libnah. 21And they journeyed from Libnah, and pitched in Rissah. [22]And they journeyed from Rissah, and pitched in Kehelah. [23]And they journeyed from Kehelah, and pitched in mount Shepher. [24]And they journeyed from mount Shepher, and pitched in Haradah. [25]And they journeyed from Haradah, and pitched in Makheloth. [26]And they journeyed from Makheloth, and pitched in Tahath. [27]And they journeyed from Tahath, and pitched in Terah. [28]And they journeyed from Terah, and pitched in Mithkah. [29]And they journeyed from Mithkah, and pitched in Hashmonah. [30]And they journeyed from Hashmonah, and pitched in Moseroth. [31]And they journeyed from Moseroth, and pitched in Bene-jaakan. [32]And they journeyed from Bene-jaakan, and pitched in Hor-haggidgad. [33]And they journeyed from Hor-haggidgad, and pitched in Jotbah. [34]And they journeyed from Jotbah, and pitched in Abronah. [35]And they journeyed from Abronah, and pitched in Ezion-geber. [36]And they journeyed from Ezion-geber, and pitched in the wilderness of Zin—the same is Kadesh. [37]And they journeyed from Kadesh, and pitched in mount Hor, in the edge of the land of Edom.— [38]And Aaron the priest went up into mount Hor at the commandment of the Lord, and died there, in the fortieth year after the children of Israel were come out of the land of Egypt, in the fifth month, on the first day of the month. [39]And Aaron was a hundred and twenty and three years old when he died in mount Hor. [40]And the Canaanite, the king of Arad, who dwelt in the South in the land of Canaan, heard of the coming of the children of Israel.— [41]And they journeyed from mount Hor, and pitched in Zalmonah. [42]And they journeyed from Zalmonah, and pitched in Punon. [43]And they journeyed from Punon, and pitched in Oboth. [44]And they journeyed from Oboth, and pitched in Ije-abarim, in the border of Moab. [45]And they journeyed from Ijim, and pitched in Dibon-gad. [46]And they journeyed from Dibon-gad, and pitched in Almon-diblathaim. [47]And they journeyed from Almon-diblathaim, and pitched in the mountains of Abarim, in front of Nebo. [48]And they journeyed from the mountains of Abarim, and pitched in the plains of Moab by the Jordan at Jericho. [49]And they pitched by the Jordan, from Beth-jeshimoth even unto Abel-shittim in the plains of Moab.

# Part IV
# Appendices

# Appendix 1
# P's Timeline

Some scholars believe that R added pre- and post-flood genealogies that were in a separate document to make the combined text more continuous. This edition initially assumed that P quoted pre-flood and post-flood genealogies in order to make P continuous, part of its experiment to see whether the texts could be continuous, but after reading the P text with these genealogies, it is clear that they are part of a key unifying element in the P text, its continuous timeline. The genealogies are the beginning of the timeline, starting at the creation, and the rest of the P text extends that timeline to the arrival in Canaan.

Here is a summary of the timeline:

- GEN 5:3 Adam lived a hundred and thirty years, and begot ... Seth.
- GEN 5:6 And Seth lived a hundred and five years, and begot Enosh.
- GEN 5:9 And Enosh lived ninety years, and begot Kenan.
- GEN 5:12 And Kenan lived seventy years, and begot Mahalalel.
- GEN 5:15 And Mahalalel lived sixty and five years, and begot Jared.
- GEN 5:18 And Jared lived a hundred sixty and two years, and begot Enoch.
- GEN 5:21 And Enoch lived sixty and five years, and begot Methuselah.
- GEN 5:25 And Methuselah lived a hundred eighty and seven years, and begot Lamech.
- GEN 5:28 And Lamech lived a hundred eighty and two years, and begot a son. 29 And he called his name Noah....
- GEN 5:32 And Noah was five hundred years old; and Noah begot Shem, Ham, and Japheth.
- GEN 11:10 Shem was a hundred years old, and begot Arpachshad two years after the flood.
- GEN 11:12 And Arpachshad lived five and thirty years, and begot Shelah.
- GEN 11:14 And Shelah lived thirty years, and begot Eber.
- GEN 11:16 And Eber lived four and thirty years, and begot Peleg.
- GEN 11:18 And Peleg lived thirty years, and begot Reu.
- GEN 11:20 And Reu lived two and thirty years, and begot Serug.
- GEN 11:22 And Serug lived thirty years, and begot Nahor.
- GEN 11:24 And Nahor lived nine and twenty years, and begot Terah.

- GEN 11:26And Terah lived seventy years, and begot Abram, Nahor, and Haran.
- GEN 21:5And Abraham was a hundred years old, when his son Isaac was born unto him.
- GEN 25:26bAnd Isaac was threescore years old when she *[Rebekah]* bore (them) *[Jacob and Esau]*.
- GEN 47:8And Pharaoh said unto Jacob *[when Israel came to Egypt]* 'How many are the days of the years of thy life?' 9And Jacob said unto Pharaoh: 'The days of the years of my sojournings are a hundred and thirty years;
- EX 12:40Now the time that the children of Israel dwelt in Egypt was four hundred and thirty years. 41And it came to pass at the end of four hundred and thirty years, even the selfsame day it came to pass, that all the host of the Lord went out from the land of Egypt.
- NUM 14:33And your children shall be wanderers in the wilderness forty years.

Notice that Pharaoh asks Jacob just one question when they meet, "GEN 47:8How many are the days of the years of thy life?" This is what is needed to continue P's timeline: before this point, the timeline is based on parents' ages when their sons were born, but after this point, the timeline is based on the number of years after Israel came to Egypt.

The P text also dates important events on this timeline. For example, it says: "GEN7:6And Noah was six hundred years old when the flood of waters was upon the earth" and "GEN 12:4bAnd Abram was seventy and five years old when he departed out of Haran."

(But note that P also gives people's ages when important events happen in cases where they do not fit on the timeline. He tells us "GEN 41:46aAnd Joseph was thirty years old when he stood before Pharaoh king of Egypt," though he does not place Joseph's birth on the timeline by telling us how old Jacob was when Joseph was born.[124] He also tells us "EX 7:7And Moses was fourscore years old, and Aaron fourscore and three years old, when they spoke unto Pharaoh," but he does not place their births on the timeline. It seems that P's pedantic attention to detail led him to create the timeline and also led him to give people's ages when available, even if their births are not on the timeline.)

It is interesting to ask whether P realized that there are rounding errors if we date events using this timeline. We say that someone is 50 years old, for example, if he is 50 years and one day, 50 years and one month, or 50 years and eleven months old. This rounding error prevents us from adding up the numbers on this timeline to get the number of years after creation. For example, the P text says:

GEN 5:3Adam lived a hundred and thirty years, and begot ... Seth.

6And Seth lived a hundred and five years, and begot Enosh.

⁹And Enosh lived ninety years, and begot Kenan.

If we simply add those numbers up, we calculate that Kenan was born 130 + 105 + 90 = 325 years after creation. But Adam actually might have been 130 years and 6 month old when Seth was born, Seth might have been 105 years and 5 months when Enosh was born, and Enosh might have been 90 years and 2 months when Kenan was born, which would mean that Kenan was born in the year 326 after creation, not 325 after creation.

If births are distributed randomly, there would be a rounding error of about 6 months in each generation, which comes to about 9 years in the 18 generations between Noah and Abraham—but 18 is a small enough number that the distribution might not be random, so we cannot calculate exactly how many years after creation Abraham was born.

In seventeenth-century England, Bishop Ussher used these genealogies as part of his calculation of the exact age of the world and concluded that the creation occurred in 4004 BC. If a well-educated English bishop did not realize that this rounding error makes it impossible to calculate the exact year after creation when people in these genealogies were born, then it is plausible that P also did not realize it and that he thought his timeline could be used to calculate the exact year after creation when the events in the Bible occurred.

Of course, we will never know for sure what P was thinking. These dates might just be another example of P's precise way of providing details, rather than an attempt to calculate how many years after creation events occurred.

# Appendix 2
# The Stages of the Exodus

Scholars agree about some additions that R made to the source texts. Most additions are added in one location and are meant to smooth over transitions between the JE and P texts or insertions of documents from other texts, but some additions are used in many places and are meant to unify the combined text.

As one pervasive addition meant to create a sense of unity in his patched together work, R added a phrase beginning with "These are the generations of …." in many places. We know that R added it because the same phrase is inserted in all of the source texts. For example,

- J text: "<sup>GEN 2:4</sup>These are the generations of the heaven and of the earth" introduces the story of the creation in the J text.
- P text: "<sup>GEN6:9</sup>These are the generations of Noah" introduces a genealogy in the P text.
- E text: "<sup>GEN 37:2</sup>These are the generations of Jacob" begins the story of Joseph and his brothers (Jacob's sons) in the E text.

"Generations" is a bit of a misleading translation of the Hebrew *toledot*, which can also mean history or records. These examples show that the phrase was not only used to introduce genealogies.

Some scholars say that R also created unity and continuity in the story of the Exodus by inserting transitional passages from an earlier document that is sometimes called the "stations" or the "itinerary" of the exodus. This earlier document is preserved whole in Numbers 33, where each step of the journey is described in the same way, as you can see in this partial quotation:

> <sup>NUM 33:5</sup>And the children of Israel journeyed from Rameses, and pitched in Succoth. <sup>6</sup>And they journeyed from Succoth, and pitched in Etham, which is in the edge of the wilderness. <sup>7</sup>And they journeyed from Etham, and turned back unto Pi-hahiroth, which is before Baal-zephon; and they pitched before Migdol.

Every step is in this form: "They journeyed from … and they pitched …." "Pitched" means "camped"; they pitched their tents.

The theory that R inserted these passages undermines the claim that the J, E, and P texts were originally continuous documents. If these transitional passages were inserted later, many locations in the original texts would simply have one story after another, without any connection or transition between them.

However, there is good reason to reject this theory. As we saw earlier, the insertions of "These are the generations of" are all in the same form, so it is plausible that they were inserted to increase the unity of the final work. By contrast, the stations of the exodus are in different forms in the narratives than they are in Numbers 33, and they are less uniform in the narratives than in Numbers 33. Here are a few examples, with a quotation from the narrative followed by a quotation from Numbers 33 in each one:

- EX 12:37a And the children of Israel journeyed from Rameses to Succoth
- NUM 33:5 And the children of Israel journeyed from Rameses, and pitched in Succoth.

- EX 16:1 And they took their journey from Elim, and all the congregation of the children of Israel came unto the wilderness of Sin,"
- NUM 33:10 And they journeyed from Elim, and pitched by the Red Sea. 11 And they journeyed from the Red Sea, and pitched in the wilderness of Sin.

- EX 17:1 And all the congregation of the children of Israel journeyed from the wilderness of Sin, by their stages, according to the commandment of the Lord, and encamped in Rephidim; and there was no water for the people to drink.
- NUM 33:12 And they journeyed from the wilderness of Sin, and pitched in Dophkah. 13 And they journeyed from Dophkah, and pitched in Alush. 14 And they journeyed from Alush, and pitched in Rephidim, where was no water for the people to drink.

And so it goes: there are places where the narrative of the exodus uses the same phrasing as the itinerary in Numbers 33, but in most places it uses different phrasing. If R inserted these verses from Numbers 33 in the narrative to make it more uniform, why would he change the phrasing in a way that makes it less uniform? Why wouldn't he keep the uniform phrasing used in Numbers 33?

There are also some stages in Numbers 33 that are not included in the narrative at all. For example, there is a long series of places beginning with Rimmon-perez where the itinerary in Numbers 33 says they pitched but which the narrative does not mention:

NUM 33:19 And they journeyed from Rithmah, and pitched in Rimmon-perez. 20 And they journeyed from Rimmon-perez, and pitched in

Libnah. [21]And they journeyed from Libnah, and pitched in Rissah. [22]And they journeyed from Rissah, and pitched in Kehelah. [23]And they journeyed from Kehelah, and pitched in mount Shepher.

And so on: this series of places not mentioned in the narrative continues all the way to verse 30, and there are other stages not mentioned in the narrative besides the ones in this series.

Perhaps R did not add these stages in the itinerary to the narrative of the exodus because he had no narrative material to connect with them, but it is much more decisive that there are also stations in the narrative of the exodus that are not present in Numbers 33: "[NUM 21:18b]And from the wilderness to Mattanah; [19]and from Mattanah to Nahaliel; and from Nahaliel to Bamoth;" These three stations, mentioned in J's account of the journey through the desert, are not mentioned in the itinerary.

There is no plausible explanation of why R would change the text of Numbers 33 to make the wording less uniform if R inserted these stations in the narrative to make it more uniform.

There is only one plausible explanation of all the differences between Numbers 33 and the narrative, explaining why some stations in Numbers 33 are not in the narrative, why some stations in the narrative are not in Numbers 33, and why the wording is different in the narrative and in Numbers. The only plausible explanation is that the stations in the narrative and the stations in Numbers 33 were based on the same traditions but were written independently.

We would expect something similar if two people were writing about any event: most of the details would be the same in the two accounts, each account would include a few details that are not in the other, and the wording describing each detail would usually be different in the two accounts.

Thus, this edition assigns the stages of the exodus in the narratives to the writers of those narratives, not to a redactor copying them from Numbers 33. As a result, the narratives are continuous, rather than jumping from one event to another without any transition.

# Appendix 3
# Passages Removed by R

RJE and R had different approaches to their source documents. When J and E told similar stories, RJE sometimes edited them together to create a text that included both, and he sometimes just included the parts he liked best, patching together the combined story from pieces of the two source texts and leaving gaps in what survives of the J and E text—with more gaps in the E text, since J is a great story-teller. By contrast, R tried to include both the JE and P texts, even when there were discrepancies between them, apparently considering the source documents so important that he did not want to remove anything.

An obvious example of R's approach is the story of Noah, where R kept both the J and the P text despite glaring contradictions about the number of clean animals Noah took on the ark, about the length of time the flood lasted, and about whether Noah sent a raven or dove to see if the water had receded.

Nevertheless, there are some cases where R removed parts of a source text, which are listed in this appendix. Apparently the contradictions were so blatant that he could not include everything from both sources,

## Pre-Flood and Post-Flood Genealogies
### Gen. 4:17-25 (J), 5:1-33 (P), 10:1-31 (J), 11:10-24 (P)

R seems to have removed much of J's pre-flood genealogy and a significant part of her post-flood ideology.

J's pre-flood genealogy has a long genealogy of Cain's descendents but much less about the descendents of Adam's other son, Seth. It says

> GEN 4:25And Adam knew his wife again; and she bore a son, and called his name Seth: 'for God hath appointed me another seed instead of Abel; for Cain slew him.' 26And to Seth, to him also there was born a son; and he called his name Enosh....

But it does not list any other descendents of in the line of Seth.

Some scholars suggest that J only wrote a genealogy of Cain's line and not of Seth's, but it does not make sense that J would provide Cain's line of descendents, which died out at the time of the flood, but not Seth's line of descendents, which survived the flood and became the ancestors of everyone living in J's time. It is more plausible that R removed J's list of Seth's descendents in Genesis 4 because it blatantly contradicted P's list in Genesis 5, and that R kept J's list of Cain's descendents because P (who just records the direct line of descent from Adam to Abraham) did not include a list of Cain's descendents to contradict J's list.

We can see very clearly that this is what R did in the post-flood genealogies.

J's post-flood genealogy includes many lines of descent from each of Noah's sons. Among others, it has the following line of descendents of Shem: Elam, Arpachshad, Shelah, Eber. Then J says: "GEN 10: 25And unto Eber were born two sons; the name of the one was Peleg; for in his days was the earth divided; and his brother's name was Joktan." Then she goes on to list the some descendents of the younger brother Joktan but does not mention the descendents of the elder brother Peleg.

P's post-flood genealogy includes the same line of descendents from Shem to Peleg— Elam, Arpachshad, Shelah, Eber, Peleg—and then it goes on to list this line of descendents of Peleg: Reu, Serug, Nahor, Terah, Abram (Gen. 11:10 to 11:24).

A later part of the J text shows us that some that some of J's post-flood genealogy has been removed, when it says "GEN 11:27Terah begot Abram, Nahor, and Haran." This is the first mention of Terah in the J text, and it makes no sense that J would end the list of Shem's descendents at Peleg and later pull in Terah without ever mentioning him before. There is one plausible explanation of why our J text has a gap in the genealogy that could have introduced Terah: J's genealogy originally extended from Shem to Terah, R included J's line from Shem to Peleg because it agreed with P, and R removed J's line from Peleg to Terah because it contradicted P. This contradiction in a genealogy, which is a list of names, presumably was so blatant that R could not keep it.

The J text also mentions Lot without any introduction: "GEN 12:4So Abram went, as the Lord had spoken unto him; and Lot went with him." This is the first mention of Lot in the J text, and it assumes that the reader knows who Lot is, implying that there is a gap in the text where Lot was introduced. The simplest explanation for this gap is that Lot was also in the post flood genealogy that R eliminated, like Terah.

Since R clearly removed the parts of J's post-flood genealogy that contradicted P, it makes sense that he also removed J's pre-flood genealogy of the descendents of Seth because it contradicted P.

# Joseph and His Brothers
## Gen. 37-41

Most scholars agree that the story of Joseph and his brothers includes this bit of P text: "GEN 41:46aAnd Joseph was thirty years old when he stood before Pharaoh king of Egypt." The mention of Joseph's age is typical of P. Some scholars have not noticed another bit of the P text in this story:

> GEN 37:2Joseph, being seventeen years old, was feeding the flock with his brethren, being still a lad even with the sons of Bilhah, and with the sons of Zilpah, his father's wives; and Joseph brought evil report of them unto their father.

Here, there is a mention of Joseph's age, typical of the P text, and there is also a hint that the P text had a story about Joseph's quarrel with his brothers that is totally different from J's and E's story. In those two texts, Joseph quarreled with all his brothers, but this snippet of the P text implies that he quarreled only with the brothers who were sons of Bilhah and Zilpah, the handmaids of Jacob's wives. P also tells us just a bit earlier which tribes these son's represent: "GEN 35:25and the sons of Bilhah, Rachel's handmaid: Dan and Naphtali; 26and the sons of Zilpah, Leah's handmaid: Gad and Asher."

Combining P's story of a quarrel with these four brothers and JE's story of a quarrel with all eleven brothers would have created such blatant contradictions that R had to remove P's story.

Even the passage that scholars agree is from P, "GEN 41:46aAnd Joseph was thirty years old when he stood before Pharaoh king of Egypt," cannot possibly have been the entirety of what the P text said about Joseph. Even if P had just the briefest summary of the Joseph story (which seems likely), it must have said more than this. Thus, it is clear that R removed part of what the P text said about Joseph and his brothers.

# The Rod of Moses or of Aaron
## Ex. 3:15-4:4, 4:21 (E) 7:8-10 (P)

In the E text, God tells Moses to cast down his rod to turn it into a serpent before Pharaoh:

> EX 3:15And God said moreover unto Moses: 'Thus shalt thou say unto the children of Israel: The Lord *[=YHWH]*, the God of your fathers, the God of Abraham, the God of Isaac, and the God of Jacob, hath sent me unto you; this is My name for ever, and this is My memorial unto all generations. EX 4:1And Moses answered and said: 'But, behold, they will not believe me, nor hearken unto my voice; for they will say: The Lord hath not appeared unto thee.' 2And the Lord said unto him: 'What is that in thy hand?' And he said: 'A rod.' 3And He said: 'Cast it on the ground.' And he cast it on the ground, and it became a serpent; and Moses fled from before it. 4And the Lord said unto Moses: 'Put forth thy hand, and take it by the tail—and he put forth his hand, and laid hold of it, and it became a rod in his hand ... EX 4:21And the Lord said unto

Moses: 'When thou goest back into Egypt, see that thou do before Pharaoh all the wonders which I have put in thy hand.

But in the P text, when they actually come before Pharaoh, it is Aaron rather than Moses who casts down his rod:

> EX 7:8And the Lord spoke unto Moses and unto Aaron, saying:
> 9'When Pharaoh shall speak unto you, saying: Show a wonder
> for you; then thou shalt say unto Aaron: Take thy rod, and cast
> it down before Pharaoh, that it become a serpent.' 10And Moses
> and Aaron went in unto Pharaoh, and they did so, as the Lord had
> commanded; and Aaron cast down his rod before Pharaoh and
> before his servants, and it became a serpent.

Presumably, there was also a passage in the E text where Moses appeared before Pharaoh and cast down his rod, as God had commanded, but R removed this passage because it blatantly contradicted the passage where Aaron cast down the rod.

# Spies to Canaan
## Num. 13

In Numbers 13, Moses sends spies to look at the land of Canaan.

The P text's version of this story, in Numbers 13:1 through 13:16, says that Moses chose one person from the heads of each tribe to act as spies.

The J text version of this story begins as follows:

> NUM 13:17And Moses sent them to spy out the land of Canaan, and
> said unto them: 'Get you up here into the South, and go up into
> the mountains; 18and see the land, what it is; and the people that
> dwelleth therein, whether they are strong or weak, whether they
> are few or many....'

But there is no previous mention of the spies in the J text: it begins with "Moses sent them" and "Moses said to them," without giving us any idea of whom he is sending and talking to.

There is clearly a gap in the J text, something that R removed when he combined these stories from J and from P.

Later, there is a clue to what R removed from the J text. When the Israelites are about to cross the Jordan into Canaan, the tribes of Reuben and Gad said that they wanted to stay on the east side of the Jordan because they had many cattle and there was good grazing land there. In the J text, Moses said to them:

> NUM 32:7And wherefore will ye turn away the heart of the children
> of Israel from going over into the land which the Lord hath given
> them? 8Thus did your fathers, when I sent them from Kadesh-

barnea to see the land. ⁹For when they went up unto the valley of Eshcol, and saw the land, they turned away the heart of the children of Israel, that they should not go into the land which the Lord had given them.

Thus, it seems that the J text said that Moses sent spies from the tribes of Reuben and Gad, who came back and told the Israelites not to invade Canaan.

By contrast, the story in the P text begins "ᴺᵁᴹ ¹³:¹And the Lord spoke unto Moses, saying: ²'Send thou men, that they may spy out the land of Canaan, which I give unto the children of Israel; of every tribe of their fathers shall ye send a man, every one a prince among them'" and continues by listing the names of the person chosen from each tribe to be a spy.

It seems that R omitted the J text about choosing spies from only Reuben and Gad because the self-contradiction would have been too blatant.

# Baal of Peor
## Num. 25

At the beginning of Numbers 25, J blames the worship of Baal of Peor on the Moabites. We have seen J's hostility to the Moabites earlier, where she says that Moab and Ammon descend from incest between Lot and his daughters,[125] and this story is another example of that hostility. In J, Moses has the judges slay those who worshipped Baal of Peor.[126]

Later in Numbers 25, P blames the matter of Peor on the Midianites rather than the Moabites.[127] In P, a plague punishes those who worshipped Baal of Peor. But P's first mention of this plague is

>⁸And he *[Phinehas, grandson of Aaron]* went after the man of Israel into the chamber, and thrust both of them through, the man of Israel, and the woman through her belly. So the plague was stayed from the children of Israel. ⁹And those that died by the plague were twenty and four thousand.

There is no mention in the Bible of this plague beginning, just this description of it ending.

There is clearly a gap in the P text here. The most recent plague in the Bible before this one, also in the P text, was punishment for the Israelites' complaining after Korah's rebellion and was ended, a plague that killed fourteen thousand and seven hundred people before Aaron ended it by burning incense.[128] In the plague of Baal of Peor kills twenty four thousand people before Aaron's grandson Phinehas ends it by murdering the Midianite woman and the Israelite man who brought her. Thus, this plague of Baal Peor is clearly a different from the plague that punished Korah's rebellion. But there is no mention of the beginning of this plague in the received text of the Bible.

There is a gap in the P text, which must have said that Midianite women led the Israelites to worship Baal of Peor and God punished them by sending a plague. R must have removed this from the P text because it contained such a blatant contradiction of the J text, which says that the Moabites caused the worship of Baal of Peor.

# Appendix 4
# Inept Editing

Why did R include blatant contradictions in some places and remove them in others? For example, we have seen that J and P contradict each other about the order of creation, the number of clean animals that Noah brought into the ark, and the length of the flood. R included these contradictions, though he could have eliminated them by removing just a few verses, less of a change than he made in other places to eliminate contradictions.

The answer might be inept editing. R did such a skillful job of weaving JE and P together that we tend to think he was perfect, but there clearly are some places where his editing was inept.

This appendix looks at places where editing is so obvious that it shows clearly that the Bible was created by editing together source documents.

## Dwelling in Booths
**Lev, 23:39-43**

There is a case where we have some external evidence that R added to his source texts, and that he placed the added text ineptly.

Many Jews today believe that the custom of eating their meals in temporary booths during the Sukkot holiday goes back to the Israelites' journey through the desert, but the book of Nehemiah tells us that it began much later, at the time when Ezra read the entire Torah to the people:

> Nehemiah 8:13 And on the second day were gathered together the heads of fathers' houses of all the people, the priests, and the Levites, unto Ezra the scribe, even to give attention to the words of the Law. 14And they found written in the Law, how that the Lord had commanded by Moses, that the children of Israel should dwell in booths in the feast of the seventh month; 15and that they should publish and proclaim in all their cities, and in Jerusalem, saying: 'Go forth unto the mount, and fetch olive branches, and branches of wild olive, and myrtle branches, and palm branches, and branches of thick trees, to make booths, as it is written.' 16So the people went forth, and brought them, and made themselves booths, every one upon the roof of his house, and in their courts, and in the courts of the house of God, and in the broad place of the water gate, and in

the broad place of the gate of Ephraim. [17]And all the congregation of them that were come back out of the captivity made booths, and dwelt in the booths; for since the days of Joshua the son of Nun unto that day had not the children of Israel done so. And there was very great gladness.

When we look at this commandment to dwell in booths in the Torah, it seems strangely out of place:

> LEV 23:39Howbeit on the fifteenth day of the seventh month, when ye have gathered in the fruits of the land, ye shall keep the feast of the Lord seven days; on the first day shall be a solemn rest, and on the eighth day shall be a solemn rest. [40]And ye shall take you on the first day the fruit of goodly trees, branches of palm-trees, and boughs of thick trees, and willows of the brook, and ye shall rejoice before the Lord your God seven days. [41]And ye shall keep it a feast unto the Lord seven days in the year; it is a statute for ever in your generations; ye shall keep it in the seventh month. [42]Ye shall dwell in booths seven days; all that are home-born in Israel shall dwell in booths; [43]that your generations may know that I made the children of Israel to dwell in booths, when I brought them out of the land of Egypt: I am the Lord your God.

Verse 41 sounds like the conclusion of the set of commandments about the holiday of Sukkot: "it is a statute for ever in your generations; ye shall keep it in the seventh month." But then another commandment is added in verse 42 about dwelling in booths.

The most plausible explanation for why the Israelites never knew about this commandment from the days of Joshua until it was discovered in the days of Nehemiah and Ezra is that it did not exist before those later days. R added it when he put together the version of the Torah that Ezra was reading, and his editing was a bit inept, so the commandment is out of place. It would fit into the text of Leviticus more seamlessly if R had put Leviticus 23:41, the conclusion about keeping the laws of this festival, after Leviticus 23:42, which has the commandment about dwelling in booths.

Richard Elliott Friedman has argued that Ezra himself, or one of his close associates, was R.[129] If it was Ezra, this incident would discredit him: he would have been deliberately deceptive, giving everyone the impression that this commandment was always in the Torah, even though he knew that he had recently inserted it. It is kinder to assume that an associate of Ezra had added it earlier, but of course, there is no way of knowing.

# Jacob and Esau
## Gen. 26-28

P's story of Jacob going to Laban to find a wife goes on for two verses and then is interrupted by a separate long story, making it difficult to follow. Here is the P text of the beginning of this story without the interruption:

> GEN 26:34And when Esau was forty years old, he took to wife Judith the daughter of Beeri the Hittite, and Basemath the daughter of Elon the Hittite. 35And they were a bitterness of spirit unto Isaac and to Rebekah. GEN 27:46And Rebekah said to Isaac: 'I am weary of my life because of the daughters of Heth. If Jacob take a wife of the daughters of Heth, such as these, of the daughters of the land, what good shall my life do me?' GEN 28:1And Isaac called Jacob, and blessed him, and charged him, and said unto him: 'Thou shalt not take a wife of the daughters of Canaan.

This continuous story is interrupted after the first two verses by Genesis 27:1-45, which is the story from J about Jacob stealing Esau's blessing, and this interruption makes it hard to follow the entire story of Jacob's going to find a wife, especially for modern readers who do not know that the Hittites are the same as the sons and daughters of Heth.

Possibly, R put the brief passage about Esau's bad marriages before the story of Jacob stealing his blessing so that Esau's misbehavior in marrying Hittites would give some justification for Jacob getting the blessing, but the combined text does not hold together. In P's story of Esau's marriages, both Isaac and Rebekah disapprove of Esau, but in J's story of the blessing, Isaac wants to bless Esau and does not show any disapproval of him at all.

In addition, in J's story of the blessing, Isaac seems to be on his death bed when he blesses Jacob: he cannot see, and he asks Esau, "GEN 27:4And make me savoury food, such as I love, and bring it to me, that I may eat; that my soul may bless thee before I die.'" In this story, Isaac is disappointed that he has blessed Jacob rather than Esau. But afterwards, in the continuation of P's story of Jacob's going to find a wife, Isaac seems to be healthy again, he deliberately blesses Jacob but not Esau, and Esau leaves because he displeased his father:

> GEN 28:1And Isaac called Jacob, and blessed him, and charged him, and said unto him: 'Thou shalt not take a wife of the daughters of Canaan. 2Arise, go to Paddan-aram, to the house of Bethuel thy mother's father; and take thee a wife from thence of the daughters of Laban thy mother's brother. 3And God Almighty bless thee, and make thee fruitful, and multiply thee, that thou mayest be a congregation of peoples; 4and give thee the blessing of Abraham, to thee, and to thy seed with thee; that thou mayest inherit the land of thy sojournings, which God gave unto Abraham.' 5And Isaac

sent away Jacob; and he went to Paddan-aram unto Laban, son of Bethuel the Aramean, the brother of Rebekah, Jacob's and Esau's mother. [6]Now Esau saw that Isaac had blessed Jacob and sent him away to Paddan-aram, to take him a wife from thence; and that as he blessed him he gave him a charge, saying: 'Thou shalt not take a wife of the daughters of Canaan'; [7]and that Jacob hearkened to his father and his mother, and was gone to Paddan-aram; [8]and Esau saw that the daughters of Canaan pleased not Isaac his father; [9]so Esau went unto Ishmael, and took unto the wives that he had Mahalath the daughter of Ishmael Abraham's son, the sister of Nebaioth, to be his wife.

These two versions of the story just do not hold together, and they were obviously patched together from two inconsistent sources. The editing is particularly inept at the beginning, where the first two verses of the story from P about Esau's wives is separated from the rest of that story by the entire story from J of Jacob stealing Esau's blessing.

# Third Story of Joseph
## Gen. 35:25

As we saw in Appendix 3, the P text gives a different account of the quarrel between Jacob and his brothers than the other two texts:

> GEN 37:2...Joseph, being seventeen years old, was feeding the flock with his brethren, being still a lad even with the sons of Bilhah, and with the sons of Zilpah, his father's wives; and Joseph brought evil report of them unto their father.

In the other two texts, Joseph offends all of his brothers by telling them his dreams and by wearing a coat of many colors; in the P text he offends only the sons of the Jacob's concubines by telling Jacob about something they did that was wrong.

Presumably, the story in the P text must have contradicted the JE text so blatantly that R removed it.

It makes sense that R added the other one of the two P passages, because it gives extra information about Joseph's age without blatantly contradicting the other texts. "GEN 41:46And Joseph was thirty years old when he stood before Pharaoh king of Egypt"

It does not make sense that R included the quarrel with only the sons of Bilhah and Zilpah when he added the P passage in Genesis 37:2. To give the extra information about Joseph's age at the time of the quarrel with his brothers, he should have included only "GEN 37:2...Joseph, being seventeen years old, was feeding the flock with his brethren, being still a lad"; apparently, it was simply a mistake to include the a bit of extra text saying "even with the sons of Bilhah, and with the sons of Zilpah, his father's wives; and Joseph brought evil report of them unto their father." It is a prime example of inept editing.

(By the way, in this passage, the Hebrew word translated as "wives of" is *nashei*, which can mean either "wives of" or "women of." In this case, it clearly means "women," since it refers to Jacob's concubines Bilhah and Zilpah, not to his wives Leah and Rachel.)

People who work as editors today might find some comfort in considering that R, undoubtedly the most influential editor of all time, was occasionally inept.

# Appendix 5
# The Early Myths

The Bible begins with a series of familiar myths: Adam and Eve, Cain and Abel, Noah's flood, and the tower of Babel. It also has brief references to other myths.

One of the most interesting facts about the E text is that it does not include any of these myths. It starts with Abraham, and it is concerned with the patriarchs and Moses. All of the earlier myths were introduced by the J text, which was strongly influenced by pagan religions of surrounding peoples, and some were also included in the P text, since P knew them from the JE text. E might have known some or all of these myths, but he left them out, showing that he did not consider them essential to the Israelite religion.

This fact is important because creationism has discredited the Bible. We know that the different species of living organisms were not created in the beginning, as Genesis says; they were formed by evolution and have changed over time. Fundamentalists who believe that the entire Bible is literally true look foolish when they contradict the scientific consensus. But, in fact, creation is not part of the E text, the text of the Bible that is closest to the religion of the earliest Israelite priests.

It is also important because, when scholars found that some of these myths are derived from the myths of surrounding peoples, this also was said to discredit the Bible. But the E text includes only the stories of the patriarchs and the exodus, which are specific to the Israelites; these earlier myths were not part of the religion of the earliest Israelite priests.

Finally, it is important because it makes the E text unique. Every other early religion includes some sort of creation myth. We have to wonder why E is so different from other early religions.

Of course, it is not surprising that J was influenced by the myths and the view of God that surrounding peoples had. As we have seen, she was the only writer of the four texts who was not a priest. She was a member of the court of Judah. She tells us that the Judah had three children from a Canaanite wife, indicating that the tribe had a strong mix of Canaanite ancestry and perhaps also of Canaanite religious traditions. The court was multi-cultural, because kings took wives from surrounding kingdoms to cement alliances, so she must have also been exposed to the religions of surrounding peoples.

The myths that she included at the beginning of the Bible come from a variety of sources. This appendix speculates about what the sources may have been.

# Expulsion from Eden

The story of the Garden of Eden seems to be based on a myth about the beginnings of farming. In Eden, humans lived without work, but the serpent convinced Eve to eat the forbidden apple, and after they were expelled from Eden, they had to do the hard work of farming to produce their food. God says to Adam:

> GEN 3:17 …cursed is the ground for thy sake; in toil shalt thou eat of it all the days of thy life. [18]Thorns also and thistles shall it bring forth to thee; and thou shalt eat the herb of the field. [19]In the sweat of thy face shalt thou eat bread.

The curse of Adam was that he had to work the ground to produce food, in other words, he had to farm.

Nearby agricultural societies have myths of mother goddesses who are associated with snakes. Many murals of the mother goddess and snake have been discovered on Crete. Nearer to home, the consort of the Canaanite god El was Asherah, who was called "the one of the serpent"; she was shown in reliefs as a nude goddess standing on a lion and holding one or more snakes.[130]

It is plausible that, in the very earliest version of the myth of Eden, Eve was a mother-earth goddess. In Hebrew, her name is *Hava*, which seems to be an archaic form of *Haya*, a feminine singular form of the Hebrew word for life (which is used in the masculine plural *hayim* in Biblical and modern Hebrew). The Bible confirms that Eve's name comes from the word for life, saying: "GEN 3:20And the man called his wife's name Eve; because she was the mother of all living." In reality, the Bible's Eve was the mother of all humans, not of all living things, but the name might date back to the days when Eve was a goddess representing mother earth, with a phallic snake as companion, and was the feminine source of all life.

Many believe that early horticultural societies were matriarchal and their religions centered on earth goddesses; later agricultural societies became patriarchal and developed new patriarchal myths that retained traces of the old matriarchal goddess. For example, the Greeks have the myth of Pandora's box, which unleashed all the world's evils when Pandora opened it. But the name Pandora means "all giver," which implies that she might have originated as mother-earth goddess of a matriarchal society, whose box contained all the good things that the earth gives to humanity.[131] In one place she is called "Pandora, the earth, because she bestows all things necessary for life"[132] When Greeks became patriarchal, they reversed the matriarchal myth and made Pandora the source of evil.[133]

Eve might have a similar history. In matriarchal society, the mother-earth goddess and her serpent were the source of fertility and sustained all life, but when society became patriarchal, the myth was reversed and Eve became the source of the evils of life.

Israel did not go through a matriarchal horticultural phase because it went from herding to patriarchal agriculture. Thus, the myth of Eve and the serpent probably originated in an earlier farming society that did go through a matriarchal phase.

# Cain and Abel

The myth of Cain and Abel also seems to be based on a myth about the beginning of food production, but while the myth of Eve was invented by farmers, the myth of Cain and Abel is told from the point of view of the herders.

Abel the herder and Cain the farmer are brothers. God accepts Abel's sacrifice but rejects Cain's, and Cain becomes so angry that he murders Abel. When Cain denies knowing where his brother is, God says:

> GEN 4:10 … 'What hast thou done? the voice of thy brother's blood crieth unto Me from the ground. [11]And now cursed art thou from the ground, which hath opened her mouth to receive thy brother's blood from thy hand. [12]When thou tillest the ground, it shall not henceforth yield unto thee her strength; a fugitive and a wanderer shalt thou be in the earth.'

This myth seems to originate with herders after the shift from hunting and gathering to farming and herding. The shift led to rapid population growth among farming societies, who had permanent settlements where it was easier to raise more children, so they had to expand their territory to feed their growing numbers. To expand, they had to conquer and cultivate lands used for grazing, which involved killing the herders who used those lands, as Cain the farmer killed Abel the herder.

This myth is told from the herders' point of view. It says that God preferred Abel and rejected the sacrifice of Cain. It gets revenge on the farmers as God punishes Cain by making the ground bear less food for him and making him into a fugitive and a wanderer. Herders were nomadic, while farmers lived in permanent settlements; this punishment makes the farmer more of a wanderer than the herder was.

Adam and Eve is the myth of a farming society, while Cain and Abel is the myth of a herding society that resents the encroachments of farming societies. It could be a myth that J borrowed from some surrounding herding society or it could be a myth that dates back to early ancestors of the Israelites, who lived long before the patriarchs.

# Noah and the Flood

Because people were evil, "GEN 6:6...it repented the Lord that He had made man on the earth, and it grieved Him at His heart." God decided to destroy life with a flood and to save one righteous man, Noah. In the J text, God told Noah to build an ark use it to save his household and seven pairs of all clean animals (animals suitable for sacrifice) and one pair of unclean animals. It rained forty days and forty nights. After the floodwater receded, Noah sacrificed some of the clean animals to thank God for saving him.

When archeologists found clay tablets that contained the Babylonian text that we call the Epic of Gilgamesh, many were surprised to hear that it contained a flood myth similar to the myth in Genesis. The god Ea tells Utnapishtim about the gods' plan to destroy the earth with a flood and commands him to build a boat and bring all beasts and animals into it. There were six days of rain that flooded the earth, and the boat settled on Mount Nimrush. On the seventh day, Utnapishtim released first a dove that came back to him, then a swallow that came back to him, and finally a raven that did not come back. Then he let the animals out of the boat and sacrificed a sheep in thanks for being saved.[134] This Babylonian epic was based on a much earlier Sumerian epic, dating back to 2100-2000 BCE, which also has a short version of the flood myth.

When the Epic of Gilgamesh was discovered, its flood myth was taken as another piece of evidence that the entire Bible was just a collection of myths, not essentially different from the myths of surrounding peoples. But through the lens of the documentary hypothesis, we can see that J often uses myths of surrounding people, while E does not.

# Tower of Babel

This myth seems to date back to the days of the earliest large cities, much earlier than Israel's patriarchs but much later than the beginnings of herding and farming. When groups of nomadic herders saw these cities, they must have been overwhelmed by their power, impressed by their tall buildings, and surprised that they contained people who spoke many different languages (because they were centers of trade among many peoples). The herders lived in small groups that all spoke the same language, so it was easy to invent the myth that the people in the cities spoke multiple languages as a punishment for their presumption, which was obvious when you looked at the large building of their cities.

Thus, this myth is an origin myth explaining why people in the cities spoke many different languages:

> GEN 11:5And the Lord came down to see the city and the tower, which the children of men builded. 6And the Lord said: 'Behold, they are one people, and they have all one language; and this is what they

begin to do; and now nothing will be withholden from them, which they purpose to do. [7]Come, let us go down, and there confound their language, that they may not understand one another's speech.'

There is a somewhat similar Sumerian myth dating back to about 2100 BCE. The goddess Innana orders Emerkar to embellish her E-ana temple, and he also asks permission to conquer and get tribute from the people of Aratta so he can build the tall Abzu temple of the god Enki. When this temple is built, "Enki ... shall change the speech in their mouths, as many as he had placed there, and so the speech of mankind is truly one."[135]

This myth is told from the point of view of Sumerians, who built cities, so it considers building the tower a good thing that unifies the world's languages. By contrast, the myth of the tower of Babel seems to be told by nomadic herders, so it considers building the tower an evil that leads to the division of the world's languages.

# Other Myths

The J text includes allusions to many other myths that are too brief to let us speculate about their origins. We can just list them:

- GEN 4:20And Adah bore Jabal; he was the father of such as dwell in tents and have cattle. [21]And his brother's name was Jubal; he was the father of all such as handle the harp and pipe. [22]And Zillah, she also bore Tubal-cain, the forger of every cutting instrument of brass and iron
- GEN 4:23And Lamech said unto his wives: "Adah and Zillah, hear my voice; Ye wives of Lamech, hearken unto my speech; For I have slain a man for wounding me, And a young man for bruising me; [24]If Cain shall be avenged sevenfold, Truly Lamech seventy and sevenfold."
- GEN 6:1And it came to pass, when men began to multiply on the face of the earth, and daughters were born unto them, that the sons of God saw the daughters of men that they were fair; and they took them wives, whomsoever they chose. ... [4]The Nephilim *[giants]* were in the earth in those days, and also after that, when the sons of God came in unto the daughters of men, and they bore children to them; the same were the mighty men that were of old, the men of renown.
- GEN 10:8And Cush begot Nimrod; he began to be a mighty one in the earth. [9]He was a mighty hunter before the Lord; wherefore it is said: 'Like Nimrod a mighty hunter before the Lord.'

These are fragments of myths. Some remind us of Greek and Roman myths. Jubal, the first musician, reminds us of Orpheus, and the "mighty men of old" remind us of the classical heroes who were supposed to be descended from gods and goddesses mating with mortals: Aeneas was the son of Venus, Perseus was the son of Zeus, Achilles was the son of Thetis, Theseus was the son of Poseidon, and so on.

Of course, these fragments remind us of Greek and Roman myths not because they originated with the Greeks or Romans but because we know more classical myths than we do middle-eastern myths. The similarities are just meant to show that they are typical pagan myths, not to show their origin. Interestingly, in the classical myths, some of the classical heroes were descended from goddesses and mortal men, while in J's myth, heroes were descended from the sons of God and mortal women.

"Sons of God" is problematic because the narrator in J does not use the word "God" as a rule. The Hebrew word for God, *Elohim*, is in the plural and can also mean "gods." The Nephilim lived in Canaan, as we learn later in J, when the Israelite spies sent to Canaan report "[Num 13:33]And there we saw the Nephilim, the sons of Anak, who come of the Nephilim; and we were in our own sight as grasshoppers, and so we were in their sight.'" Rather than uncharacteristically using the word *Elohim* to mean God, J is probably referring to myths about the sons of Canaanite gods and the daughters of men producing renowned heroes of Canaanite myth such as Anak.

# Myths in E, J and P

If we want to reconstruct the early history of the Israelite religion, it is important to remember that all these early myths came from pagan sources.

The E text reflects the religion of the earliest Israelite priests, and it is about the patriarchs and Moses, without any mixture of earlier myths.

The J text, produced in the multi-cultural Judean court, added these myths and had a much more anthropomorphic view of God than E, also influenced by pagan sources.

The Aaronid priests officiated at the Temple in Jerusalem, so they might have been familiar with these myths that were circulating in the Judean court in Jerusalem. Or perhaps they incorporated these pagan myths in their religion after the combined JE text was produced; P was aware of the JE text and wrote versions of a couple of its myths (creation and flood) with a much less anthropomorphic God.

Finally, the JE and P texts were edited together, along with some shorter texts, to form the Torah that we have today—with the inconsistencies that result from combining three sources—and these pagan myths became part of the Israelite religion.

# Notes

1. Thomas Hobbes, *Leviathan*, published 1651, Chapter 33, "Of the Number, Antiquity, Scope, Authority, and Interpretation of the Bible." Baruch Spinoza, *Tractatus Theologico-Politicus*, published posthumously in 1677, Chapter 8, "Of the Authorship of the Pentateuch and the Other Historical Books of the Old Testament." For a summary of Spinoza's positions, see Ursula Goldenbaum, "Liebniz as a Lutheran" in Allison P. Coudert, Richard H. Popkin, and Gordon M. Weiner ed,. *Liebnez, Mysticism and Religion* (International Archive of the History of Ideas, Kluwer Academic Publishers, 1998) p. 182-186.

2. Jean Astruc, *Conjectures sur les mémoires originauz dont il paroit que Moyse s'est servi pour composer le livre de la Genèse. Avec des remarques qui appuient ou qui éclaircissent ces conjectures* (Conjectures on the original documents that Moses appears to have used in composing the Book of Genesis. With remarks that support or throw light upon these conjectures). Brussels, 1753.

3, Johann Gottfried Eichhorn, *Introduction to the Old Testament* (*Einleitung in das Alte Testament*), Leipzig, 1780-82.

4. Julius Wellhausen, *Prolegomena zur Geschichte Israels* (*Prologue to the History of Israel*) 1883.

5. Israel Finkelstein and Neil Asher Silberman, *The Bible Unearthed: Archaelology's New Vision of Ancient Israel and the Origin of its Sacred Texts* (Simon & Schuster, 2002) p. 114 ff.

6. For example, the tribe of Gilead (later called Gad) on the east side of the Jordan, was attacked by Ammon, also on the east side of the Jordan, and organized an impromptu army: "[JUD 11:5]And it was so, that when the children of Ammon made war against Israel, the elders of Gilead went to fetch Jephthah out of the land of Tob. [6]And they said unto Jephthah: 'Come and be our chief, that we may fight with the children of Ammon.'"

7. Famously, when the tribe of Gilead on the east side of Jordan fought with Ephraim on the west side of the Jordan, "[JUD 12:5]And the Gileadites took the fords

of the Jordan against the Ephraimites; and it was so, that when any of the fugitives of Ephraim said: 'Let me go over, 'the men of Gilead said unto him: 'Art thou an Ephraimite?' If he said: 'Nay'; ⁶then said they unto him: 'Say now Shibboleth'; and he said 'Sibboleth'; for he could not frame to pronounce it right; then they laid hold on him, and slew him at the fords of the Jordan; and there fell at that time of Ephraim forty and two thousand."

8. Judges 13-16.

9. I Samuel 3:3.

10. I Samuel 4:17.

11. II Samuel 6:13-16.

12. II Samuel 8:17.

13. I Kings 1:8, 1:34.

14. I Kings 1:7.

15. I Kings 2:26.

16. I Kings 5:27-32.

17. I Kings 9:11.

18. I Kings 12:14.

19. II Chronicles 2:9.

20. II Chronicles 10:11.

21. 1 Kings 12.

22. Finkelstein and Silberman, *The Bible Unearthed*, p. 229 ff.

23. 1 Kings 11:4-7.

24. Frank Moore Cross, *Canaanite Myth and Hebrew Epic: Essays in the History of the Religion of Israel* (Harvard University Press, 1973) p. 206.

25. Jeremiah 1:1.

26. Exodus 32:1-28.

27. Genesis 49.

28. Genesis 43:8 ff.

29. Genesis 19:30-38.

30. Genesis 27.

31. Genesis 31:35.

32. Genesis 38.

33. Genesis 19:8.

34. Genesis 3:16.

35. Harold Bloom and David Rosenberg, *The Book of J* (Grove Weidenfeld, 1990).

36. "¹ CHRON 5:26And the God of Israel stirred up the spirit of Pul king of Assyria, and the spirit of Tilgathpilneser king of Assyria, and he carried them away, even the Reubenites, and the Gadites, and the half tribe of Manasseh, and brought them unto Halah, and Habor, and Hara, and to the river Gozan, unto this day." "2 KINGS 15:29In the days of Pekah king of Israel came Tiglathpileser king of Assyria, and he took Ijon, and Abelbethmaachah, and Janoah, and Kedesh, and Hazor, and Gilead, and

Galilee, all the land of Naphtali, and carried them captive to Assyria."

37. "[2 KINGS 17:6]In the ninth year of Hoshea the king of Assyria took Samaria, and carried Israel away into Assyria, and placed them in Halah and in Habor by the river of Gozan, and in the cities of the Medes." "[2 KINGS 18:11]And the king of Assyria carried Israel away unto Assyria, and put them in Halah, and in Habor, on the river of Gozan, and in the cities of the Medes; [12]because they hearkened not to the voice of the Lord their God, but transgressed His covenant, even all that Moses the servant of the Lord commanded, and would not hear it, nor do it."

38. "[HOS 3:4]For the Israelites will live many days without king or prince, without sacrifice or sacred stones, without ephod or household gods. ... [5]Afterward the Israelites will return and seek the Lord their God and David their king. They will come trembling to the Lord and to his blessings in the last days." Hosea wrote in the 8th century BCE, after the exile of Israel and before the exile of Judah. "[JER 30:3]'The days are coming,' declares the Lord, 'when I will bring my people Israel and Judah back from captivity and restore them to the land I gave their ancestors to possess,' says the Lord."

39. Edwin Thiele, *The Mysterious Numbers of the Hebrew Kings*, 3rd edition (Grand Rapids: Zondervan/Kregel, 1983) p. 217.

40. II Kings 18:3-7.

41. I Kings 6:16, 20, 21, 23–28.

42. I Kings 7:25, II Chronicles 4:4.

43. I Kings 7:29.

44. Numbers 21:8-9

45. II Kings 19:4.

46. II Kings 18:13-16.

47. II Kings 19:35-36.

48. I Chronicles 21:14-17.

49. II Kings 21:2, 21:20.

50. II Kings 23.

51. II Kings 22:3-11.

52. II Kings 23:29.

53. II Kings 25.

54. II Kings 25:25-26.

55. Nehemiah 8:1-8.

56. Martin Noth first advanced the theory that these books form a unified work, which he called the Deuteronomistic history. Martin Noth, *Überlieferungsgeschichtliche Studien* (1943). The theory is now widely accepted.

57. To see which parts of Deuteronomy were by Dtr1 and Dtr2, see Richard Elliott Friedman, *The Bible with Sources Revealed: A New View into the Five Books of Moses* (HarperSanFrancisco, 2005) pp. 309-368.

58. Deuteronomy 5:17, quoted in the familiar form though they are translated slightly differently in the JPS translation.

59. Genesis 41:45, 50-52.

60. Exodus 2:21.

61. Exodus 4:10-12.

62. Exodus 6:10-7:2.

63. Exodus 17:1-7.

64. Numbers 20:1-13.

65. Numbers 25:17-18.

66. Numbers 25:16-18.

67. Numbers 25:1-3.

68. Exodus 3:1.

69. Exodus 2:18.

70. Exodus 18.

71. The arguments for this earlier date are summarized in Richard Elliot Friedman, *Who Wrote the Bible* (Harper and Row, 1989) pp. 207-214.

72. Genesis 31:45.

73. Genesis 31:46.

74. The only place in the E text where God changes his mind in in the story of the golden calf, where God says he will destroy the Israelites and Moses convinces Him not to by appealing to His vanity (Ex. 32:9-14). But this story might be a later addition; see page 27.

75. Exodus 33:20.

76. Exodus 13:1-16.

77. Exodus 20:19-23:33.

78. In E, the Israelites accept the covenant in Exodus 24:3-8. The story of the golden calf is in Exodus 32:1-35.

79. Exodus 32:9-14.

80. Genesis 38:2-5.

81. Exodus 34-17-26.

82. Genesis 19:30-38.

83. Genesis 27.

84. Genesis 31.

85. Genesis 38.

86. Genesis 27.

87. Genesis 30:31-43.

88. Genesis 3:22.

89. Genesis 11:5.

90. Genesis 18:20-21.

91. Genesis 3:8.

92. Genesis 18:1-5.

93. Exodus 24:1-9.

94. Genesis 43:29-31.

95. Genesis 18:24-32.

96. Bloom, *Book of J*, p. 16.

97. Richard Elliott Friedman, *The Hidden Book in the Bible: The Discovery of the First Prose Masterpiece* (HarperSanFrancisco, 1998).

98. Genesis 38.

99. Genesis 7:2, 8:20.

100. Genesis 6:19.

101. Leviticus 17:1- 26:46.

102. Exodus 20:1-14.

103. Genesis 1:1-2:1.

104. Genesis 1.

105. Genesis 6:9-9:28.

106. Genesis 17:1-27.

107. Genesis 23:1-20.

108. Genesis 27:46-28:9.

109. Genesis 48:3-7, 49:29-33.

110. Leviticus 17:1-12.

111. Genesis 9:8-17.

112. Genesis 17:1-10.

113. Genesis 2:7.

114. Genesis 1.

115. Genesis 23:1-20.

116. Genesis 26:34-35, Genesis 27:46 ff.

117. Genesis 48:3-7, 49:29-33.

118. The supplementary hypothesis was introduced in John Van Seters, *Abraham in History and Tradition* (Yale University Press, 1975). Other early exponents of the supplementary hypothesis were Hans Heinrich Schmid, *Der sogenannte Jahwist*, 1976 (translated as *The So-called Yahwist*) and Rolf Rendtorff, *Das überlieferungsgeschichtliche Problem des Pentateuch*, 1977 (translated by John J. Scullion as *The Problem in the Process of Transmission of the Pentateuch*).

119. Genesis 18:16-33.

120. Genesis 19:1-26.

121. John Van Seeters, *Abraham in History and Tradition*, pp. 305, 311.

122. Genesis 23:7-20.

123. Friedman, *Sources Revealed*, p. 266.

124. Genesis 35:22-23.

125. Genesis 19:36-38.

126. Genesis 25:5.

127. Numbers 25:17-18.

128. Numbers 17:9-14.

129. Friedman, *Who Wrote the Bible*, p. 224.

130. Frank Moore Cross, *Canaanite Myth and Hebrew Epic*, pp. 31-32.

131. See Jane Ellen Harrison, *Prolegomena to the Study of Greek Religion,* second edition (Cambridge University Press, 1908) pp 283–285 and A.H. Smith, "The Making of Pandora" *The Journal of Hellenic Studies* 11 (1890, pp. 278–283) p 283.

132. In a scholium to line 971 of Aristophanes' *The Birds*. See Jeffrey M. Hurwit, "Beautiful Evil: Pandora and the Athena Parthenos" *American Journal of Archaeology 99.2* (April 1995: 171–186).

133. Jane Ellen Harrison, *Prolegomena to the Study of Greek Religion.*

134. *Epic of Gilgamesh*, Tablet XI, lines 1-203.

135. Wikipedia, "Enmerkar and the Lord of Aratta."

CPSIA information can be obtained
at www.ICGtesting.com
Printed in the USA
BVHW042202090719
553029BV00002B/3/P